# Economic Pluralism

*Economic Pluralism* explores the evolving meanings and consequences of pluralism in contemporary economics. Its 20 original essays reflect the breadth and maturity of pluralist discourse among economists, including new perspectives on pluralism in mainstream and heterodox economics, pluralist innovations in undergraduate and graduate economics education, and pluralist analyses of economic heterogeneity (commercial and communal, capitalist and non-capitalist). It is a volume sure to elicit fresh thinking about academic economics and real-world economies in the twenty-first century.

**Robert Garnett** is Associate Professor of Economics at Texas Christian University. **Erik K. Olsen** is Assistant Professor of Economics and member of Doctoral Faculty at the University of Missouri Kansas City. **Martha Starr** is Associate Professor of Economics at American University in Washington, DC.

# Routledge frontiers of political economy

1 **Equilibrium Versus Understanding**
Towards the rehumanization of economics within social theory
*Mark Addleson*

2 **Evolution, Order and Complexity**
*Edited by Elias L. Khalil and Kenneth E. Boulding*

3 **Interactions in Political Economy**
Malvern after ten years
*Edited by Steven Pressman*

4 **The End of Economics**
*Michael Perelman*

5 **Probability in Economics**
*Omar F. Hamouda and Robin Rowley*

6 **Capital Controversy, Post Keynesian Economics and the History of Economics**
Essays in honour of
Geoff Harcourt, volume one
*Edited by Philip Arestis, Gabriel Palma and Malcolm Sawyer*

7 **Markets, Unemployment and Economic Policy**
Essays in honour of
Geoff Harcourt, volume two
*Edited by Philip Arestis, Gabriel Palma and Malcolm Sawyer*

8 **Social Economy**
The logic of capitalist development
*Clark Everling*

9 **New Keynesian Economics/ Post Keynesian Alternatives**
*Edited by Roy J. Rotheim*

10 **The Representative Agent in Macroeconomics**
*James E. Hartley*

11 **Borderlands of Economics**
Essays in honour of
Daniel R. Fusfeld
*Edited by Nahid Aslanbeigui and Young Back Choi*

12 **Value, Distribution and Capital**
Essays in honour of
Pierangelo Garegnani
*Edited by Gary Mongiovi and Fabio Petri*

13 **The Economics of Science**
Methodology and epistemology
as if economics really mattered
*James R. Wible*

14 **Competitiveness, Localised
Learning and Regional
Development**
Specialisation and prosperity in
small open economies
*Peter Maskell, Heikki Eskelinen,
Ingjaldur Hannibalsson,
Anders Malmberg and
Eirik Vatne*

15 **Labour Market Theory**
A constructive reassessment
*Ben J. Fine*

16 **Women and European
Employment**
*Jill Rubery, Mark Smith,
Colette Faga and
Damian Grimshaw*

17 **Explorations in Economic
Methodology**
From Lakatos to empirical
philosophy of science
*Roger Backhouse*

18 **Subjectivity in Political
Economy**
Essays on wanting and choosing
*David P. Levine*

19 **The Political Economy of
Middle East Peace**
The impact of competing trade
agendas
*Edited by J.W. Wright, Jnr*

20 **The Active Consumer**
Novelty and surprise in consumer
choice
*Edited by Marina Bianchi*

21 **Subjectivism and
Economic Analysis**
Essays in memory of
Ludwig Lachmann
*Edited by Roger Koppl and
Gary Mongiovi*

22 **Themes in Post-Keynesian
Economics**
Essays in honour of
Geoff Harcourt, volume three
*Edited by Claudio Sardoni and
Peter Kriesler*

23 **The Dynamics of Technological
Knowledge**
*Cristiano Antonelli*

24 **The Political Economy of Diet,
Health and Food Policy**
*Ben J. Fine*

25 **The End of Finance**
Capital market inflation, financial
derivatives and pension fund
capitalism
*Jan Toporowski*

26 **Political Economy and the
New Capitalism**
*Edited by Jan Toporowski*

27 **Growth Theory**
A philosophical perspective
*Patricia Northover*

28 **The Political Economy of the
Small Firm**
*Edited by Charlie Dannreuther*

29 **Hahn and Economic Methodology**
*Edited by Thomas Boylan and Paschal F. O'Gorman*

30 **Gender, Growth and Trade**
The miracle economies of the postwar years
*David Kucera*

31 **Normative Political Economy**
Subjective freedom, the market and the state
*David Levine*

32 **Economist with a Public Purpose**
Essays in honour of John Kenneth Galbraith
*Edited by Michael Keaney*

33 **Involuntary Unemployment**
The elusive quest for a theory
*Michel De Vroey*

34 **The Fundamental Institutions of Capitalism**
*Ernesto Screpanti*

35 **Transcending Transaction**
The search for self-generating markets
*Alan Shipman*

36 **Power in Business and the State**
An historical analysis of its concentration
*Frank Bealey*

37 **Editing Economics**
Essays in honour of Mark Perlman
*Edited by Hank Lim, Ungsuh K. Park and Geoff Harcourt*

38 **Money, Macroeconomics and Keynes**
Essays in honour of Victoria Chick, volume 1
*Edited by Philip Arestis, Meghnad Desai and Sheila Dow*

39 **Methodology, Microeconomics and Keynes**
Essays in honour of Victoria Chick, volume 2
*Edited by Philip Arestis, Meghnad Desai and Sheila Dow*

40 **Market Drive and Governance**
Reexamining the rules for economic and commercial contest
*Ralf Boscheck*

41 **The Value of Marx**
Political economy for contemporary capitalism
*Alfredo Saad-Filho*

42 **Issues in Positive Political Economy**
*S. Mansoob Murshed*

43 **The Enigma of Globalisation**
A journey to a new stage of capitalism
*Robert Went*

44 **The Market**
Equilibrium, stability, mythology
*S.N. Afriat*

45 **The Political Economy of Rule Evasion and Policy Reform**
*Jim Leitzel*

46 **Unpaid Work and the Economy**
*Edited by Antonella Picchio*

47 **Distributional Justice**
Theory and measurement
*Hilde Bojer*

48 **Cognitive Developments in
Economics**
*Edited by Salvatore Rizzello*

49 **Social Foundations of Markets,
Money and Credit**
*Costas Lapavitsas*

50 **Rethinking Capitalist
Development**
Essays on the economics of
Josef Steindl
*Edited by Tracy Mott and
Nina Shapiro*

51 **An Evolutionary Approach to
Social Welfare**
*Christian Sartorius*

52 **Kalecki's Economics Today**
*Edited by Zdzislaw L. Sadowski
and Adam Szeworski*

53 **Fiscal Policy from Reagan to
Blair**
The left veers right
*Ravi K. Roy and
Arthur T. Denzau*

54 **The Cognitive Mechanics of
Economic Development and
Institutional Change**
*Bertin Martens*

55 **Individualism and the Social
Order**
The social element in liberal
thought
*Charles R. McCann Jnr*

56 **Affirmative Action in the
United States and India**
A comparative perspective
*Thomas E. Weisskopf*

57 **Global Political Economy and
the Wealth of Nations**
Performance, institutions,
problems and policies
*Edited by
Phillip Anthony O'Hara*

58 **Structural Economics**
*Thijs ten Raa*

59 **Macroeconomic Theory and
Economic Policy**
Essays in honour of
Jean-Paul Fitoussi
*Edited by K. Vela Velupillai*

60 **The Struggle Over Work**
The "end of work" and
employment alternatives in
post-industrial societies
*Shaun Wilson*

61 **The Political Economy of
Global Sporting Organisations**
*John Forster and Nigel Pope*

62 **The Flawed Foundations of
General Equilibrium Theory**
Critical essays on economic
theory
*Frank Ackerman and
Alejandro Nadal*

63 **Uncertainty in Economic
Theory**
Essays in honor of David
Schmeidler's 65th birthday
*Edited by Itzhak Gilboa*

64 **The New Institutional Economics of Corruption**
*Edited by Johann Graf Lambsdorff, Markus Taube and Matthias Schramm*

65 **The Price Index and its Extension**
A chapter in economic measurement
*S.N. Afriat*

66 **Reduction, Rationality and Game Theory in Marxian Economics**
*Bruce Philp*

67 **Culture and Politics in Economic Development**
*Volker Bornschier*

68 **Modern Applications of Austrian Thought**
*Edited by Jürgen G. Backhaus*

69 **Ordinary Choices**
Individuals, incommensurability, and democracy
*Robert Urquhart*

70 **Labour Theory of Value**
*Peter C. Dooley*

71 **Capitalism**
*Victor D. Lippit*

72 **Macroeconomic Foundations of Macroeconomics**
*Alvaro Cencini*

73 **Marx for the 21st Century**
*Edited by Hiroshi Uchida*

74 **Growth and Development in the Global Political Economy**
Social structures of accumulation and modes of regulation
*Phillip Anthony O'Hara*

75 **The New Economy and Macroeconomic Stability**
A neo-modern perspective drawing on the complexity approach and Keynesian economics
*Teodoro Dario Togati*

76 **The Future of Social Security Policy**
Women, work and a citizen's basic income
*Ailsa McKay*

77 **Clinton and Blair**
The political economy of the third way
*Flavio Romano*

78 **Marxian Reproduction Schema**
Money and aggregate demand in a capitalist economy
*A.B. Trigg*

79 **The Core Theory in Economics**
Problems and solutions
*Lester G. Telser*

80 **Economics, Ethics and the Market**
Introduction and applications
*Johan J. Graafland*

81 **Social Costs and Public Action in Modern Capitalism**
Essays inspired by Karl William Kapp's theory of social costs
*Edited by Wolfram Elsner, Pietro Frigato and Paolo Ramazzotti*

82 **Globalization and the Myths of Free Trade**
History, theory and empirical evidence
*Edited by Anwar Shaikh*

83 **Equilibrium in Economics**
Scope and limits
*Edited by Valeria Mosini*

84 **Globalization**
State of the art and perspectives
*Edited by Stefan A. Schirm*

85 **Neoliberalism**
National and regional experiments with global ideas
*Edited by Ravi K. Roy, Arthur T. Denzau and Thomas D. Willett*

86 **Post-Keynesian Macroeconomics**
Essays in honour of Ingrid Rima
*Edited by Mathew Forstater, Gary Mongiovi and Steven Pressman*

87 **Consumer Capitalism**
*Anastasios S. Korkotsides*

88 **Remapping Gender in the New Global Order**
*Edited by Marjorie Griffin Cohen and Janine Brodie*

89 **Hayek and Natural Law**
*Eric Angner*

90 **Race and Economic Opportunity in the Twenty-First Century**
*Edited by Marlene Kim*

91 **Renaissance in Behavioural Economics**
Harvey Leibenstein's impact on contemporary economic analysis
*Edited by Roger Frantz*

92 **Human Ecology Economics**
A new framework for global sustainability
*Edited by Roy E. Allen*

93 **Imagining Economics Otherwise**
Encounters with identity/difference
*Nitasha Kaul*

94 **Reigniting the Labor Movement**
Restoring means to ends in a democratic labor movement
*Gerald Friedman*

95 **The Spatial Model of Politics**
*Norman Schofield*

96 **The Economics of American Judaism**
*Carmel Ullman Chiswick*

97 **Critical Political Economy**
*Christian Arnsperger*

98 **Culture and Economic Explanation**
Economics in the US and Japan
*Donald W. Katzner*

99 **Feminism, Economics and Utopia**
Time travelling through paradigms
*Karin Schönpflug*

100 **Risk in International Finance**
*Vikash Yadav*

101 **Economic Policy and Performance in Industrial Democracies**
Party governments, central banks and the fiscal–monetary policy mix
*Takayuki Sakamoto*

102 **Advances on Income Inequality and Concentration Measures**
*Edited by Gianni Betti and Achille Lemmi*

103 **Economic Representations**
Academic and everyday
*Edited by David F. Ruccio*

104 **Mathematical Economics and the Dynamics of Capitalism**
Goodwin's legacy continued
*Edited by Peter Flaschel and Michael Landesmann*

105 **The Keynesian Multiplier**
*Edited by Claude Gnos and Louis-Philippe Rochon*

106 **Money, Enterprise and Income Distribution**
Towards a macroeconomic theory of capitalism
*John Smithin*

107 **Fiscal Decentralization and Local Public Finance in Japan**
*Nobuki Mochida*

108 **The 'Uncertain' Foundations of Post-Keynesian Economics**
Essays in exploration
*Stephen P. Dunn*

109 **Karl Marx's Grundrisse**
Foundations of the critique of political economy 150 years later
*Edited by Marcello Musto*

110 **Economics and the Price Index**
*S.N. Afriat and Carlo Milana*

111 **Sublime Economy**
On the intersection of art and economics
*Edited by Jack Amariglio, Joseph W. Childers and Stephen E. Cullenberg*

112 **Popper, Hayek and the Open Society**
*Calvin Hayes*

113 **The Political Economy of Work**
*David Spencer*

114 **Institutional Economics**
*Bernard Chavance*

115 **Religion, Economics and Demography**
The effects of religion on education, work, and the family
*Evelyn L. Lehrer*

116 **Economics, Rational Choice and Normative Philosophy**
*Edited by Thomas A. Boylan and Ruvin Gekker*

117 **Economics Versus Human Rights**
*Manuel Couret Branco*

118 Hayek Versus Marx and
   Today's Challenges
   *Eric Aarons*

119 Work Time Regulation as
   Sustainable Full Employment
   Policy
   *Robert LaJeunesse*

120 Equilibrium, Welfare and
   Uncertainty
   *Mukul Majumdar*

121 Capitalism, Institutions and
   Economic Development
   *Michael Heller*

122 Economic Pluralism
   *Edited by Robert Garnett,
   Erik K. Olsen, and Martha Starr*

# Economic Pluralism

Edited by Robert Garnett,
Erik K. Olsen, and Martha Starr

 Routledge
Taylor & Francis Group

LONDON AND NEW YORK

First published 2010
by Routledge
2 Park Square, Milton Park, Abingdon, Oxon OX14 4RN

Simultaneously published in the USA and Canada
by Routledge
711 Third Ave, New York, NY 10017

*Routledge is an imprint of the Taylor & Francis Group, an informa business*

Typeset in Times by Wearset Ltd, Boldon, Tyne and Wear
First issued in paperback in 2013

*British Library Cataloguing in Publication Data*
A catalogue record for this book is available from the British Library

*Library of Congress Cataloging-in-Publication Data*
Economic pluralism/edited by Robert Garnett, Erik K. Olsen, and Martha
Starr.
p. cm.

1. Economics. 2. Pluralism. I. Garnett, Robert F. II. Olsen, Erik K., 1966–
III. Starr, Martha.

HB171.E243 2009
330.1–dc22                                              2009008115


ISBN13: 978-0-415-74741-7 (pbk)
ISBN13: 978-0-415-77703-2 (hbk)
ISBN13: 978-0-203-87181-2 (ebk)

# Contents

*Notes on contributors*                                                       xvi
*Acknowledgments*                                                             xxii

**Economic pluralism for the twenty-first century**                             1
ROBERT GARNETT, ERIK K. OLSEN, AND MARTHA STARR

**PART I**
**Pluralism and economic inquiry**                                             17

*Pluralism and heterodoxy*

1  **Pluralism in heterodox economics**                                        19
   FREDERIC S. LEE

2  **Moving beyond the rhetoric of pluralism: suggestions for an**
   **"inside-the-mainstream" heterodoxy**                                      36
   DAVID COLANDER

3  **Is convergence among heterodox schools possible,**
   **meaningful, or desirable?**                                               48
   WILLIAM WALLER

4  **Raising dissonant voices: pluralism and economic heterodoxy**            61
   DIANA STRASSMANN, MARTHA STARR, AND
   CAREN A. GROWN

*Theorizing pluralism*

5  **Is Kuhnean incommensurability a good basis for pluralism**
   **in economics?**                                                          74
   GUSTAVO MARQUÉS AND DIEGO WEISMAN

 6  Why should *I* adopt pluralism?                                     87
    ROGIER DE LANGHE

 7  Ontology, modern economics, and pluralism                          99
    TONY LAWSON

 8  The Cambridge School and pluralism                                 114
    VINCA BIGO


PART II
**Pluralism and real-world economies**                                 127

*Economic democracy and the common good*

 9  America beyond capitalism: the Pluralist Commonwealth              129
    GAR ALPEROVITZ

10  From competition and greed to equitable cooperation:
    what does a pluralist economics have to offer?                     145
    ROBIN HAHNEL

11  Growth, development, and quality of life: a pluralist
    approach                                                           160
    DAPHNE T. GREENWOOD AND RICHARD P.F. HOLT

12  Beyond the status quo, in the world and in the discipline:
    the comments of an Austrian economist                              176
    EMILY CHAMLEE-WRIGHT

*Economic cooperation: commercial and communal*

13  Hayek and Lefebvre on market space and extra-catallactic
    relationships                                                      181
    VIRGIL HENRY STORR

14  The plural economy of gifts and markets                            194
    IOANA NEGRU

15  Communities and local exchange networks: an Aristotelian
    view                                                               205
    PHILIP KOZEL

**PART III**
**Pluralism and economics education** 219

16 Promoting a pluralist agenda in undergraduate economics
   education 221
   KIMMARIE MCGOLDRICK

17 The illusion of objectivity: implications for teaching
   economics 236
   ALISON BUTLER

18 A pluralist teaching of economics: why and how 250
   GILLES RAVEAUD

19 Economic pluralism and skill formation: adding value to
   students, economies, and societies 262
   ROD O'DONNELL

20 A most peculiar success: constructing UADPhilEcon, a
   doctoral program in economics at the University of Athens 278
   YANIS VAROUFAKIS

   *Index* 293

# Contributors

**Gar Alperovitz** is the Lionel R. Bauman Professor of Political Economy at the University of Maryland and serves as President of the National Center for Economic and Security Alternatives. Previously he was a Fellow of King's College at Cambridge University, a founding Fellow of the Institute of Politics at Harvard University, a Fellow of the Institute for Policy Studies, a Guest Scholar at the Brookings Institution, and a Guest Professor at Notre Dame University. He has also served as a Legislative Director in the U.S. House of Representatives and the U.S. Senate, and as a Special Assistant in the Department of State. Dr. Alperovitz was a Marshall Scholar and a Guggenheim Fellow.

**Vinca Bigo** received her Ph.D. from the University of Cambridge, U.K. She is an active member of the Cambridge Social Ontology Group. Her research centers on feminist epistemology, ontology, pluralism, and psychology in economics, on the nature of care, and the ethics of care.

**Alison Butler** received her Ph.D. from the University of Oregon and has taught at several different public and private universities across the country. Her outlook is shaped by many factors, including her upbringing as a white Jewish woman raised across different economic classes and living in an interracial household; her experiences teaching in settings of very different racial and economic diversity and her time spent working in the highly structured professional environment of the Federal Reserve Bank of St. Louis. Her current research focuses on alternative pedagogies and issues relating to gender and race in the classroom.

**Emily Chamlee-Wright** is Professor of Economics at Beloit College in Beloit, Wisconsin, and a senior research scholar at the Mercatus Center in Fairfax, Virginia. She earned her Ph.D. in Economics from George Mason University. Her primary research interests concern the ways in which cultural and market processes affect one another. Her books include *The Cultural Foundations of Economic Development* (Routledge 1997) and *Culture and Enterprise*, co-authored with Don Lavoie (Routledge 2000). She is currently completing a new book, *The Learning Society: Social Coordination in Post-Katrina New Orleans*

(Routledge, Advances in Heterodox Economics), which examines intersections between markets and social capital with particular attention to the roles of culture and social capital in communities recovering from Hurricane Katrina.

**David Colander** received his Ph.D. from Columbia University and has been the Christian A. Johnson Distinguished Professor of Economics at Middlebury College, Middlebury, Vermont since 1982. In 2001–2002 he was the Kelly Professor of Distinguished Teaching at Princeton University. He has authored, co-authored, or edited over 35 books and 100 articles on a wide range of topics. His books have been, or are being, translated into a number of different languages, including Chinese, Bulgarian, Polish, Italian, and Spanish. He has been president of both the Eastern Economic Association and History of Economic Thought Society and is, or has been, on the editorial boards of numerous journals, including the *Journal of Economic Perspectives* and *Journal of Economic Education*.

**Robert Garnett** is Associate Professor of Economics at Texas Christian University. His writings on the philosophy of economics and economics education have appeared in *Rethinking Marxism*, the *Journal of Economic Issues*, the *Atlantic Economic Journal*, the *Review of Political Economy*, the *Review of Austrian Economics*, the *Review of Social Economy*, the *Journal of Markets and Morality*, *Studies in Philosophy and Education*, and the *Post-Autistic Economics Review*. His current projects focus on economics education as liberal education, the meaning and requirements of pluralism in economic inquiry, and the relationship between commercial and philanthropic forms of economic cooperation.

**Daphne T. Greenwood** is Professor of Economics at the University of Colorado at Colorado Springs.

**Caren A. Grown** is Economist-In-Residence at American University. Previously, she directed the Poverty Reduction and Economic Governance team at the International Center for Research on Women, and was a Senior Program Officer at the John D. and Catherine MacArthur Foundation in Chicago, Illinois. She has written and edited several books including *The Feminist Economics of Trade* (Routledge 2007, with Diane Elson, Irene Van Staveren, and Nilufer Cagatay), *Trading Women's Health and Rights: The Role of Trade Liberalization and Development* (Zed Books 2006, with Elissa Braunstein and Anju Malhotra), *Taking Action: Achieving Gender Equality and Empowering Women* (Earthscan Press 2005, with Geeta Rao Gupta), and *Development, Crises and Alternative Visions: Third World Women's Perspectives* (Monthly Review Press 1987, with Gita Sen). Her current research focuses on assets and women's well-being, gender issues in public finance, and international trade and gender. She holds M.A. and Ph.D. degrees in economics from New School for Social Research and a Bachelor's degree in political science from UCLA.

**Robin Hahnel** is Professor of Economics at American University. He has written extensively with *Z Magazine* editor Michael Albert, including a co-authored book, *The Political Economy of Participatory Economics* (Princeton 1991). His other recent books include *The ABCs of Political Economy: A Modern Approach* (Pluto 2002) and *Economic Justice and Democracy: From Competition to Cooperation* (Routledge 2005). His research in economic theory and analysis is informed by the works of Marx, Keynes, Sraffa, Kalecki, and Robinson, among others. He has actively participated in various social movements and organizations over the years, most recently with the Southern Maryland Greens and the U.S. Green Party. He also has served as a visiting professor or economist in Cuba, Peru, and England.

**Richard P.F. Holt** is Professor of Economics at Southern Oregon University. He received his Ph.D. in Economics from the University of Utah. Among the scholarly outlets that have published his work are the *Review of Political Economy, Journal of Post Keynesian Economics, Eastern Economic Journal*, and *American Journal of Economics and Sociology*. His recent books include *Empirical Post Keynesian Economics: Looking at the Real World*, co-authored with Steven Pressman (M.E. Sharpe 2006) and *Quality of Life, Sustainability and Economic Development: State and Local Options*, co-authored with Daphne Greenwood (M.E. Sharpe, forthcoming).

**Philip Kozel** received his Ph.D. in Economics from the University of Massachusetts, Amherst. As an Assistant Professor at Rollins College, he has helped his department to complete an extensive reform of the economics major. His current research is on the economics of piracy from the high seas to DVDs.

**Rogier De Langhe** is a Ph.D. fellow of the Research Foundation of Flanders (FWO) and works in the field of philosophy of social science, exploring such topics as models, explanation, and economic methodology.

**Tony Lawson** lectures in the Faculty of Economics at the University of Cambridge, U.K. He is organizer of the Cambridge Social Ontology Group, and the Cambridge Realist Workshop, and until recently was Executive Director of the Cambridge Centre for Gender Studies. He has published various articles and books, the latter including *Economics and Reality*, and *Reorienting Economics*, both with Routledge.

**Frederic S. Lee** is Professor of Economics at the University of Missouri Kansas City and the Executive Director of the International Confederation of Associations for Pluralism in Economics (ICAPE). He has published in numerous heterodox economics journals, including the *Journal of Economic Issues, Review of Radical Political Economy, Review of Social Economy, Journal of Post Keynesian Economics, Review of Political Economy*, and *Journal of Australian Political Economy*. He is also the editor of the widely circulated Heterodox Economics Newsletter.

**Gustavo Marqués** is Magister in Philosophy and Doctor in Philosophy (University of Buenos Aires). He is full Professor of Methodology of the Social Sciences and Epistemology of Economics (Faculty of Economic Sciences, UBA and UNLZ). He has written and published many books and articles about methodology and epistemology of the social sciences and economics, most of them in Spanish. His paper, "Criticizing Dow and Chick's Dualism: The Case of the Dual 'Rational/Irrational' in the Stock Market" appeared in English in the *Post Autistic Economics Review*, issue 35.

**KimMarie McGoldrick** is Professor of Economics in the Robins School of Business at the University of Richmond in Virginia. Her passion for developing her students' research skills led her to develop a new economics capstone experience in which students apply, assess, and extend the theoretical and applied models they have encountered in their economics coursework. Over the past seven years she has (co)coordinated many teaching and learning workshops including five CeMENT regional mentoring workshops, several IAFFE teaching workshops, a Service Learning in Economics workshop, and an Annual Teaching Workshop in Wilmington, NC. She is a member of the staff of the Teaching Innovations Program, an NSF funded project designed to improve undergraduate education in economics by offering instructors an opportunity to expand their teaching skills and to participate in the scholarship of teaching and learning. She also serves on the Editorial Board of the *Journal of Economic Education*. She is currently completing an edited volume (with David Colander) on *Educating Economists: The Teagle Discussion on Reevaluating the Undergraduate Economics Major* (Edward Elgar, 2010).

**Ioana Negru** is Lecturer in Economics at Anglia Ruskin University, Cambridge. She has recently published in the area of economic methodology and pluralism. Her main research interests include the economics of gift exchange and altruism, Austrian economics, the philosophy of economics, and economic methodology.

**Rod O'Donnell** completed his Ph.D. at Cambridge University in 1982 and was Professor of Economics at Macquarie University from 1995 to 2007. He is now Professor of Economics at the University of Technology, Sydney. His varied research interests include the thought of J.M. Keynes (economics, philosophy, and politics), macroeconomics, pluralist economics, skill formation in graduates, and the teaching of economics.

**Erik K. Olsen** is Assistant Professor of Economics and member of Doctoral Faculty at the University of Missouri Kansas City. He teaches Political Economy, Urban Economics, Mathematical Economics, and Microeconomics at both the graduate and undergraduate levels. He received his Ph.D. in Economics from the University of Massachusetts Amherst in 2005.

**Gilles Raveaud** was a post-doctoral fellow at Harvard University at the time of this writing. He is currently Assistant Professor at the Institute of European Studies at the University of Paris Saint-Denis. He received his Ph.D. in

Economics from the Université Paris-X Nanterre (France). He was in June 2000 one of the founders of the Post-Autistic Economics Network (PAEN) which mobilized students and lecturers to contest the hegemony of neo-classical economics at the universities. His research critically examines the discourses of mainstream economists and of the European Union on unemployment. His work has been published in the *Journal of Common Market Studies*.

**Martha Starr** is Associate Professor of Economics at American University in Washington, D.C. Prior to joining AU, she was a senior economist at the Federal Reserve Board of Governors. Her research is centrally concerned with issues of culture and social values in economic life, and has covered such subjects as consumerism and the media, lifestyle and consumption norms, gender and economic identity, "self-control" problems in consumer spending, socially responsible investment and consumption, and household saving. She is also strongly interested in macroeconomics and monetary policy, especially as they relate to globalization and development. Her work has appeared in a wide range of journals, with recent articles having appeared in the *Review of Social Economy*, *Review of Radical Political Economy*, *Economic Inquiry*, *Contemporary Economic Policy*, *Journal of Comparative Economics*, and *Global Society*. She is a co-editor of the *Review of Social Economy*.

**Virgil Henry Storr** is Senior Research Fellow and the Director of Graduate Student Programs at the Mercatus Center and the Don C. Lavoie Research Fellow in the Program in Philosophy, Politics and Economics, Department of Economics, George Mason University. He holds a Ph.D. in Economics from George Mason University and a B.A. from Beloit College. Virgil's book on the Bahamas' economic culture, *Enterprising Slaves and Master Pirates*, was published by Peter Lang. He is currently working on a new book, *The Culture of Markets*, to be published by Routledge in their Advances in Heterodox Economics series.

**Diana Strassmann** is the founding editor of *Feminist Economics*, the journal of the International Association for Feminist Economics (IAFFE) and a co-founder of IAFFE. After receiving her A.B. in economics from Princeton University and her M.A. and Ph.D in economics from Harvard University, she joined the Rice University faculty in 1983. She is currently Professor of the Practice in Rice University's Center for Women, Gender, and Sexuality Studies, a faculty affiliate at Rice's Chao Center for Asian Studies, and director of Rice's Program in Poverty, Social Justice, and Human Capabilities. She has published widely in the fields of economic regulation, environmental policy, and feminist economic theory. Her current research focuses on the impact of feminism on economics.

**Yanis Varoufakis** was born in Athens in 1961, where he received his secondary education prior to completing his university studies. He has held academic appointments at the University of Essex, University of East Anglia, University of Sydney, and University of Glasgow. Since 2000, he has taught political economy at the University of Athens where he directs UADPhilEcon, an international doctoral program in economics. His books include *Rational Conflict* (Blackwell 1991), *Foundations of Economics* (Routledge 1998), and *Game Theory: A Critical Text* (Routledge 2004). He is currently working on a book entitled *Modern Political Economy*, also to be published by Routledge.

**William Waller** is Professor of Economics and Director of Wine Studies at Hobart and William Smith Colleges where he has taught since 1982. He received his B.S (1978) and M.A. (1979) in economics from Western Michigan University. He received his Ph.D. in economics from the University of New Mexico (1984). He is past-president of the Association for Evolutionary Economics and past-president of the Association for Institutional Thought. He has served as a trustee of the Association for Social Economics, a member of the editorial board of the *Journal of Economic Issues*, and as member of the board of directors of the Association for Evolutionary Economics, where he served for a year as acting Secretary-Treasurer. He is currently a trustee of the Association for Evolutionary Economics. He has co-edited two books, *Alternatives to Economic Orthodoxy* (M.E. Sharpe, 1987) and *The Stratified State* (M.E. Sharpe, 1992). His articles on institutionalist methodology, feminist economics, public policy, and the work of Thorstein Veblen have been published in *Journal of Economic Issues*, *Review of Social Economy*, *History of Political Economy*, and *Review of Institutional Thought* as well as a number of edited collections. He is active in the Association for Evolutionary Economics, the Association for Institutional Thought, the Association for Social Economics, and the International Association for Feminist Economics.

**Diego Weisman** has a degree in Economics and in Philosophy from the University of Buenos Aires, where he is undertaking postgraduate studies in the field of Epistemology of Economics. In the last five years, he has been a research fellow of the Research Center for the Epistemology of Economic Sciences (CIECE), where he has been involved in many studies of the Epistemology of Economics.

# Acknowledgments

This volume would not exist but for the extensive collaboration that brought 200 economists from 29 countries to the University of Utah in early June 2007 for a three-day conference on Economic Pluralism for the 21st Century. Special recognition and thanks are due to the International Confederation of Associations for Pluralism in Economics (ICAPE) for sponsoring the conference and to the ICAPE conference organizing committee: Al Campbell (University of Utah), Wilfred Dolfsma (Utrecht School of Economics), Edward Fullbrook (University of the West of England), Robert Garnett (Texas Christian University), Neva Goodwin (Tufts University), John Henry (University of Missouri, Kansas City), Mary King (Portland State University), Frederic Lee (University of Missouri, Kansas City), Judith Mehta (University of East Anglia), Edward McNertney (Texas Christian University), Erik K. Olsen (University of Missouri, Kansas City), and Martha Starr (American University). Equally crucial were the heroic contributions of the University of Utah: Al Campbell, Korkut Erturk, Becky Guillory, Julie Robinson, Scott Kjelstrom, Rogier Kamerling, Ozge Ozay, Carlos Schonerwald da Silva, Yongbok Jeon, Ozden Birkan, and Adem Yavuz Elveren.

In our attempt to craft a thematically cogent volume, we were able to select only a small subset of the conference papers. We are grateful to all conferees who submitted their papers for possible inclusion in this volume, and to each of our contributors for their gracious responses to our extensive requests for revision.

Finally, we thank Terry Clague, Tom Sutton, Sarah Hastings, and Beth Lewis at Routledge and Allie Waite at Wearset for their generous assistance in the production and marketing of this collection.

# Economic pluralism for the twenty-first century

*Robert Garnett, Erik K. Olsen, and Martha Starr*

Half a century ago, a book exploring the value of pluralism in economic inquiry, institutions, and education would have seemed anomalous, particularly in the United States. In the wake of World War II, economists were "covered in glory" (Morgan and Rutherford 1998: 13), having solved many wartime policy problems with their newly acquired mathematical and statistical expertise (Sent 2006: 83). The economist was increasingly regarded as a "neutral, professional scientist, offering expert, value-free advice" (Morgan and Rutherford 1998: 11); and the economists' new tools – formal modeling, econometric testing, and hypothetico-deductive reasoning – were widely admired as the *sine qua non* of a rigorous, objective social science (ibid.: 9). Scientific monism thus emerged as the mainline ethos of postwar economics (Weintraub 2002), in marked contrast to the pluralist atmosphere of the 1920s and 1930s in which "it was possible to hold a number of different economic beliefs and to do economics in many different ways without being out of place or necessarily forfeiting the respect of one's peers" (ibid.: 4).

Many proponents of scientific monism in postwar U.S. economics saw themselves as freedom fighters. They defended the singularity of Truth and Method as "a wall against irrational and authoritarian threats to inquiry" (McCloskey 1998: 169; Richardson 2006: 14–16).

> For the immigrants who lived through the interwar period in Europe – and some, like Marschak, who fled first Lenin and then Hitler – this hope of building a *wertfrei* social science, immune to propaganda of every kind, gave motivating force to the econometrics movement.
> (Leijonhufvud and Craver 1987: 181; see also Hutchison 1960 [1938] and Popper 1945).

In this broader context, postwar U.S. economics and its ascendant monism were part of a "grand crusade against fascism and totalitarianism" (Bernstein 1999: 108). Noble aims notwithstanding, however, advocates of these new analytical methods often crossed the lines that divide scholarly enthusiasm from illiberal zeal; they "adopted a crusading faith, a set of philosophical doctrines, that made them prone to fanaticism and intolerance" (McCloskey 1998: 140). Circa 1965, mainstream economists' elevated social status and methodological hubris predisposed them to dismiss alternative theories *tout court* as unscientific.

Dissenters objected to the mainstream's hegemonic intolerance in a variety of ways. One group of challengers pursued a "fight science with science" strategy. Leading Austrian, Marxian, Sraffian, post Keynesian, institutionalist, and new classical theorists in the 1970s and early 1980s developed paradigmatic altern-atives to prevailing micro- and macroeconomic orthodoxies (cf. Dolan 1976; Desai 1979; Steedman 1977; Kregel 1975; Eichner 1979; and Tool 1979).[1] These critics were monist in their pursuit of stand-alone alternatives to mainstream theory. Yet they were also pluralist in one important sense. Against the grain of the modernist unity-of-science movement, they sought to make truth and method contestable in economic inquiry. We therefore regard their diverse heterodox projects as a first wave of pluralism in contemporary economics.

By the early 1990s, however, dissatisfaction with this Kuhnian school-of-thought-ism gave rise to a new genre of pluralism, "not just polite tolerance among parallel schools, each with its own truth" but "active dialogue and mutual learning among self-consciously partial perspectives" (Fullbrook 2005). Philo-sophically, the second-wave pluralists stood atop a wide raft of post-positivist work on economic ontology and epistemology that had flourished in the 1980s. This included the work of pragmatists, postmodernists, Marxists and post-Marxists, Keynesians and post Keynesians, feminists, realists, hermeneuticists, institutionalists, post-structuralists, and others (Tribe 1978; Resnick and Wolff 1982; McCloskey 1983; Klamer 1983; Amariglio 1984; Ruccio 1984; Amariglio 1988; Mirowski 1987; Mäki 1989; Dow 1990; Lavoie 1990; Samuels 1990; Strassmann 1993; Lawson 1994).

Second-wave pluralists were dissatisfied with the notion of science as empire building or paradigmatic one-upmanship, a monist view they ascribed to many mainstream economists as well as to their first-wave critics. In seeking to explain the broad embrace of this monist view by postwar economists, some new plural-ist writers (Fullbrook 2001; Garnett 2006; Marqués and Weisman this volume) pointed to the influence of Thomas Kuhn's *Structure of Scientific Revolutions* (Kuhn 1962). Cold War language and logic permeate Kuhn's text (Fuller 2000; Fullbrook 2001), most notably in Kuhn's analogy between scientific paradigms and rival political systems: "Like the choice between competing political institu-tions, the choice between competing paradigms proves to be a choice between incompatible modes of community life" (Kuhn 1962: 94). On Fullbrook's reading of Kuhn's *Structure*,

> Kuhn's book methodically transposes the Cold War narrative onto the competing-theories narrative of science.... Kuhn's narrative makes the defense of one's paradigm community, through the elimination or marginal-ization of rival ones, the scientist's overriding goal.... It is this emotionally-charged us-or-them, all-or-nothing mentality which Kuhn's book seems to legitimate as the ethos of science.
>
> (Fullbrook 2001)

Post-Kuhnian pluralism gained wide visibility in 1992, when Geoffrey Hodgson, Uskali Mäki, and Donald McCloskey published a petition in the *American Economic Review* (signed by 44 leading economists, including four Nobel laureates) calling for "a new spirit of pluralism in economics, involving critical conversation and tolerant communication between different approaches" and demanding that this new pluralism be "reflected in the character of scientific debate, in the range of contributions in its journals, and in the training and hiring of economists" (Hodgson *et al.* 1992). One year later, Hodgson, John Adams, Terry Neale, and several other economists created an international consortium, ICARE (the International Confederation of Associations for the Reform of Economics), to serve as an institutional voice for the new pluralism. By 2000, ICARE had been joined by the U.K.-based Association for Heterodox Economics, pluralistic journals like the *Review of Political Economy*, and pluralistic organizations like the European Association for Evolutionary Political Economy – all creating new spaces for dialogue and collaboration among previously segregated schools of thought (Lee 2002).

The new pluralism gained additional momentum in 2000 and 2001, when a series of petitions from young economists in France, the United Kingdom, the United States, and Italy ignited the international Post-Autistic Economics (PAE) movement (Fullbrook 2003).[2] This student-led movement called for a more open and scientific economics, guided by a philosophically principled pluralism:

> [a pluralism] that regards the various "schools" of economics, including neoclassicalism, as offering different windows on economic reality, each bringing into view different subsets of economic phenomena ... [and] rejects the idea that any school could possess final or total solutions, but accepts all as possible means for understanding real-life economic problems.
>
> (Fullbrook 2003: 8–9)

The pluralistic ethos of the PAE movement struck a resonant chord with economics students and faculty around the world, giving rise to what Fullbrook describes as a "peace movement," an historic attempt to forge unity among dissenting economists who despite being "a sizable and growing minority" had long been divided into separate schools of thought (Fullbrook 2003: 2). Sheila Dow concurs:

> The interesting new work among young scholars is synthetic in nature, exploring the middle ground between schools of thought and developing new ideas as a result of cross-fertilization.
>
> (Dow 2008: 9)

Our strict juxtaposition of first- and second-wave pluralism is of course stylized. Many economists today would identify with key elements of both perspectives. Yet the epistemological perspectives of first- and second-wave pluralism are sufficiently divergent to warrant a distinction. First-wave pluralists place a high value on paradigmatic self-sufficiency. Their ideal is the analytically unified and self-contained school of thought whose practitioners need not engage in scholarly dialogue beyond the boundaries of their own tradition. Second-wave pluralists, in contrast, aspire to a Millian pluralism: a "positive valuing of a diversity of views in the minimal sense that one who is so committed would not want to reduce the number of available narratives or views" (Hargreaves-Heap 2001: 356; see also Mill 2001 [1859]). From this perspective, the value of interparadigmatic conversation never ends since there is no possibility, even in principle, that "any school could possess final or total solutions" (Fullbrook 2003: 8–9).

As economics enters the twenty-first century, tensions between these monist and pluralist ideals – unity and difference, closure and openness, self-sufficiency and interdependence – are generating important new lines of thought and discovery. The shifting terrain of post-Cold War economic theory is posing novel questions, for example, about the meaning and value of paradigms and pluralism. Is it any longer accurate or useful to classify neoclassical economics as a single body of thought (Colander 2000)? Are mainstream economists becoming more pluralistic (Davis 2006)? Are heterodox economists as pluralistic as they claim to be (cf. Sent 2003; Van Bouwel 2004; Lee this volume)? Does the mainstream/heterodox serve to affirm and protect non-mainstream traditions, or does it only deepen their marginality and hasten their dissolution (Lee 2009; Colander this volume)? Should non-mainstream economists seek to produce a "single correct alternative to neoclassical economics" or should they pursue pluralist objectives (King 2002)? Is scientific progress in economics enhanced or retarded when individual scholars abide by pluralist norms (De Langhe this volume; Boettke 2007)?

Economics education is a second area in which critical synergies between pluralist and monist perspectives are giving rise to new conversations. Economics educators increasingly agree, for instance, that students' intellectual development is inhibited by the authoritarian monism of conventional economics textbooks, curricula, and pedagogies. At the same time, sharp disagreements remain over whether or not "economics students are entitled to a solid disciplinary training in prevailing economic theory" (Vromen 2007: 64). These disputes are the latest in a long-running debate over the goals of the undergraduate economics major. Critics have rightly objected to the paradigmatic parochialism embedded in the standard goal of teaching students to "think like economists" (Siegfried *et al.* 1991). But rather than rejecting the traditional mantra, recent work on these questions has followed the "mend it, don't end it" path proposed two decades ago by Bartlett and Feiner (1992). Leading economics educators are speaking across the mainstream/heterodox divide, trying to restate the concept of thinking like an economist to convey not "thinking like a traditional microeconomist" but the broader liberal art of reaching reasoned economic conclusions in the face of analytical, empirical, or normative uncertainties (Colander and McGoldrick 2008; Becker 2004; Knoedler and Underwood 2003; Feiner 2002; Earl 2000; Ferber 1999).

A third nexus of pluralist rethinking lies in the rapidly evolving field of comparative economics. Postwar development economists posited a tripartite classification of national economies: capitalist (First World), socialist-communist (Second World), and other (Third World). This venerable continuum, along with the very idea of an economic system, are being recast in distinctly pluralist ways today by feminist, Marxist, institutionalist, Austrian, and human development economists, all of whom emphasize the historical-institutional complexity, contingency, and path-dependence of every economic system (cf. Gibson-Graham 1996; Resnick and Wolff 2002; Hodgson 1999; Buchanan 1991; Koppl 2008; Sen 1999). Roger Koppl (2008: 925), for example, writing in the free-market tradition of Austrian economics, argues that

> Little is said when we declare the superiority of "the free market" over "intervention." Any market is governed by formal and informal rules, and no one set of rules is uniquely able to render markets "free." It is easy enough to see the difference between Soviet-style socialism and Western democratic capitalism. It is not always easy to decide when a marginal change in the rules diminishes freedom.

The old debates – capitalism vs. socialism and the like – are still present in economic discourse; but they are gradually being eclipsed by new debates about the relative (dis)advantages of untidy economic hybrids such as gift economies, basic income grants, and ethically inspired market action (e.g., ethical consumption, investment, or production practices).

This volume offers a snapshot of contemporary pluralist thinking in each of these important domains. Its 20 essays, all previously unpublished, reflect the creativity and controversy that currently surround discussions of economic pluralism. The first eight chapters address questions of pluralism in the philosophical realms of epistemology, ontology, and methodology; the remaining 12 chapters explore the roles and consequences of pluralism in real-world economies and economics education, respectively. Innovative reforms in all of these areas promise to add substantial value to economics and economies in the twenty-first century. In support of these transformative efforts, *Economic Pluralism* aims to encourage critical conversations about the role and value of pluralism in all forms of economic institutions, knowledge, and learning.

## Pluralism and economic inquiry

The first eight chapters examine conceptual and philosophical aspects of economic pluralism. Pluralism in this context refers to the claim that there is no uniquely warranted theoretical lens through which to view the world, no single methodology for characterizing it empirically, and no single set of questions worthy of investigation (Kellert *et al.* 2006). Chapters 1–4, "Pluralism and heterodoxy," offer contentious perspectives on the value of broadening the circles of economic conversation among heterodox schools of thought, or between heterodox and mainstream discourses, and how this might productively be done.

The first chapter, by current ICAPE president Frederic Lee ("Pluralism in heterodox economics"), looks at evidence for the existence of pluralism within heterodox economics. He argues that economics is divided into two distinct alternative perspectives: mainstream economics and heterodox economics. For some time now, mainstream economists have demonstrated a pronounced anti-pluralism toward their heterodox colleagues by refusing to engage with heterodox theories, progressively excluding heterodox economists from academic positions, preventing heterodox economists from gaining influence in professional organizations, and denigrating heterodox journals and departments in ranking exercises. In contrast, Lee finds that heterodox economists (Post Keynesian, institutionalist, Marxist, feminist, and others) have made pluralism a core value. Not only do these economists maintain a level of proficiency in mainstream economics, they also engage meaningfully with one another. Lee documents the extent to which heterodox economists belong to multiple professional associations, routinely cite work in journals from different heterodox perspectives, and participate in conferences sponsored by diverse heterodox economics organizations. Lee argues that while the different traditions that constitute heterodox economics have distinct identities, there is such sustained integration of the different heterodox approaches that they can be considered a "pluralistic, integrative whole." Heterodox economics is thus a living example of how pluralist dialog can enrich the participating viewpoints and perhaps yield a coherent body of analysis that transcends the individual perspectives.

David Colander, whose own work successfully straddles mainstream and heterodox discourses, argues ("Moving beyond the rhetoric of pluralism: suggestions for an 'inside-the-mainstream' heterodoxy"), in contrast to Lee, that heterodox calls for pluralism are unlikely to change the mainstream's disinterest in heterodox work. Mainstream economists are so busy competing with each other for the highly limited access to the profession's highly regarded outlets that heterodox work simply never makes it onto their radar screens. Colander proposes several strategies to change this fact, centered on possibilities of articulating heterodox work more effectively along the innovative edges of mainstream research.

William Waller ("Is convergence among heterodox schools possible, meaningful, or desirable?") looks at the pluralism/heterodoxy relationship through an evolutionary lens, arguing that forces of selection tend to produce convergences in ideas, interests, and methods across schools of thought. This selection mechanism makes increased cross-talk among heterodox schools not only likely but inevitable.

Diana Strassmann, Martha Starr, and Caren Grown ("Raising dissonant voices: pluralism and economic heterodoxy") point out that, in both heterodox and mainstream circles, participation in the production of economic knowledge is dominated by people with certain characteristics: men over women, people of European over African or Latino ancestry, and people from wealthy countries over the rest of the world. Since knowledge production is inevitably shaped by the life experiences, positions, and judgments of its participants, efforts to foster pluralism in economics risk being hollow if they aim only to diversify theoretical and methodological approaches, without also broadening the range of voices regularly heard in economic discourse.

The remaining chapters in Part I, collectively titled "Theorizing pluralism," examine conceptual, theoretical, and pragmatic dimensions of pluralism in economic inquiry. For Gustavo Marqués and Diego Weisman ("Is Kuhnean incommensurability a good basis for pluralism in economics?"), pluralism has two distinct meanings: a diversity of paradigms, and an attitude of engagement and open mindedness. They argue that the work of J.S. Mill provides stronger support for both types of pluralism than does Kuhn's incommensurability thesis, which many heterodox economists (notably Sheila Dow) have invoked in support of economic pluralism. Kuhn's incommensurability thesis provides only a negative basis for recommending pluralism. We cannot entirely rule out viewpoints incommensurable with our own because we lack the epistemological grounds to do so; but this does not mean that these viewpoints have merit or can contribute to knowledge production within one's preferred paradigm. Marqués and Weisman also read Kuhn as arguing that paradigms develop because of convergent thinking within the paradigm, not from conversation across paradigms. Mill, on the other hand, provides positive reasons for embracing pluralism. For Mill, liberty of expression requires an attitude of openness and engagement among people and society, i.e. a pluralist orientation. Further, since human knowledge is fallible, dissenting ideas must not be silenced. Encounters between different viewpoints are necessary to fully develop and grasp one's own ideas. Hence pluralism must not only be tolerated but embraced as an active catalyst for knowledge production. Heterodox economists should therefore reconsider their de facto reliance upon Kuhn's incommensurability thesis and look instead to Mill as a basis for pluralism.

Rogier De Langhe ("Why should *I* adopt pluralism?") points out that lack of consensus, or dissensus, is both ubiquitous and enduring across the social and natural sciences. It is better understood as a stylized fact of scientific endeavor rather than an anomalous and transient state between normal periods of consensus. The task for communities of scholars and for science policy, therefore, is to manage this diversity of views without halting or distorting knowledge production. Pluralism provides a means to do this, but De Langhe also sees a paradox. Individual-level pluralism entails an "anything goes" attitude that prevents a scholar from taking a robust stance and defending a position. So while pluralism provides a way to manage diversity, it may inhibit knowledge production. De Langhe proposes to resolve this paradox by distinguishing between individual and community levels of pluralism. Individual scholars can make warranted, albeit subjective, choices among competing alternatives, but diverse communities of scholars cannot. Hence pluralism is a desirable characteristic of *groups* of scholars, and provides a way to manage diversity while promoting knowledge production, even though *individual* level pluralism is not desirable.

Tony Lawson ("Ontology, modern economics, and pluralism") addresses the charge of anti-pluralism that is sometimes leveled against projects – such as his own critical realism – that aim to provide an integrated, scientific alternative to mainstream economics. He sees this criticism as misguided if, as in the case of critical realism, the proposed alternative is itself pluralist. Vinca Bigo ("The Cambridge School and pluralism") confronts the related argument that critical realists are anti-pluralist because of their unwavering preference for "open" rather than "closed" conceptions of economic and social systems. Bigo contests this claim, arguing that a critical realist stance does not entail the rejection of all work done from a closed-system perspective; rather, it rejects the insistence that all economic analysis must be conducted within a closed-system framework.

## Pluralism and real-world economies

The seven chapters in Part II consider pluralism in economic structures, institutions, and relations. They address several related themes: What are the desired characteristics of a pluralistic economy? What are the advantages of an economy that recognizes and encourages diverse economic arrangements? To what extent are these pluralist features found in existing economies? How might the desired features of pluralist economies become more prevalent? How can a plurality of economic theories contribute to this? These questions are all the more apt in light of the financial turmoil across the globe and economic downturn unfolding in 2009. The bounds of what is possible, desirable, and indeed necessary in terms of reform and public action seem to be broader now than at any time in a generation, and this calls for discussion that is open not only to diverse perspectives but also to diverse institutional forms.

The first four essays ("Economic democracy and the common good") focus on the characteristics of a pluralist economy. Gar Alperovitz ("America beyond capitalism: the Pluralist Commonwealth") considers the question of what the U.S. economy might look like *beyond* capitalism. He finds that while long-term trends have left people less free, less equal, and less in control of their own futures, a new mosaic of ideas and policies has been taking shape at the state, local, and firm level that can counter these trends. This new mosaic contains the building blocks of a democratic political-economic system that differs from the capitalisms and socialisms we have known in the past. Alperovitz calls this the "Pluralist Commonwealth." Large-scale public ownership of corporate equity, worker-owned and community-benefitting enterprises, Community Development Corporations, nonprofit corporations, and enterprising state and local public agencies all have a role to play in this commonwealth. These are not utopian hopes; all of these institutions exist and are thriving in some form in the U.S. today. Alperovitz claims that some kind of systemic transformation, while not necessarily imminent, may be emerging as a spontaneous, evolutionary response to the manifest ills of contemporary U.S. capitalism.

Robin Hahnel's essay ("From competition and greed to equitable cooperation: what does a pluralist economics have to offer?") begins with the provocative claim that the movements for economic justice, economic democracy, and environmental sustainability have failed miserably over the past quarter century. Hahnel argues that heterodox economists have contributed to this failure through their misconceptions about the nature of capitalism, lack of clarity about what is required to achieve progressive economic change, and flawed visions of the desired alternatives. The key to reversing a generation of defeat is fundamental change in the way economists understand capitalist economies, as well as new strategies for seeking change. Like Alperovitz, Hahnel sees glimmers of hope in an otherwise unpleasant economic reality – already-existing "experiments in equitable cooperation" within the prevailing capitalist economy such as local currency systems, cooperative enterprises, and intentional communities that should be recognized and cultivated. While imperfect and incomplete, these experiments are indispensible as pilot programs for a progressive economics movement that seeks to replace capitalism with equitable cooperation.

Daphne Greenwood and Ric Holt ("Growth, development and quality of life: a pluralist approach") argue for a new way of thinking about quality of life and sustainability at the community level. They note that mainline economic theory tends to obscure the distinction between growth and development. Economic growth has yet to be proven sustainable, and rising aggregate income tells us very little about human health, inequality, power, culture, or human relationships. Growth itself is a poor and misleading indicator of quality of life. Greenwood and Holt call for a new approach to economic theory that integrates social development, economic growth, and "strong sustainability." They see elements of this new approach in ecological, feminist, post-Keynesian, Marxist, and institutionalist economic theories – in the diverse yet complementary perspectives of Veblen, Ayres, Galbraith, Georgescu-Roegen, Boulding, Daly, and Nelson. These different traditions all have something to contribute to the new pluralist approach to human well-being that Greenwood and Holt advocate.

Finally, Emily Chamlee-Wright ("Beyond the status quo, in the world and in the discipline: the comments of an Austrian economist") approaches the arguments of Alperovitz, Hahnel, Greenwood, and Holt from the perspective of an Austrian economist. One might expect an Austrian to be mostly satisfied with the political-economic status quo, given the broad support accorded to market-based solutions in recent decades. But this is not the position taken by Chamlee-Wright. Like many left-leaning heterodox economists, she is deeply dissatisfied with the current state of both political-economic affairs and the economics profession, and argues that important theoretical and policy changes are needed in order to advance the common good. She also agrees with Alperovitz and Hahnel that civil society (the non-governmental public realm) offers rich possibilities for cooperation and experimentation, and calls for a pluralistic conversation among economists over the role of civil society as a means to remedy pressing social problems. Where Chamlee-Wright differs from the other contributors is in her vision of the state. Rather than turn to government as a complement to civil society, Chamlee-Wright proposes turning to radically de-politicized market processes in which the winners and losers are not preordained. For her the appropriate way forward is Tocquevillian – fostering complex forms of voluntary community, civic and commercial – rather than the Alperovitz/Hahnel solution of civil society plus government.

The final three chapters in Part II ("Economic cooperation: commercial and communal") explore alternatives to monolithic conceptions of economy, particularly the notions of market economy or capitalism as all-pervasive systems that colonize and destroy all other forms of economic cooperation. Virgil Storr ("Hayek and Lefebvre on market space and extra-catallactic relationships") offers an unorthodox Austrian account of market processes as sources of commercial and communal cooperation. Storr's emphasis on the communal aspects of commerce is inspired by a creative joint reading of the Austrian economist Friedrich Hayek and the Marxist economic geographer Henri Lefebvre. While noting that Hayek and Lefebvre both fail to theorize the communal externalities of markets, Storr shows how their respective modes of analysis can be creatively combined to bring "extra-catallactic" relations into our theories and assessments of commercial societies.

Ioana Negru ("The plural economy of gifts and markets") examines the evolving relationship between gift and market forms of economic cooperation, both historically and within economic theory. Viewing gift exchange as a form of economic interaction that is never fully supplanted by a market economy, Negru challenges established economic and anthropological narratives that posit a linear progression gift to market modes of provisioning. She envisions instead a gift/market nexus, a behaviorally and institutionally diverse network of cooperation, as a lens through which to analyze economic life in historical and contemporary societies.

Philip Kozel ("Communities and local exchange networks: an Aristotelean view") analyzes two institutional innovations that arguably enhance the virtues and outcomes of market exchange: local currencies and local exchange trading systems. Against critics who see markets as necessarily entailing certain negative effects, Kozel argues, *pace* Aristotle and latter-day Aristoteleans like Amartya Sen, that the effects of markets are contingent upon the social arrangements in which they are embedded. Kozel's essay speaks to the virtues of pluralism both in terms of economic organization (commercial and communal forms of economic cooperation) and economic theory/philosophy (reaching across the left/right divide).

## Pluralism and economics education

Economics education is an emerging frontier in the economic pluralism movement. These final five chapters draw from the authors' diverse backgrounds and interests to describe innovative pedagogical, curricular, and professional reforms through which intellectual pluralism might become (and in some spaces is already) a valued goal and tool of graduate and undergraduate economics education.

KimMarie McGoldrick ("Promoting a pluralist agenda in undergraduate economics education") proposes creative strategies for pluralistic reform in undergraduate economics education. Over the past two decades, educators in economics and across the disciplines have increasingly embraced the goals of active learning, inclusive classrooms, and critical analytical thinking. These trends, McGoldrick suggests, open the door for pluralist reform in undergraduate economic education. She encourages mainstream and heterodox economists to form a "teaching commons," both to enlarge the professional dialog about economics education and to cultivate their shared goals and values as liberal educators.

Alison Butler ("The illusion of objectivity: implications for teaching economics") explores issues of inclusion and exclusion in the introductory economics classroom. While standard textbooks put forth a single, "objective" understanding of economic principles, Butler enumerates the diverse ways that economic phenomena are perceived depending upon an individual's race, gender, class, and other axes of social and economic difference. She offers concrete suggestions for how to enrich student learning by fostering inclusive, multi-perspectival discussions of economic ideas.

Gilles Raveaud ("A pluralist teaching of economics: why and how") reflects on the lessons he gained through a decade of work as a student, teacher, and active participant in the international post-autistic campaign for pluralistic reform in graduate and undergraduate economics education. He proposes an intelligent rethinking of introductory economics as a problem-centered course that includes but does not privilege standard neoclassical theory.

Rod O'Donnell ("Economic pluralism and skill formation: adding value to students, economies, and societies") argues that well-designed pluralist courses provide a broader and richer set of transferable thinking skills than their orthodox counterparts (e.g., learning to judge the relative value of competing claims when no single correct answer is available). He illustrates his claims with reference to his Contending Perspectives in Economics course at the University of New South Wales, Australia. O'Donnell's argument is exceptionally useful for instructors or administrators in need of a concrete rationale for pluralistic reform of undergraduate curricula.

Yanis Varoufakis ("A most peculiar success: constructing UADPhilEcon, a doctoral program in economics at the University of Athens") delivers a colorful first-hand account of the formation and structure of the Ph.D. program at the University of Athens. By virtue of its unique curriculum, learning goals, and pedagogy, the UADPhilEcon program is an exceptional model of pluralist education. Varoufakis argues that UADPhilEcon students achieve higher levels of intellectual autonomy via the "universal skills" they acquire through required courses in political philosophy, economic history, and the history of economic ideas, in addition to basic microeconomics, macroeconomics, mathematics, and econometrics courses.

## Parting words

This volume, while seeking to advance larger discussions of economic pluralism within and beyond the discipline of economics, is ultimately limited in scope. Its

20 chapters are devoted almost exclusively to pluralism as currently defined and debated by heterodox economists. Such a narrow focus may seem inconsistent with a pluralist ethos. To be clear, however, we see heterodox pluralism as merely one part of economic pluralism, not the whole. We are keenly aware of pluralist currents within mainstream economics, for example Davis (2006). We also do not regard heterodox economists as always and everywhere more pluralistic than their mainstream counterparts, or vice versa. We are excited by the pluralistic rethinking of human nature, well-being, and cooperation across the social sciences today, and believe that all economists can and should contribute to the overlapping conversations made possible by these emerging developments.

That said, we also believe that heterodox economists are well positioned to exercise leadership in the ongoing campaign to foster pluralism in all areas of economic discourse. Some observers claim that professional economics is no more pluralistic today than when Hodgson *et al.* published their "Plea for a Pluralistic and Rigorous Economics" petition in 1992. Others (ourselves included) point to the community of heterodox economists as one segment of the discipline in which a significant tilt toward pluralism has demonstrably occurred since the early 1990s (Lee 2002; Dow 2000; Fullbrook 2003; Lawson 2003). The chapters in this volume add breadth and nuance to this pluralist turn in heterodox economics. In so doing, we hope they might elicit broader conversations about the value of pluralism in economic inquiry, institutions, and education among economists at large.

## Notes

1 We do not classify feminist economics as a first-wave (Kuhnian) pluralist project, in part because feminist economics per se did not emerge until the late 1980s and because feminist economists have generally defined and conducted their project in a more open-handed manner than many of their heterodox counterparts.
2 The initial petitions from French students (2000) and professors (2001) as well as the 2001 petitions from Ph.D. students at Cambridge University and from an international gathering of economics students and faculty at the University of Missouri at Kansas City appear in Fullbrook (2003). A 2002 petition of Ph.D. students in Siena, Italy is available at www.debating.it/siena2003/conf_phd_econ2003/manifesto.htm. A 2003 petition by Harvard undergraduate students seeking a more pluralistic introduction to economics is recorded in Lee (2003). A similar 2008 petition by undergraduate and graduate students at the University of Notre Dame is available at: http://openeconomics.blogspot.com/.

## References

Amariglio, J. (1984) "Economic History and the Theory of Primitive Socio-Economic Development," Unpublished Ph.D. thesis, Department of Economics, University of Massachusetts, Amherst.
—— (1988) "The Body, Economic Discourse, and Power: An Economist's Introduction to Foucault," *History of Political Economy*, 20 (4): 583–613.
Bartlett, R.L. and Feiner, S.F. (1992) "Balancing the Economics Curriculum: Content, Method, and Pedagogy," *American Economic Review*, 82 (2): 559–64.

Becker, W.E. (2004) "Economics for a Higher Education," *International Review of Economics Education*, 3 (1): 52–62.

Bernstein, M.A. (1999) "Economic Knowledge, Professional Authority, and the State," in R.F. Garnett, Jr. (ed.) *What Do Economists Know?*, 103–23, London: Routledge.

Boettke, P.J. (2007) "Methodological Pluralism and the Austrian School of Economics?" Unpublished essay. Available at http://austrianeconomists.typepad.com/weblog/2007/12/methodological.html (accessed November 20, 2008).

Buchanan, J.M. (1991) *The Economics and the Ethics of Constitutional Order*, Ann Arbor: University of Michigan Press.

Colander, D. (2000) "The Death of Neoclassical Economics," *Journal of the History of Economic Thought*, 22 (2): 127–43.

Colander, D. and McGoldrick, K. (2008) "The Economics Major and a Liberal Education," Working paper, Department of Economics, Middlebury College.

Davis, J.B. (2006) "The Turn in Economics: Neoclassical Dominance to Mainstream Pluralism?" *Journal of Institutional Economics*, 2 (1): 1–20.

Desai, M. (1979) *Marxian Economics*, Oxford: Basil Blackwell.

Dolan, E.G. (1976) "Austrian Economics as Extraordinary Science," in E.G. Dolan (ed.) *The Foundations of Modern Austrian Economics*, 3–18, Kansas City: Sheed and Ward.

Dow, S. C. (1990) "Beyond Dualism," *Cambridge Journal of Economics*, 14 (2): 143–57.

—— (2000) "Prospects for the Progress in Heterodox Economics," *Journal of the History of Economic Thought*, 22 (2): 157–70.

—— (2008) "A Future for Schools of Thought and Pluralism in Heterodox Economics," in J.T. Harvey and R.F. Garnett, Jr. (eds.) *Future Directions for Heterodox Economics*, 9–26. Ann Arbor: University of Michigan Press.

Earl, P.E. (2000) "Indeterminacy in the Economics Classroom," in P.E. Earl and S.F. Frowen (eds.) *Economics as an Art of Thought: Essays in Memory of G.L.S. Shackle*, 25–50, London: Routledge.

Eichner, A. (1979) *A Guide to Post-Keynesian Economics*, White Plains, NY: M.E. Sharpe.

Feiner, S.F. (2002) "Toward a Post-Autistic Economics Education," *Post-Autistic Economics Review*, issue 12, March 15, article 2.

Ferber, M.A. (1999) "Guidelines for Pre-College Economics Education: A Critique," *Feminist Economics*, 5 (3): 135–42.

Fullbrook, E. (2001) "Real Science is Pluralist," *Post-Autistic Economics Review*, issue 5, March 13, article 5.

—— (ed.) (2003) *The Crisis in Economics. The Post-Autistic Economics Movement: The First 600 Days*, London: Routledge.

—— (2005) "The Rand Portcullis and PAE," *Post-Autistic Economics Review*, volume 32, July 5, article 5.

Fuller, S. (2000) *Thomas Kuhn: A Philosophical History for Our Times*, Chicago: University of Chicago Press.

Garnett, R.F., Jr. (2006) "Paradigms and Pluralism in Heterodox Economics," *Review of Political Economy*, 18 (Fall): 521–46.

Gibson-Graham, J.-K. (1996) *The End of Capitalism (as we knew it)*, Cambridge, MA: Blackwell.

Hargreaves-Heap, S. (2001) "Postmodernism, Rationality, and Justice," in S. Cullenberg, J. Amariglio, and D. Ruccio (eds.) *Postmodernism, Economics, and Knowledge*, 354–73, London: Routledge.

Hodgson, G.M. (1999) *Economics and Utopia: Why the Learning Economy is Not the End of History*, London: Routledge.

Hodgson, G.M., Mäki, U., and McCloskey, D.N. (1992) "Plea for a Pluralistic and Rigorous Economics," *American Economic Review*, 82 (May): xxv.

Hutchison, T.W. (1960 [1938]) *The Significance and Basic Postulates of Economic Theory*, Second edition, New York: Kelley.

Kellert, S.H., Longino, H.E., and Waters, C.K. (eds) (2006) *Scientific Pluralism*, Minneapolis: University of Minnesota Press.

King, J.E. (2002) "Three Arguments for Pluralism," *Journal of Australian Political Economy*, 50: 82–88.

Klamer, A. (1983) *Conversations with Economists*, Totowa, NJ: Rowman and Allanheld.

Knoedler, J. and Underwood, D. (2003) "Teaching the Principles of Economics: A Proposal for a Multi-paradigmatic Approach," *Journal of Economic Issues*, 37 (3): 697–725.

Koppl, R. (2008) "Computable Entrepreneurship," *Entrepreneurship Theory and Practice*, 32 (5): 919–26.

Kregel, J. (1975) *The Reconstruction of Political Economy: An Introduction to Post-Keynesian Economics*, London: Macmillan.

Kuhn, T.S. (1962) *The Structure of Scientific Revolutions*, Chicago: University of Chicago Press.

Lavoie, D. (ed.) (1990) *Hermeneutics and Economics*, London: Routledge.

Lawson, T. (1994) "A Realist Theory for Economics," in R.E. Backhouse (ed.) *New Directions in Economic Methodology*, 257–85. London: Routledge.

—— (2003) *Reorienting Economics*, London: Routledge.

Lee, F.S. (2002) "The Association for Heterodox Economics: Past, Present, and Future," *Journal of Australian Political Economy*, 50 (December): 29–43.

—— (2009) "A Note on the Pluralism Debate in Heterodox Economics." Unpublished paper, Department of Economics, University of Missouri Kansas City.

Lee, M. (2003) "Mission Statement," Cambridge, MA: Students for a Humane and Responsible Economics.

Leijonhufvud, A. and Craver, E. (1987) "Economics in America: The Continental Influence," *History of Political Economy*, 19 (2): 173–82.

Mäki, U. (1989) "On the Problem of Realism in Economics," *Ricerche Economiche*, 43 (1–2): 176–98.

McCloskey, D.N. (1983) "The Rhetoric of Economics," *Journal of Economic Literature*, 31 (June): 434–61.

—— (1998) *The Rhetoric of Economics*, Second edition, Madison: University of Wisconsin Press.

Mill, J.S. (2001) [1859] *On Liberty*, London: Electric Book Company.

Mirowski, P. (1987) "The Philosophical Bases of Institutionalist Economics," *Journal of Economic Issues*, 21 (September): 1001–38.

Morgan, M.S. and Rutherford, M. (eds) (1998) *From Interwar Pluralism to Postwar Neoclassicism*, Durham: Duke University Press.

Popper, K. (1945) *The Open Society and its Enemies*, London: Routledge.

Resnick, S.A. and Wolff, R.D. (1982) "Marxist Epistemology: The Critique of Economic Determinism," *Social Text*, 6 (Fall): 31–72.

—— (2002) *Class Theory and History: Capitalism and Communism in the USSR*, London: Routledge.

Richardson, A.W. (2006) "The Many Unities of Science: Politics, Semantics, and Ontology," in S. Kellert, H. Longino, and K. Waters (eds) *Scientific Pluralism*, 1–25, Minneapolis: University of Minnesota Press.

Ruccio, D.F. (1984) "Optimal Planning Theory and Theories of Socialist Planning," Unpublished Ph.D. thesis, Department of Economics, University of Massachusetts, Amherst.

Samuels, W.J. (1990) "Introduction," in W.J. Samuels (ed.) *Economics as Discourse*, 1–14, Boston: Kluwer Academic Publishers.

Sen, A. (1999) *Development as Freedom*, New York: Alfred A. Knopf.

Sent, E.-M. (2003) "Pleas for Pluralism," *Post-Autistic Economics Review*, volume 18, February 4, article 2.

—— (2006) "Pluralisms in Economics," in S. Kellert, H. Longino, and K. Waters (eds.) *Scientific Pluralism*, 80–101, Minneapolis: University of Minnesota Press.

Siegfried, J.J., Bartlett, R.L., Hansen, W.L., Kelley, A.C., McCloskey, D.N., and Tietenberg, T.H. (1991) "The Status and Prospects of the Economics Major," *Journal of Economic Education*, 23 (3): 197–224.

Steedman, I. (1977) *Marx After Sraffa*, London: New Left Books.

Strassmann, D. (1993) "The Stories of Economics and the Power of the Storyteller," *History of Political Economy*, 25 (1): 147–65.

Tool, M.R. (1979) *The Discretionary Economy: A Normative Theory of Political Economy*, Santa Monica, CA: Goodyear Publishing Co.

Tribe, K. (1978) *Land, Labour, and Economic Discourse*, London: Routledge and Kegan Paul.

Van Bouwel, J. (2004) "Explanatory Pluralism in Economics: Against the Mainstream?" *Philosophical Explorations*, 7 (3): 299–315.

Vromen, J. (2007) "In Praise of Moderate Plurality," in J. Groenewegen (ed.) *Teaching Pluralism in Economics*, 64–94, Cheltenham, UK and Northampton, MA: Edward Elgar.

Weintraub, E.R. (2002) *How Economics Became a Mathematical Science*, Durham: Duke University Press.

# Part I

# Pluralism and economic inquiry

# 1    Pluralism in heterodox economics

*Frederic S. Lee*

Throughout the twentieth century, economics has been divided into at least two alternative theoretical approaches (with numerous internal differences), mainstream economics and heterodox economics. Mainstream economists practice ecumenicalism or "internal pluralism" and hence treat their heretical brethren with tolerance. This is because they employ many of the same theoretical tools, models, and accompanying discourse and because many theoretical advances in mainstream theory started out as heretical ideas. One-time heretical economists thus often become well-respected mainstream economists.[1] In this sense, mainstream economics practices internal pluralism (Davis 2006). But once economists "cross the line" and became associated with heterodox economics, their work is unlikely to be regarded as serious or relevant by their mainstream colleagues.

Against this backdrop of disciplinary division and conflict, this chapter explores the foundational role of pluralism in heterodox economics. The first section examines the pluralism or lack of pluralism in the relationship between mainstream and heterodox economics in the United States and the United Kingdom. The second section surveys evidence of pluralism and integration within heterodox economics over the past century. Heterodox economics is a multi-level term that refers to (1) a group of broadly commensurable economic theories – specifically Post Keynesian-Sraffian, Marxist-radical, Institutional-evolutionary, social, feminist, Austrian, and ecological economics – each of which holds a non-commensurable position vis-à-vis mainstream economics; (2) a community of economists who engage with and are associated with one or more of the heterodox approaches; and (3) a coherent, distinct, evolving body of economic theory that draws upon various theoretical contributions by heterodox approaches and from which heterodox economic policy recommendations can be drawn. Within heterodox economics, pluralism therefore refers to engagement across different heterodox approaches and to the commitment to build a community of heterodox economists through professional and theoretical integration. The chapter concludes with an overview of pluralism and heterodox economics today.

## Anti-pluralism in economics

From 1900 to the 1970s, the intolerance and anti-pluralism of mainstream economists was directed at Marxist and Institutionalist economists in the United
States and at Marxist economists in the United Kingdom. Through the use of
state power – exemplified by the post-1918 Red Scare and later McCarthyism in
the United States and the state control of funding for adult education in the
United Kingdom, the power of the business community, and the class-elite
power vested in institutions of adult and higher education – Marxist economists
were not hired, or, if hired, often arbitrarily dismissed. Moreover, mainstream
economists took advantage of this power to denigrate Marxists and Institutionalists, to exclude them from their departments, and to silence them within their
professional organizations. After 1970, state power played a more indirect role
and professional power became more predominant in controlling heterodoxy
within the discipline. In particular, in the face of heterodox economists being
hired, heterodox associations being formed, heterodox journals being established, and heterodox departments with graduate programs being created after
1970, additional professional-based mechanisms for containing and eliminating
heterodox economics had to be found. In the United States the ranking of economic journals and departments by the National Research Council and/or economists became the mechanism, while in the United Kingdom, the
government-backed Research Assessment Exercise and Quality Assurance
Agency for Higher Education subject benchmarks and reviews, which were captured by the mainstream, became the mechanisms.

The consequences of these mechanisms were that mainstream economists
(often in conjunction with university administrators) used them to cleanse their
departments of heterodox economists, to not hire heterodox economists, and to
restrict and constrain teaching to mainstream economics and research to mainstream topics. The first example of this occurred at the University of Houston in
the early 1970s, but it also occurred at the University of Texas and the University of Connecticut, and most recently at the University of Notre Dame. Moreover, in the 1990s, the University of Manchester and University of Cambridge
explicitly dismissed the importance and relevance of heterodox economics and
made well-advertised efforts to hire only mainstream economists (and many
other old and new universities also made the same anti-pluralistic decisions).

By the end of the twentieth century, the hegemony of mainstream theory in
doctoral programs (as well as undergraduate programs) was seemingly so complete in the United States that the American Economic Association Commission
on Graduate Education in Economics simply did not recognize that economic
theories other than mainstream economic theory existed, while also noting that
graduate programs were virtually identical in terms of the core theory taught at
both the graduate and undergraduate level.[2] Similarly, in the United Kingdom,
approximately 60 percent of undergraduate and 77 percent of graduate students
receive no exposure to heterodox economics, over 40 percent of the departments
have no heterodox economists on staff (including nearly all the top-ranked

departments), and only approximately 10 percent of undergraduate and graduate students (located mostly in low or no-ranked departments) receive a significant and positive engagement to heterodox economics and encouragement to do heterodox dissertations. Such intellectual insularity and dominance is the end product of the century-long anti-pluralistic attitude that promoted the repression of heterodox economics and its complement of indoctrinating students with mainstream theory (Lee 2004, 2006, 2007a, and 2007b; Strassman 1993; and Klamer and Colander 1990).

## Anti-pluralism and heterodox economics

The outcome of the anti-pluralism of mainstream economists is an asymmetrical critical scholarly engagement with heterodox economics, which would further reinforce the mainstream proclivities for anti-pluralism (if this is possible). Since both mainstream and heterodox economics provide alternative, incommensurable explanations for the same economic phenomena and social scientists, politicians, and government officials use them to develop economic and social policies, then critical scholarly engagement between the two approaches would seem reasonable. Moreover, such critical scholarly dialogue might promote theoretical developments within each paradigm that otherwise would not occur. However, being monolingual, mainstream economists can not and hence do not engage with their heterodox brethren as evident by the fact that core mainstream journals form a closed self-referencing group. That is to say, these journals cite other core mainstream journals and vice versa; but these journals in general do not cite core heterodox journals (see Lee and Harley 1998; Lee 2008a; and Appendix I in Lee 2009), especially ignoring the Marxist, Institutionalist, and interdisciplinary journals.[3] Thus mainstream economists who publish in the core mainstream journals are influenced only by those journals and are ignorant of any views that are not carried by them, which imply that they are completely ignorant of the current developments in heterodox economics.

In contrast, because all heterodox economists have been trained in mainstream economics and hence know its language, many attempt to critically engage with mainstream economists and hence devote part of their research time to keeping up with the current developments in mainstream economics, to understanding what they are saying, to criticizing their theoretical and empirical arguments, and to explaining why there needs to be an alternative paradigm. It follows that many of the articles by heterodox economists that are published in heterodox journals are concerned with issues in mainstream economics. Heterodox economists are also concerned with issues within heterodox economics and therefore write articles dealing with them which appear in heterodox journals. The heterodox journals reflect (hence empirically verify) this twofold agenda by citing both mainstream and heterodox journals. In particular, the percentage of citations imported on average from mainstream journals by the generalist and specialized heterodox journals range from 4.2 to 13.1 percent per year, which is generally greater than the percentage of citations imported from other heterodox journals each year (see Appendix I in Lee 2009).

By 2000 mainstream economists and their associations had acquired the social power needed to cleanse the discipline of heterodox economists and economics. Moreover, they do not communicate and otherwise engage with heterodox economists and hence have isolated themselves from engaging in contested scientific inquiry. Thus, mainstream economists have ceased to consider heterodox economists as economists but as astrologers perhaps (Hayes 2007), and thus have no qualms with their anti-pluralistic attitudes or the naked use of power to academically lynch heterodox economists and eliminate them from institutions of higher education and the economics profession. They enjoy the sweet smell of a cleansed profession and take no notice of the strange fruit hanging from the tree. Of course heterodox economists can avoid this fate if they just become mainstream. In contrast, heterodox economists and their associations do not have any such power and therefore are incapable of defending their academic right to exist; in fact they do not have the academic right to exist. Hence, pluralism in economics does not exist and in its place are implicit, socially constructed blasphemy "laws" that are used to defend mainstream economics and to suppress the heterodox alternative.[4]

### Pluralism and integration in heterodox economics

As noted above, heterodox economics includes a number of different heterodox approaches. Thus pluralism within heterodox economics refers to the "academic right" of any particular approach to exist (Lee 2008b). However, because none of the different approaches have acquired the social power needed or even sought to suppress a particular heterodox approach, the "academic rights" meaning of pluralism has only a minor importance within heterodox economics. Consequently, pluralism takes on a different meaning, that of professional and theoretical integration across the different but largely commensurable heterodox approaches. In this manner, pluralism contributes to building a community of heterodox economists and providing a more comprehensive theoretical explanation of the social provisioning process than any one heterodox approach. Hence what is anti-pluralism is the claim that one particular heterodox approach is superior to all others and that heterodox economics and economists should be reduced to that one approach. Rejecting professional sectarianism and theoretical isolation, pluralism is a core value of heterodox economics, embedded in its community of heterodox economists and in the development of its economic theory (Garnett 2005a, 2005b, and 2006; Mäki 1997; and Lawson 2006).

For a pluralistic community of heterodox economists to exist, it must be grounded in a social system of work that produces economic knowledge that contributes to a heterodox understanding of the economy and the social provisioning process. Since a social system of work implies that participants are dependent on each other for the production of scientific knowledge, how strong or weak pluralism qua community is, in part, a function of how dependent heterodox economists are on each other's research and on the extent to which they work on common research goals, and, in part, is dependent on the degree of integration of their social activities. Therefore, while a heterodox economist may find one particular heterodox approach to his/her liking, he/she also professionally and theoretically engages with economists who are perhaps partial to other heterodox approaches. Pluralism in the form of professional integration includes attendance at heterodox conferences, membership in multiple heterodox associations, subscribing to and/or serving on boards of multiple heterodox journals, and participating in cross-approach collective efforts to support and promote heterodox economics. Pluralism in terms of theoretical integration extends from at least reading and teaching alternative heterodox approaches, to partaking in multi-approach theoretical discussions, and to actively synthesizing different heterodox approaches, especially in collaboration with heterodox economists associated with the different approaches, so to develop a comprehensive, coherent explanation of the social provisioning process.[5]

### *Professional integration*

While it is sometimes claimed that the various heterodox approaches practiced strict professional segregation in the 1970s and up to almost the present day, there is in fact little support for this anti-pluralism. There are three kinds of professional segregation: legal, informal, and voluntary. First, "legal" segregation occurs when an association accepts or rejects applicants solely on the basis of their theoretical views and expels members if their theoretical views become questionable. This form of segregation has not been instituted by any heterodox (or mainstream) economics association past or present. Moreover, since 1988 a number of new heterodox associations have formed, such as the European Association for Evolutionary Economics (1988), International Association for Feminist Economics (1992), Progressive Economics Forum (1998), Association for Heterodox Economics (1999), and Society of Heterodox Economists (2002), and have adopted explicit non-segregationist approaches toward their name, membership, and conference participation. Second, "informal" segregation exists when members of an association define its agenda in a manner that creates significant pressure on members not in favor of it to leave the association and on potential new members who are not in favor of the agenda not to join. This has occurred in two heterodox associations, Union for Radical Political Economics (URPE) and Conference of Socialist Economists (CSE), in the mid-1970s; however, by the mid-1990s the impact of these two incidents had dissipated and hence informal segregation has not been a disruptive factor within the heterodox community in either country for the past decade (Wrenn 2004; Lee 2007b).

A third kind of segregation that promotes anti-pluralism takes the form of a voluntary lack of professional engagement across heterodox approaches and associations. However, the evidence of this kind of segregation is not supported by the evidence, which shows American heterodox economists engaging in professional integration across heterodox associations and journals.[6] That is, for the period 1987–95, approximately 1538 heterodox economists in the United States belonged to the Association for Evolutionary Economics (AFEE), Association for Social Economics (ASE), Association for Institutionalist Thought (AFIT), URPE, and/or subscribed to the *Journal of Post Keynesian Economics* (JPKE) – see Table 1.1.[7] Each heterodox association and journal had from 8 to 88 percent of its members and subscribers belonging to a least one other heterodox association or subscribing to the JPKE and from 2.7 to 33.9 percent belonging to three or more. Overall 11 percent of the 1538 heterodox economists belonged to two or more associations or subscribed to the JPKE while 2.3 percent belonged to three or more – see Table 1.1. Moreover, the thirty-five economists that belonged to three or more associations or subscribed to the JPKE included Marxists, Institutionalists, social economists, and Post Keynesians – see Appendix III, Table 1, in Lee (2009).

From circa 1990 to circa 2000, in spite of an apparent 51 percent decline in American membership, these four associations and the JPKE experienced significant growth in professional engagement, with an overall 19 percent of their members belonging to two or more and 5.3 percent belonging to three or more associations or subscribing to the JPKE – see Table 1.1. The forty American heterodox economists that belonged to the latter included those who clearly have the reputations of engaging across heterodox associations and heterodox journals – see Appendix III, Table 2, in Lee (2009). So by 2000 a community of heterodox economists that were professionally engaged had clearly emerged in the United States in the sense that a significant minority, if not majority, of the members of each association and the JPKE were engaged with one other and more than 5 percent and up to 28 percent were engaged with two or more associations. And in 2006, the overall degree of professional engagement remained

*Table 1.1* American heterodox economists membership in AFEE, ASE, AFIT, URPE, JPKE, 1987–2006

| Association/ journal | Total membership | | | Membership in two or more (%) | | | Membership in three or more (%) | | |
|---|---|---|---|---|---|---|---|---|---|
| | 1987–95 | 2000–01 | 2006 | 1987–95 | 2000–01 | 2006 | 1987–95 | 2000–01 | 2006 |
| AFEE | 608 | 306 | 239 | 25 | 44 | 50 | 5.5 | 12.7 | 13.8 |
| ASE | 416 | 142 | 128 | 25 | 38 | 41 | 7.2 | 19.0 | 18.8 |
| JPKE | 79 | 103 | 90 | 24 | 28 | 22 | 12.7 | 16.5 | 15.6 |
| AFIT | 59 | 101 | 120 | 88 | 78 | 63 | 33.9 | 27.7 | 20.8 |
| URPE | 585 | 294 | 312 | 8 | 16 | 17 | 2.7 | 6.5 | 7.1 |
| Overall[1] | 1,538 | 750 | 707 | 11 | 19 | 19 | 2.3 | 5.3 | 5.1 |

Source: Derived from Appendix III, Tables 1–3, in Lee (2009).

Notes
1 Excludes double accounting.
  AFEE – Association for Evolutionary Economics; ASE – Association for Social Economics; JPKE – *Journal of Post Keynesian Economics*; AFIT – Association for Institutional Thought; URPE – Union for Radical Political Economics.

about the same, even though American membership in the associations and subscriptions to the JPKE declined by 6 percent. More significantly, the percentage of the professional engagement of the membership of AFEE, ASE, and URPE increased. Consequently, an important characteristic of these associations is that a significant minority of their members embrace pluralism by becoming increasingly professionally engaged – see Table 1.1.

The above indicates that, even though individual heterodox associations and the JPKE continue to exist, heterodox economists in the United States coalesced into a professional community by 2000 and remained so. If we go beyond AFEE, ASE, AFIT, URPE, and the JPKE to include the International Association for Feminist Economics (IAFFE), the total number of American heterodox economists for 2000–01 and 2006 increases, although the overall percentage of membership in two or more and three or more associations and the JPKE do not. However, for individual associations and the JPKE the percentages do increase for 2000–01 and 2006 – see Table 1.1. Hence, the core of American heterodox economists who were professionally engaged increased their professional engagement, that is, the network that emerged between the professionally engaged economists became denser. This fact becomes even clearer when the number of heterodox associations are increased to include the Association for Heterodox Economics (AHE), Progressive Economics Forum (PEF), Outline on Political Economy (OPE), and *Heterodox Economics Newsletter* (HEN). In this case, for 2006 the number of heterodox economists in the United States increases to 1020, with 28.7 percent having membership in two or more associations, JPKE, OPE, and HEN and 9.6 percent in three or more – see Table 1.2. The

*Table 1.2* American heterodox economists memberships or subscriptions to AFEE, ASE, AFIT, URPE, IAFFE, AHE, PEF, OPE, JPKE, and HEN, 2006

| Association/journal | Total membership | Membership in two or more (%) | Membership in three or more (%) |
|---|---|---|---|
| AFEE | 239 | 55.6 | 28.0 |
| ASE | 128 | 52.3 | 29.7 |
| JPKE | 90 | 34.8 | 18.9 |
| AFIT | 120 | 69.2 | 33.3 |
| URPE | 312 | 42.9 | 18.6 |
| IAFFE | 288 | 23.3 | 9.4 |
| AHE | 20 | 85.0 | 50.0 |
| HEN | 223 | 78.0 | 32.8 |
| PEF | 12 | 33.3 | 25.0 |
| OPE | 26 | 61.5 | 34.6 |
| Overall[1] | 1020 | 28.7 | 9.6 |

Source: Derived from Appendix III, Table 6, in Lee (2009).

Notes
1 Excludes double counting.
AHE – Association for Heterodox Economics; HEN – *Heterodox Economics Newsletter*; PEF – Progressive Economic Forum; OPE – Outline on Political Economy List.

point is that, as measured, nearly 30 percent of heterodox economists in the United States are professionally engaged with nearly 10 percent being significantly engaged. And these 10 percent or ninety-six heterodox economists represent those whose publications, intellectual arguments, and conference engagement have created a heterodox economics community and given it its pluralism, personality, and persona – see Appendix III, Table 3, in Lee (2009).

## Theoretical integration

Theoretical segregation involves the isolation of a particular theoretical approach and its adherents from all other approaches and their adherents; that is to say, theoretical segregation occurs where there is no engagement across different theoretical approaches that are commensurable to some degree. Throughout the twentieth century, there has been theoretical engagement between the various heterodox approaches. In the first half of the twentieth century the development of Institutional economics did not occur independently of engagement with Marxism and the economics of Keynes; and Marxists were not adverse to drawing on Thorstein Veblen and also engaging with Keynes. Moreover, Marxism, and particularly Paul Sweezy and the monopoly capital school, drew upon the work of Michael Kalecki and Josef Steindl, who also contributed to the development of Post Keynesian economics. Finally, the development of Post Keynesian economics from the 1930s onwards engaged with Institutionalism and Marxism directly or indirectly through Gardiner Means, Kalecki, Steindl, and Piero Sraffa.

This general proclivity for pluralistic theoretical engagement and integration continued unabated from the 1960s through the 1980s with various endeavors by heterodox economists to engage, integrate, or synthesize Institutional, Post Keynesian, and Marxist-radical approaches, Institutional and Post Keynesian approaches, Post Keynesian and Marxian-radical approaches, Post Keynesian and Austrian, Austrian and Institutionalists, Feminist and Marxist-radical approaches, Institutional and Marxist-Radical Approaches, Institutional and Social Economics, ecological and Marxian-radical approaches, and social and Marxian economics. Thus by 1990 theoretical integration proceeded to such an extent that many heterodox economists could no longer see distinct theoretical boundaries between the various approaches, an outcome that mirrored the professional integration already taking place (Lee 2007b).

From 1990 to the present day, heterodox economists continued the past integration efforts of engaging across the various heterodox approaches – see Table 1.3.[8] The theoretical engagement between Post Keynesian, Institutional, social, Marxian/radical, and feminist economics is unsurprising since, as noted above, many heterodox economists are members of more than one heterodox association. In addition, we find that there are engagements between ecological and Marxian, social, and Institutional economics as well as between Austrians and Marxian/radical, Post Keynesian, Institutional, and feminist economics. Moreover, there are creative mixtures of heterodox approaches that are best described by their own names, such as the social structures of accumulation school, the French conventions school, and economic sociology. Finally to reinforce the theoretical integration obvious in Table 1.3, the informal but de facto editorial policies adopted by editors of heterodox economics journals have resulted in papers being accepted for publication that engaged with the full range of heterodox approaches. Consequently, from 1993 to 2003 the nine principal English-language generalist heterodox journals[9] cited each other so extensively that no single journal or sub-set of journals is isolated – see Appendix II in Lee (2009). Hence they form a completely interdependent whole where all heterodox approaches have direct and indirect connections with each other.

It is clear that the heterodox community is not segregated along theoretical lines, but rather there is cross-approach engagement to such an extent that the boundaries of the various approaches do not simply overlap, they are, in some cases, not there at all. The ensuing theoretical messiness of cross-approach

*Table 1.3* Theoretical work that engaged two (or more) heterodox approaches (representative sample for the period, 1990–2006)

| Post Keynesian institutionalism | Post Keynesian feminism | Post Keynesian Marxism/radical | Post Keynesian Austrian |
|---|---|---|---|
| Lavoie (1992) | Levin (1995) | Dutt (1990) | Runde (1993) |
| Jennings (1994) | Danby (2004) | Crotty (1993) | Prychitko (1993) |
| Arestis (1996) | van Staveren (2006) | Lavoie (2006) | Mongiovi (1994) |
| *Institutionalism feminism* | *Institutionalism Marxism/radical* | *Institutionalism social economics* | *Feminism Marxism/ radical* |
| Peterson and Brown (1994) | Garnett (1999) | Stanfield (1994) | Matthaei (1996) |
| Waller (2005) | Mouhammed (2000) | Merrett (1997) | Gibson-Graham (1996) |
| | Dugger and Sherman (2000) | Niggle (2003) | Barker and Feiner (2004) |
| *Feminism social economics* | *Social economics ecological* | *Austrian institutionalism* | *Austrian Marxism/ radical* |
| Emami (1993) | Gowdy (1994) | Horwitz (1998) | Adaman and Devine (1996) |
| Nelson (1993) | Ropke (2005) | | Burczak et al. (1998) |
| | | | Prychitko (2002) |
| *Ecological institutionalism* | *Ecological Marxism/radical* | *Austrian feminism* | *Other* |
| Söderbaum (2000) | Gowdy (1988) | Horwitz (1995) | Kotz et al. (1994) |
| Vatn (2005) | Martinez-Alier (2003) | Levy (2002) | Smelser and Swedberg (2005) |
| | Burkett (2006) | | |

engagement is evidence to detractors of the theoretical incoherence of heterodox economics, whereas to supporters of progress towards a more theoretically coherent heterodox economics – a glass half-empty of coherence vs. a glass half-full of coherence (O'Hara 2007a, 2007b; King 2002; Palermo 2005; Ropke 2004, 2005; and Waller this volume).

## Heterodox economics today

The absence of professional and theoretical segregation means that the hetero-dox community is a pluralistic integrative whole. Some heterodox economists hold distinct theoretical views while maintaining a broad professional engage-ment, while others hold broad theoretical views but maintain a narrower profes-sional engagement. In any case, all heterodox economists have much in common that is positive (as opposed to holding only a critique of mainstream economics in common), which means they are all capable of producing scientific knowledge about the economy and the social provisioning process that is of direct and/or indirect interest to each other. This combination of professional and theoretical engagement has two important implications for heterodox economics. The first is that the community is distinct from the community of mainstream economists; and the second is that it generates the central value that underpins the commun-ity of heterodox economists: that is the value of pluralism – the right of different theoretical approaches to exist without qualification and that engagement with the different approaches is a positive social value.

So what does this pluralist community of heterodox economists look like in terms of its members, associations, publication outlets, work sites, conferences, and communications? First of all it is both a national and world-wide commun-ity. That is, it consists of at least twenty-seven heterodox associations, some of which were formed over thirty years ago while others were formed in the last decade; and those identified are located in the United States, United Kingdom/ Ireland, Japan, Brazil, Europe, and seven other countries around the world – see Table 1.4. In addition, there are many heterodox economists who are not members of these associations but simply subscribe to heterodox journals, such as the JPKE, subscribe to heterodox newsletters such as HEN, or are members of particular heterodox e-mail lists such as OPE. Consequently, heterodox econo-mists are found around the world – see Table 1.5 (this chapter) and Appendix IV in Lee (2009). Some associations and e-mail lists are specific to particular coun-tries because of language or particular focus, which means that the number of their members who belong to other associations may be low. However, other associations are not so constrained and hence 28 to 68 percent of their member-ship belong to two or more other heterodox organizations and from 15 to 34 percent belong to three or more – see Appendix V in Lee (2009). Furthermore every heterodox organization has at least a few members who belong to four or more such organizations; and these fifty-five heterodox economists are well known for their professional engagement and leadership, with forty located in the United States, four in the United Kingdom, two each in Canada and

*Table 1.4* Heterodox economics associations, 2007[1]

| Name | Date formed | Country or region of primary activity | Membership 2006 (if known) |
|---|---|---|---|
| Association d'Economie Politique (AEP) | 1980 | Canada | 250 |
| Association for Economics and Social Analysis (AESA) | Late 1970s | United States | |
| Association for Evolutionary Economics (AFEE) | 1965 | United States | 360 |
| Association for Heterodox Economics (AHE) | 1999 | United Kingdom and Ireland | 167 |
| Association for Institutionalist Thought (AFIT) | 1979 | United States | 128 |
| Association for Social Economics (ASE) | 1970 | United States | 181 |
| Association pour le Developement Des Estudes Keynesiennes (ADEK) | 2000 | France | 54 |
| Association Recherche et Regulation | 1994 | France | |
| Belgian-Dutch Association for Institutional and Political Economy | 1980 | The Netherlands and Belgium | |
| Conference of Socialist Economists (CSE) | 1970 | United Kingdom | |
| European Association for Evolutionary Political Economy (EAEPE) | 1988 | Europe | |
| German Association of Political Economy | | Germany | |
| German Keynes Society | | Germany | 100 |
| International Association for Feminist Economic (IAFFE)s | 1992 | World | 624 |
| International Confederation of Associations for Pluralism in Economics (ICAPE) | 1993 | United States/world | |
| Japan Association for Evolutionary Economics (JAFEE) | 1996 | Japan | |
| Japan Society of Political Economy (JSPE) | 1959 | Japan | |
| The Japanese Society for Post Keynesian Economics (JSPKE) | 1980 | Japan | |

*Table 1.4* Continued

| Name | Date formed | Country or region of primary activity | Membership 2006 (if known) |
| --- | --- | --- | --- |
| Korean Social and Economic Studies Association (KSESA) | 1987 | Korea | 179 |
| Progressive Economics Forum (PEF) | 1998 | Canada | 183 |
| Society for the Advancement of Behavioral Economics (SABE) | 1982 | United States | |
| Society for the Advancement of Socio-Economics (SASE) | 1989 | World | |
| Society for the Development of Austrian Economics (SDAE) | 1996 | United States | |
| Society of Heterodox Economists (SHE) | 2002 | Australia | 86 |
| Sociedade Brasileira de Economia Politica (SEP) | 1996 | Brazil | |
| Union for Radical Political Economics (URPE) | 1968 | United States | 363 |
| US Society for Ecological Economics (USSEE) | 2000 | United States | |

Note
1 This list of heterodox associations is not exhaustive.

Australia, and seven scattered around the world – see Table 1.5 and Appendix V in Lee (2009).

The heterodox community also includes some thirty generalist heterodox journals, seventeen specialist journals, twenty-six interdisciplinary journals, and a whole host of popular journals. Some of the journals are national in orientation while others are international, particularly the *Post-Autistic Economics Review* with its 9512 subscribers from over 150 countries. Moreover, there are approximately fourteen heterodox book series and at least eight international publishers, including Ashgate, Cambridge, Edward Elgar, Pluto Press, Routledge, M.E. Sharpe, and Verso, and a large number of national publishers that have a specific interest in publishing heterodox economics books. In addition, there are a large number of work sites, that is, academic departments in many different countries where the production and teaching of heterodox economics takes place without prejudice. The number of departments around the world that offer post-graduate qualifications, such as a M.A. or Ph.D., in which heterodox economics is an important component is more than thirty; and it is the graduates of these post-graduate programs that will determine the character and personality of the heterodox community over the next two decades.[10] Finally, as a rough estimate, there

*Table 1.5* Heterodox economists by country, 2006

| Country | Number of heterodox economists | Membership/subscription in four or more heterodox organizations |
|---|---|---|
| United States | 1026 | 40 |
| United Kingdom | 233 | 4 |
| Canada | 231 | 2 |
| Korea | 187 | 1 |
| Mexico | 113 | |
| Australia | 105 | 2 |
| France | 77 | |
| Japan | 58 | 1 |
| Italy | 44 | 1 |
| Germany | 39 | |
| Brazil | 35 | |
| India | 33 | |
| The Netherlands | 32 | 1 |
| Austria | 30 | 1 |
| Turkey | 25 | |
| New Zealand | 24 | 1 |
| Spain | 23 | |
| Greece | 21 | |
| Rest of Europe | 117 | |
| Rest of World | 106 | 1 |
| Total | 2559 | 55 |

Source: Derived from Appendix IV and V in Lee (2009).

are at least thirty-five heterodox conferences a year around the world, including the annual conferences of many of the above heterodox associations, supplemented by AESA's and ICAPE's triennial conferences.

The significance of the many conferences is that they promote and maintain social relationships between heterodox economists and hence help glue the community together. And when not attending conferences, heterodox economists, especially those in relatively isolated situations, rely on association newsletters or more generally the HEN to remain part of the community (Lee *et al.* 2005).

The anti-pluralist response of mainstream economists to individual heterodox economists in recent years has not changed from the responses in earlier times. Such responses, while painful to individuals and threatening their continued membership in the community, do not necessarily affect the structural and relational components that maintain the community of heterodox economists. However, in the past decade the mainstream has threatened the actual structures of the community by attacking, through assessment exercises, subject benchmarking statements, and ranking of departments and journals, the work site and production of doctoral students.

Responding to this anti-pluralism requires that heterodox economists promote cross-paradigm pluralism more by continuing to attempt engagement with mainstream economics, that heterodox economics be taught to more students, that more heterodox doctoral students be produced, and that heterodox economists strengthen pluralism within their community by becoming more professionally and theoretically engaged and integrated through joining multiple heterodox associations, subscribing to multiple heterodox journals, attending multiple heterodox conferences, and engaging in open pluralistic, integrative theoretical dialog with other heterodox economists. All this requires is the will to act with pluralism, and there are many members of the heterodox economics community today who have such capabilities.

## Acknowledgments

I would like to thank John Davis, John Henry, John King, Terry McDonough, Robert McMaster, Julie Nelson, and Jouni Paavola for comments on an earlier version of the chapter. The arguments in the chapter are those of the author and do not represent the views of ICAPE or its affiliated member associations.

## Notes

1  For example, see the essays in Holt and Pressman (1998) on Barbara Bergmann, James Buchanan, John R. Commons, Milton Friedman, Frank Knight, and Thomas Schelling.
2  To put it another way, the Commission simply assumed that all economists spoke the same language, that is, were intellectually-theoretically the same – a conclusion that clearly emerges from the work of Klamer and Colander (1990). This clearly suggests that mainstream economists are language-challenged in that they are unable to communicate in a different theoretical language.
3  The data in Appendix I pertains only to those selected Diamond List core mainstream journals. However, further examination of the *SSCI: Citation Reports* reveals that the other Diamond List Journals as well as all the lesser mainstream journals do not cite heterodox economic journals.
4  For further discussion of pluralism and academic rights, see Lee (2008b).
5  Theoretical integration addresses the concern of many heterodox economists that a comprehensive alternative theory for explaining the social provisioning process that draws upon all the different heterodox approaches is needed if heterodox economics is going to survive in the contested theoretical world of economics.
6  The association membership and journal subscription data used in the rest of the section was, over a fifteen year period, obtained from public and private-confidential sources. The latter provided the data on the condition that individual memberships and subscriptions would not be revealed.
7  Because there is no American association for Post Keynesian economists, the JPKE is used to identify American Post Keynesians.
8  The last fifteen years also witness the publication of encyclopedias on various heterodox approaches, where Post Keynesians refer to Institutionalism and Austrianism (King 2003), Institutionalism refers to feminism and Post Keynesianism (Hodgson *et al.* 1994), and feminist economics refers to Institutionalism, Marxism, and Post Keynesian economics (Peterson and Lewis 1999).
9  The journals include *Cambridge Journal of Economics, Capital and Class, Feminist Economics, Journal of Economic Issues, Journal of Post Keynesian Economics, Metroeconomica, Review of Political Economy, Review of Radical Political Economics,* and *Review of Social Economy.*

10 It should be noted that every one of the post-graduate programs takes a pluralistic-integrative approach to teaching heterodox economics.

## References

Adaman, F. and Devine, P. (1996) "The Economic Calculation Debate: Lessons for Socialists," *Cambridge Journal of Economics*, 20(5): 523–537.

Arestis, P. (1996) "Post-Keynesian Economics: Towards Coherence," *Cambridge Journal of Economics*, 20(1): 111–135.

Barker, D.K. and Feiner, S.F. (2004) *Liberating Economics: Feminist Perspective on Families, Work, and Globalization*, Ann Arbor: The University of Michigan Press.

Burczak, T., Cullenberg, S., Prychitko, D., and Boettke, P. (1998) "Socialism, Capitalism, and the Labor Theory of Property: A Marxian-Austrian Dialogue," *Rethinking Marxism*, 10(2): 65–105.

Burkett, P. (2006) *Marxism and Ecological Economics*, Boston: Brill.

Crotty, J.R. (1993) "Rethinking Marxian Investment Theory: Keynes-Minsky Instability, Competitive Regime Shifts, and Coerced Investment," *Review of Radical Political Economics*, 25(1): 1–26.

Danby, C. (2004) "Toward a Gendered Post Keynesianism: Subjectivity and Time in a Nonmodernist Framework," *Feminist Economics*, 10(3): 55–75.

Davis, J.B. (2006) "The Turn in Economics: Neoclassical Dominance to Mainstream Pluralism?" *Journal of Institutional Economics*, 2(1): 1–20.

Dugger, W.M. and Sherman, H.J. (2000) *Reclaiming Evolution: A Dialogue Between Marxism and Institutionalism on Social Change*, New York: Routledge.

Dutt, A.K. (1990) *Growth, Distribution, and Uneven Development*, Cambridge: Cambridge University Press.

Emami, Z. (1993) "Challenges Facing Social Economics in the Twenty-First Century: A Feminist Perspective," *Review of Social Economy*, 51(4): 416–425.

Garnett, R.F. (1999) "Postmodernism and Theories of Value: New Grounds for Institutionalist/Marxist Dialogue?" *Journal of Economic Issues*, 33(4): 817–834.

—— (2005a) "Whither Heterodoxy?" *Post-Autistic Economics Review*, 34, article 1: 2–20.

—— (2005b) "Sen, McCloskey, and the Future of Heterodox Economics," *Post-Autistic Economics Review*, 35, article 3: 19–31.

—— (2006) "Paradigms and Pluralism in Heterodox Economics," *Review of Political Economy*, 18(4): 521–546.

Gibson-Graham, J.K. (1996) *The End of Capitalism (as we knew it): A Feminist Critique of Political Economy*, Cambridge: Blackwell Publishers.

Gowdy, J.M. (1988) "The Entropy Law and Marxian Value Theory," *Review of Radical Political Economics*, 20(2–3): 33–40.

—— (1994) "The Social Context of Natural Capital," *International Journal of Social Economics*, 21(8): 43–55.

Hayes, C. (2007) "Hip Heterodoxy," *The Nation*, (June 11): 18, 20–25.

Hodgson, G.M., Samuels, W.J., and Tool, M.R. (eds) (1994) *The Elgar Companion to Institutional and Evolutionary Economics*, Aldershot: Edward Elgar.

Holt, R.P.F. and Pressman, S. (eds.) (1998) *Economics and its Discontents: Twentieth Century Dissenting Economists*, Edward Elgar: Cheltenham.

Horwitz, S. (1995) "Feminist Economics: An Austrian Perspective," *Journal of Economic Methodology*, 2(2): 259–279.

—— (1998) "Hierarchical Metaphors in Austrian Institutionalism: A Friendly Subjectivist Caveat," in R. Koppl and G. Mongiovi (eds) *Subjectivism and Economic Analysis: Essays in Memory of Ludwig M. Lachmann*, 143–162, London: Routledge.

Jennings, A.L. (1994) "Toward a Feminist Expansion of Macroeconomics: Money Matters," *Journal of Economic Issues*, 28(2): 555–565.

King, J.E. (2002) *A History of Post Keynesian Economics Since 1936*, Cheltenham: Edward Elgar.

King, J.E. (ed.) (2003) *The Elgar Companion to Post Keynesian Economics*, Cheltenham: Edward Elgar.

Klamer, A. and Colander, D. (1990) *The Making of an Economist*, Boulder: Westview Press.

Kotz, D.M., McDonough, T., and Reich, M. (eds) (1994) *Social Structures of Accumulation: The Political Economy of Growth and Crisis*, Cambridge: Cambridge University Press.

Lavoie, M. (1992) *Foundations of Post-Keynesian Economics*, Aldershot: Edward Elgar.

—— (2006) "Do Heterodox Theories Have Anything in Common? A Post-Keynesian Point of View," *Intervention: Journal of Economics*, 3(1): 87–112.

Lawson, T. (2006) "The Nature of Heterodox Economics," *Cambridge Journal of Economics*, 30(4): 483–505.

Lee, F. S. (2004) "To Be a Heterodox Economist: The Contested Landscape of American Economics, 1960s and 1970s," *Journal of Economic Issues*, 38(3): 747–763.

—— (2006) "The Ranking Game, Class and Scholarship in American Mainstream Economics," *Australasian Journal of Economics Education*, 3(1–2): 1–41.

—— (2007a) "The Research Assessment Exercise, the State and the Dominance of Mainstream Economics in British Universities," *Cambridge Journal of Economics*, 31(2): 309–325.

—— (2007b) "Challenging the Mainstream: Essays on the History of Heterodox Economics in the 20th Century," unpublished manuscript.

—— (2008a) "The Citation Impact of Feminist Economics: Two Comments," *Feminist Economics*, 14(1): 137–142.

—— (2008b) "A Note on the Pluralism Debate in Heterodox Economics," unpublished paper.

—— (2009) "Pluralism and Heterodox Economics: Appendices," available at http://cas.umkc.edu/econ/economics/faculty/Lee/docs/icape2b.doc.

Lee, F.S. and Harley, S. (1998) "Peer Review, the Research Assessment Exercise and the Demise of Non-Mainstream Economics," *Capital and Class*, 66 (Autumn): 23–51.

Lee, F.S., Cohn, S., Schneider, G., and Quick, P. (2005) *Informational Directory for Heterodox Economists: Journals, Book Series, Websites, and Graduate and Undergraduate Programs*. 2nd Edition.

Levin, L. (1995) "Toward a Feminist, Post-Keynesian Theory of Investments," in E. Kuiper and J. Sap with S. Feiner, N. Ott, and S. Tzannatos (eds) *Out of the Margins: Feminist Perspectives on Economics*, 100–119, London: Routledge.

Levy, T. (2002) "The Theory of Conventions and a New Theory of the Firm," in E. Fullbrook (ed.) *Intersubjectivity in Economics: Agents and Structures*, 254–272, London: Routledge.

Mäki, U. (1997) "The One World and the Many Theories," in A. Salanti and E. Screpanti (eds) *Pluralism in Economics*, 37–47, Cheltenham: Edward Elgar.

Martinez-Alier, J. (2003) *The Environmentalism of the Poor: A Study of Ecological Conflicts and Valuation*, Cheltenham: Edward Elgar.

Matthaei, J. (1996) "Why Feminist, Marxist, and Anti-Racist Economists Should be Feminist-Marxist-Anti-Racist Economists," *Feminist Economics*, 2(1): 22–42.

Merrett, S. (1997) *Introduction to the Economics of Water Resources: An International Perspective*, Lanham: Rowman and Littlefield.

Mongiovi, G. (1994) "Capital, Expectations, and Economic Equilibrium: Some Notes on Lachmann and the so-called 'Cambridge School'," *Advances in Austrian Economics*, 1: 257–277.

Mouhammed, A.H. (2000) "Veblen's Economic Theory: A Radical Analysis," *Review of Radical Political Economics*, 32(2): 197–221.

Nelson, J.A. (1993) "Gender and Economic Ideologies," *Review of Social Economy*, 51(3): 287–301.

Niggle, C.J. (2003) "Globalization, Neoliberalism and the Attack on Social Security," *Review of Social Economy*, 61(1): 51–71.

O'Hara, P.A. (2007a) "Principles of Institutional-Evolutionary Political Economy-Converging Themes from the Schools of Heterodoxy," *Journal of Economic Issues*, 61(1): 1–42.

—— (2007b) "Heterodox Political Economy Specialization and Interconnection-Concepts of Contradiction, Heterogeneous Agents, and Uneven Development," *Intervention: Journal of Economics*, 4(1): 99–120.

Palermo, G. (2005) "Are We All Post-Keynesians?" *History of Economic Ideas*, 13(1): 145–162.

Peterson, J. and Brown, D. (eds) (1994) *The Economic Status of Women under Capitalism: Institutional Economics and Feminist Theory*, Aldershot: Edward Elgar.

Peterson, J. and Lewis, M. (eds) (1999) *The Elgar Companion to Feminist Economics*, Cheltenham: Edward Elgar.

Prychitko, D.L. (1993) "After Davidson, Who Needs the Austrians? Reply to Davidson," *Critical Review*, 7(2–3): 371–380.

—— (2002) *Markets, Planning and Democracy: Essays after the Collapse of Communism*, Cheltenham: Edward Elgar.

Ropke, I. (2004) "The Early History of Modern Ecological Economics," *Ecological Economics*, 50: 293–314.

—— (2005) "Trends in the Development of Ecological Economics from the Late 1980s to the Early 2000s," *Ecological Economics*, 55: 262–290.

Runde, J. (1993) "Paul Davidson and the Austrians: Reply to Davidson," *Critical Review*, 7(2–3): 381–397.

Smelser, N.J. and Swedberg, R. (eds.) (2005) *The Handbook of Economic Sociology*, 2nd edition, Princeton: Princeton University Press.

Söderbaum, P. (2000) *Ecological Economics*, London: Earthscan Publications Ltd.

Stanfield, J.R. (1994) "Learning from Japan about the Nurturance Gap in America," *Review of Social Economy*, 52(1): 2–19.

Strassman, D. (1993) "Not a Free Market: The Rhetoric of Disciplinary Authority in Economics," in M.A. Ferber and J.A. Nelson (eds) *Beyond Economic Man: Feminist Theory and Economics*, 54–68, Chicago: The University of Chicago Press.

van Staveren, I. (2006) "Post Keynesianism Meets Feminism," unpublished paper.

Vatn, A. (2005) *Institutions and the Environment*, Cheltenham: Edward Elgar.

Waller, W. (2005) "Accidental Veblenian, Intentional Institutionalist, and Inevitable Feminist," *Journal of Economic Issues*, 39(2): 327–334.

Wrenn, M.V. (2004) "What is Heterodox Economics?" Unpublished Ph.D. diss., Department of Economics, Colorado State University.

# 2 Moving beyond the rhetoric of pluralism

## Suggestions for an "inside-the-mainstream" heterodoxy

*David Colander*

## Introduction

Most observers would agree that a healthy field of study needs diversity and a vibrant and open market for ideas. Thus, it would seem that calls for pluralism in economics, such as have been made by self-described heterodox economists, would be welcomed by the mainstream economics profession. They haven't been; the calls have been essentially ignored by the mainstream, leading some heterodox economists to argue that the mainstream of economics is unpluralistic, closed-minded, and ideologically biased. In turn, heterodox calls for pluralism are seen by many in the mainstream as simply calls for the mainstream to listen to the heterodox economist's particular point of view, and not as true calls for pluralism.

Because it fails to achieve the desired ends, I find the rhetoric of pluralism unhelpful. Heterodox calls for pluralism do not increase openness or foster communication between heterodox and mainstream economists because such calls suggest that mainstream economists somehow do not favor openness to alternative views, and that the reason why mainstream economists are not open to heterodox ideas is because mainstream economists are closed-minded. Seeing the mainstream's rejection of their ideas as due to the mainstream's closed-mindedness may make heterodox economists feel better, but it is not a way to open up dialog between mainstream and heterodoxy. Some mainstream economists may indeed be closed-minded, just as some heterodox economists are. But that's life. Other mainstream economists are open-minded, and, in my view, it is toward those open-minded economists that heterodox economists should be directing their arguments. It is time for heterodox groups to move beyond the rhetoric of pluralism.

One can debate endlessly whether the mainstream of the profession is pluralistic. In some ways it is, and in other ways it isn't. For heterodox groups to dwell on ways in which the profession is unpluralistic doesn't gain them anything in terms of furthering their views with those mainstream economists who are open to change. While I agree with heterodox critics that mainstream economics has entrenched views, and has developed structures to protect those views, I do not see this as unusual or something unique to the field of economics. It is simply how the real world works. The heterodox groups with which I am familiar have as entrenched views as does the mainstream, and oftentimes the institutional protections are stronger within heterodox groups than they are within mainstream groups. So, in my view, it makes little sense to rail against such structures that naturally develop within any ongoing system.

In this chapter I advocate an alternative strategy – what might be called an "inside-the-mainstream" heterodoxy. As opposed to emphasizing the non-pluralistic aspects of the mainstream, this strategy emphasizes opening up dialog with that part of the mainstream that is open to change. As we discuss in Colander *et al.* (2004) this part of the mainstream is much larger than is often portrayed by heterodox economists. Mainstream economics is not neoclassical and cannot usefully be seen as a monolithic group with a single "orthodox" view. Instead it is a complex adaptive system of many competing views – views often as diverse as those held by heterodox economists. The mainstream is characterized by multiple layers of distinctions and gray areas of understanding about scope, method, and interpretation of results. At any one time, one view in the mainstream may be dominant, but that dominance does not necessarily reflect an entrenched orthodoxy, and it is not necessarily the view of all in the mainstream; it simply represents the way the intellectual forces play out at this particular time. Because of the multifacetedness of the mainstream, it is not *beliefs* that separate mainstream from heterodoxy; it is *attitude* and willingness to compete within a given set of rules and institutional structures. Mainstream economists are willing to compete within those rules; heterodox economists aren't.

Because mainstream economists are limited by implicit and explicit institutional norms and rules, their beliefs, their research, and their teaching, all may differ (Colander 2005a). For example, just because one works on general equilibrium models does not mean that one accepts that general equilibrium is an acceptable description of the economy. Similarly, just because one works on game theory does not mean that one believes most people are perfectly rational. Research and beliefs can differ. Mainstream researchers' decisions about the subject matter they will study, the methods they use, and what they teach are part of a complicated set of practical, strategic decisions that do not necessarily reflect their deep views about how the economy works or what are interesting questions.

Because the mainstream has highly restrictive limitations on method and scope, for them, many ideas and issues are outside the purview of economics. But in the best of the mainstream economists, underneath any seeming orthodoxy is often an openness to ideas and a desire to see economics progress and consider these difficult issues. But to be open to any one else's ideas about such questions, these open-minded mainstream economists must be convinced that the person raising the questions understands the reasoning that led mainstream economics to avoid that question and to follow a more traditional mainstream approach.

In my view too many heterodox economists begin with the premise that mainstream economists don't understand the problems and limitations with "orthodox" mainstream arguments, and that it is the heterodox economist's job to point them out. That approach stops dialog. Such heterodox economists have little chance of communicating with open-minded mainstream economists since, almost by definition, that heterodox critic has not recognized the deep understanding of the issues that these open-minded mainstream economist have, or at least think they have. Communication fails, natural allies are kept apart, and entrenched views are reinforced rather than attacked.

The alternative strategy for heterodox economists that I support is a strategy built on opening lines of communication. It does not emphasize distinctions between heterodoxy and mainstream but rather deemphasizes them. It attempts to establish lines of communication among all economists. I suggest that young heterodox-leaning future economists will be more effective critics if they follow this alternative strategy.

## Why a change in heterodox approach is needed

Mainstream economics would benefit from much more interaction with heterodox economists. That isn't happening. Heterodox economics is losing ground, and their ideas are not getting a hearing from the mainstream profession. In fact, heterodox economics is not only losing ground, it is not even holding its own; it is being squeezed out of the university academy, as deans and other decision makers respond to pressure from mainstream economists to support mainstream economics, not heterodox economics. The case of Notre Dame is but the most recent case, and now the squeeze on heterodox views is moving to Europe as well. This is leading to a loss in diversity in the profession, which I see as bad for economics.

In trying to understand what can be done about this squeeze, it is important to think about it from an administrator's perspective. Few administrators are in a position to make judgments about what economic ideas are best, so he or she naturally turns to a ranking or to outside experts for guidance. Numerous published rankings have developed, which all come to quite similar results because they all reflect the same natural science ranking system, which is a system that determines rankings on quality-weighted journal article publications and citations, in an attempt to determine importance and influence.

I fully agree with heterodox economists that the existing ranking approach that has developed in economics is far from optimal and is in many ways perverse. It deemphasizes subjective valuation of ideas. It encourages fads. It directs research away from major ideas that will improve society and directs research toward clever, but relatively unimportant, publishable articles. It gives no value to books and little or no value to traditional publishing outlets for heterodox economists. It also gives no value to the many other contributions economists make, such as teaching and policy advising. It leads researchers to focus their research output on a selected set of journal article publications, even though efficient scholarly communication on many issues would take place through Internet discussion and postings.

Unfortunately, the system is what it is, and I am not sure how it can be changed without the development of an alternative ranking system. (That's why I think that developing alternative ranking systems that administrators would find both acceptable and compelling, as achieving the ends that they want to achieve, should be a front burner research issue for heterodox economics groups). But despite any unfairness, even if the current ranking system is unfair, it is a system that heterodox economists will have to live with and operate within.

One reason why no better ranking system has developed is that it is extremely difficult to independently judge the "best" research in a field where empirical data are generally insufficient to guide researchers in choosing the "best" idea. What is "best" will be, to some degree, internally defined within the profession and will have some degree of arbitrariness to it. The context within which the idea is expressed, and by whom it is expressed, will both contribute to its being considered a "good" idea. A second reason why is that, for all its faults, the current ranking system has a number of advantages. First, it is transparent. All economists, heterodox and orthodox, know what it is and how it is calculated, and can choose to play by it or not. Second, it is a ranking system that is not directly tied to any particular ideology. The higher you score on the "rankings" the more desirable you are to economics departments. To most departments it matters less what you have to say and matters more that you have said it in the right journals. The ideology is there, as it inevitably will be in any research, but it is indirect, not direct.[1]

Most mainstream journal editors would gladly create controversy and do not see themselves as promoting any specific orthodoxy, although implicitly I agree they often do. They are open to new ideas if those ideas are expressed in the right form. That means that the ideas are embedded in a formal model or are buttressed by rigorous statistical analysis (even if that analysis requires the use of poor proxies for what one is trying to measure), and/or are pushing the envelope on a statistical or analytical technique. As I discuss in Colander (2007), graduate economics students at top schools do not feel limited by any orthodoxy in what issues they look at, and the directions that the top mainstream economists convey to their graduate students are to "tell me something I don't already know," not to "tell me something that fits an orthodox mold."[2]

I'm not saying that the mainstream is openly looking to modern heterodox economics for ideas. Telling anyone "something they don't already know" is difficult, and telling extremely bright economists who have succeeded in the profession, and who are being given the accolades of the profession, "something they don't already know" is very hard indeed. But I am saying that the best of the mainstream are open to new ideas and will work hard to see that new ideas get nurtured, as long as those ideas fit their view of science and of what "good economics" are.[3]

It is that openness to competing ideas that has led to the recent turmoil within mainstream economics. Today mainstream economics should not be thought of as a static entity, but rather as a complex adaptive system in which a variety of ideas and approaches compete. Within the mainstream, broadly defined, we have econophysicists developing models of zero-rationality agents, behavioral economists developing models of non-rational choice, and complexity economists arguing that the stochastic dynamic general equilibrium model is almost useless in providing insight into the macro economy. We also have experimental economists changing the way economics is done and evolutionary game theorists changing the overall frame of vision of economics. The mainstream profession is abuzz with competing ideas and approaches. While almost none of these new ideas and approaches are core mainstream, they are acceptable to the mainstream, despite the fact that they are "heterodox" ideas in reference to the orthodox neoclassical thought, which is what most heterodox economists have in mind when they talk about orthodoxy.

In my use of the term "mainstream" I include all these ideas, and more. While many mainstream economists consider these new ideas stupid, and many of the closed-minded ones, of which I agree there are many, will not even consider them, the best of that mainstream will. What I am arguing is that heterodox economists should promote a dialog with this "best of the mainstream" group, and that there is an environment at the edge of the mainstream where heterodoxy can exist and possibly even prosper.

## Two paths for heterodoxy

If the mainstream is open to heterodox ideas, at least on the edge of the mainstream, what accounts for the difficulty that most self-defined heterodox economists face? I see two reasons. The first is that all ideas face enormous competition in the economics profession; it is not easy getting one's ideas heard. The top graduate schools recruit very bright students and train them in how to write papers with the right combination of technique and content that will get them a job, get them published, and get them tenure. They create graduates who will succeed in the existing environment. Heterodox programs have not done that; they have tended to see themselves as outside of the mainstream. Heterodox graduate programs generally have trained students in their particular heterodox tradition and have not given significant training in the latest developments in mainstream economics, in advanced analytical or empirical techniques, or in how to write an article that will advance them in a mainstream-controlled environment.

That would be fine if these heterodox students were being sent out into an environment that valued that heterodox tradition, but all too often these heterodox students are sent out into an environment controlled by the mainstream that is hostile to the heterodox tradition and to the way in which they were trained. All too often these heterodox students aren't being equipped with the tools necessary to survive in that environment outside of some protected heterodox niches, which are becoming smaller generation by generation. Regardless of how bright these heterodox economists are, in competition with the mainstream-trained young economists who have been primed to survive in the existing environment, most of the young heterodox economists naturally lose out. The reality is that effective "inside-the-mainstream" heterodoxy requires not only solid technical skills, but rather superior technical skills. The only ones who are allowed to break the rules are those who have demonstrated a full command of them.

A related reason why young heterodox economists have such a hard time is that while the mainstream is open to ideas, it is not open to the form that those ideas take. Mainstream economics is a highly restricted conversation, with a strong commitment to limiting the conversation to those ideas that fit into a formal mathematical model and which allow econometric consideration. To enter the mainstream conversation, models and econometrics have to be blended in just the right way to convince the mainstream profession that the author has something to add.

This limitation of form of expression leads mainstream economists to work on only those sets of ideas that their tools can shed some light on. Other issues are not worked on, not because they are not considered important, but because the mainstream economists believe that they cannot say anything about them in a way that can enter the economics conversation. Mainstream graduate students recognize that the conventions that have developed in economics are highly limiting. As one graduate student noted in discussions with me, sociologists look at important issues that they can't say anything about, while economists look at unimportant issues that they can say something about.

Heterodox economists rail against these conventions, and they violate them; they choose to talk about what they consider important issues, even if they don't have the tools to do it in a manner that fits the mainstream conventions. That unwillingness to accept mainstream conventions about form is in large part what separates out what might be called an "inside-the-mainstream" heterodox economist from an "outside-the-mainstream" heterodox economist. In my view, it is primarily heterodox economists' unwillingness to accept the mainstream conventions about form, less than the particular ideas or ideology that they hold, that is the distinguishing characteristic of the "outside-the-mainstream" heterodox economics.

I am not criticizing heterodox economists for not accepting mainstream conventions; I am simply pointing out that in doing so they are essentially shutting themselves out of the mainstream conversation and making it very difficult for them, and more importantly for their students, to succeed in an environment controlled by the mainstream.[4]

Despite my concerns, my preferred form of communication is much closer to the heterodox approach than it is to the mainstream economic approach. Thus, I am highly sympathetic to the heterodox complaints about form. I agree that just because the available tools can't handle an issue does not mean that the issue should not be considered by economists. I also agree that somehow the profession should be broad enough to include multiple frames of communication, so that when the tools become available, there is a framework of economic thought to tie together with those tools. The question is how best to bring that about.

Here is where I differ from most heterodox economists. Even though I share many of the concerns of self-described heterodox economists, I work hard to carry on a dialog with the mainstream and to put the heterodox concerns in a way that the mainstream will hear and will consider. I admit; I seldom succeed, but at least they will talk to me.[5] My approach is different from that of many self-described heterodox economists. They carry on their own conversation and seldom enter into the mainstream conversation. In the long run, I suspect that for most heterodox groups, it is a losing strategy – a strategy that will result in heterodox traditions being further squeezed from the profession. Hence, I suggest that heterodox groups consider an alternative "inside-the-mainstream" strategy. Specifically, my suggested approach is that some heterodox economists consider seeing themselves within this environment, rather than seeing themselves as existing solely in the heterodox environment. Essentially, I am suggesting a Fattah-type approach to the mainstream rather than a Hammas-type approach. This "inside-the-mainstream" approach would engage the mainstream as much as possible and be more open to accepting mainstream conventions about form than most heterodox economists are willing to do.

I don't expect many of those who are established in the heterodox movement to choose this approach. The wounds of the battles are too raw. And it is true that they are providing an important service; there are benefits to the profession from an "outside-the-mainstream" heterodoxy that points out its foibles and creates an alternative – benefits that do not exist for an "inside-the-mainstream" heterodoxy, who are always close to being co-opted. But being an "outside-the-mainstream" heterodox economist is a tough life, especially for young heterodox economists. I present these ideas in the hope that some of the younger heterodox economists will consider it as an alternative.

Below, I list some suggestions for those in the heterodox community who are interested in exploring this approach or in opening a dialog with the mainstream and becoming part of the "inside-the-mainstream" heterodoxy.[6]

## Suggestions for an "inside-the-mainstream" heterodoxy

### *Criticize the best of the profession, not the worst*

As I have discussed above, the economics profession has much diversity of thought and play of ideas. Heterodox criticisms of a mainstream orthodoxy that do not take that diversity into account are unlikely to be heard. Criticisms that see the profession as a complex adaptive system are much more likely to be heard. Whenever I hear a heterodox economist criticizing the "neoclassical orthodoxy," I can only feel that they are speaking to the converted and will not have any chance of entering into a conversation with the mainstream.

### *Concentrate on areas where you can make a difference*

As I have argued in Colander (2005a), principles textbooks are full of neoclassical ideas and often are not consistent with much of the latest thinking in the profession. One of the reasons textbooks are inconsistent with the best thinking in the profession is that the mainstream does not focus on teaching or pedagogy. This lack of concern about teaching by the mainstream leaves an opening for "inside-the-mainstream" heterodox economists. By addressing their arguments to the narrow issue of what economists teach in their textbooks and not to the issue of economists' research, heterodox economists are on much firmer ground and can get a better hearing from mainstream journals.

### See the heterodox conversation as an incubator for ideas

I am sympathetic to those heterodox economists who want to stay out of the mainstream debate. Ideas need nurturing, and the environment for ideas within mainstream economics is unfriendly. Its requirement that ideas be formally modeled make it hard for novel ideas to develop. Heterodox economics communities provide an incubator environment within which ideas can germinate and sprout. They develop their own institutional structure which provides institutional validation of their ideas and support mechanisms which allow the ideas to thrive within its limited environment. They are wonderful idea incubators, which allow people to have more friendly critics around who treat their ideas more gently than they would be treated in mainstream economics. This gentle treatment gives the ideas a chance to germinate and perhaps even to sprout. Thus, the "outside-the-mainstream" heterodox community plays an important role.

### Prepare your ideas to leave the incubator

Ideas cannot remain in the incubator forever, and for the heterodox communities to serve the function of incubator, they must transfer the idea, developed in heterodoxy, up to the mainstream. All too often, what happens with ideas developed in heterodox economics is that they remain in their incubator and do not cross-pollinate with mainstream ideas. Both heterodox and mainstream economics are worse off for it. Thus, for the most part, the new ideas that have entered the mainstream in recent years, even though they parallel ideas heterodox economists have pushed for years, did not enter through heterodoxy, and the mainstream work almost never cites heterodox work.

For example, until recently the analytic and computational tools to consider uncertainty were not developed, and Post Keynesian economists who emphasized uncertainty fell outside-the-mainstream conversation. With the development of complexity tools in mathematics, today the ideas of Post Keynesians are being integrated without any reference to Post Keynesians. Similarly with Institutional Economics' concern with socioeconomic aspects and institutional feedback on individuals. Before the development of evolutionary game theory, such concerns could not be integrated into mainstream theory; today they can be, and are. But it is being done with almost no reference to Institutionalists who kept these ideas alive as mainstream economics completely ignored them.

To make the transfer from the heterodox incubator to the mainstream, the ideas must be developed in a formal model and buttressed by technical empirical work. This transfer is difficult; often, the reason the mainstream has shied away from the complicated issues that heterodox economists see as important is highly likely to have been that mainstream economists thought the issues were intractable given the existing tools, not because the mainstream did not believe such issues were important. What this means is that for the heterodox ideas to enter the mainstream, the tools must change. They can only be dealt with formally by bringing more sophisticated mathematics and statistics to bear on the issue than the mainstream is currently using.

### *See mathematicians and technical economists as your allies, not your nemesis*

Mainstream economics is a formal modeling field; it is not going to change. It has chosen the issues it has because the tools it has available could be used to shed light on those issues. Advanced mathematicians can bring in new ideas because they have new ways of looking at issues that mainstream economists know were important, but shied away from because they didn't have the techniques to handle them. Thus, there is a natural symbiosis of heterodox economics with advanced applied mathematical economics and statistics. That symbiosis has not been developed, in part because heterodox economists have been anti-math. In my view heterodox economists should be precisely the opposite – they should welcome higher and higher levels of mathematical and statistical formalization into economics because that is what will allow the formal consideration of the issues they want considered.

Most heterodox economists don't have the skills to do that formal mathematical work, and I am not arguing that they should develop them. But I am arguing that "inside-the-mainstream" heterodox economics should have a working knowledge of what is going on in high-level mathematics and statistics, with an eye to see if new analytic techniques may be able to address some of the issues they believe should be addressed. Where there are, the "inside-the-mainstream" heterodox economists should be exploring possibilities for joint work with ultra mathematicians and ultra statisticians, who do have the skills and the interest in ideas. There is a natural connection between these two groups.

### *Become involved in mainstream organizations*

Organizations such as the American Economic Association and European Economic Association are generally controlled in theory by the members, but in practice they are controlled by a small group of mainstream economists. Few people vote in elections, and the nominating committees keep the control in the hands of a small group of elite graduate school economists. Whereas individual departments and economists don't have to be pluralistic, these organizations must at least appear to be. "Inside-the-mainstream" heterodox economists would become involved in these organizations; they would vote in them and, if they have enough support, would influence the profession through their role in these organizations. I see heterodox economists volunteering to serve on committees and coming up with suggestions for new programs to "broaden" the education and training of economists that could get support in the broader mainstream community.

### *Worry less about methodology*

Many heterodox economists focus on methodological issues. For an "inside-the-mainstream" heterodox economist, that is a mistake. Unless he or she is a philosopher specializing in methodology, just about everything to be said about methodology has been said. To think that anyone but a specialist is going to have much to add on methodology is similar to a neophyte thinking he can do better than an index fund in investing.

Instead of complaining or discussing methodological problems, an "inside-the-mainstream" heterodox economist would be working on specific institutional problems that both underlie and affect methodology, such as creating an alternative ranking system. If the current ranking system does not put heterodox research in an appropriate light, he or she would develop a research agenda designed to create an alternative ranking system that does, and explain why it is a better system. There are many foibles with the current ranking systems, especially as a ranking system for economists who are primarily teachers of economics or are involved in "hands-on" applied policy. Heterodox interests fit much better into what undergraduate teaching needs, and were a separate "teaching-oriented" research ranking system developed, heterodox economics would come out much better in the rankings.

### *Don't dwell on unfairness*

If there is to be a dialog, it has to originate from heterodox economists. The mainstream has the power and has little incentive to give it up, and for the most part is totally unaware of a heterodoxy even existing.[7] Heterodox economists today find themselves in precarious positions and are being squeezed out institutionally both in the United States and in Europe. Is it fair that most of the effort toward communication will have to be on the heterodox economist's side? Absolutely not. But so what? Regardless of how unfair the profession is to you, it does not help to feel sorry for yourself.

I fully agree, heterodox economics are discriminated against and ill-treated. But complaining about it will not change the situation when the other side has the power. So, I see no other option than to live with it. If you define your role in a way that allows you to succeed within the institutions that exist, you have more of a chance of changing the institutions than you do if you are marginalized. Toward that end, I do not see it as especially helpful to distinguish oneself as a heterodox economist, and not just as an economist who has certain beliefs. To differentiate oneself as heterodox places one in opposition to an orthodoxy that the mainstream doesn't believe exists, and thereby reduces the possibility of communication with the very people who I believe heterodox economists should be communicating with.

## Conclusion

I do not expect my suggestions to be well received by the heterodox community, just as my ideas are generally not well received in the mainstream community. I offer them in the hope of establishing better lines of communication between mainstream and heterodox economists. I am not arguing that all, or even most, established heterodox economists should become "inside-the-mainstream" heterodox economists. Most established heterodox economists have found a comfortable institutional niche for themselves, which allows them to expound their ideas to a friendly group of fellow economists and students. They can do quite well as an "outside-the-mainstream" heterodox economist.

The reason I wrote this chapter is that the trend I see occurring in the profession is one in which the heterodox community is increasingly marginalized. It is becoming harder and harder for heterodox students to exist in the "outside-the-mainstream" heterodox niches. In my view, the heterodox niche that currently exists may not be a sustainable niche within the economics profession. In any case heterodox students should expect that the niche will come under increasing competitive pressures from the mainstream. Unless the heterodox program expands within the economic profession, or otherwise grows through interdisciplinary programs which establish themselves outside of economists' normal niches (as feminist economics has done), heterodox students will generally have a harder time than their professors, and their students' students will have an even harder time existing in that niche.

In my view a dynamic profession is a blend of many different ideas, all competing to be heard. Currently self-described heterodox ideas are not being heard. The "inside-the-mainstream" heterodoxy approach suggested in this chapter offers a way for young heterodox economics to exist in the mainstream environment and for heterodox ideas to become blended in with mainstream ideas. It is a heterodoxy that is continually changing and multifaceted. It is opportunistic and concentrates on those niches where heterodox ideas can flourish. The theoretical part of this heterodoxy would likely integrate with researchers from physics, math, and statistics programs that allow heterodox economists to push the frontier of techniques as well as ideas. The non-technical part of this heterodoxy would concentrate on teaching undergraduate economics and would provide an undergraduate teaching of economics that is much broader than that which is currently taught. Improving that teaching would be a major contribution to both the profession and the society.

## Notes

1 I discuss my view of how ideology enters mainstream economics in Colander (2005b).
2 There is, of course, no shortage of closed-minded mainstream economists, just as there is no shortage of closed-minded heterodox economists. In my considerations of mainstream and heterodox economists, I am talking about the best of both groups.
3 For example, Ken Arrow played a critical role in guiding and nurturing the Santa Fe complexity work, and in supporting Brian Arthur's attempt to broaden economics, even though he was associated with the general equilibrium theory that it was meant to replace.
4 Were mainstream economists to accept this broader form of communication, new methods of deciding what is good or not, including new rankings, would have to develop. I suspect that these alternative rankings and methods of choosing among ideas would likely be *as* discriminatory to heterodox ideas and to heterodox economists, *or more so*, than the current ones. In any case, the economics profession would be a far different profession than it is now. But I am not sure that it would be a better profession. From the vantage point of a supporter of heterodox ideas, a commitment to form over content in limiting the conversation has much to be said for it because it makes it less likely that ideology will limit the conversation.
5 My tendency to try to promote dialog between different groups has made me the only white male Anglo Saxon protestant token that I know of. When heterodox economists are looking for a token mainstream economist to talk to they often invite me. When mainstream economists are looking for a token heterodox economist to invite, they often invite me.
6 The suggestions here are an expansion of the argument developed in Colander (2003) and Colander, Holt, and Rosser (2007).
7 I initially entitled this chapter "What does mainstream economics think of heterodox economics?" I changed it because my honest answer to that question was that they don't think about it. For the most part, the mainstream is unaware of the existence of an "outside-the-mainstream" heterodoxy.

## References

Colander, D. (2003) "Post Walrasian Macroeconomics and Heterodoxy: Thinking Outside the Heterodox Box," *International Journal of Political Economy*, 33(2): 68–81.
—— (2005a) "What Economists Teach and What Economists Do," *Journal of Economic Education*, 36(3): 249–260.
—— (2005b) "Economics as an Ideologically Challenged Science," *Revue de Philosophie Economique*, 1: 3–24.
—— (2007) *The Making of an Economist Redux*, Princeton, NJ: Princeton University Press.
Colander, D., Holt, R.P.F., and Rosser, Jr., B. (2004). *The Changing Face of Economics: Conversations with Cutting Edge Economists*, Ann Arbor: University of Michigan Press.
—— (2007). "Live and Dead Issues in the Methodology of Economics," *Journal of Post Keynesian Economics*, 30 (2): 303–312.

# 3 Is convergence among heterodox schools possible, meaningful, or desirable?

*William Waller*

## Introduction

This chapter explores the issue of convergence among disparate approaches to economic issues, both theoretical and practical. By *convergence*, I mean when two fairly distinct branches of economic thought (either different schools of thought or different strands within a school of thought), which have distinct and discrete developmental, intellectual histories, independently arrive at the same, or very similar, positions on questions of theory, practice, and/or interpretations of observations. Convergence can occur between two strands of economic thought at any time. The significance of convergence for pluralism in economics occurs when at least the members of one strand become aware of the convergence.

In a recent article in the *Journal of Economic Issues*, Philip O'Hara (2007: 5) labeled me as a "Major Heterodox Converger," which stimulated me to think about the benefits of convergence (Waller 1999, 2005). Some economists react negatively to arguments that there have been examples of convergence among different schools of thought, which have at times been fruitful. Such reactions, which range from taking mild offence to genuine fury and vitriol, are surprising and a bit dispiriting for advocates of economic pluralism and suggest issues that need to be addressed.

The basic idea of convergence is exemplified by Oliver E. Williamson's general observation that institutions are important and his recognizing that John R. Commons (1990 [1934]) had made similar observations (Williamson 1975: 3). What is significant here is that Williamson, at the time of his initial remarks on Commons, would generally have been considered a neoclassical economist and Commons was one of the co-founders of original institutional economics. This is an instance of convergence.

Williamson's (1975) acknowledgment of the shared character of his focus on transactions with Commons became the opportunity for an ongoing dialogue between those who identify their work with the new institutional economics (NIE) and those who identify their work with original institutional economics (OIE). This communication has led to additional areas of convergence between these two strands of economic thought, particularly evidenced by the work of Richard Nelson (2007) and Douglas North (2005), to the mutual benefit of both strands of thought. Theoretical and conceptual contributions from both strands – such as cumulative causation, path dependency, the role of technology in social change, the significance of routines and habits, and evolutionary processes – are the subject of lively exchanges within and among the participants in these strands of economic thought.

It should be noted that in the example above, while Williamson noted the convergence between his ideas and Commons', he did almost nothing with that observation. His observation of the convergence created the opportunity for others to follow up on his observation. There are many such cases of convergence, but it is not the case that all such occurrences lead to any discernable change in either strand of economic thought.

Convergence's consequences for pluralism in economics then are dependent upon these opportunities being exploited in the larger community of economic discourse. The important question is, under what circumstances are such opportunities likely to be exploited in such a way as to enhance the conversation and enhance pluralism in economics more generally? I suspect there are many such circumstances, as when the stagflation of the 1970s – a problem that was not solvable with conventional theoretical and conceptual apparatus – led to a broader discussion among economists, including exchanges of ideas between mainstream and heterodox economists, and an increase in pluralism within the economics profession (Albelda *et al.* 1984; Sherman 1976). Indeed, it would be fairly surprising if honest scholars from alternative perspectives never came up with commensurate observations, theories, or conclusions when observing the same behavior, among the same population, in the same culture, around the same time. Thought of in this way, it is surprising that convergence is not noticed more often.

## The problem

The concerns expressed about convergence are less about its occurrences and more about the perception of what happens after convergences occurs. Several years ago, I presented a paper at a joint panel of Association for Social Economics and the Association for Evolutionary Economics at the Allied Social Science Association meetings, where I argued that institutional and social economics were inevitably converging with feminist economics. The shared elements creating that convergence, I argued, were the shared definition of economics as the study of provisioning and the recognition of gender as a cultural construction. While the details of the argument are unimportant here, a comment made in response to the paper was that this line of argument "erased" one of these intellectual traditions. Because I was focusing on the convergences, I certainly emphasized the common elements among these three very different traditions (Waller 2006). But I did not propose that convergence leads to the merging of these three traditions, or one of them subsuming the other two. However, that comment helped me understand the concern underlying some of the less measured opposition to the idea of convergence.

In this same vein, a recent comment in the *Journal of Economic Issues*, in my view, perfectly illustrates what convergence should not be. Baldwin Ranson (2007) in a note entitled "Heterodox Theoretical Convergence: Possibility or Pipe Dream?" points out that a large number of papers at the 2006 Association for Evolutionary Economics meeting addressed convergence. Moreover, he notes correctly that many of these papers assessed the likelihood and desirability of the merger of disparate research programs into a common approach.

Ranson's title foreshadows his conclusions: pipe dreams – dreams induced by indulging in opiates – are generally not considered accurate representations of the real world. But the character of his argument is also instructive. He begins with a questionable assertion: "Veblen rejected the preconception of other theoretical positions, and any convergence with Veblenian theory requires theoretical preconceptions compatible with his" (Ranson 2007: 243–244). Why? I can think of no reason that this is logically the case. Veblen rejected those preconceptions because he was convinced they were factually incorrect. If core tenets of Veblen's theory of human nature were found to be significantly out of line with empirical evidence on human behavior, institutionalists would not use them. If the combined preconceptions of Veblen were discovered to be incompatible or incoherent, the methodological prescriptions of contemporary institutional economics would require institutional economists to clarify, improve, and reconstitute their understanding of human behavior.

However, Ranson proceeds with an internally inconsistent demonstration of non-convergence. Convergence for him is other heterodox approaches converging upon his preferred rendering of Veblenian institutionalism. What makes this odd is that Ranson is a proponent of a particular variant on the Veblen–Ayres tradition (usually associated with the University of Texas) as modified by J. Fagg Foster of the University of Denver. This Veblen/Ayres/ Foster variant is currently articulated in the scholarship of a total of seven living institutionalists – though to be fair it has been an influential bunch.[1] I point this out because Ranson himself agrees with (and cites) Geoffrey Hodgson's observations that" ... by 1945 American institutionalism was fractured and diverse, and lacking a consensus on its own methodological and theoretical foundations" (Hodgson 2004: xvii). Ranson adds: "We judge that observation still to be true" (Ranson 2007: 261). But the point remains that, in Ranson's assessment, the measure of all things is Ranson's preferred approach to institutional economics, fixed and immutable, an ideal to be approximated if convergence is to be realized.

## Another view of convergence

Is there another way to understand the possibility of convergence among heterodox thought: one that does not involve the erasure of other approaches; one that does not establish one's traditions or approach as the immutable standard that the others will approximate; one that maintains an open and pluralist economics discipline? I think there is such an understanding of convergence. To make this case I will argue in favor of two propositions. First, convergence is inevitable. Second, convergence is an opportunity.

### *Inevitability*

Since I am by training and disposition an institutional economist, the argument that convergence is inevitable will be an evolutionary argument. There are two ways of constructing evolutionary theory in institutional economics: the generalized Darwinian approach (sometimes referred to as "universal Darwinism") as articulated by Geoffrey Hodgson (2002; Hodgson and Knudsen 2006) among others; and an alternative approach suggested by Ulrich Witt (2004, 2008) and others, referred to as an "ontological continuity" approach to evolution or, more recently, focusing on the processes of novelty emergence and dissemination. The generalized Darwinian approach describes economic and social evolutionary processes in terms of variation, selection, and retention. The ontological continuity approach eschews this framework, arguing that developing evolutionary arguments requires deriving the framework from the social processes under examination. This chapter adopts as a matter of expository convenience the ontological continuity approach, which will entail using the term "meme" largely metaphorically rather than analogically.

I begin by borrowing from Daniel Dennett's (1995) characterization of Richard Dawkin's concept of a "meme" as described in his book *Darwin's Dangerous Idea*. Dawkin introduced the concept of a meme in his 1976 book, *The Selfish Gene*. A meme is what Dawkin's calls the "unit of cultural transmission." He argues that the meme is the analogue to the gene in biological evolution and serves the same purpose as the gene in the process of cultural evolution. To develop the concept of the meme, we must first note something about evolution.

Genes, or units of biological transmission, must reproduce themselves or become extinct. Organisms are the vessels that carry genes. The only criterion that matters in selection is differential rates of reproduction of the gene. The gene's reproduction may or may not be particularly beneficial for the organism that carries it. Differential rates of reproduction over incredibly long periods of time lead to natural selection. Dennett notes that there are many cases of "convergent evolution" – for example, eyes have evolved in many lineages or powered flight in four lineages in two different phyla. He attributes these cases of convergent evolution to the fact that these particular biological characteristics are good solutions to recurring needs or problems that enhance the reproductive capacity of particular genes (Dennett 1995: 306–307). Successful design strategies are likely to recur in evolutionary design space to meet recurring or ongoing challenges to gene reproduction, with random variations occurring over extremely long periods of time.

When we move to the cultural sphere, the likelihood of convergence increases dramatically. If we think of a meme as a physical, mental, or linguistic artifact, we observe that there is no need to depend on random variations: the meme can be transmitted intentionally; it can be changed intentionally; and we can intentionally engage in experimentation to speed up adaptation. And similar to genes, we know from the history of technology that innovation comes from the recombination of existing elements of earlier technology. For example, Samuel Colt added the steamboat's paddlewheel to a pistol to create the revolver. Once the component parts of an invention are present in a society, the invention becomes almost inevitable. For example, once the high output internal combustion engine was available, within a few years, it was put in a cart, on a railcar, in a boat, on a bicycle and on a glider – by many different people. This leads to the phenomenon of simultaneous invention. These components are the "memes" of technology that account for the variations that are the source of modification over time. They can be grand recombinations or very small ones, resulting in major innovations or minor improvements.

In the realm of ideas, like technology, new things often come from the recombination of existing components in new arrangements. New ideas are very rare. Most scholarly activity (a subset of human behavior directed at ideas) is not, as is commonly thought, directed at new ideas. Instead, scholarly activity is usually focused on minor refinements on well-worn ideas generated by imitating the work of our predecessors.

The components of new ideational combinations are not always understood as being of the same character. We have a very complex taxonomy for particular ideational pieces that make up "memes" at this level of generalization. Some are ideas, some are concepts, some are definitions, and some are techniques and methods. We regularly recombine these elements to explore new things old ways, old things new ways, old things old ways, and sometimes serendipitously – with the ever so rare leap of imagination – new things new ways. While biological evolution can look to the physical recombination of genes (itself once a concept with no physical counterpart) for variation, the resulting changes in phenotypes occur at many different levels. In the world of ideas, the components available for recombination leading to variation are all mental constructs we have (in our particular language) separated into many different categories, so calling them all "memes" for our purposes is somewhat helpful rhetorically, to downplay the differences that are emphasized by our taxonomy of mental constructs.

These ideational memes are transmitted through human communication and are retained in memory and in mechanical storage devices of many kinds, so once a new component is available it generally remains available. If the scholarly community is operating purposefully to solve a problem, then the meme is likely to be explored for possible use in this process. Persuasion and demonstration will be key to its incorporation and use in the body of warranted knowledge. Memes, like genes, will be selected on the basis of their differential reproduction. A problem can emerge when the meme is an idea, as an idea does not have to be correct in order to reproduce.

Fortunately, not all memes that survive and reproduce will be incorrect. If we consider that economists are generally people of good will, seriously trying to understand the human behaviors necessary for people to provision themselves, then within that community it is certain that with random variation over extremely long periods of time, there will be moments of inevitable convergence, just as there are in biological evolution.

Thorstein Veblen is well known for his attempt to incorporate evolutionary theorizing into economics. In trying to understand the likelihood of any particular results of convergence being incorporated into economic discourse more widely and any impacts this may have on pluralism within economics, Veblen may be of some help. Scholarly activity, like all human behavior, can either be intentional and teleological in character, or it can "drift blindly," to use Veblen's terminology. Veblen thought human behavior was motivated by instincts. Purposeful behavior directed at accomplishing some end in view or solving a problem was motivated by the "instinct of workmanship." However, human beings were also motivated by the instinct of "idle curiosity." These different motives for scholarly activity (whether instinctual or not) could lead to very different behavior that is relevant to the likelihood of any idea or concept being adopted or adapted into a scholarly community's discourse. The solving of a particularly intransigent or important problem is more likely to lead to an expansion of the search for knowledge, including looking in some unlikely places, in order to solve the problem. Idle curiosity, while important to motivating disinterested scholarly pursuit of basic research for its own sake, may in the absence of some other more compelling motive, lead to blind drift, or alternatively to the elaboration of existing frameworks; completing well understood research programs; baroque elaboration of theoretical possibilities; and/or to use Barbara Wootton's (1937: 130) wonderful term, "umbilical contemplation."

If we consider that human intellectual pursuits are not dominated by blind drift, but instead are the result of the purposeful pursuit of warranted knowledge, then we might do better than random variation in our pursuit of understanding, and then convergence will not require such vast periods of time. Warranted knowledge is a term of art in institutional economics. Knowledge is, in the pragmatic tradition, provisional. It is the best understanding of how the world works that we have at a particular point in time. It is always changing. There are a number of criteria used to establish the warrant of a particular component of knowledge, including but not limited to empirical verification, coherence with other components of knowledge, and success in application. What we use to comprehend and act in our world is the body of knowledge currently accepted as the most likely correct understanding of how things work by the community of people who study such things. This body of knowledge changes over time. It is added to by new research. It is rearranged by new conceptual schemes. It even changes because of reinterpretation due to the inherent ambiguity in the languages in which it must be expressed and is continually reconstructed. Warranted knowledge is a thoroughly social construct. Either intentionally or through blind drift – fast or slow – convergence is inevitable.

## *Opportunity*

Occasions of convergence create opportunities. But not all opportunities are taken. The opportunity for knowledge creation through convergence is most interesting when the convergence leads to a restructuring of the meaning of a strand of thought as a *result* of the convergence. Different strands of economic thought borrow from one another all the time. Much of this borrowing is trivial and hackneyed at best – as when a particular term or concept is borrowed and incorporated for expository effect. Often when a concept is "shared," there is little convergence in the way of shared meaning as a result of the sharing, as in the difference between the meaning of "rationality" in mainstream neoclassical economics and its meaning in Austrian economics – where rationality means maximization of net returns and purposeful human behavior respectively. To consider a few examples:

### *Post Keynesians and institutionalists*

Mark Lavoie (1992) has argued (as have others) that the microeconomic foundations of Post Keynesian economics can be found in Institutional economics. Gardiner Means's work on administered prices (Samuels and Medema 1990; Lee and Samuels 1992), John Kenneth Galbraith's (1967) extensions of those ideas in his major works, and Alfred Eichner's (1976) analysis of the "megacorp" provide examples of fruitful convergences that have stimulated thinking in both frameworks. As L. Randall Wray (2007) has noted, there are convergences between the monetary approaches of John R. Commons and John Maynard Keynes that both recognized contemporaneously. He recently noted the unexploited convergence between Keynes's monetary theory of production and Thorstein Veblen's analysis in *The Theory of Business Enterprise* (1978 [1904]).

In the case of Post Keynesian economics, the convergence was the recognition that institutional economics could serve as the underlying disaggregated theory of economic behavior. This moved Post Keynesian economics from an approach to macroeconomics into a full-blown alternative school of thought with an underlying approach to ontology, epistemology, methodology, value theory, and independently warranted research methods.

### *Feminist economics*

The advances in feminist economics since the creation of the International Association for Feminist Economics constitute a premiere example of fruitful convergence. Consider that what brought the members of this group together was not a shared approach to research (though there are increasing commonalities and a vigorous debate about methods), but instead a set of common concerns about the inclusion of gender in economic analysis and the removal of androcentric bias from both theory and methods in economics regardless of the research tradition (see, for example, Barker and Feiner 2004; Grapard 1999; Whalen and Whalen

1994). This characterization is unsettling for some feminist economics – a concern that seems to emerge from confounding use of the term "methodology" in the sense of shared tools and techniques of analysis and shared goals of analysis, with "methodology" in the sense of shared ontological, epistemological, and axiological (value) commitments that are generally understood to define separate schools of thought. As Ulla Grapard (1999: 544–545), who distinguishes between these two uses of the term methodology, concludes in her essay on feminist methodology, "Although feminist economists do not necessarily share a common ideological and philosophical perspective, they do have a commitment to methodologies that help formulate theoretical models and practical proposals that will lead to emancipatory change for women." This convergence of interests and goals with the variety of methodologies, methods, and philosophical perspectives from many strands and schools of thought within feminist economics has generated the most fruitful cross-research tradition discussions within economics in the post-World War II period.

*Institutional economics and feminist economics: the missed opportunity*

In the late nineteenth century, both Thorstein Veblen and Charlotte Perkins Gilman produced evolutionary analyses of modern industrial culture that explicitly employed a concept of gender as a cultural construction. Both carefully explored patriarchy as an ongoing system of economic oppression that exploited women to the advantage of men and frustrated attempts by women to lead productive and fulfilling lives outside the control of men. They both identified this as an extension of women's enslavement by men and the inclusion of women in the category of property. There are of course also profound differences in their analyses. For example, Veblen is more interested in the role of patriarchy in the development of the institutions of modern industrial culture, whereas Gilman is primarily concerned with the consequences of these institutional developments on the social and biological circumstance under which women were exploited in modern industrial culture. Two extremely popular and widely read books, Gilman's *Women and Economics* (1994 [1898]) and Veblen's *The Theory of the Leisure Class* (1934 [1899]) appear at approximately the same time, sharing important commonalities.

Briefly, for those unfamiliar with Veblen's analysis of the role of women in the development of modern economies, it should be noted that gender analysis is at the core of Veblen's theoretical work (see Peterson 1998 for a discussion of this claim). Veblen's preparatory work for *The Theory of the Leisure Class* involved publishing two articles on the role of women in economics (see Veblen 1964 [1894], 1964 [1899]). In *The Theory of the Leisure Class*, he uses ethnographic research to show the development of the leisure class emerging out of the gendered division of labor prevalent in technologically primitive (neolithic) societies. He shows how his gendered analysis of contemporary (1890s) leisure class behavior evolves from these earlier forms. Veblen returns to the central role of the social construction of gender in explaining the evolution of economic behavior in what he considered his most important theoretical contribution in *The Instinct of Workmanship and the State of the Industrial Arts* (1990 [1914]). In that book, he argues that the development of the industrial arts and the cultivation of the instinct of workmanship evolve from women's work. The ethnographic foundations of his analysis are carefully documented in *The Instinct of Workmanship*, unlike *The Theory of the Leisure Class* (see Waller 1994).

Additionally, both Veblen and Gilman were important figures among the emerging philosophical school of Pragmatism, documented by Seigfried (1996). Dorfman (1934: 194, 196) and Dimand (1999: 402) both note that they were aware of one another's work through Lester Ward who gave Gilman a copy of *The Theory of the Leisure Class* about which she commented favorably. Margaret Lewis and David Sebberson (1997: 424) have argued:

> Gilman and Veblen are writing at a time when American philosophy is seriously challenging enlightenment thought with pragmatism, which legitimates theory not on the grounds of universality, logical validity, or mathematical elegance, but rather on the grounds of how the theory will undergird human action and lead to richer living. By grounding their economics in pragmatism, Gilman and Veblen are reconceiving economics as a human science situated within human action rather than as an enlightenment science that objectifies economics and abstracts it from human action.

Dimand (1999:402) concurs that Gilman's approach was congenial to Veblen's institutional economics with its pragmatic philosophical foundations.

So what was the missed opportunity? While it is often argued that Gilman's work was dismissed as unscientific because it contained no models or mathematical formalisms, this is not a correct reading of the history of economic thought of the time. Both Veblen and Gilman were widely read, their books were both best sellers, both were influential public intellectuals of their times, and both were participants in a major development in philosophy – Pragmatism – that was entering its heyday at precisely this time. But most importantly, the hegemony of formalist approaches to economics did not dominate American economic thought or even American academic economic thought until after the Great Depression. So there was a congenial discursive space, even within economics, to address the role of gender in the economy from their similar perspectives. Unfortunately, other institutional economists did not add or expand upon Veblen's analysis of the role of women until the early 1970s. And only after that reawakening did any institutional economists return to reconsider Gilman's work from an institutionalist perspective. Feminist thought continued to develop in its own intellectual constellation with no discernable impact as a result of subsequent developments in institutional economics.

## Conclusions

So what are the general characteristics of the opportunities I believe are useful for a healthy pluralist economics? They grow out of a particular view of the world – that is, ontological realism. First, there is a real world that economists are trying to understand – to figure out how it works. Second, economists are serious about this scholarly endeavor and believe it to be important. Or alternatively economic analysis is not a performative enterprise whose participants produce their work for the purpose of dazzling their peers. The real world exists independent of, but is not unaffected by, this scholarly enterprise. And the third characteristic is that our knowledge of how the real world works is always partial, provisional, and incomplete. Convergences allow scholars in one tradition to see another tradition, at those points of convergence, a bit more clearly. They provide a comprehensible alternative perspective.

Ordinarily economists work within a research tradition that has boundaries, preconceptions, approved methods, priorities – all the components of an independent research program – that, taken together, structure the way particular economists approach their subject of inquiry. When economists view the work of other economists outside their own traditions, they do so from within their own tradition and consequently do not always appreciate what it is that the economists in the other tradition find fascinating about the insights they develop. When there is a convergence like the ones mentioned above, there is a moment where conversation and enhanced understanding can take place on a different level than normal circumstances.

To understand the significance of convergence, a consideration of the underlying necessities of any argumentative discourse is helpful. First, the participants must agree that there is a disagreement. Then they must agree on rules and starting points. Part of this will be some assumptions that are shared, though the participants will probably understand these assumptions differently. The important point for the purpose of understanding the potential outcomes of convergence is that "something" must already be agreed upon in order for any conversation to take place among those who disagree. Once some level of agreement or shared understanding is in place, there is a possibility of meaningful exchange and the expansion of the range of shared understanding.

When convergence occurs, there is a moment of real or apparent shared understanding of a phenomenon. All the participants in the converging analytic traditions have for that moment the shared understanding that is a prerequisite for meaningful conversation and exchange. This creates an opportunity to discuss shared meanings, shared or convergent concepts, and possibly shared goals of research. Additionally it gives members of one tradition an entry point to the other tradition. The paths that led to the convergence can be explored to see how each perspective got to the same place. Is there more common ground on that path than was previously suspected? Does this moment of convergence suggest that maybe the path beyond this convergence can be fruitfully explored in a context of continual shared conversations? These are moments to see a little further, understand a little better, understand a little differently, or at least celebrate a little success for all.

When ideas, concepts, and theories are passed as memes from one tradition to another, the consequences can be dramatic, as with the borrowing of ideas of physics within the mainstream of economics or the borrowing of evolution by institutional economics (and others). Borrowers have the advantage as Veblen pointed out in his book, *Imperial Germany and the Industrial Revolution* (1964 [1915]), that they are not inhibited in their use of the borrowed material by the constraints that arose with its development in its original context. Borrowers do not have to repeat mistakes, proceed down blind alleys, or remove the lens of the original context from their eyes. They can see things afresh. When the diffusion goes both ways (as it always does to some degree), both parties to the exchange can benefit – gains from intellectual trade so to speak. Most variation results in no significant change, but small variations over a very long period of time have the potential for dramatic impacts.

So on some occasions these moments are lasting influences on both traditions, as in the Post Keynesian-Institutional approaches. Sometimes the moments pass, leaving both traditions unaffected as in the Veblen–Gilman case. Sometimes it leads to new communities of shared research interest and understanding as in Feminist economics. I can think of no case where it has been harmful.

So when convergences occur we have a choice to make. To illustrate this choice consider that when the "new institutional economics" began to emerge, there were two responses by "original institutional economists." One response was dismissal ("old wine in new bottles") and scorn ("after a mere one hundred years, neoclassical economics has discovered institutions"). The other response was to greet this development as a sign of success and opportunity, as notably done by John Adams in his Association for Evolutionary Economics presidential address (1994) and J. Ron Stanfield in his Veblen–Commons Award Address (2006). We can always ignore the convergence or we can embrace it as an opportunity. I know of no heterodox tradition that is so complete, so influential, and so well developed, that in can prudently ignore these opportunities. So I remain a "converger" and a pluralist and an institutionalist and for the most part an optimistic economist. So pass the pipe.

## Note

1  Here I refer to Marc Tool, Paul Dale Bush, Edythe Miller, Gladys Foster, Baldwin Ransom, Ann Jennings, and myself. Jennings and Waller are students of Louis Junker, one of Foster's students. The others were students of Foster. There are others influenced by Foster and Foster's students – but we are not talking about a large number of active scholars.

## References

Adams, J. (1994) "Economy as an Instituted Process," *Journal of Economic Issues*, 28(2): 331–356.

Albelda, R., Gunn, C., and Waller, W. (1984) "The Resurgence of Political Economy," in Albelda, R., Gunn, C., and Waller, W. (eds) *Alternatives to Economic Orthodoxy*, 3–17, Armonk: M.E. Sharpe.

Barker, D. and Feiner, S. (2004) *Liberating Economics: Feminist Perspectives on Families, Work, and Globalization*, Ann Arbor: University of Michigan Press.

Commons, J.R. (1990 [1934]) *Institutional Economics*, New Brunswick: Transactions Press.

Dawkins, R. (1976) *The Selfish Gene*, Oxford: Oxford University Press.

Dennett, D. (1995) *Darwin's Dangerous Idea: Evolution and the Meaning of Life*, New York: Simon and Schuster.

Dimand, M.A. (1999) "Charlotte Perkins Gilman," in O'Hara, P. (ed.) *Encyclopedia of Political Economy*, Vol. 1, 400–403, New York: Routledge.

Dorfman, J. (1934) *Thorstein Veblen and His America*, New York: Viking.

Eichner, A. (1976) *The Megacorp and Oligopoly*, Cambridge: Cambridge University Press.

Galbraith, J.K. (1967) *The New Industrial State*, Boston: Houghton Mifflin.

Gilman, C.P. (1994 [1898]) *Women and Economics*, Amherst, NY: Prometheus Books.

Grapard, U. (1999) "Methodology," in Peterson, J. and Lewis, M. (eds) *The Elgar Companion to Feminist Economics*, 544–555, Northampton, MA: Edward Elgar.

Hodgson, G.M. (2002) "Darwinism in Economics: From Analogy to Ontology," *Journal of Evolutionary Economics*, 12(2): 259–281.

—— (2004) *The Evolution of Institutional Economics: Agency, Structure and Darwinism in American Institutionalism*, New York: Routledge.

Hodgson, G.M. and Knudsen, T. (2006) "Why We Need a Generalized Darwinism: And Why a Generalized Darwinism is Not Enough," *Journal of Economic Behavior and Organization*, 61(1): 1–19.

Lavoie, M. (1992) *Foundations of Post Keynesian Economics*, Cheltenham, UK: Edward Elgar Publishing.

Lee, F. and Samuels, W. (1992) *The Heterodox Economics of Gardiner C. Means: A Collection*, Armonk, NY: M.E. Sharpe.

Lewis, M. and Sebberson, D. (1997) "The Rhetoricality of Economic Theory: Charlotte Perkins Gilman and Thorstein Veblen," *Journal of Economic Issues*, 31(3): 417–424.

Nelson, R. (2007) "Institutions and Economic Growth," *Journal of Economic Issues*. 51(2): 313–323.

North. D. (2005) *Understanding the Process of Economic Change*, Princeton: Princeton University Press.

O'Hara, P.A. (2007) "Principles of Institutional-Evolutionary Political Economy: Converging Themes from Schools of Heterodoxy," *Journal of Economic Issues*, 42(1): 1–42.

Peterson, J. (1998) "Veblen and Feminist Economics: Valuing Women's Work in the Twenty-First Century" in Brown, D. (ed.) *Thorstein Veblen in the Twenty-First Century*, 117–129, Northampton, MA: Edward Elgar.

Ranson, B. (2007) "Heterodox Theoretical Convergence: Possibility or Pipe Dream?" *Journal of Economic Issues*, 42(1): 243–264.

Samuels, W. and Medema, G. (1990) *Gardiner Means: Institutionalist and Post Keynesian*, Armonk, NY: M.E. Sharpe.

Seigfried, C. (1996) *Pragmatism and Feminism: Reweaving the Social Fabric*, Chicago: University of Chicago.

Sherman, H. (1976) *Stagflation*, New York: Harper and Row.

Stanfield, J.R. (2006) "From OIE to NIE toward EE," *Journal of Economic Issues*, 40(2): 249–260.

Veblen, T. (1934 [1899]) *The Theory of the Leisure Class*, New York: Modern Library.

—— (1964 [1894]). "The Economic Theory of Women's Dress," in Ardzrooni, L. (ed.) *Essays in Our Changing Order*, New York: Augustus M. Kelley.

—— (1964 [1899]). "The Barbarian State of Women," in Ardzrooni, L. (ed.) *Essays in Our Changing Order*, New York: Augustus M. Kelley.

—— (1964 [1915]). *Imperial Germany and the Industrial Revolution*, New York: Augustus M. Kelley.

—— (1978 [1904]) *The Theory of Business Enterprise*, New Brunswick, NJ: Transactions Books.

—— (1990 [1914]) *The Instinct of Workmanship and the State of the Industrial Arts*, New Brunswick, NJ: Transactions Books.

Waller, W. (1994) "Technology and Gender in Institutional Economics," in Peterson, J. and Brown, D. (eds) *The Status of Women under Capitalism: Institutional Economics and Feminist Theory*, 55–77, Brookfield VA: Edward Elgar.

—— (1999) "Institutional Economics, Feminism, and Overdetermination," *Journal of Economic Issues*, 33(4): 835–844.

—— (2005) "Accidental Veblenian, Intentional Institutionalist, and Inevitable Feminist," *Journal of Economic Issues*, 39(2): 327–334.

—— (2006) "The Convergence of Feminist and Institutional/Social Economics." Paper presented at a joint session of the Association for Evolutionary Economics and the Association for Social Economics at the annual meetings of the Allied Social Science Associations, Boston (Jan.).

Whalen, C., and Whalen, L. (1994) "Institutionalism: A Useful Foundation for Feminist Economics," in Peterson, J., and D. Brown (eds) *The Status of Women under Capitalism: Institutional Economics and Feminist Theory*, 19–34, Brookfield VA: Edward Elgar.

Williamson, O. (1975) *Markets and Hierarchies*, New York: The Free Press.

Witt, U. (2004) "On the Proper Interpretation of 'Evolution' in Economics and its Implications for Production Theory," *Journal of Economic Methodology*, 11: 125–146.

—— (2008) "Ontology and Heuristics in Evolutionary Economics: Back to Veblen?" Paper presented at a session of the Association for Evolutionary Economics at the annual meetings of the Allied Social Science Associations, New Orleans (Jan.).

Wootton, B. (1937) *Lament for Economics*, London: George Allen and Unwin.

Wray, L.R. (2007) "Veblen's *The Theory of Business Enterprise* and Keynes's Monetary Theory of Production," *Journal of Economic Issues*, 41(2): 617–624.

# 4    Raising dissonant voices

## Pluralism and economic heterodoxy

*Diana Strassmann, Martha Starr, and*
*Caren A. Grown*

As part of an agenda to improve economics, heterodox economists have sought to promote the virtues of pluralism. However, the tendency to affiliate with similarly situated people and the preference for talking disproportionately with those who share similar perspectives appears to afflict not just the orthodox. Heterodox intellectual communities themselves demonstrate some of the same patterns of insularity so often seen among the mainstream, such as numerous conference sessions containing few women or scholars of non-European descent. Similarly, based on the papers they publish in heterodox journals or their books, it seems that many male heterodox authors apparently feel little compunction to engage substantively with women and feminist scholars. Indeed, except for their more casual clothes, a group of heterodox economists chatting at a reception is often indistinguishable from its mainstream counterpart in gender, race, and ethnicity.

Is the goal of pluralism simply to bring greater legitimacy to the points of view of marginalized, disproportionately male, European-descended economists who are currently clamoring for more legitimacy for their heterodox points of view? If so, this would seem to be a self-interested stance oriented toward enhancing the perceived importance of the existing hierarchy of heterodox scholars. Or does pluralism have the broader goal of enhancing human well-being in the world, with the goal of building an economics that is more responsive to the needs of all people, as some promoters of pluralism claim?

In imagining an economics that considers the well-being of all people, Amartya Sen has been a pioneer. In 1990, he stunned the world with his estimates that more than a 100 million women have died disproportionately to men during the twentieth century because of a lack of equal access to food, medical attention, and other resources (Sen 1990a). This horrific death toll – larger than the combined casualties of both World Wars, confirmed by Stephan Klasen and Claudia Wink (2003) – reveals an ongoing catastrophe of devastating proportions. Any effort to improve the well-being of all people, which some promoters of pluralism claim as a key goal, must therefore acknowledge that gender bias is one of the most critical economics issues of our time.

The tendency, however, has generally been for heterodox economists to think about pluralism not as greater openness to marginalized or underrepresented topics (however important), but rather as diversity in theoretical and methodological approaches to economics. For instance, why have heterodox economists not by and large applied heterodox approaches to gender equality issues? Is it because heterodox economists do not see that gender relations and gender inequality have much explanatory power in explaining how capitalism or globalization works? Or, do they still think that class is more important than gender and do not understand intersectionality – of class, gender, race, and so forth?

Indeed it is by their approaches, such as institutionalism, Marxism, post-Keynesian economics, that some key U.S. heterodox groups label themselves. An approach-based definition of pluralism takes the position that neoclassical economics provides an insufficient explanatory approach and that the field would benefit from being more open to alternative conceptual frameworks.

But a focus on approaches, by its very nature, is not a focus on economic problems, including those oriented toward improving human lives. This is not to say that the problems and topics addressed by such heterodox groups are not important and compelling. However, there is a difference between an association organized around shared approaches, for example, institutionalism, and one organized around a set of perceived economic concerns where a variety of approaches, including those that use very orthodox theoretical and methodological approaches, are treated as valuable within the framework of scholarship the heterodox group identifies as part of its mission.

The omission of concerns relating to gender inequality from the vast majority of economic papers, by the heterodox and orthodox alike, treats gender concerns as not worthy of substantive space in conference sessions, journals, and edited books. A classic example of a heterodox economist omitting feminist perspectives is Geoffrey M. Hodgson's 2001 book *How Economics Forgot History: The Problem of Historical Specificity in Social Science*. The book includes 1,150 citations, but only sixteen to women and only one to a feminist economist. An alternative book might be written entitled *How a Heterodox Economist Forgot Women*. Among heterodox books, this book is not unique in its neglect of gender, nor are papers by heterodox economists that fail to cite more than one or two (if any) feminist scholars.

Amartya Sen points out that a key reason for the neglect of attention to gender inequality is that the inequality is viewed as "natural."[1] He writes that the notion that an inequality is "natural" or "just" is key to the operation and survival of these arrangements (Sen 1990b: 137, 145). Although feminist thought has emerged and found proponents among heterodox scholars (just as it has among some mainstream scholars), the lack of interest shown by many heterodox economists to research into the causes of and solutions to gender inequality or to the ideas of women and feminists suggests that they, too, believe that gender inequality is perhaps natural, and certainly not so outrageous as to be a research priority. That said, we do acknowledge that some heterodox sessions are diverse, and that a number of male heterodox economists care deeply about these issues, including the chief organizers of the International Confederation of Associations for Pluralism in Economics (ICAPE). This chapter, for example, would never have been included in a mainstream volume.

As Sen shows, claims that observed inequalities are "natural" inherently accept social and institutional arrangements underlying the observed inequalities. Further, he argues that such structures can only persist if the legitimacy of the unequal order is not challenged (Sen 1990b: 137, 145). In this context, it is also worth noting what the "approach" definition of pluralism implicitly does not ask, and how this very definition itself may serve as a deterrent to the participation of differently situated participants.

The approach definition does not, for example, inquire into the diversity of participants, and ask, "Why are women and women's perspectives represented so sparsely in heterodox forums?" or "Why are the vast majority of participants in heterodox sessions, conferences, and scholarly publications male? Or European-descended? Or heterosexual?" Nor does it investigate the consequences of this framework and ask, "How do our life experiences influence the economic topics we choose to investigate and consider important?" or "Is it possible that people who are different from me may find different topics of greater immediate urgency, and that perhaps their views merit attention?" It also does not ask, "What can we do to open the door to bring people into economic conversations who are very unlike us? How can we engage with scholars from the South or those who may have a different ethnicity, race, sexual orientation, or gender?"

A "natural" explanation in economics for the lack of diversity in its forums is that there are few Ph.D. women economists, or few African-descended, or Southern scholars – that the problem is with the pipeline, or with skill deficiencies, or with the quality and importance of the work being done by the scholars who fit those demographics. If the conference session or journal under consideration has a particular theme, say methodology or history of thought, another natural explanation might be that women (or scholars of color, etc.) do not write in this area or submit to the journal, or participate in the association. The typical view is that this is unfortunate and should be changed, but that the situation is most likely unavoidable given the relative shortage of such scholars and the apparent lack of interest of such scholars in those topics.

Although many important economics conferences are held around the world, a look at sessions at the Allied Social Science Association (ASSA) meetings, the most important annual meetings of economists in the United States, is instructive because of the hegemonic influence of American economists. At the same time, we acknowledge that the ASSA is by no means representative of economic meetings in many other parts of the world.

Table 4.1 provides a snapshot of women's representation in sessions at the ASSA meetings during 2006 through 2008, and compares sessions of the main North American groups often labeled or self-identified as heterodox [the Association for Evolutionary Economics (AFEE), the Association for Social Economics (ASE), the International Association for Feminist Economics (IAFFE), and the Union of Radical Political Economics (URPE)] with American Economics

*Table 4.1* Female authors as a share of all authors of papers presented at the Allied Social Science Associations' annual meetings, by sponsoring organization

| Session sponsor | 2006 | 2007 | 2008 |
|---|---|---|---|
| 1  American Economics Association (AEA)[1] | 24.5 | 17.6 | 23.6 |
| 2  All heterodox organizations[2] | 32.9 | 37.7 | 31.2 |
| 3  Heterodox excluding IAFFE sessions | 26.8 | 29.3 | 25.5 |
| 4  Heterodox excluding IAFFE and IAFFE co-sponsored sessions | 21.1 | 22.3 | 17.8 |

Notes
1  1:5 sample.
2  Heterodox organizations include the Association for Evolutionary Economics (AFEE), the Association for Social Economics (ASE), the International Association for Feminist Economics (IAFFE), and the Union of Radical Political Economics (URPE).

Association (AEA) sessions.[2] Regrettably, name data does not permit a comparable analysis of participation by other demographic groups of scholars.

Except for sessions organized by feminist economists working within heterodox traditions, sessions at the ASSA meetings not only generally contain no engagement with feminist thought, but most also contain few women (or African-descended scholars, Latino/a scholars, or Southern scholars). As shown in line (4) of the table, women in 2006–2008 comprised only 17.8–22.3 percent of participants in non-IAFFE or IAFFE co-sponsored heterodox economic sessions – a range comparable to and in some years even lower than the share of women in AEA sessions (line 1). Although the overall share of women in heterodox sessions is substantially higher (line 2), this result is only obtained through the defining of IAFFE, an organization devoted to feminist inquiry, as a heterodox organization, and to the willingness of some heterodox organizations to share their session allotments with IAFFE in the form of co-sponsored sessions (many of which are actually organized by society members who also happen to be IAFFE members).

While the willingness of some heterodox societies to co-sponsor sessions with IAFFE shows good intent and is to be strongly commended – especially as their co-sponsorship of sessions with IAFFE comes at the expense of other sessions they might run – the non-IAFFE sponsored or IAFFE co-sponsored sessions do not show a greater percentage of women than in AEA sessions on average. This pattern of divided discourse suggests that, even in the more theoretically and methodologically "open-minded" heterodox world, heterodox discourse is fractured into separate communities, with the more predominant participants tending to converse together on topics that engage little with the issues of central concern to feminist scholars or other scholars not well represented in heterodox forums.

Perhaps it might also be said that some narrowness is inevitable in a discursive community and that any intellectual community will have a set of shared assumptions, goals, and interests. Scholarly associations typically organize conferences and panels with member participants, who by virtue of their affiliation are inherently screened to fit within the conception of the association. Ditto for society journals, which typically expect some acknowledgment of the core ideas around which the association builds its identity. Or perhaps it may be argued that it is natural for women and men (or for Northerners and Southerners, etc.) to have different interests insofar as our backgrounds and bodies shape our priorities and knowledge.

However, while supportive intellectual communities can nourish ideas and scholars, knowledge constructed in insular intellectual communities is less likely to consider and embrace paradigm-shifting insights. A narrow demographically restricted group of scholars is not likely to identify the most pressing concerns and needs of all people, without giving some platform to their voices. If knowledge is understood to be partial and situated,[3] economists, like other knowledge producers, construct accounts of the world colored by their own positions and judgments about the relative importance of various phenomena.

Therefore, the very logic behind a call for pluralism, the claim that economic knowledge will be improved through greater openness to alternative perspectives, must also acknowledge that true openness requires more than diversity in theoretical and methodological approaches from people of the same demographic group as the dominant practitioners. A truly substantive, or *deep* pluralism, must also insist on holding the door open to scholars with different lives and bodies and call for greater diversity in the people who participate in scholarly conversations. Such a pluralism must also anticipate that differently situated practitioners will have different priorities about what economic concerns are the most pressing and even what should count as legitimate inquiry. An inclusive heterodoxy, one that is deeply rather than superficially pluralistic, must therefore seek not just pluralism in theoretical and methodological approach, but also pluralism in knowledge production and pluralism in the topics of investigation.

Those who might worry that such pluralism lacks legitimacy or may lead to relativism should be reassured by philosophers of science, who increasingly recognize the social character of knowledge and the importance of pluralism (Longino 2002: 1). Moreover, the idea of knowledge as situated in human experience does not imply that all accounts have to be taken as equally valid, but rather that the authority of each account is limited. Helen Longino argues that scientific method "must be understood as a collection of social, rather than individual, process" with the quality or "objectivity" of the practice depending on "the extent to which a scientific community maintains critical dialogue" and "to the degree that it permits *transformative* criticism" (Longino 1990: 76). In short, we fail the ideals of free and open inquiry and those we claim to adhere to in promoting pluralism if we fail to engage with scholars whose ideas, backgrounds, and perspectives may rock the foundations of what we believe.

## Toward a more inclusive pluralism

If the heterodox community indeed is committed to seeking out those who are missing, what steps should be taken? How can we better empower those whose ideas we cannot yet fathom and may not even agree with?

Reaching out to the scholars who are missing from heterodox sessions, and making them feel valued and welcome, requires more than a willingness to accept them into the community. Several fields of thought provide insight into strategies that might help heterodox economic groups (or any group of scholars) become more inclusive and pluralistic. These include capabilities theory, socio-linguistics, and social studies of science.

The capabilities approach pioneered by Amartya Sen and Martha Nussbaum directs us to consider how to enable people to be and do all that they potentially can (see for example, Sen 1999 and Nussbaum 2003). This theory may be applied to consider how to enable differentially situated scholars to participate more fully in heterodox intellectual communities. Beyond the ways in which intellectual communities may signal their willingness to engage with such schol-ars, there are practical realities as well. Some barriers can seriously limit the par-ticipation of certain voices. For example, countries where educational opportunities are very limited are less likely to produce scholars who can learn how to participate successfully in international forums. Universities with hostile climates toward women or minorities are less likely to provide a nurturing home for them.

One common explanation offered for the lack of diversity in American eco-nomic forums, however, is therefore that women, scholars of color, and other underrepresented groups are scarce in the field. For example, Figure 4.1 shows the percentages of newly awarded doctorates in the United States earned by women, African Americans, and Latino Americans in 2006. Figure 4.1 shows that women earned 30 percent of the Ph.D.s in economics during 2006; these numbers are strikingly lower for African Americans and Latino Americans, who during the same year earned only 3.9 and 4.9 percent of those degrees.

In response to this perception, the AEA established a "Pipeline Program" in the 1970s. The centerpiece of this program is a summer institute to strengthen the technical (i.e., math) skills of "underrepresented minority groups in the U.S. context," for example, African Americans, Latinos, Native Americans, and those with demonstrated financial needs. In the mid-1990s, a mentoring program was created for students enrolled or accepted in an economics Ph.D. program in order to strengthen student progress through graduate school and the transition to research and teaching. Related, the AEA's willingness to provide funds to its Committee on the Status of Women in the Economics Profession (CSWEP) shows some good faith efforts to bring more women into the economics discip-line in the United States.

Despite the "natural" explanations for the scarcity of certain demographic groups in the United States, one only has to attend a National Economic Associ-ation (NEA) session at the Allied Social Science Association (ASSA) meetings to notice that it is possible to have a conference panel that attracts and welcomes African American scholars. Ditto for IAFFE sessions, where women and femin-ist scholars participate in abundance. So what can we learn from these organiza-tions to better welcome, attract, and populate heterodox sessions with scholars of color, Southern scholars, women, and other underrepresented groups? First, we

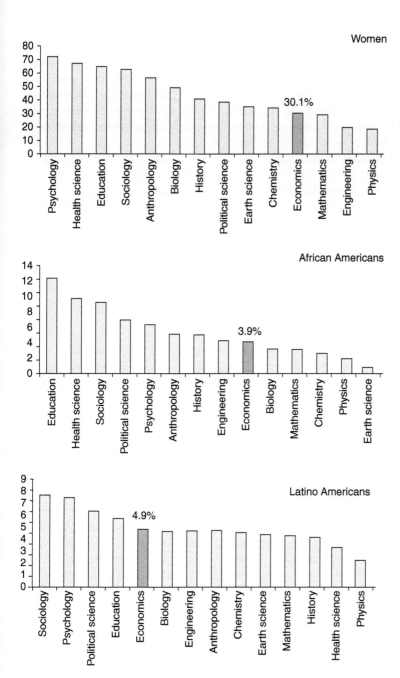

*Figure 4.1* Share of newly awarded doctorates earned in 2006 by women, African Americans, and Latino Americans (source: National Science Foundation, *Survey of Earned Doctorates*, 2006).

can gain insight from the websites of some of the associations containing scholars missing from so many other heterodox and orthodox sessions, including the NEA, which contains primarily African American economists, IAFFE, whose membership includes feminist economists from over forty countries around the world (primarily women but also many men), and the Human Development and Capabilities Association (HDCA), which contains diverse scholars from around the world (including a large percentage from Southern countries) whose work explicitly focuses on human well-being.

The NEA states on its website, "We are particularly interested in producing and distributing knowledge of economic issues that are of exceptional interest to native and immigrant African Americans, Latinos and other people of color" (NEA 2008). Among the examples listed on the website are children's issues, criminal justice, gender, employment and labor, health, teen pregnancy, education, housing, welfare and poverty, and environmental/ecological economics. The IAFFE website says, "We are a continually expanding group of scholars, policy professionals, students, advocates and activists interested in empowering and improving the well-being of women – and other under-represented groups – around the world" (IAFFE 2008a). Finally, consider the focus of the work of the HDCA. Its website states that the association

> shall promote high quality research ... [on] ... the quality of life, poverty, justice, gender, development and environment ... [and] shall further work in all disciplines – such as economics, philosophy, political theory, sociology and development studies – where such research is, or may be, pursued.
>
> (HDCA 2008)

For all these organizations, the primary focus is a particular set of crucial issues, rather than a methodological loyalty. In fact, scholars with a strong agenda to promote research on particular issues tend to be diverse among themselves, with some embracing new theoretical and methodological approaches and others finding it more strategic to use traditional tools in research areas other economists may view as peripheral. A large percentage of African American economists, for example, use traditional economic approaches in pursuing scholarship oriented toward ending U.S. poverty and discrimination. Similarly, many feminist economists choose to use mainstream methods in pursuing work oriented toward enhancing gender equality. Many scholars feel that changing policy on a serious or neglected problem may be more critical than holding an allegiance to a particular theoretical approach.

However, because conceptual frameworks enhance the centrality of some research topics while deemphasizing others, they can limit the possibility of theories that fully address certain neglected concerns. Therefore, research on neglected topics often goes hand in hand with theoretical and methodological innovations. Feminist economists, for example, have pointed to gendered omissions from economic theory, raising issues such as gender relations, unpaid work, market-home interdependencies, and so forth that have implications for both economic theory and methodology. Similarly, scholars working in the framework of human capabilities focus on human well-being, raising a broad set of theoretical and methodological concerns about both measurement and theory. And yet, interestingly, heterodox scholars who focus on economic methodology do not always count such work as important in the field of economic methodology; indeed, scholarship on capabilities and feminist theory appears to have comparatively little visibility in the conference sessions, journals, and books of scholars who identify as economic methodologists. For example, Wade Hands (2001), in his important and widely recognized book on economic methodology, only finds two feminist economists whose work is worth citing and does not even refer to work on capabilities and post-colonial theory.

Research from social studies of science and sociolinguistics provides insights into the significance and meaning of such economics works. The social studies of science literature (see for example, the work of Traweek 1988, 1992) calls attention to social behavior in scholarly communities and shows its importance in the construction of knowledge. Whom we speak with in the halls, how our scholarly societies are governed, whom we meet with at conferences, and so forth influence our ideas and reflect the values we place on insights from various people. The record of acknowledgments at the beginning of a book and the list of citations at the end are often clues as to whom an author has been speaking with and listening to.

Sociolinguistic analysis emphasizes that words have intended audiences and that texts and speech are rich in social signals, so that studying their patterns can help illuminate relationships of power, inclusion, exclusion, and distance that are produced and re-produced through communication (Strassmann and Polanyi 1995). Sociolinguistic examination of texts and utterances – particularly those that members of a scholarly community find *unremarkable* – can uncover the positioning of various members in terms of race, ethnicity, gender, social status, location, and historical moment (Labov 1972; Goffman 1981). This methodology is well documented and accepted in linguistics, and takes the position that a written or spoken text that seems normal to community members reveals the rules and conventions of the community considered to be acceptable and fully appropriate.[4]

This analytical framework permits us to make inferences about the significance of the frequent publication of works that do not give substantive space to scholarship by women, such as the book by Hands, or more recently, the collection edited by Edward Fullbrook (2008), entitled *Pluralist Economics*, which contains thirteen chapters, all by men. That the publication of such books is unremarkable, at least in certain heterodox circles, is telling. It signals that, for those who write, edit, review, and publish such books, it is quite business as usual for conversations on these topics to be all male.

Similarly, women who attend conferences cannot fail to notice if the other papers at the workshop do not cite the work of other women or feminists. Or scholars of color or those from the South notice if there are no others like them. Indeed, any scholar can tell by such clues whether she or he falls into the category of persons that the other scholars are generally consulting with and listening to, regardless of whether there may be an occasional high-profile session featuring such participants. What matters is not the official position of a scholarly society or whether there may be some welcoming places or people in the organization, but rather what are the subtle day to day, article to article, book to book, or conference to conference patterns of engagement.

More generally, in reading a text or listening to a conversation, those who experience no dissonance will tend to remain oblivious to how their easy acceptance of unwritten assumptions and arguments enables them to feel like expected and welcome participants in the intellectual community. For example, an article that describes how U.S. tax policies influence labor force participation in the United States, but which leaves out the term United States, makes the default assumption that all readers will know that the author is referring to the phenomena in the United States and implicitly signals the expectation that the readers will be American.

Since all scholars have situated perspectives, we cannot always anticipate how our words or judgments may signal to others that they do not belong in our community of engaged scholars. However, academic associations, journals, and other scholarly institutions can take actions to minimize the likelihood and extent of such behaviors. For example, the journal, *Feminist Economics*, has developed a policy designed to ensure that all papers published in the journal are oriented to an international audience (see Appendix). To further ensure adherence to the policy and to enhance the international character of the journal, the journal's peer review process requires international diversity among reviewers. IAFFE also requires a member of its International Committee to participate or liaise with each board committee to further enhance the extent to which the organization is attuned to the broader international needs and goals. That said, IAFFE remains dominated by North American and European scholars and could do much more to enhance the ethnic, racial, and geographic diversity of its members.

Heterodox organizations committed to change must carefully consider the impact of all that its organization and members do. What structures and procedures can be implemented to enhance the diversity of voices? For example, how are the boards of associations and journals constructed? Does the association have a systematic form of self-study, consultation, and reflection to consider new efforts and structures that might further ensure and welcome the participation of differently situated scholars? How can established scholars better listen to underrepresented scholars about institutional changes that may enhance organizational diversity and about ideas that may merit more visibility?

Economists who would like to promote pluralism should think beyond the promotion of ideas they consider to be underrepresented, to think instead more deeply about how to nurture the conversations that will open up the discipline to people with different backgrounds and experiences, and what they and their societies and journals can do to ensure the fuller participation of scholars from the broader world community.

## Acknowledgment

We gratefully thank Gemini Wahhaj for her thoughtful and very useful suggestions.

## Appendix: IAFFE policy on orienting papers for an international audience

*Feminist Economics* is an international journal, with over half of its readers and institutional subscribers living outside the United States. It is therefore important that papers be oriented to a broad international audience rather than to just the audience of any specific country. Although U.S.-oriented articles are overwhelmingly the most common form of inappropriately oriented articles, the points that follow apply to articles oriented to the audience of any other specific country or region. Papers are not appropriately oriented to an international audience in the following circumstances:

- Authors assume that people from all over the world should be interested in a particular country's economic phenomena, without either arguing why or framing the issues in the context of broader feminist economic concerns. At a minimum, correcting this problem requires rewriting the introduction and conclusion.
- Authors treat a phenomenon as though a particular country's experience is universal. Often the assumption is subtle and implicit and might be acceptable for a paper in a national journal, but is not appropriate for an international journal. Articles are culturally biased if they do not recognize that the experience of a particular country is not the world's experience.
- Authors refer to a phenomenon in a particular country without explicitly noting that it is a country-specific phenomenon or that a particular country's version of the phenomenon might not be the same elsewhere. Examples: references to statistics, patterns, or phenomena without appropriate modifications, e.g. "the labor force participation rate" or the "national goal" etc. In all such cases, modifications referring to the particular country are needed.
- Authors assume that people all over the world have heard of an organization or law in a country and do not explain the law or organization appropriately for an international audience.
- Authors provide an overview of the relevant literature on their topic, referring solely to contributions from one geographical region (e.g. North America). This approach may not be acceptable to an international audience, particularly where there have been significant contributions from other geographical regions, or if the issue under discussion is not primarily or solely concerned with that region or country.

A useful way for authors to revise their papers for an international audience is to imagine themselves as a reader from another country and then to revise the paper appropriately.

Source: IAFFE (2008b)

# Notes

1 Sen's focus was on gender equality, although his points apply to all forms of inequality.
2 Deducing genders from names is not necessarily straightforward, since some names are used by both genders and/or many are of non-Western origin; however, excluding or making assumptions about such cases could introduce biases into the analysis. Thus, we made extensive use of the Internet to determine gender when it was not obvious, with photos on homepages, biographical notes, lists of names by gender for different nationalities, we resolved almost all uncertainties, out of more than 1,200 persons, we were unable to determine the gender of less than half a dozen. Nonetheless, because this process is time-consuming, we coded a 1:5 sample of the AEA's more than 150 sessions per year rather than the whole pool.
3 For a more detailed review of this perspective, see Haraway (1988) and Strassmann (1996).
4 See Strassmann and Polanyi (1995) for a detailed explanation of this methodology and its application to economics through exploration of a popular American economics textbook.

# References

Fullbrook, E. (2008) *Pluralist Economics*, London: Zed Books.

Goffman, E. (1981) *Forms of Talk*, Philadelphia: University of Pennsylvania Press.

Hands, D.W. (2001) *Reflection without Rules: Economic Methodology and Contemporary Science Theory*, New York: Cambridge University Press.

Haraway, D. (1988) "Situated Knowledges: The Science Question in Feminism and the Privilege of the Partial Perspective," *Feminist Studies*, 14 (3): 575–99.

Hodgson, G.M. (2001) *How Economics Forgot History: The Problem of Historical Specificity in Social Science*, London: Routledge.

Human Development and Capabilities Association (HDCA) (2008) Available at www.capabilityapproach.com (accessed September 4, 2008).

International Association for Feminist Economics (IAFFE) (2008a) Available at www.iaffe.org (accessed September 4, 2008).

—— (2008b) Available at www.feministeconomics.org/instructions_policies.cfm (accessed September 5, 2008).

Klasen, S. and Wink, C. (2003) "Missing Women: Revisiting the Debate," *Feminist Economics*, 9 (2/3): 263–99.

Labov, W. (1972) "The Transformation of Experience in Narrative Syntax," in *Language in the Inner City*, 354–95, Philadelphia: University of Pennsylvania Press.

Longino, H. (1990) *Science as Social Knowledge*, Princeton, NJ: Princeton University Press.

—— (2002) *The Fate of Knowledge*, Princeton, NJ: Princeton University Press.

National Economic Association (NEA) (2008). Available at www.neaecon.org (accessed September 4, 2008).

National Science Foundation (2006) *Survey of Earned Doctorates*, Arlington, VA: National Science Foundation.

Nussbaum, M. (2003) "Capabilities as Fundamental Entitlements: Sen and Social Justice," *Feminist Economics*, 9 (2/3): 33–59.

Sen, A. (1990a) "More Than a Hundred Million Women Are Missing," *New York Review of Books*, December 20: 61–66.

—— (1990b) "Gender and Cooperative Conflicts," in I. Tinker (ed.) *Persistent Inequalities: Women and World Development*, 123–49, New York: Oxford University Press.

—— (1999) *Development as Freedom*, New York: Anchor Books.

Strassmann, D. (1996) "How Economists Shape Their Tales," *Challenge*, 39 (1): 13–20.

Strassmann, D. and Polanyi, L. (1995) "The Economist as Storyteller: What the Texts Reveal," in E. Kuiper and J. Sap (eds.) *Out of the Margin: Feminist Perspectives on Economics*, 129–50, London: Routledge.

Traweek, S. (1988) *Beamtimes and Lifetimes: The World of High Energy Physics*, Cambridge: Harvard University Press.

—— (1992) "Border Crossings: Narrative Strategies in Science Studies among Physicists at Tsukuba Science City, Japan," in A. Pickering (ed.) *Science as Practice and Culture*, 429–66, Chicago: University of Chicago Press.

# 5    Is Kuhnean incommensurability a good basis for pluralism in economics?

*Gustavo Marqués and Diego Weisman*

## Introduction

Two forms of pluralism lie at the heart of many theoretical and methodological discussions in economics: (1) the defense of a plurality, which in our case may consist in theories or methods; and (2) the promotion of an attitude characterized by open mindedness and engagement. These two senses are very different, indeed. The first is better approached as an epistemological claim, the second as a humanist and political demand. In this chapter we explore what kind of foundations (if any) Thomas Kuhn's vision of science and knowledge provides for endorsing pluralism in either of the two senses described. To highlight its shortcomings, we will contrast Kuhn's view to John Stuart Mill's conception of pluralism.

Kuhn's view of science provides the main foundation of Sheila Dow's Babylonian mode of thought and her proposal of a modified pluralism, which guides the work of many heterodox economists. Contrary to Dow, we argue that Mill's ideas are better suited for serving pluralist economists' goals. Specifically, we argue that Mill's fallibilism is a more suitable foundation for both forms of pluralism than Kuhn's incommensurability thesis. In addition, we contend that Dow's conception of a Babylonian mode of thought and her proposal of a modified pluralism is spoiled by her strong commitment to Kuhn's incommensurability thesis. Contrary to her expectations, the assumption of incommensurability weakens the possibilities for fruitful communication among members of different schools of thought.

## Kuhn's vision of science

### *Pluralism as a defense of a plurality*

Borrowing from Mäki (1997: 39), the first meaning of pluralism may be found in the following definition:

> Pluralism: *P is an instance of pluralism about X if and only if it is a theory or principle which either justifies an actually obtaining plurality of Xs or prescribes an actually non-obtaining plurality of Xs by appealing to reasons Y.*

Two points call for attention. First, to recommend something implies to have *positive* reasons for it. For example, to promote a plurality of discourses of type X means to have reasons that indicate that the larger the number of discourses belonging to X the better for the acquisition of some posited goal assumed to be desirable. Second, such plurality should be conformed by *conflicting* elements: those that are incompatible (not just complementary) with each other.[1]

Nowhere does Kuhn promote a plurality of paradigms, because he lacks *positive* epistemic reasons in its favor. At most his work suggests *negative* reasons: given the assumed impossibility of choosing among rival views, there are no grounds against the coming up of new proposals. But negative reasons give rise at best to an attitude of tolerance. Tolerance is not bad, but involves a passive stance: neither condemnation nor promotion.

But, perhaps, Kuhn's view of science is important in another sense. The issue of pluralism is connected to the problem of *demarcation*. Traditional methodology draws two different demarcation lines: (1) between science and non science; (2) between better and worse scientific theories. The competing methodologies proposed different criteria of demarcation, but they all belong to what, following Lakatos (1981), could be called the demarcationist research program in scientific methodology.

However, these criteria have been objected to and considered flawed for economics and few people currently believe it would be of any use to keep them. Even more, many economists and methodologists of economics think that finding adequate criteria of demarcation is an unattainable goal. Some pluralists go even further and find the demarcationist program authoritarian and, consequently, unacceptable on moral and political bases.

Regarding the rules for acceptance and elimination, Kuhn's position appears to be more suitable to be part of a pluralist vision of science. In fact, he rejects any possibility of finding an objective meta-rule designed to choose rationally among rival paradigms. Here is where incommensurability plays a fundamental role: it allows those scientists who have been segregated by a demarcation criterion to deny methodological prescriptions any positive role in normal scientific decisions. Supposedly, this might explain the favorable reception that a fraction of the pluralist community dispensed to Kuhn's ideas. But, as will be shown further on, the consequences of assuming incommensurability far exceed the results desired by its supporters and lead to conclusions that jeopardize the attainment of pluralism, particularly in the second sense of the term.

### *Pluralism as a defense of a certain attitude*

Kuhn's main message was that any time researchers go beyond the limits of their own paradigm serious communication problems arise, the difficulties become more and more severe with time, and the net utility of this out-looking approach is probably *negative* in terms of a cost–benefit appraisal. This is bad news for pluralists, who encourage people to become engaged in a multilingual conversation. We will elaborate a little more on these points.

First, for Kuhn, communication with other points of view is difficult even if a light notion of incommensurability, like the one sustained in "The Road since *Structure*," is assumed. The breakdown of communication is now restricted to some (sometimes very limited) group of terms (called "lexicons"). This allows Kuhn to assert that it is always possible to communicate with outsiders if one is ready to learn and master the foreign paradigm as a "native" speaker does. His new position provides an argument against the supposed impossibility of communication among rival paradigms, and, particularly, against the necessity of translation for doing it successfully. According to Kuhn (1990: 9), for communication to be possible without translation all that is needed are bilingual abilities. However, though it is true that bilingualism makes successful communication *possible in principle*, the *practical* significance of this possibility-argument is dramatically reduced by the many difficulties involved in acquiring bilingual capacities.

Second, these practical problems will be aggravated in the future given the historical conditions in which knowledge takes place and grows. Kuhn warned us that "despite occasional spectacular successes, communication across the boundaries between scientific specialties becomes worse and worse" (Kuhn 1977: 289). The reason for this gloomy view is that the advance of knowledge requires specialization and the incorporation of a very sophisticated language, which diverges from other specialized languages in at least some lexicons. This trend of increasing differentiation seems to be unavoidable and implies that in the future scientific communities will work in an environment of growing isolation.

Third, the increasing practical difficulties pointed out were some of the reasons that underpinned his rather pessimistic vision about the *utility* of engaging in communication with members of foreign paradigms. He makes this point quite clear in his paper "Logic of discovery or psychology of research":

> My object in these pages is to juxtapose the view of scientific development outlined in my book, *The Structure of Scientific Revolutions*, with the better known views of our chairman, Sir Karl Popper. *Ordinarily I should decline such undertaking, for I am not so sanguine as Sir Karl about the utility of confrontations.*
>
> (Kuhn 1977: 267; our emphasis)

These remarks should be of concern for pluralists. Is not a positive stance to "the utility of confrontation" of ideas an essential part of any position that deserves to be called pluralist? But he had another reason for dismissing confrontations and for praising concentration on just one point of view, which has no relation with the practical problems referred to above. Kuhn distinguished between (1) divergent thinking, that involves "freedom to go off in different directions ... rejecting the old solution and striking out in some new directions," and (2) "convergent thinking," which rejects "flexibility and open-mindedness" and focuses instead on only one point of view (Kuhn 1977: 226). At first sight, he seems prepared to claim that both dispositions are required, but a careful reading of his work reveals that his main intention is to highlight the vital importance of the second attitude. As Kuhn himself recognizes, his "central thesis" asserts that "in the sciences ... it is often better to do one's best with the tools at hand than to pause for contemplation of divergent approaches," (ibid.: 225).

For Kuhn, science consists of solving puzzles and doing research. These activities, if successful, add a new piece to the existing scientific body (be it a theoretical or empirical result). This is the main result of *convergent* thinking. Critical debate is a completely different matter:

> Philosophers regularly criticize each other's work and the work of their predecessors with care and skill. Much of their discussion and publication is in this sense Socratic: *it is a juxtaposition of views forged from each other through critical confrontation and analysis.* (In philosophy) there is nothing quite like research.
>
> (Kuhn 1977: 9)

The difference between convergent and divergent thinking is quite clear. Because research and solving puzzles add new pieces of knowledge, their contribution is *positive*. Confrontation (critical debate), instead, is mainly *negative* and consists in analysis of the work made by someone else. Convergent thinking, then, produces positive contributions for the development of a paradigm, and is its main engine of knowledge acquisition and accumulation.

In many passages Kuhn seems to *equate* science with convergent thinking and consider critical debate as an undesired detour that scientists unable to keep doing research as they always did are forced to undertake to regain the ability of doing normal science. Kuhn explicitly rejected the point of view developed by Popper in "Back to the Presocratics," where "the tradition of claims, counterclaims, and debates over fundamentals which, except perhaps during the Middle Ages, have characterized philosophy and much of social science ever since" was considered the foundation of modern science. He emphasizes the opposite view: "to turn Sir Karl's view on its head, *it is precisely the abandonment of critical discourse that marks the transition to a science*" (Kuhn 1977: 273).

It might be argued that he is not really dismissing the importance of critical debate, because he was not a prescriptivist. However, he recognized that some of his historical descriptions had also a prescriptivist content (Kuhn 1970: 207).[2]

It is more than likely that his bold ideas about normal science and convergent thinking convey this twofold character. Besides, words like "scientific practice" and "rational" carry a strong normative baggage: they recommend what they designate. To say that somebody proceeds rationally or scientifically is describing as well as recommending his practice. To describe what the successful scientific practice is, prescribes in turn what is needed to do in order to become a successful scientist. Given that most of Kuhn's "descriptions" of the scientific practice strongly underline the key role played by convergent thinking, it is hard to dismiss the implicit recommendation involved in such passages.

Fourth, if we are true and Kuhn defines science in terms of features that characterize convergent thinking and normal science, expressions like "scientists start making extraordinary research" are misleading. Going to the doctor is something that sportsmen are forced to do any time they are unable to keep playing. In this sense, extraordinary research is as characteristic of science as going to the doctor is characteristic of a sportsman. It would be also unfair to describe divergent thinking as a second-best scientific activity, because there is no other alternative when normal research becomes impracticable. Is going to the doctor a second best of practicing our favorite sport? Although *scientists* do sometimes practice divergent thinking, *science* is not made of it. Scientists only stop practicing convergent thinking when they are unable to. Only in these special situations do they pay attention to other approaches.

According to Kuhn, extraordinary research is nothing good in itself. It is just an unwilling step undertaken with the expectation of going back to normalcy as soon as possible. If the practice of solving puzzles is working well, scientists have no incentives to engage themselves in divergent thinking. If the practice of solving puzzles is failing, the incentives to explore other views arise from their hope that this transitory detour paves the way to go back to normal science. Solving puzzles is the goal, divergent thinking is just a transitory mean.

Fifth, we have showed that the main message of Kuhn's philosophy of science is that inter-paradigmatic communication is *problematic*, that it is *increasingly* problematic, and that even if bilingual capacities *could* be acquired and aptly exercised along the time, the *fruitfulness* of engaging in this practice is in question. We wonder why someone who gets the message and shares this point of view is going to undertake the extremely difficult task of becoming a multilingual speaker! It is highly improbable that people will invest time in gaining such skills, and it is difficult to see how they *could believe* that they might profit by adopting a pluralist stance.

Kuhn's philosophy is corrosive of pluralism. If incommensurability generates a communication problem, *assuming* incommensurability considerably aggravates this very problem: those who believe in incommensurability (even in its weaker sense) will lack the incentives for engaging in a conversation with "foreign" positions and will probably refuse to waste their time in an extremely difficult and highly inefficient task. Kuhn's views fuel precisely the sort of attitude that pluralists oppose.

## Mill's vision of the utility of confrontations

As we said earlier, to be committed to pluralism means at least two different things: (1) to defend plurality and (2) to defend an attitude on the part of the people. Mill defended both sorts of pluralism. In his *On Liberty*, paragraph IV, he asserts that diversity is a crucial human resource that has to be protected from state interference and the tyranny of society. The richness of a society lies in the diversity of its members and their opinions. This shows that, ultimately, Mill is not directly interested in theories or methods. His main concern is not epistemological. *The plurality which he promotes is that of human characters, disposi-tions, and inclinations.* His is a Humanistic position. Liberty of expression means precisely diversity of behaviors. To put it in a nutshell, he is promoting *individualism.*

> Where, not the person's own character, but the traditions and customs of other people are the rule of conduct, there is wanting one of the principal ingredients of human happiness, and quite the chief ingredient of individual and social progress.... If it were felt that the free development of individu-ality is one of the leading essentials of well-being; that it is not only a co-ordinate element with all that is designed by the term civilization, instruction, education, culture, but is itself a necessary part and condition of all those things; there would be no danger that liberty should be under-valued.... But the evil is that individual spontaneity is hardly recognized by the common modes of thinking, as having any intrinsic worth, or deserving any regard on its own account.
>
> (Mill 1993 [1869]: 65–66)

Unfortunately, social consensus and conventional judgment set limits to indi-vidual expression. Against these attitudes Mill advances an *epistemological* thesis: we are *fallible* and so we are not in a position to shout down those opin-ions which are different from the prevailing ones. Since the present opinions may be false, it is licit to express any view inconsistent with them. What has to be limited are not the unusual conceptions, but the power of society to reduce non-conventional views to silence. In this way Mill links an epistemological thesis about the limitations of our knowledge to a defense of human individual diversity. Although Mill restricted his discussion to daily life and moral values, all he says is also pertinent for scientific practice. Mill's remarks can be read as a passionate promotion of a plurality of *theories*. If we are right, a plurality of theories is defended in order to encourage a plurality of individualities. Theoret-ical pluralism is not an end in itself; instead, it is put at the service of individual-ism. It will pay to have a closer look at the way in which he defends these ideas.

At first sight, his argument seems to be merely *negative*: it is grounded on the limitations of our knowledge. Plurality of opinions should be tolerated because we do not know for sure which of them are false. Pluralism is the price to be paid for our inability to reach and recognize the truth. But Mill also advances a *positive* argument in favor of theoretical pluralism. In his view the proposal of a plurality of visions has a twofold benefit: (1) gives us more chances for reaching true knowledge; and (2) improves our comprehension of those theories that we hold. He was unable to sustain his first claim, but in his failure he is not alone, because a coherent epistemological foundation for theoretical pluralism – as well as for any other position – is still lacking. But, regarding his second claim he advances a cogent argument for promoting a plurality of theories: our under-standing of our own points of view is enhanced when other approaches are considered.

This kind of understanding requires taking into consideration those theories which are rivals of the one we embrace, inspecting their contents and credentials for claiming truth. A constant comparison among them is wanted and needed.[3] People are unable to reach all the implications of their own views, and also unable to understand them deeply, if no alternative theory exists or, providing its existence, has not been thoroughly considered. According to Mill, proliferation is welcome because it increases *our understanding* of our own beliefs.

It is easy to defend the plurality of theories during the state in which the human mind is still "imperfect."[4] Mill's positive argument in favor of theoretical pluralism is in this sense analogous to Caldwell's defense of it in terms of epistemological uncertainty (Caldwell 1988: 243). But Mill has a second, positive argument, which goes beyond this assumption. According to him, the existence of a plurality of opinions is not a simple sub-product of our ignorance, a result of intellectual unrest that we should accept until the truth is acquired and recognized, and the falsehood of some ideas can be definitely shown. Mill says that *even if we had such certainties* we should nevertheless pay attention to false conceptions, because they contribute to improve our knowledge. We need them to build our knowledge and to make it better.

The key word here is "knowledge." Though truth is important, just saying something which is true is not enough to have knowledge. To know is something more than to assert a sentence which is true. Knowledge, properly understood, requires the clear perception of the motives and the very reasons which give rise to (and come in support of) the idea one takes as true, something which is lost when the contrary views are silenced.[5] It crucially involves the permanent confrontation with opposite ideas. Rival theories and points of view are, then, something valuable by themselves, even when we know that they are wrong. Plurality not only should be tolerated; it must be systematically promoted.

The previous considerations lead us to the second meaning of pluralism. To be pluralist in this sense has nothing to do with the promotion of a plurality of reactions. On the contrary, pluralism is associated with just one kind of behavior and attitude. Though it looks paradoxical at first, pluralists do not embrace demarcationist and authoritarian attitudes (even when these particular attitudes are members of the plurality constituted by the whole range of human reactions). Pluralism would be better described now as the promotion of just one response: sympathy for other people and a disposition for listening to other opinions and becoming engaged in a fruitful conversation.

It is interesting to underscore that Mill's commitment to this second sense of pluralism is precisely the one assumed by ICAPE and most of their members. We think most practitioners of heterodox economics sustain pluralism because they favor the peaceful (and polite) coexistence of the many existing theories (Garnett 2006; Freeman and Kliman 2006). They are mainly interested in encouraging people to dispense a tolerant treatment to the different existing theories (and to adopt a sympathetic stance toward them). For lack of a better term, we would say that for them pluralism is more a political and humanistic vindication than an epistemological thesis. Pluralism is here related with respect, dignity, and engagement in conversation, not with truth.

## Dow's modified pluralism

Sheila Dow's modified pluralism intends to be an intermediate position between traditional demarcationism and anything goes. Relying in Thomas Kuhn's thinking, and more specifically, in his incommensurability thesis, Dow rejects both positions. Apparently, she seems attracted by incommensurability mainly for three reasons: First, because it rules out the existence of epistemological meta-criteria which compel strict observance on the part of any specific paradigm (Dow 1997). Second, the awareness of incommensurability might alert economic practitioners of the serious communication problems that arise any time they consider other discourses, and, presumably, this recognition would give them the patience to keep talking to each other, and the willingness to try even harder in spite of repeated misunderstandings (Dow 2004). These reasons underpin her conviction about the possibility of constructing a workable notion of a Babylonian mode of thought, which includes a number of heterodox schools. Third, Kuhn's vision allows that scientific contributions made inside a given scientific community must be evaluated only by its members (Dow 2008). It seems to be a good way for "recovering the practice" of the members of the different schools belonging to the Babylonian mode of thought, and preserving discussion and rational criticism within it.

We concede that traditional methodology is unworkable if Kuhn is right. But her next claims can hardly be substantiated on this basis. To start, her Babylonian mode of thought is a very problematic notion. Dow says that "economic schools of thought are most effectively identified at the methodological level as paradigms. Methodological differences had to be understood if communication between schools of thought was to succeed" (Dow 2001: 13). It is an odd remark. If any school is considered a paradigm and incommensurability is taken seriously, communication between them faces all the problems described at length above. As was showed there, the unpleasant consequences of incommensurability are revealed in the later Kuhn, who described the scientific family as divided into many small groups or scientific communities, each one with its own language and its own vision of the world, isolated from each other and unable to communicate effectively with one another. The growing sophistication of specialized languages implies that the dialogue between different communities is getting more and more unsuccessful.

If this position is taken as granted, why should a member of a paradigm be concerned with the difficult task of becoming a bilingual speaker? Kuhn does not offer us a single word in support of this disposition. He certainly alerts us over the many difficulties involved in communication, but this message has a *discouraging* (rather than a fueling) effect. Dow offers some suggestive indications in support of the supposed beneficial results of inter-paradigmatic communication. In her view, "cross fertilization" will result in "innovation." Though it might be true that cross-fertilization aided innovation and the progress of knowledge, our point is that there is no basis in Kuhn's work for sustaining such a claim.

In fact, according to Kuhn only when scientists are in big trouble, and cannot pursue their research in a normal (fruitful) way any more, do they start looking for different alternatives, aiming at something like "cross fertilization." *Crises*, and the unpleasant feelings that accompany them, are the *only incentives* for engaging in inter-paradigmatic communication. Are the many schools of thought that are supposed to be members of the Babylonian mode of thought in such a desperate situation?

Let us move now to her third claim. Dow wants to discuss and criticize other modes of thinking: the demarcationist project, constructivism, and the methodology and epistemology that underpin mainstream economics. She also wants to say the mainstream is unable to reach what is considered the main purpose of economic science: to illuminate or explain (in a sense essentially linked to understanding) social phenomena. We tend to agree with this value judgment, but it cannot be founded on Kuhn's philosophy.

Incommensurability jeopardizes the possibility of any criticism – internal or external – to a competing mode of thinking. Even conceding that understanding or illuminating social phenomena should be the "real" aim of economics, the degree to which this goal is achieved by mainstream economics can not be assessed from the outside if the Kuhnean vision of science is right. As Dow remarks, "it was Kuhn (1962) who captured the imagination with his argument that understanding is paradigm-specific" (Dow 1997: 92). But this condemns all *external* criticisms to failure. From the outside it is impossible to appreciate the significance of the aims pursued within a paradigm. If any external (i.e., mainstream) criticism does not help to illuminate post-Keynesian or neo Austrian problems, the same could be said of any heterodox models regarding the typical aims of mainstream economists. As it happens with ideas, the full appreciation of epistemic values is also "paradigm-specific." Even worse, incommensurability may inhibit also *internal* criticism. How can an outsider (who cannot appreciate properly mainstream goals) know the degree in which different mainstream contributions help to reach mainstream aims? How can an outsider know that mainstream models are not illuminating or do not reach the aims intended by their builders? In spite of Dow's intentions, if one opts for incommensurability it is difficult to see on which grounds one could object that "anything goes." Incommensurability is a notion designed to give any scientific community enough freedom to do its job without interference from any external point of view. No external or internal criticisms are permissible if the critic is a foreigner.

Dow could say that communication may be accomplished by becoming an insider. But remember that there are many difficulties involved in the practical task of exercising multilingualism. Even more important, there are also the incentive problems already pointed out: if you do not accept the golden rule of communication as a value in itself (something that could be grounded on Mill's thinking, rather than on Kuhn's incommensurability), why might heterodox economists be so anxious to master other languages, but for the fact that they are repeatedly failing at doing their job properly? Is Dow ready to assume this uncomfortable implication? As long as her arguments are based on incommensurability she seems to need this assumption to be cogent.

The previous considerations help to explain why not all the practitioners of heterodox economics can easily fit within the Babylonian mode of thought. The existence of intolerance is reflected in the attitude of some heterodox economists towards axiomatic systems, mathematics, classical logic, local closures, and many other mainstream techniques. For some heterodox economists, "formalism" or "deductivism" (the label under which, according to Lawson, all relevant features of mainstream methodology are grouped) is something one has to break up with, not having a single ingredient worth of being incorporated or even considered. They do not show a disposition to listen and be engaged in a clarifying dialogue with the dominant point of view and, consequently, they do not fit Babylonian standards.

Some heterodox economists go even further. They are also wary of schools of thought that, according to Dow, belong to the Babylonian world. Holt (2007), for instance, regrets that the Babylonian spirit could pave the way for too many unnecessary (and maybe dangerous) points of view. He is mainly concerned with excessive diversity within the so-called post-Keynesians. His view is in line with Davidson (2004). Both of them underrate the dialogue not only with mainstream economics, but also with traditions of economic thinking that many post-Keynesians considered as true members of the family. Those, like Holt and Davidson, who look at modified pluralism with suspicion because they think it allows an excessively wide range of points of view, find support in Kuhn's philosophy. Diversity of opinions is considered a source of contamination, not a source of inspiration. Although they do not swear by Kuhn, they are truly normal scientists in a Kuhnean sense. And, contrary to Dow's expectations, they reject Dow's proposal for sharing Babel city with unwelcome neighbors.

In some recent contributions to the *Post Autistic Economic Review*, the opposite viewpoint about how to understand pluralism has come to the surface. Without naming them overtly, Sent (2003) and Van Bouwel (2005) contest Holt and Davidson's positions, taking for granted that post-Keynesians should interact with Kaleckians, Sraffians, institutionalists, and other groups of heterodox economists. Van Bouwel also insists on the importance of considering in some cases the use of mainstream techniques, like equilibrium analysis. These approaches will surely fit Dow's expectations, but, unfortunately for her, they are mainly Millian and inconsistent with Kuhn's philosophy. For them pluralism should incorporate tolerance and willingness to listen to other opinions. Otherwise, it is difficult for both authors to avert the idea that the plea for pluralism is just a strategic move made by people who find themselves in a weaker position.[6] Both papers stressed the important issue that it is not necessary to be mainstream in order to be a normal scientist. We add that a Kuhnean post-Keynesian may be (indeed, should be, if he has grasped the main message of *The Structure of*

*Scientific Revolutions*) as intolerant as a typical mainstream economist.[7] This helps to understand where the shortcomings of a Kuhn-based pluralism lie.

## Conclusions

In the current methodological discussions in economics, "pluralism" is mainly used for (1) claiming for the proliferation of theories, or (2) denoting an open-minded attitude and a full disposition to interact with other perspectives. Interpreted in the first sense pluralism may be defended by means of *negative* arguments. For instance, one reason to sustain pluralism is that human know-ledge is fallible. This is enough for the interplay of different views to be admit-ted. It might also be defended if one believes there are no universally valid criteria for discriminating between science and non-science, or between good and bad scientific procedures or results. As was shown, both Mill and Kuhn pro-vided arguments of this sort. But negative reasons are not enough. Tolerance is a necessary but insufficient condition for being committed to pluralism. In this sense, Mill supercedes Kuhn in that he advances *positive* (though *subjective*) reasons for endorsing pluralism.

Regarding the second sense of pluralism, we find it completely alien to Kuhn's thinking. Though Kuhn's notion of incommensurability puts an end to the demarcationist project (a result which makes Kuhnean philosophy so attrac-tive for some heterodox economists), it has far reaching consequences: any other interference of rival groups is also dismissed. If pluralism is grounded on incom-mensurability the pluralist thinker can not find incentives for listening to differ-ent points of view or for engaging in a useful conversation among people with different perspectives. Such incentives, according to Kuhn, may only come from a state of complete disarray, something that heterodox economists are more prone to impute to mainstream economics than to their own practice. As was shown, "innovation" for its own sake can not be seriously considered a goal without assuming that the discipline is in a crisis. Incommensurability gives rise to an unwelcome sort of pluralism, conformed by a diversity of insulated com-munities, each of them behaving autistically. This means that no connection with the outside world will be needed or welcomed. It is curious that Dow could think that Kuhn is a crucial referent for promoting pluralism.

In *On Liberty*, Mill provides an extensive argument for attitudes and disposi-tions consistent with the second sense of pluralism. Being more optimistic about the prospects of undertaking an exchange of ideas with people who hold differ-ent opinions, he advises conversation, tolerance, and a common effort toward the integration of different approaches. He provides a promising foundation for grounding pluralists' claims and for the diffusion of a pluralist behavior into the heterogeneous group of heterodox economists.

# Notes

1 It is easy to defend a plurality of *complementary* elements. The real challenge for a pluralist position is to advance positive reasons for the existence of a proliferation of *rival* components. This, at least, is especially important in the case of theories.
2 Though Kuhn rejects a sharp demarcation between description and prescription, he accepts that a difference exists. He *has to* proceed in such a way: if one assumes that no demarcation line exists between description and prescription, it ensues that *any* sentence has a prescriptivist content! This seems to be a self-defeating argument.
3 ."..the peculiar evil of silencing the expression of an opinion is, that it is robbing the human race; posterity as well as the existing generation; those who dissent from the opinion, still more than those who hold it. If the opinion is right, they are deprived of the opportunity of exchanging error for truth: if wrong, they lose, what is almost as great a benefit, the clearer perception and livelier impression of truth, produced by its collision with error" (Mill 1993 [1869]: 20–21).
4 ."..in an imperfect state of the human mind, the interest of truth require the diversity of opinions" (Mill 1993 [1869]: 59).
5 "There is a class of persons ... who think it enough if a person assents undoubtingly to what they think true, though he has no knowledge whatever of the grounds of the opinion, and could not make a tenable defense of it against the most superficial objections ... this is not the way in which truth ought to be held by a rational being. This is not knowing the truth. Truth, thus held, is but one superstition the more, accidentally clinging to the words which enunciate a truth" (Mill 1993 [1869]: 41–42).
6 "The appeals to pluralism on the part of heterodox economics may be seen as an instance of strategic pluralism.... [the appeals] could be primarily inspired by efforts to achieve professional power and dominance" (Sent 2003).
7 For a denunciation of "normal" (non-pluralist) attitudes inside the Marxist community see Freeman and Kliman (2006).

# References

Caldwell, B. (1988) "The Case for Pluralism," in De Marchi, N. (ed.) *The Popperian Legacy in Economics*, 231–244, Cambridge: Cambridge University Press.

Davidson, P. (2004) "A Response to King's Argument for Pluralism," *Post Autistic Economics Review*, volume 24, March 15, article 1.

Dow, S. (1997) "Methodological Pluralism and Pluralism of Method," in Salanti, A. and Screpanti, E. (eds.) *Pluralism in Economics – New Perspectives in History and Methodology*, 89–99, Cheltenham, UK: Edward Elgar.

—— (2001) "Post Keynesian Methodology," in Holt, R.P.F. and Pressman, S. (eds.) *A New Guide to Post Keynesian Economics*, 11–20, London: Routledge.

—— (2004) "Structured Pluralism," *Journal of Economic Methodology*, 11(3): 275–290.

—— (2008) "A Future for Schools of Thought and Pluralism in Heterodox Economics," in Harvey, J. and Garnett, R. (eds.) *Future Directions for Heterodox Economics*, 9–26, Ann Arbor: University of Michigan Press.

Freeman, A. and Kliman, A. (2006) "Beyond Talking the Talk: Towards a Critical Pluralist Practice," *Post Autistic Economics Review*, volume 40, December 1, 31–53.

Garnett, R.F. (2006) "Paradigms and Pluralism in Heterodox Economics," *Review of Political Economy*, 18 (4): 521–546.

Holt, R.P.F. (2007) "What is Post Keynesian Economics," in Pressman, S., Forstater, M., and Mongiovi, G. (eds.) *Post-Keynesian Macroeconomics: Essays in Honor of Ingrid Rima*, London: Routledge.

Kuhn, T.S. (1970) *The Structure of Scientific Revolutions*, Second Edition, Chicago: University of Chicago Press.

—— (1977) *The Essential Tension: Selected Studies in Scientific Tradition and Change*, Chicago: University of Chicago Press.

—— (1990) "The Road since *Structure*," *PSA: Proceedings of the Biennial Meeting of the Philosophy of Science Association*, volume 2: 3–13.

Lakatos, I. (1981) *Philosophical Papers*, Vol. 2, Cambridge, Cambridge University Press.

Mäki, U. (1997) "The One World and the Many Theories," in Salanti, A. and Screpanti, E. (eds.) *Pluralism in Economics – New Perspectives in History and Methodology*, 37–47, Cheltenham, UK: Edward Elgar.

Mill, J.S. (1993) [1869] "On Liberty," in *On Liberty and Utilitarianism*, New York: Bantam Books.

Sent, E.M. (2003) "Pleas for Pluralism," *Post Autistic Economics Review*, volume 18, February 4, article 1.

Van Bouwel, J. (2005) "Towards a Framework for Pluralism in Economics," *Post Autistic Economics Review*, volume 30, March 21.

# 6    Why should *I* adopt pluralism?

*Rogier De Langhe*

## Introduction

If the most perplexing thing in the world is a lack of theory, the second most perplexing must be an abundance of it. The latter is what we witness in economics today. A broad range of schools strive for scholarly attention: neoclassical, social, feminist, institutionalist, Sraffian, Marxian, Austrian, Post Keynesian, etc. They not only differ in their answers but also in the way they frame their questions, rendering an unbiased comparison extremely difficult, if not impossible. This issue is clearly not economics specific. Whether it is quantum mechanics, international relations theory, or indeed even forest management, diversity is ubiquitous across the spectrum of the sciences. Even highly formalized sciences like logic and mathematics are divided into different schools of thought, debating fundamental issues such as the acceptability of certain kinds of inconsistencies or the existence of numbers. This strongly suggests that dissensus is not a transient matter. I consider it to be a stylized fact about scientific research and as such the related issue of pluralism becomes of key importance. I take pluralism to be an epistemic position which acknowledges the validity of different possible perspectives on reality in an active way, which means that they are not only tolerated but also taken into account when goals of knowledge (prediction, problem-solving, truth, curiosity, policy advice, funding decision,…) are to be achieved.

Given the ubiquity of divergent views, it is indispensable to develop strategies to handle them without halting or distorting knowledge production. How to manage this multiplicity of views constitutes the basic problem at hand. Of course, discrimination among views is often best dealt with by scholars from within the respective disciplines themselves. But given its common occurrence in virtually any science, an across-the-board story remains to be told. What are the causes of pluralism? Does it result from the nature of the world or from the way we investigate that world? How should scientists manage diversity? What does pluralism mean for science policy? What can a general analysis contribute to the solution of discipline-specific problems of theory choice?

I introduce a crucial but often neglected distinction between different levels at which pluralism can be situated. From this framework I address the general question of how to manage divergence of views, a matter intricately connected to pluralism. Basically, my argument is the following. I maintain that pluralism is a desideratum at the aggregate level, but not necessarily at the individual level. *We* should be pluralists, but not *me* and neither should *you*. I argue that an individual scholar should take a stance, i.e. come up with an original, robust, and consistent position from which he develops and defends his results. A personal stance, biased as it can be, is the only way to obtain sufficient informative guidance for question-resolving inquiry.

## Framing pluralism

I have introduced dissensus as a stylized fact about scientific practice. It could be argued that dissensus does not deserve this status because, for instance, dissensus might swiftly be eliminated by engaging in rational constructive debate. But this misses the point. Divergence might cease for a certain problem, but it will never cease for science in general. Since divergence in this sense will always be around, it is not sufficient to look for ways to bring different views together. Most of the time the real problem scholars will face is how to manage divergence *in the meantime.* Only a small group of specialists are concerned with fundamental discussions that could possibly eliminate divergence with respect to a certain issue, while a lot of scholars in fundamental and applied research use assumptions about the issue on which divergence exists in their own research. This is where science is no longer a matter of discriminating between or reconciling views, but of managing diversity. Most contributions on pluralism seem to focus on ways to make different views somehow compatible, believing that this will enable dialogue and new insights. Considering dissensus as a given allows us to skip this and pass right on to the problem of managing diversity, an aspect of pluralism I believe to be of much greater importance to practitioners in the field.

Interestingly, dissensus (or diversity or divergence of views – I use these interchangeably) is actually not supposed to appear. If there's only one world out there, as most will concede, there should be a trend toward increasing consensus as knowledge advances and science comes closer to the Truth. But this kind of linear view of an ever-growing body of knowledge and consensus is not what we observe. As it turns out, diversity is a stylized fact about science. The literature offers a number of explanations for this gap between one world and the multiplicity of views. These might be seen as causes of dissensus.[1]

*Underdetermination*    Theories are never completely determined by the data they are built upon. The most famous instance of this is Hume's problem of induction, formulated by Born (1949) as ."..no observation or experiment, however extended, can give more than a finite number of repetitions"; therefore, "the statement of a law – B depends on A – always transcends experience. Yet this kind of statement is made everywhere and all the time, and sometimes from scanty material."[2]

*Ontology*   The complexity of the world necessitates pluralism. This argument has been put forth in economics, e.g. Caldwell (2004) "Some may agree with Lawson and me that pluralism makes good sense; the complex nature of social reality may also mean that it is inevitable."; in philosophy of science, e.g. Giere (1999: 28) "This great complexity implies, I think, that it is impossible to obtain an adequate overall picture of science from any one perspective. [...] The only adequate overall pictures will be collages of pictures from various perspectives"; as well as *in tempore non suspecto*, with a paraphrase of Voltaire: "in a subject as difficult as economics, a state of doubt may not be very comfortable, but a state of certainty would be ridiculous."[3]

*Cognition*   Conversely it is argued that it is not the complexity of the world but the limitations of our own mind that necessitate us to simplify and specialize. Theories and models typically highlight a number of salient features while obscuring others lest they become as complex as reality itself and hence uninformative (like a map on a 1–1 scale). Our representations of the world are thus inevitably partial.

*Situatedness*   There is no view from nowhere. Every scholar necessarily occupies a certain place in the world historically, geographically, socially,... Shapin (1982: 4) writes "Reality seems capable of sustaining more than one account given of it, depending upon the goals of those who engage with it." Hacking (1999) calls this the *contingency thesis*.

*Experiential diversity*   Everyone has a unique set of experiences. According to Rescher (1993) this leads to a perspectival rationalism in which one person can conclude p and another ~p with both claims being rationally warranted against their respective sets of experiences. Different experiences also lead to learning different languages. The impact this has is debatable;[4] the linguistic relativity hypothesis for instance suggests that differences in categorization of the world can lead to a different perception of the world. In other words, people speaking different languages might have different world views.

*Pragmatism*   Different goals and interests constitute different perspectives on the world (Kitcher, 2001: 55–62). Explanations are affected by what kind of an answer you want from it, e.g. "technical" interests of planning, prediction and control; "practical" interests of mutual understanding; and "emancipatory" interests of liberation, freedom from domination, and autonomy. Weber and Van Bouwel (2002) show how this can be understood for the social sciences.

*Path dependence*   Knowledge has a history; it is not produced from nothing. The past determines how an issue is conceptualized in the present. Past problems for instance determine which instruments have been devised, which institutions have been set up, and how they work. But also scholars have a knowledge history. Their past research interests, education, jobs, contacts,... As such, the past affects both future paths and current stances.

## A first cut

Now that I have set out the scope of the problem and listed a number of causes of diversity, it is time for a first cut at the problem of how to handle diversity.[5] I start with the two limiting alternatives: to accept all views simultaneously (syncretism) and to accept none (skepticism). Although these views are extremes and thus rarely held, they will prove to be useful beacons.

*Syncretism* is an all-embracing position that comes down to accepting a conjunction of the alternatives. As there is something to be said for each of the contenders, judgment is suspended and all are kind-heartedly adopted as constituting the sum of our knowledge of the subject. The problem with this position is that it runs aground on its own inconsistencies. The answer to any question would be both yes and no, rendering syncretism ultimately uninformative. You can't have your cake and eat it too.

Perhaps a more cynical response is the one which sees the alternatives as cancelling each other out. The *skeptic* stands perplexed when confronted with the multitude of views. While the syncretist still made a decision (be it an empty one), the skeptic refrains completely. If all inquirers were to adopt this stance, science itself would come to a full stop. Their situation would be comparable to that of the ass of Buridan, the poor creature that starved while sitting between two equally appealing stacks of hay. Skepticism seems to be driven by a precautionary principle ("in dubio, abstine")[6] that leaves its advocates not only unspoiled but also in ignorance.

Both the skeptic and the syncretist have a safe but unfruitful stance. Since the options of accepting all and rejecting all must be rejected, the only alternative left to reach an informative stance is to make a selection after all. Now let's presume we do this in the most minimalist of ways, making a choice just for its own sake (e.g. by flipping a coin). This leads to a very extreme form of *relativism*.[7] This extreme relativist resigns himself to the necessity of choice, but denies the existence of any ground for picking one alternative over another. In the end the relativist is indifferent toward the alternatives; he only chooses because he feels he has to. His commitment is contingent and varies independently from good arguments for or against it. He has no tool whatsoever to convince others of his stance, except for his all-encompassing indifference. More importantly, he has no reason for a protracted exploration of a particular point of view, for the perspective he holds might change with every coin flip. An arbitrary choice is thus not sufficient, not for the scholar himself nor for his colleagues. So we need something more; some kind of a warrant.[8]

This first cut already enables us to derive a few useful hints of how a credible view on the management of theoretical diversity should look. The first two positions, syncretism and skepticism, suggested that choice cannot be dispensed with. Additionally, the third position made clear that choice will somehow need to be warranted in order to avoid extreme relativism. So a first general conclusion is that we need to make some kind of a warranted choice when faced with divergent views. This creates two notorious problems: (1) How can we be pluralists if we need to make a choice? Pluralism's inability to choose leads its critics to declare that it is *self-defeating* because pluralism claiming its own truth is a very un-pluralist thing to do. (2) How can choice be warranted if multiple divergent views are rationally justifiable (from the epistemic context as sketched in the seven points listed in "Framing pluralism")? It is argued that this lack of warrant associated with pluralism leads to an *anything goes*.

## A matter of levels

Already after a first cut, the problem of how to manage diversity seems to run aground on its own assumptions. It was shown that the only way to avoid syncretism, skepticism, and relativism (which I evaluated as unfruitful positions) was to make some warranted choice, but this apparently contradicts with the very nature of pluralism. As a consequence, it seems as if every fruitful research will need to retreat into monism in order to avoid an unfruitful position characterized by self-defeat and "anything goes."

This, I contend, is a false impression. What this contradiction points to is not so much a flaw in the concept of pluralism itself, but rather a failure on the part of theoreticians to distinguish between two different levels at which pluralism can be situated: the individual and the aggregate level. I will show that this multi-level distinction solves the two problems and gives the notion of pluralism more conceptual clarity.

Pluralism was characterized as follows:

> Pluralism is to acknowledge the validity of different possible perspectives on reality in an active way, which means that they are not only tolerated but also taken into account when goals of knowledge (prediction, problem-solving, truth, curiosity, policy advice, funding decision,…) are to be achieved.

The introduction of levels actually splits this up into an individual version and an aggregate version. The latter says that diversity of views should be respected and accommodated at the level of groups of scientists, conference organizers, editorial boards, science policy, etc. The former looks at pluralism from the standpoint of the individual scientist: "Should *I* adopt pluralism?," "Should *I* mark alternative views merely as plausible or actually endorse them?"

To my knowledge, this distinction is at least not frequently being made in the literature on economic methodology. The introduction of levels removes the apparent tension associated with the two problems. The first problem occurred when pluralism appeared to be incompatible with the choice for one particular view, leading to the criticism that pluralism is self-defeating. When looked at from a two-level perspective, this problem disappears because holding a stance (on the individual level) does not disqualify diversity (at the aggregate level) any longer. Hence, pluralism on the aggregate level is not self-defeating.

Now that it has been shown that choice does not preclude diversity, the question remains how it is possible for that choice to be warranted in the face of the defined insolubility of divergence, thus avoiding an "anything goes." The introduction of an individual and an aggregate level once again offers a solution.

The way to proceed is to note that the inconclusiveness between views exists at the aggregate level. To make this point I start by referring back to the seven causes of divergence of views I enumerated earlier. Apart from an ontological cause, a cognitive cause, and underdetermination, I mentioned situatedness, pragmatics, path dependency, and experiential diversity. Interestingly, in terms of the individual/aggregate-distinction, all seven obtain at the aggregate level, but only the first three obtain at the individual level. The reason why situatedness, pragmatics, path dependency, and experiential diversity caused divergence is that when scholars are aggregated, the result is that a multiplicity of different situations, interests, paths, and experiences come together. However, from the point of view of an individual scholar, this multiplicity collapses: it is *your* situation, *your* epistemic interest, *your* path, and *your* experience.[9] As such, contrary to the aggregate level where all seven factors mentioned are causes of dissensus, these latter four factors stop causing divergence from the standpoint of the individual scholar. This means that the individual has more tools available to make a warranted choice. It is this additional determination which provides leeway for a warranted choice at the individual level even if this warrant is not available at the aggregate level.[10] From the individual perspective a choice might be made on grounds not available at the aggregate level. The result is a solution for the second problem. Choice can be warranted (on the individual level) in the face of insolvability (at the aggregate level).

## How to manage diversity

Divergence of views is a basic feature of the practice of science (stylized fact, in the "Introduction"). It is therefore indispensable to manage it in a way that does not impede on knowledge production. The three strategies I have treated in "A first cut" did not meet this condition. However, they did suggest that a credible view on how to manage diversity could be obtained by allowing a warranted choice. The two problems associated with this statement could be countered by introducing a multi-level version of pluralism, leading to the solution that holding a stance on the individual level does not disqualify diversity at the aggregate level; and choice can be warranted on the individual level due to reduced indeterminacy, in the face of insolvability at the aggregate level. Warranted choice can go hand in hand with pluralism on the condition that pluralism is confined to the aggregate level. In other words, the cost of warranted choice is individual level pluralism.

Note that the framework I've sketched only points out the trade-offs that obtain. Whether or not we actually want to give up individual level pluralism for warranted choice is something that remains to be shown separately. This assessment will proceed in two stages. First I give five reasons to prefer warranted choice over individual level pluralism. Then I take away a number of fears that could be associated with dropping individual level pluralism.

### The benefits of warranted choice at the individual level

*Soundness*    I have already shown how warranted choice enables us to resolve two notorious problems associated with pluralism. A pluralism enabling warranted choice will hence be more sound.

*Realism*    The naive assumption that the parts need to be pluralist in order for the whole to be pluralist is abandoned; social systems are not just the sum of their parts.

*Best of both worlds*    Warranted choice at the individual level allows one to exploit the increased determinacy at the individual level while retaining the benefits of diversity.

*Transparency*    Individuals voicing their preferences loud and clear improves market efficiency. Clear stances result in an increased transparency, actually boosting compatibility rather than limiting it.

*Condition of possibility*    For pluralism to be possible, different well-elaborated perspectives are already presupposed, which makes the presence of different separate but coherent views at some lower level a condition of possibility for higher level pluralism.

### Costs of dropping individual level pluralism

*Loss of scope?*    From a statement like that of Kurz and Salvadori (2000: 37) one would be inclined to conclude that dropping individual level pluralism is not a good idea: "[T]o seek dominance for one theory over all the others with the possible result that all the rival theories are extinguished amounts to advocating scientific regress." Of course, Kurz and Salvadori have a genuine concern when they suggest that making a choice limits the scope of research. However, I compare it to the point the dove has when it states that it could fly much faster, if only the wind wouldn't hinder it so much. Of course, should the air disappear it would not fly faster but drop dead on the ground.[11]

The point is that boundaries not only restrict but also define. For the individual scholar, taking stance offers a way to cut a path through the desert of data. It provides him with a lens through which he can see; and although every lens has its distortions, without it he is blind. More technically, taking a personal stance, boosted by increased determinacy on the individual level but biased as it can be, seems to offer a unique way to obtain more informative guidance in inquiry. The increased determinacy at least partially renders individual pluralism obsolete. Also, it is important to note that prospects for individual pluralism are limited by the fact that personal bias isn't always a matter of choice for the individual. Limits of scope are often not a personal choice at all. One's proper situatedness, epistemic interests, path dependency, and experiential diversity determine one's perspective. As such, the individual is "trapped" within it. It is impossible, for example, to *have had* a different history.

*Inconsistency is lost as a tool*    One of the main problems related to individual level pluralism is that inconsistency is lost as a tool. This is an important logical device for the individual to structure his inquiry. Whenever meeting something inconsistent with his own ideas, he will either have to reframe it to fit those ideas or change them altogether. Festinger's (1957) theory of cognitive dissonance supports the view that the mind actively engages in reducing tension between dissonant cognitions. So whether we like it or not, the tool of inconsistency might well be something that just "is there" at the individual level and which we can't reason away no matter what kind of view we hold on how to deal with pluralism.

*Isolationism?*    One still might bring in that making too clear a choice is unacceptable, not from a scientific point of view but from a social perspective. How can a scientific community function if all scholars have their own private stance which they themselves feel to be the best game in town? How can we foster compatibility and avoid isolationism? In other words, having abandoned a naive view on social structure, it remains to be shown how a community of autonomous scholars can add up to the scientific community we observe, with its divergence of views but not totally fragmented.

First, actively reacting against alternative views might be more useful than tacit tolerance. At least the former means both parties are still on speaking terms with each other, hence it might turn out to be more constructive to be a paradigm warrior than to be a tolerant pluralist. Second, no scientist can cover a whole discipline (see cognitive limitations argument), so he will have to rely on the work of others and choose among their contributions in order to get a view of the whole. The isolation, if any, will thus be rather mild. New information will most often be woven into the fabric of the old, leading for example Sir Isaac Newton to state he was "standing upon the shoulders of giants." Third, it was stated that knowledge production is mostly path dependent (see path dependence in "Framing pluralism"). Scholars will mostly be choosing among frameworks of others instead of producing their own. A fourth factor that can be indicated which has less to do with knowledge than with group dynamics is the occurrence of herding behavior. In any group, it is to be expected that a number of scholars will choose for the safety of the most common stance, no matter what their personal stance is. In sum, taking a stance is mainly a matter of positioning oneself *within* the diversity of views already available in the community of scholars and as such it is to be expected that their individually taken positions will nonetheless cluster around a number of well-elaborated and incommensurable perspectives that already exist.

Dropping individual pluralism does not lead to the extremes of isolationism. Indeed, the argument could even be turned upside down by stating that *not* taking a stance on the individual level might lead to isolationism. Although I am wary of pushing the analogy between science and markets too far, a market works more efficiently when every participant voices his preferences loud and clear; only then can an optimal aggregation of needs take place. Similarly, I believe a point might be made for the increased transparency which results from taking a stance. As such, individuals making a warranted choice can actually boost compatibility rather than limit it.

*Impossibility of eclecticism?* Taking a stance, i.e. making a warranted choice, in no way presupposes that you do this neatly within the boundaries of a certain perspective or a certain school. This is the way the aggregate level influences the individual level. Views don't just fall from the sky. Taking a stance involves the individual positioning himself within the diversity of views already available, constructing a base from which to engage in his own research activities.

*Implausibility?* But if knowledge ultimately is perspectival, then why should individual scholars choose to take a stance while at the same time realizing that their position is a priori at best only partially true? Because he can do no other. The reasons why knowledge is perspectival are reduced at the individual level (from seven to three) exactly because, for the individual, a number of elements concerning his perspective are not a matter of choice. It's not possible to *have had* another personal history; it's not possible for a woman to momentarily stop being a woman, etc. So given a perspectival knowledge the individual might still feel compelled to a position from his personal position. However, this does not settle the matter completely, because the scholar might be compelled to a point of view, but still realize it is just a point of view. For this it is necessary to refer to the difference between belief and pursuit.[12] Pursuing a certain line does not rule out that you believe your knowledge is bound to be perspectival. And as Kitcher (1990: 8) notes, the scientific community doesn't care what you believe, but only what beliefs you pursue.[13] Finally, scholars might also be motivated by their belief that elaborating a certain stance benefits the aggregate level (and it is at this higher level that the goals of science will ultimately need to be situated),[14] supported by the insight that individual specialization, independence, and decentralization in the end often tend to offer better results at the aggregate level.[15]

## Where to go?

The cost for warranted choice turns out to be surprisingly low, its benefits being underrated and its costs overestimated. Hence, I believe there to be good reasons to prefer warranted choice to individual pluralism. A reason for the proliferation of individual pluralism might simply be that it inadvertently sneaks into the discourse of well-meaning pluralists being unaware of the conceptual boundary between different levels of pluralism. For them, individual level pluralism brings

little benefit at a huge cost. As such, advocates of pluralism might consider reformulating their position since I hope to have demonstrated that a pluralist has
little to lose and much to gain from dropping individual level pluralism.

As a guideline for practice I infer that advocates of pluralism should not
bother trying to convince individual scientists of adopting pluralism in their own
research nor blame them for not doing so. Instead, from the point of view I have
advocated here, the true challenge for pluralists is to concentrate their efforts
toward designing the aggregate structures in such a way that they reflect the
diversity at the individual level.

The claim that an advocate of pluralism needn't be a pluralist himself might
become more tangible when formulated from a political point of view: to be an
advocate of democracy does not rule out having a clear stance. Indeed, it is even
expected of politicians to have a clear stance on the individual level. The extent
to which a politician can also be an advocate of democracy[16] is probably comparable with the extent to which a scientist can take a stance at the individual level
while still being an advocate of pluralism. So along with different levels come
different roles to be played. The different roles a scientist will need to fulfill are
then individual roles like writing articles, giving lectures, etc. and aggregate
roles like editor, reviewer, conference organizer, dean, etc. Individuals have been
shown to be able to sustain both individual and aggregate roles (with their
respective goals and rules of conduct) at the same time. Of course it would be
naive to assume that these different roles are totally separate if fulfilled by the
same person, but all the same this is what people like prime ministers, judges,
and referees do. An individual level pluralist could perhaps even be seen as the
scientific equivalent of a populist: someone who wishes to please everybody but
whose policy perspectives are very restricted because he is tied to all kinds of
incommensurable commitments.

A general lesson to be drawn is that the shortest way to reach a desideratum
at the higher level is not necessarily to desire it at the individual level. Like individual level pluralism in politics leads not to democracy but to populism, I have
contended that individual pluralism in science might not be the best way to reach
aggregate pluralism. A principle being illustrated in its most well-known form
by the prisoner's dilemma: both prisoners do the most rational thing on the individual level but end up with a suboptimal outcome.

Finally, it should be noted that the sketch of pluralism I have presented here
has only set out a few beacons, namely those which I thought were useful for the
purpose at hand. Many great challenges concerning pluralism have remained
unmentioned; perhaps the biggest of them all is to get a clearer view on aggregation and how it actually proceeds or should proceed.[17]

## Acknowledgments

The author acknowledges the support of the Research Foundation Flanders
(FWO). Thanks also to Jeroen Van Bouwel, Maarten Van Dyck, Erik Weber,
and the participants in the 2007 ICAPE and AHE conferences.

# Notes

1  Of course it is extremely difficult to be exhaustive here. I can do no more than present what I believe is a representative sample of the literature. These points elaborate on a similar enumeration by Van Bouwel (2005: 1).
2  Born (1949: 6) as quoted in Popper (1992: 54).
3  A paraphrase of Voltaire, quoted from Kurz and Salvadori (2000: 235–58).
4  For a classic critique of conceptual relativism, see Donald Davidson (1973–1974).
5  I owe the distinction between syncretism, skepticism and relativism to Rescher (1993).
6  A principle originating from medicine, meaning "abstain when in doubt."
7  Indeed, relativism needn't be arbitrary, but in this case it is; hence the adjective "extreme." Again it must be stressed that these extreme views are only to be used as beacons, not as representations of the (undoubtedly more subtle) views actually held by real scholars.
8  A warrant has so far only been defined in a negative way, namely as anything which is not arbitrary. This is sufficient for this first cut. Later on in the paper, a positive account will be suggested by referring to the reduced indeterminacy at the individual.
9  Epistemic interests might also vary on the underlying level of different problems an individual is faced with, but the point is that singularity obtains when an individual is faced with a certain problem or view.
10  Note that while subjectivity was traditionally seen as an impediment to knowledge, it follows from the way I have constructed my argument that here it is assigned a constitutive role instead. While at the aggregate level there are no grounds for discrimination between perspectives, individual scientists can turn to the constitutive force of their individual situatedness, epistemic interests, pragmatics, and experience to provide grounds for a warranted choice. Turning to their own interests, experience, etc. scholars can pick a perspective, not on the basis of its being the "right" perspective, but because it allows them to spend time using the methods they master best, answering the questions they themselves deem most relevant... The point is that is doesn't really matter which perspective is chosen (there's no answer to that question at that moment), as long as the scholar makes a choice which he himself stands for. A choice (and the resulting specialization) is needed in order to develop a certain stance thoroughly, devise the best arguments for it, come up with critical test, and eventually perhaps even allowing it to be falsified in the future.
11  "The light dove, cleaving the air in her free flight, and feeling its resistance, might imagine that its flight would be still easier in empty space" Kant (2003 [1787]: 47).
12  Introduced by Laudan (1977: 108–14).
13  Kitcher (1990: 8) claims "what the community cares about is the distribution of pursuit not the distribution of belief."
14  Or how else could the billions in tax money that are spent on research be accounted for?
15  This statement refers to the comprehensive body of literature on collective decision making and collective action. A number of caveats are in order here. For example, a good method of aggregation is required for this mechanism to work.
16  In line with Voltaire's famous quote: "I disapprove of what you say, but I will defend to the death your right to say it."
17  It might be inferred from not tackling this issue that I implicitly assume the view that the individual level simply adds up to the aggregate level. However, this bottom-up view is not self-evident. Taking stance is mainly a matter of positioning oneself *within* the diversity of views already available in the community of scholars. To address this issue thoroughly is not necessary for the purpose at hand; it will however be taken up in future publications as it is intricately related to the distinction I have introduced.

## References

Born, M. (1949) *Natural Philosophy of Cause and Chance*, Oxford: Clarendon Press.

Caldwell, B. (2004). "Some Comments on Lawson's *Reorienting Economics*: Same Facts, Different Conclusions," *Post-Autistic Economics Review*, issue 28, October 25, article 3.

Davidson, D. (1973–1974) "On the Very Idea of a Conceptual Scheme," *Proceedings and Addresses of the American Philosophical Association*, 47: 5–20.

Festinger, L. (1957) *A Theory of Cognitive Dissonance*, Stanford, CA: Stanford University Press.

Giere, R. (1999) *Science without Laws*, Chicago: Chicago University Press.

Hacking, I. (1999) *The Social Construction of What?* Cambridge, MA: Harvard University Press.

Kant, I. (2003) [1787] *The Critique of Pure Reason*, New York: Palgrave Macmillan.

Kitcher, P. (1990) "The Division of Cognitive Labor," *Journal of Philosophy*, 87(1): 5–22.

—— (2001) *Science, Truth, and Democracy*, Oxford: Oxford University Press.

Kurz, H. and Salvadori, N. (2000) "On Critics and Protective Belts," in H. Kurz and N. Salvadori (eds.) *Understanding "Classical" Economics: Studies in Long-Period Theory*, 235–58, London: Routledge.

Laudan, L. (1977) *Progress and Its Problems*, Berkeley: California University Press.

Popper, K. (1992) *Conjectures and Refutations: The Growth of Scientific Knowledge*, New York: Routledge.

Rescher, N. (1993) *Pluralism: Against the Demand for Consensus*, New York: Oxford University Press.

Shapin, S. (1982) "History of Science and Its Sociological Reconstructions," *History of Science*, 20: 157–211.

Van Bouwel, J. (2005). "Towards a Framework for Pluralism in Economics." *Post-Autistic Economics Review*, issue 30, March 21, article 3.

Weber, E. and Van Bouwel, J. (2002) "Can We Dispense With Structural Explanations of Social Facts?" *Economics and Philosophy*, 18 (2): 259–75.

# 7 Ontology, modern economics, and pluralism

## *Tony Lawson*

In *Reorienting Economics* (Lawson 2003a) and elsewhere (e.g. Lawson 2006a), I defend a specific ontological conception and use it to interpret the nature of both the mainstream and heterodox traditions in economics. Various commentators suggest that my position in all this is insufficiently pluralist. In this short chapter, I hope to convince otherwise. Specifically, I will seek to allay any concern that I defend a conception in which heterodoxy is somehow discouraged from engaging others, is necessarily oriented to replacing the mainstream with an undesirably monolithic paradigm, and/or is encouraging of isolationism.

### A conception of heterodoxy in contemporary economics

Let me start by briefly summarizing the position defended in *Reorienting Economics*. I take it to be analytic to the notion of heterodoxy that it involves the rejection of some doctrine held to be true by a prevailing orthodoxy. That is simply what it means to be heterodox. And it is clear that the self-identifying heterodox traditions in modern economics not only all ardently oppose the mainstream output currently but also have done so persistently over a lengthy period of time, even through changes in the mainstream forms. Thus, it seems reasonable to conclude that the heterodox opposition stands against some feature that is enduring and central to the modern mainstream; certainly it is opposed to something common to, or presupposed by, all its contributions.

In order to distinguish the modern economic heterodoxy qua heterodoxy I thus start by identifying the (set of) feature(s) of the modern orthodoxy or mainstream that is common to all its contributions. The assessment I defend in *Reorienting Economics* and elsewhere is the following. The project that has dominated the discipline of economics for the last forty years or so is one that, although highly heterogeneous in detail, and fluid in revising its manifest form, is united and stable in, *but only in*, adhering to the following single doctrine or edict. This is an insistence that mathematical methods be more or less always employed in the study of economic phenomena. This insistence often runs over to claiming that any contribution that does not take the form of a mathematical model is not proper economics (see Lawson 2003a, chapter 1).

This is not to say that there is not an elite within the mainstream who feel their privileged positions allow them sometimes to set out some less-than-overly formalistic pieces, especially in presidential addresses and such like. But it is only in virtue of their previous, and other, formalistic contributions that such deviations are rendered legitimate. Such individuals may even introduce their favorite non-mathematical associates into the mainstream scene. But whilst the latter chosen few are few indeed, they are not really part of the mainstream as such and are seemingly mostly included/tolerated only because of their associations with powerful others who are. Even here, though, the mathematical contributions of their patrons (or matrons) constitute the essential condition.

If an oppositional stance to the noted orthodox doctrine (that formalism is normally compulsory) is the nominal essence of the current heterodoxy, what is its real essence, the explanation of this opposition? It is the recognition (albeit one that is often no more than implicit) that the universal application of the sorts of mathematical methods that mainstream economists formulate presupposes an untenable account of social reality as everywhere composed of systems of isolated atoms.

In *Reorienting Economics*, I argue that underpinning this heterodox oppositional stance is an implicit (and sometimes reasonably explicit) commitment to the alternative sort of social ontology I defend in that book. According to the latter, social reality is appropriately viewed as *structured*, in that it does not reduce to atomistic human practices but is constituted in large part by *emergent* social properties including social rules, relations, institutions, and so forth; as intrinsically *dynamic* or *processual*, in that its mode of being is a continual process of becoming; and as ubiquitous in *internal relationality* in that economic agents are what they are and/or can do what they do, by virtue of the constitutive relations in which they stand to each other (e.g. as in relations between employer and employee, parent and child, landlord or -lady and tenant, buyer and seller, etc.) (see Lawson 2006a).

So in short, if the only common and so distinguishing feature of the current mainstream is its continuing insistence upon forms of mathematical deductivist reasoning, the real essence of the heterodox opposition (qua heterodox opposition) is an accepted (but rarely explicitly acknowledged) ontological conception. It is a conception that is at odds with the implicit (closed-system and atomistic) ontology of mainstream deductivist reasoning, and so ultimately accounting for the heterodox oppositional stance.

Notice, though, that I do *not* distinguish the individual heterodox traditions from each other according to ontological commitments; indeed I suggest that ontological presuppositions are something they broadly hold in common. Nor, incidentally, do I believe that the features that serve to identify the heterodox groups as separate and distinct traditions lie at the level of substantive theories, results, methodologies, principles, policy stances, and such like. Rather my assessment is that old institutionalism, post Keynesianism, feminist economics, Austrianism, Marxian economics, etc., are each best distinguished/identified in terms of *questions and issues traditionally addressed* within their own program.

Thus old institutionalism, I argue, is an economics project concerned first and foremost with questions of stability and change. Hence its traditional and ongoing concerns are especially with technology (perceived as an important source of change), habits and institutions (seen as important sources of stability), evolutionary science, and so forth (see *Reorienting Economics* chapter 8, and also Lawson 2002, 2003a). I return to this issue of characterizing the different heterodox traditions below.

With this heterodox emphasis on questions and interests (rather than principles, methods, or answers and so forth), there is scope both for different members of any given heterodox tradition to produce competing accounts of some phenomenon, as well as for the best-substantiated contributions to be continually improved upon. So the conception I defend is quite consistent with the sort of (shifting) variety of contributions we find within any heterodox tradition.

Notice, too, that I do not suggest that heterodox contributors do not, or should not, experiment with mathematical deductive techniques and the like. Social conditions may occasionally arise that are locally of a sort presupposed by methods of formalistic modeling. If I characterize the mainstream in terms of its usual *insistence* that (for a contribution to count as economics) various sorts of mathematical deductivist methods be everywhere and always employed, I conceive heterodoxy as an (implicitly) ontologically motivated rejection of *the universalizing and dogmatic aspects of this stance*, not as a refusal ever to experiment with formalistic methods or to employ them where conditions indicate their relevance.

The mainstream itself is pluralistic within its constituting constraint, of course. Despite the best advice of those economists associated with the Bourbaki school, it is impossible to pursue a mathematical economics purely in the abstract. There has to be content, and this is found to be highly variable. Indeed, both the substantive programs pursued by the mainstream and the sorts of mathematical deductivist methods employed (along with their interpretation) are highly variable (Lawson 2005). There are those who argue that *within* orthodoxy there exists a dominant and relatively enduring (though by no means fixed) "neoclassical core" or some such. But assessments of what this entails vary quite significantly (see, for example, Fine 2006, Hodgson 2006, Arnsperger and Varoufakis 2006, or Fullbrook 2005). For the purposes at hand, I do not need to consider these matters further here.

## Pluralism

Before turning to prominent criticisms of my position that contend that I am not sufficiently pluralistic, let me indicate the type of pluralism that I believe to be of concern here. I take it that, generally speaking, by pluralism is meant something like the affirmation, acceptance, and encouragement of diversity. Clearly, such a notion itself has a plurality of meanings or inflections, of which two in particular are worth distinguishing.

One such is the notion of pluralism as description, as a claim about the way (some domain of) reality is. It is important to realize that any claim to be a pluralist in this sense needs a fair bit of elaboration. Consider for example the notion of *ontological pluralism*, which is sometimes mentioned by those who question my own orientation. This can have various meanings. One such conception designates the claim that multiple non-overlapping worlds exist (see Erlich 1986: 527). A second notion of *ontological pluralism* has it that our *one* reality contains an (at least synchronically) irreducible multiplicity of constituents.[1]

Now a *prima facie* oppositional position to an ontological pluralism is the idea that at the base of everything is one substance, say energy, or vibrations. To hold to this is to be a monist rather than pluralist in some metaphysical sense. Many Eastern religions support a monistic rather than a pluralistic philosophy. But it seems to me that, allowing for the phenomenon of emergence, either of the two conceptions of ontological pluralism just described may (or may not) be consistent with such a monistic metaphysics.

Clearly, this is not the place to attempt to elaborate an account of all the various kinds of descriptive pluralisms imaginable, and to indicate where I might stand with respect to them. I mention the foregoing merely to indicate the complexities of the topic, and ambiguities of any personal declaration to be a pluralist.

A second inflection on the term pluralism interprets it as a (normative) orientation, one of inclusiveness, of supporting and encouraging the acceptance of all interested parties, whatever their differences, within some process. The latter could be a society, or an academic conversation, a sports club, or whatever.

It is possible that because this second notion expresses an orientation rather than a state of affairs it is best captured by the adjective pluralistic. In any case, the two conceptions appear distinct. For it seems to me that no matter how pluralistic an individual might be in the second sense, they could still be led to the view that some domain of reality is, as a matter of fact, monistic in nature.

In any case, it is this second inflection of pluralism, or "being pluralistic," that seems most relevant here. For we shall see that each of the commentaries to be discussed is motivated by the worry that, by virtue of my conceiving heterodoxy in oppositional terms, my position is necessarily insufficiently pluralistic in the sense of somehow excluding, or showing insufficient respect or tolerance for or engagement with (the views of) certain others in the academic conversation. Let me then address the relevant critics. Below I examine in turn the concerns of John Davis, Robert Garnett, and Jeroen Van Bouwel.

## Replies to critics

### John Davis

In his recent *Post-Autistics Review* critique of my *Reorienting Economics*, Davis (2006) suggests that traditional heterodox economists have two options: to "look inwards" within the discipline and engage the mainstream (his preferred strategy) or to look outwards and develop alternatives of a different sort. Davis presents this as a choice between "chipping away at the core on a gradualist schedule" or "betting on a big scientific revolution." Davis prefers the former fearing that if the traditional heterodox programs do not take this route, any future change in the mainstream will be on terms determined by those pushing the "new approaches" to economics (behavioral economists, experimentalists, neuroeconomists, etc.), an outcome that is likely to be undesirably more conservative:

> traditional heterodox economists have two choices. They can maintain their outward-orientation, so that if change occurs in economics it will likely be on the terms determined by behavioral economists, experimentalists, and others in the new approaches. The risk here is that these movements may become more conservative as their success at influencing the core improves. Alternatively they can reverse their orientation, and turn to trying to shift what exists in the core, looking for allies in the "new heterodoxy" along the way, so as to improve the chances of successful change for both.
>
> (Davis 2006: 28)

From this perspective, I am criticized both as preventing the emphasized choice from emerging and for unhelpfully counseling an outward orientation:

> Lawson's view of heterodoxy, in my view, does not allow this choice to emerge. As a point-in-time, shared characteristics conception, it misses the heterogeneity and dynamics of heterodoxy, both traditional and new. Moreover, by asserting, "there is a set of characteristics by virtue of which any tradition qualifies as heterodox" (Lawson 2006a: 484), and by associating these shared characteristics with the rejection of the core of economics, he counsels an outward orientation. And with the recommendation of an outward orientation, he bets on the unlikely big scientific revolution, so that, should traditional heterodox economists in any great number accept his advice, the chances of gradual change in economics being more conservative are increased."
>
> (Davis 2006: 28–9)

The problem, as Davis perceives things here, is that I adopt the wrong strategy. Indeed, he finds the approach I adopt to be insufficiently pluralistic. Instead of looking for unity within the differences found amongst the heterodox (and other) projects, a position Davis attributes to me, we should accept a pluralism of strategies for changing economics. Thus in his final paragraph, Davis (2006: 29) asserts:

> For many [an expression of pluralism] seems to mean an open stance toward the different heterodox research programs associated with ICAPE [the International Confederation for Pluralism in Economics] that seeks to promote a unity within difference. This stance seems to me to be shortsighted and anti-pluralist in important respects.

And Davis ends by hoping that "ICAPE will become an increasingly pluralist organization in strategy as well as membership."

*Engaging the mainstream: a reply to Davis*

Davis essentially focuses upon strategies adopted in the effort to transform modern economics. As noted, he himself counsels an inward orientation of engaging with the mainstream. He criticizes me for supporting the traditional heterodox stance of advancing an alternative approach to the mainstream, rather than trying to gradually amend the latter from within. Davis advances his position in the name of both pluralism and efficacy in bringing about a more successful economics. Let me consider these two aspects (pluralism and efficacy) of his critique in turn.

First, just because heterodox traditions are constituted as heterodox traditions through their rejection of some orthodox doctrine, it does not follow that engagement with orthodox practitioners is thereby rendered necessarily infeasible or undesirable. Nor need communication be other than open and respectful. The possibilities for exchange will depend on context and on the nature of the differences. But this will be so however heterodoxy is constituted. I myself have never wished to discourage respectful engagement with others. The stance is not inherently anti-pluralist.

To be more concrete, it is clear that a rejection of the defining doctrine of contemporary orthodoxy does not involve a rejection of all endeavors to explore the usefulness of formalistic methods. Heterodoxy qua heterodoxy, as I conceive it, involves a necessary opposition *not* to the use of formalism, but only to *the dogmatic insistence that only these sorts of methods be used, irrespective of their ability to illuminate.* I do not see how a pluralist can accept this insistence, this orthodox doctrine, in the circumstances. Indeed, in rejecting this one enduring orthodox doctrine, heterodoxy, qua heterodoxy, is inherently pluralistic in its very constitutive orientation (whether or not specific heterodox contributions remain pluralistic in all other respects). If, however, individuals within or outside the traditional heterodox groups wish to explore new formalisms, or methods of any kind, who is going to object?

To date, formalistic methods that presuppose an atomistic ontology have met with very little success, and from the perspective of the ontological framework I defend, this is none too surprising. But even if the ontology I defend is roughly right, there may yet be pockets of social reality that provide the appropriate conditions for successes when utilizing methods of formalistic modeling, as I regularly acknowledge. In addition, of course, I recognize that the ontological conception I defend may yet turn out to be significantly mistaken in various ways; all knowledge claims are fallible. So no one wants to inhibit any serious methodological experimentation, whether involving formal techniques or otherwise. All that is being rejected by heterodoxy, on my conception, is the orthodox constraint on a pluralistic approach to economic analysis. This takes on a special significance just because the mainstream is constituted through this constraint.

But if that is the nature of the beast, we just have to accept that opposing the mainstream (rejecting its constitutive doctrine) is a pro-, not an anti-, pluralistic stance.

I turn to the question of the efficaciousness of different strategies. Let me first emphasize that any desire to engage does not mean heterodox economists must resort to constructing formalistic models (although of course there is no reason not to try that route if there is thought to be some promise of success). In particular, meta-theoretical discussion is at least as valid, where feasible. This can take the form of engagement via publications. Other forms depend on context.

I well understand the problems. As Richard Lipsey reminds us, if anyone presents an economics seminar without formulating a mathematical model it is not unknown for the mainstream economists "to turn off and figuratively, if not literally, to walk out" (Lipsey 2001: 184). But not all mainstream contributors are like this, especially the more thoughtful ones, despite appearances. While I was originally formulating my critique of the mainstream, Frank Hahn was head of the Cambridge (UK) economics faculty in which I am located. Hahn's commitment to the mainstream is clear enough from his retirement speech to the *Royal Economic Society*, where he famously gave advice to students to "avoid discussions of 'mathematics in economics' like the plague" (Hahn 1992a, see also Hahn 1992b), adding that we should "give no thought to methodology." Elsewhere, as I have often observed, Hahn writes of any suggestion that the emphasis on mathematics may be a problem that it is "a view surely not worth discussing" (Hahn 1985: 18). But appearances or rhetoric can mislead. This set of beliefs did not prevent Hahn himself, on various occasions, accepting invitations to talk at the *Cambridge Realist Workshop*[2] that I co-ordinate. In that forum, a genuine exchange of ideas took place on the sorts of issues here in contention, with large audiences of mostly Ph.D. students listening (and indeed joining) in. I mention this just to reinforce the idea that possibilities for engagement depend very much on people and context. In particular, there should be no presumption that we always hide our real critique, or perpetuate approaches we actually think are very unlikely to reveal insight, to be able to engage.

Davis, though, believes it strategically more efficacious to engage the orthodoxy on its own terms. He seems to contend that a failure to do so, and specifically if the traditional heterodox traditions maintain their outward-orientation, then any change achieved will be on the terms determined by the "new programs," namely: behavioral economists, experimentalists, and others in the new approaches. He worries that the "risk here is that these movements may become more conservative as their success at influencing the core improves." He believes that if the traditional heterodoxy changes its orientation and challenges the core, meaning the sort of formalism practiced, this would "improve the chances of successful change."

This statement begs various questions. What does it mean to say the new programs are likely to become more "conservative" as they influence the core? Why are the new programs likely to become more "conservative" as/if they influence the core? Is there any reason to suppose that if the traditional heterodoxy oriented itself more towards the core it could thereby achieve changes worth having?

I presume that by "more conservative," Davis means something like becoming more sympathetic to, and having minimal or reduced impact on, the current mainstream insistence that formalism be everywhere used.[3] If so, Davis is surely correct that it is only through adopting such an inward orientation that proponents of the new programs will be accepted by the mainstream. But this is the case whatever orientation is adopted by the traditional heterodoxy. Putting forward a formalistic program is the only basis on which the current mainstream has been found to accept change. Furthermore, the traditional heterodoxy is, by its nature, opposed to the insistence that formalism be everywhere involved. The only way it could thus orientate itself to the mainstream in the manner Davis suggests is to drop this opposition and relinquish its generalist heterodox status. But then it is unclear why any changes subsequently wrought by such a transformed project, should any occur, should be any less "conservative" than any brought about by the new approaches acting alone.

Fundamental to all this is the question of the sort of plurality we seek. If it is a plurality of mainstream approaches, if the goal is a variety of modeling endeavors pursued by those who insist that formalistic methods only be followed, then Davis's approach seems appropriate. Having said that we should acknowledge that at this level the mainstream is already pluralistic; the sorts of mathematical-deductivist endeavors being followed within the mainstream are regularly shifting. Our real difference here seems to be that I am more concerned that we create increased space for that which is largely absent: nonformalistic approaches to economics. These are lacking because of the anti-pluralistic maneuvers of the dominant mainstream. It is not yet clear that engaging the mainstream on the question of which form of formalism to use in conditions where none seem especially appropriate will bring about much of an improvement.

In any case, I hope it is clear that there is nothing in my approach that discourages active engagement with the mainstream. I do not think that formulating mathematical programs is the only way of doing this. Nor do I think such engagement is likely to be extremely fruitful. But there is nothing in my position that argues against it happening. On grounds of efficacy, as well as in the interests of pluralism, let a multitude of strategies be followed.

### *Rob Garnett*

In addition to some of the sorts of views aired by Davis, Rob Garnett (2006), the ICAPE Secretary and Conference Organizer from 1999 through 2007, provides a further line of criticism. In an important and wide-ranging (and I believe overall a very fair) contribution, Garnett criticizes those heterodox "paradigmist economists" who seek to replace a mainstream paradigm with their own hopefully superior one, Garnett worries that my own approach carries residual traces of such a vision:

Even the open system pluralisms of [...] Lawson carry residual traces of this paradigmist vision, insisting that heterodox economics define itself as the Other of orthodox economics. This is Cold War paradigmism in a different guise but still the same oppositional project, with the same truncated pluralism: offering intellectual openness and respect to persons and arguments within our own paradigm communities but not to outsiders. To define heterodox economics in this way is to warrant the charge that heterodox economics has no positive identity, that it defines itself only in terms of what it is not, rather than in terms of what it is (Colander *et al.* 2004: 491). This keeps us in the reactive position of "permitting the mainstream to set the heterodox agenda for heterodox economics ... to define its structure and content" (King 2004). It also demonstrates that our professed commitments to pluralism are fundamentally ill-conceived, insincere, or both.

(Garnett 2006: 531–2)

### Paradigms and the like: a reply to Garnett

In response to Garnett, I must emphasize that it does not follow that, just because heterodoxy is characterized by its rejection of some orthodox doctrine, heterodox conceptions need be monolithic, monist, paradigmist, or whatever. In principle, such heterodox projects can be as small, partial, open, multifaceted, fragmented, transitory, and inclusive as you like. Having said that, I see nothing inherently anti-pluralistic about specific individuals exploring the possibility of creating a successful substantive paradigm of any sort.

Perhaps, though, it will be said that I am being less than pluralistic in supporting one specific social ontological conception above others. I hope it is clear that the conception I defend is consistent with many modes of explanation and forms of substantive theorizing. Indeed, I would describe my position as one that is, if ontologically bold, then epistemologically and substantively very cautious. But still some might worry that my defense of a specific ontology, and my resting my arguments for inter-, or across-, group collaboration upon it, constitutes an undesirably anti-pluralistic stance in itself.

I do not think it does though. No one is saying that alternative ontological conceptions are not possible. Clearly they are. And to the extent that competing conceptions are produced, the point, once more, is to do whatever it takes to encourage all parties to constructively engage. But if one ontological conception can be shown to be better grounded than available alternatives, is that not a reason for drawing on it? Would anyone counsel a different approach in any other walk of life? Yes, let us leave options open. Let us also (repeatedly) try out alternatives, where appropriate. Certainly, let us include everyone in the conversation, whether it is oriented to the nature of ontology, substantive work, the nature of pluralism or being pluralistic, or whatever, and seek to do so with respect for, and encouragement of, each other. But *if,* when the time comes to make use of an ontological conception, one such conception (whatever the focus) seems to be significantly more appropriate than others, not least because it is found to be far more explanatorily grounded, then it seems reasonable (for at least those that believe in it) to make use of the latter. This applies to our theories of the natures(s) of pluralism(s), of how we ought to be pluralistic, as well as to everything else.

Concerning Garnett's further point that to "define heterodox economics" in opposition to orthodoxy is to warrant the charge that heterodox economics has no positive identity, it does not follow for any heterodoxy characterized by its rejection of specific orthodox doctrine(s) that it must thereby be a purely reactive program, lacking identity and defining itself purely in terms of the orthodoxy. It does mean that heterodoxy can be *identified as heterodox* in virtue of the opposition (its nominal essence). But if the opposition is to a specific set of doctrines, rather than opposition for opposition's sake, there will typically be a determinate cause, or set of causes, of this opposition rooted in the nature of the opposed doctrine(s), revealing something more fundamental about the heterodoxy qua heterodoxy (its real essence).

And over and above any rejection of specific orthodox doctrine, including the reasons for this rejection, any heterodoxy or heterodoxies can be as complex and heterogeneous as you like. As a project in its own right, each separate heterodox grouping can have its own identity, set its own agenda, and be continually evolving. Moreover, this can be so even if, throughout this variety and evolution, a rejection of fundamental orthodox doctrine is sustained.

Now this, indeed, *is precisely my conception of the situation of modern heterodox economics*. As I understand it, heterodoxy is a (group of) project(s), each primarily motivated by its own agenda (not by any desire to oppose the mainstream per se), and each concerned with questioning social reality without supposing the latter's nature everywhere conforms to the closed worlds of isolated atoms that the mainstream insistence on formal modeling presupposes. More positively, my assessment is that contemporary heterodoxy is a set of projects concerned to develop substantive theories consistent with the sort of social ontology that I believe receives the most philosophical grounding.

As I say, only if it were the case that any opposition to orthodox doctrine was caused solely by a desire to be oppositional for opposition's sake irrespective of doctrine would it follow that heterodoxy is purely reactive. If some commentators do hold to such a conception of the heterodoxy of modern economics, I am not amongst them.

Rather, on my understanding contemporary economic heterodoxy possesses deep-seated and valid reasons for its enduring and widespread opposition to specific orthodox doctrine. But this is an *a posteriori* response to a mainstream insistence that methods other than mathematical deductivist modeling are inappropriate. If the relevant orthodox doctrine were to be abandoned, this would be reason for the traditional heterodoxy to abandon the heterodox ascription, not for its seeking some other doctrine to oppose, nor for its abandoning the constructive endeavor by virtue of which each division of this heterodoxy constitutes one particular heterodox group rather than another.

## Jeroen Van Bouwel

Somewhat more trenchant in his criticism is Jeroen Van Bouwel (2005). After distinguishing five different motivations for declaring oneself a pluralist (the ontological, the cognitive limitations, the historical and geographical, the pragmatic, and the strategic motivations), Van Bouwel worries about the motivation for my support for pluralism:

> Lawson's quest for heterodox economics is not so much focusing on elaborating compatibility and complementarity with *mainstream* (or neo-classical) economics, but rather creating his own alternative, that would be the new (monist) standard.
>
> If we call Lawson's contribution pluralist, as he does, we can distinguish two different forms or conceptions of pluralism. Firstly, Lawson's work is pluralist in the sense that it provides us with an alternative to the mainstream, and as such we have more than one alternative (hence we have plurality). Secondly, we can understand pluralism as engaging in a conversation, as exchanging ideas, and not merely developing different isolated (and essentially monist) alternatives.
>
> Lawson's account does not defend this second kind of pluralism. He does not develop a form of pluralism that shows how the different schools or alternatives can be used for different occasions. He rejects the *mainstream* completely, without considering possible positive contributions. He does not elaborate a form of pluralism that might show the complementarity of the schools or make us understand the origin of the differences between [them].
>
> (Van Bouwel 2005)

In his conclusion, Van Bouwel adds:

> I claim that a *really* pluralistic approach should engage in a conversation, in spelling out compatibilities and complementarities between the mainstream and the heterodox approaches (both sides should be engaged). The pluralism of Lawson risks leading us to an isolated diversity, to a lack of exchange of ideas.
>
> (Van Bowel 2005)

### Isolationism: a reply to Van Bouwel

As well as airing the concern (addressed in my responses to Davis and Garnett) that I discourage engagement with the mainstream, Jeroen van Bouwel further complains that my approach encourages an isolationist stance within the heterodoxy. According to Van Bouwel, specifically, I do not "develop a form of pluralism that shows how the different schools or alternatives can be used for different occasions," that I do "not elaborate a form of pluralism that might show the complementarity of the schools or make us understand the origin of the differences between [them]." I have actually had much to say on this not only in

*Reorienting Economics* (Lawson 2003a), but also in Lawson (2004, 2006a). Let me briefly outline my position.

The basic thesis I advance concerning the (traditional) heterodox projects is that they are actually best conceived as divisions of labor in one overall project. Remember I do not think the heterodox projects can be distinguished by the answers given (within any given tradition these are far too variable, both at any point in time and over time). Rather I argue that the individual heterodox traditions, like, I think, research endeavor in almost all other disciplines, are identifiable more by the sorts of questions asked (see Lawson 2003a, 2006a). It is with this understanding of heterodoxy in mind that we can view the separate traditions as divisions of labor.

Central to this interpretation is the ontological conception that I defend, one that I also believe these heterodox traditions mostly implicitly presuppose. This conception has many facets. Social phenomena are, for example, viewed as bearing emergent powers, being structured, open, processual, highly internally related, comprising value, carrying meaning, and so forth. The various heterodox traditions I believe are best viewed as exploring, if implicitly, specific aspects of this ontology (whilst maintaining a commitment to the whole).

Post Keynesians, for example, make fundamental uncertainty a central category. This clearly presupposes an ontology of openness as many post Keynesians have in recent years come increasingly to acknowledge. Such a focus has involved examining the implications of uncertainty or openness for the development of certain sorts of institutions, including money, for processes of decision-making, and so forth. At the level of policy, the concern may well include the analysis of contingencies that recognize the fact of pervasive uncertainty, given the openness of social reality in the present and to the future, etc. For those influenced by Keynes, especially, a likely focus is how these matters give rise to collective or macro outcomes, and how they in turn impact back on individual acts and pressures for structural transformation, etc. (see Lawson 1994, 2003a, chapter 7).

By similar reasoning, and as already noted earlier in this chapter, I believe that it is best to distinguish (old) Institutionalism, following Veblen especially, as concerned with the processual nature of social reality, and so as focusing especially on those forces working for stability and on others working for change. This orientation has taken the manifest form of a traditional concern with evolutionary issues, and with studying those aspects of social life that are most enduring, such as institutions and habits, along with those that are most inducing of continuous change, such as technology (see Lawson 2002, 2003a, chapter 8; 2003b, 2006b).

Feminist economics, I believe, is best distinguished in terms of a focus on social relationality. Relations of care are of course a central issue. But relationality in itself seems central to most feminist concerns. Very often feminist economists have identified their own project as one that first of all concerns itself with women as subjects (which may include, for example, giving attention to differences among women, as well as between genders) and takes a particular orientation or focus, namely on the position of women (and other marginalized groups) within society and the economy. In practice this project includes an attention to the social causes at work in the oppression of, or in discrimination against, women (and others), the opportunities for progressive transformation or emancipation, questions of (relations of) power and strategy, and so forth.[4]

Austrians may perhaps be best identified in some part according to their emphasis on the role of inter-subjective meaning in social life (see Lawson 1997, chapter 10), and so on.

I suggest, then, that at least some heterodox traditions are most easily viewed as primarily (though not exclusively) concerned with different aspects of the properties of social phenomena (openness, processuality, internal relationality) uncovered and explicitly systematized through philosophical ontology.

Others traditions, though, seem to be more interested in elaborating the nature of specific social categories, and in particular how the features uncovered through philosophical ontology (openness, relationality, process, etc.) coalesce in certain social items of interest within that particular tradition. An obvious example is Marxian economics, a project primarily concerned to understand the nature of the relational totality in motion that is capitalism. But we also find a significant Austrian interest in the nature of "the market process" and entrepreneurship in particular. And as already noted there is significant post Keynesian interest in the nature of money, institutionalist interest in institutions and technology, feminist interest in care, and so forth.

How does the current mainstream join the party? Clearly its *insistence* that mathematical deductivist methods be more or less always and everywhere used and by all of us, is ill fitted to this pluralistic picture. Of course, the argument that only formalistic methods be used can be heard, but there can be no compulsion for anyone to follow. But those who experiment with formalistic methods, without insisting that others always and everywhere do so, certainly have a place. It is my assessment that formalistic endeavor will likely be most fruitful where social conditions most approximate the atomistic ontology that such endeavor presupposes. In *Reorienting Economics* (chapter 1), I sketch the sorts of scenarios under which the emergence of such conditions appears most feasible and wherein, indeed, some successes seem occasionally to have been achieved.

I hope it is clear, then, that there is a place for more or less all types of existing research practice on the conception I defend; I am not at all advancing a vision of (or seeking to encourage) isolated practices.[5] To the contrary, according to the conception I am advancing it is actually vital that the various divisions perpetually keep in touch with each other's contributions and developments. For all are working on aspects of the same whole, and each tradition requires some understanding of the whole (and so of each other's contributions) in order to carry out its own division of labor competently.

## Conclusion

My view that heterodoxy is most appropriately identified through its opposition
to a specific orthodox doctrine does not, I believe, preclude or undermine the
possibility of maintaining pluralistic orientations of the sort that most seem to
concern Davis, Garnett, Van Bouwel, and others.[6] In fact, the realizing of a more
pluralistic discipline, I hope it is clear, is something towards which, in advancing
the position defended, I too aspire.

## Acknowledgments

I am grateful to Vinca Bigo and an anonymous referee for helpful comments on
an earlier draft.

## Notes

1 Typically, it is also held that each constituent or entity can be known only fallibly and
   partially, in various ways, under various competing descriptions, with all ways of
   knowing reflecting the situatedness and specific capacities of the "knower," etc.
2 For a listing of the program for the last ten years or so, including several presentations
   by Hahn, see www.econ.cam.ac.uk/seminars/realist/previous_workshops.htm.
3 Thus, I assume Davis does not mean politically conservative. Davis explicitly rejects
   the idea that we should relate distinctions in the sorts of economic programs pursued
   (and in particular any differentiations as to whether they are orthodox or heterodox) to
   political differentiations/allegiances.
4 In turn, of course, this focus, reflexively adopted, has come to affect the ways some
   feminists at least are committed to developing pedagogical approaches that acknowledge and explore (typically hierarchical) relations not just in society at large but also
   within the academy.
5 This indeed is something I have endeavored to emphasize over and again (see, for
   example, Lawson 2006a).
6 This is not, of course, to imply that things couldn't be improved (for an argument that
   heterodoxy could be more pluralistic, see Holcombe 2008).

## References

Arnsperger, C. and Varoufakis, Y. (2006) "What is Neoclassical Economics?" *Post-
   Autistic Economics Review*, issue 38, July: 2–13.
Colander, D., Holt, R.P.F., and Rosser, J. (2004) "The Changing Face of Mainstream
   Economics," *Review of Political Economy*, 16: 485–99.
Davis, J. (2006) "The Nature of Heterodox Economics," *Post-Autistic Economics Review*,
   issue 40, December 1, 23–30.
Erlich, B. (1986) "Amphibolies: On the Critical Self-Contradictions of 'Pluralism,'" *Crit-
   ical Inquiry*, 12(3), spring: 521–49.
Fine, B. (2006) "Critical Realism and Heterodoxy," unpublished paper, University of
   London, School of Oriental and African Studies.
Fullbrook, E. (2005) "The RAND Portcullis and PAE," *Post-Autistic Economics Review*,
   issue 32, July 5, Article 5.
——— (2006) "Paradigms and Pluralism in Heterodox Economics," *Review of Political
   Economy*, 18(4): 521–46.

Hahn, F. (1985) "In Praise of Economic Theory," the *1984 Jevons Memorial Fund Lecture*, London: University College.

—— (1992a) "Reflections," *Royal Economics Society Newsletter*, 77.

—— (1992b) "Answer to Backhouse: Yes," *Royal Economic Society Newsletter*, 78: 5.

Hodgson, G.M. (2006) "An Institutional and Evolutionary Perspective on Health Economics," unpublished paper, presented at the *Cambridge Realist Workshop*, November.

Holcombe, R.G. (2008) "Pluralism versus Heterodoxy in Economics and the Social Sciences," *Journal of Philosophical Economics*, 1(2): 51–72.

King, J.E. (2004) "A Defense of King's Argument(s) for Pluralism," *Post-Autistic Economics Review*, issue 25, March 18, 16–20.

Lawson, T. (1994) "The Nature of Post Keynesianism and its Links to other Traditions," *Journal of Post Keynesian Economics*, 16: 503–38. Reprinted in Prychitko, D.L. (ed.) (1996) *Why Economists Disagree: An Introduction to the Contemporary Schools of Thought*, New York: State University of New York Press.

—— (1997) *Economics and Reality*, London: Routledge.

—— (2002) "Should Economics Be an Evolutionary Science? Veblen's Concern and Philosophical Legacy," The 2002 Clarence Ayres Memorial Lecture, *Journal of Economic Issues*, 36(2): 279–91.

—— (2003a) *Reorienting Economics*, London: Routledge.

—— (2003b) "Institutionalism: On the Need to Firm up Notions of Social Structure and the Human Subject," *Journal of Economic Issues*, 37(1): 175–201.

—— (2004) "On Heterodox Economics, Themata and the Use of Mathematics in Economics," *Journal of Economic Methodology*, 11(3): 329–40.

—— (2005) "Reorienting History (of Economics)," *Journal for Post Keynesian Economics*, 27(3): 455–71.

—— (2006a) "The Nature of Heterodox Economics," *Cambridge Journal of Economics*, 30(2): 483–507.

—— (2006b) "The Nature of Institutionalist Economics," *Evolutionary and Institutional Economics Review*, 2(1): 7–20.

Lipsey, R. (2001) "Successes and Failures in the Transformation of Economics," *Journal of Economic Methodology*, 8(2): 169–202.

Van Bouwel, J. (2005) "Towards a Framework for Pluralism in Economics," *Post-Autistic Economics Review*, issue 30, March 21, article 3.

# 8 The Cambridge School and pluralism

*Vinca Bigo*

## Introduction

Economics has recently taken an "ontological turn," at least among its avowedly heterodox traditions. One group of researchers that has been very much involved in this is that referred to by various commentators as the "Cambridge School."[1] Central here is the ontologically oriented project instituted under the auspices of the *Cambridge Social Ontology Group* (or CSOG).[2] A key feature of the project is its conception and analysis of open and closed systems. The Cambridge School has done much to try and clarify and overcome problems encountered in the modern discipline of economics. In doing so, the Group draws extensively on the categories of open and closed systems. In particular, it utilizes the terms open and closed systems to reference relevant ontological and methodological distinctions and to voice specific criticisms of mainstream economics.

There are alternative approaches to utilizing the categories of open and closed systems in economics. Chick and Dow (2005) and Mearman (2005), for example, start out by examining how terms such as openness and closure are used in other disciplines. These authors do not centrally concern themselves with event regularities. Instead they explore the possibilities of introducing these terms and their given meanings in economics. Chick and Dow (2005: 364), for instance, examine the notions of open and closed systems found in the *Oxford English Dictionary*.

Contributors to the different positions openly profess a pluralistic orientation. Given the critical stance taken by the Cambridge School, some may (and do) doubt (the legitimacy of) its claim to pluralism. Such doubts will be encouraged by any explicit charges of lack of pluralism leveled at the Cambridge School. I am thinking perhaps especially those advanced by Mearman, an important contributor to the alternative approach to analyzing open and closed systems. Specifically, his concern is that the School's approach to defining open and closed systems results in methodological recommendations that are insufficiently pluralist in orientation.

To reassure Mearman and others who may reach similar conclusions, I shall concentrate my efforts here on dispelling what is essentially a misunderstanding of the Cambridge position. In doing so, I first provide an account of the conceptions of open and closed systems defended by the Cambridge Group. Second, I discuss the implications of these conceptions for pluralism. In particular, I show that neither the conceptions themselves, nor the methodological recommendations that follow, conflict with the Group's claim to adopting an overtly pluralist orientation.

## A dualistic conception?

In this section, I introduce the Cambridge Group's conceptions of open and closed systems. In the Cambridge conception, a *closure* is defined as a *system* in which event regularities occur. Note that the closure is *identified by* events and their regularities. The system is however not reducible to the events that occur in it. Event regularities here are a reference to an essential component of the explanatory approach referred to as deductivism. Specifically, deductivism is

> a type of explanation in which regularities of the form "whenever event x then event y" (or stochastic near equivalents) are a necessary condition. Such regularities are held to persist, and are often treated, in effect, as laws, allowing the deductive generation of consequences, or predictions, when accompanied with the specification of initial conditions. *Systems in which such regularities occur are said to be closed.*
>
> (Lawson 2003: 5, my emphasis)

The usefulness of deductivism requires that event regularities are ubiquitous:

> It is clear, in fact, that if the theory of explanation and science in question turns upon identifying or positing regularities of the form "whenever event x then event y" – let us refer to systems in which such constant conjunctions of events arise as *closed* – then a precondition of the universality, or wide applicability, of deductivism is simply that reality is characterized by a ubiquity of such closures.
>
> (Lawson 1997: 19)

Once we conceive of a closure in terms of events, specifically in terms of event, and specifically in terms of systems in which event regularity occurs, we can move to identify the (ontological) conditions under which such systems can be found. And indeed, a central feature of the Cambridge project has been to seek to identify conditions associated with closed systems. Two such conditions in particular have been singled out. They are the intrinsic and extrinsic closure conditions.

The intrinsic closure condition requires individuals or mechanisms to have a fixed internal structure, constraining them to act in identical ways in repeated conditions. Extrinsic closure lays down that such individuals or mechanisms in any theory act in conditions of relative insulation from, or are orthogonal to, other causal factors in play. When these two conditions are satisfied, an event regularity is the outcome; that is, when an intrinsically stable and isolated mechanism is "triggered" (and clearly the triggering is itself in effect part of any sufficiency conditions),[3] an event regularity is guaranteed. Let me turn for now, though, to Cambridge School's conception of an *open system*. Specifically, let me begin by focusing on Mearman's worry that the Cambridge Group defines open systems in a merely negative (and seemingly dualistic) fashion as "not closed."

Neither the Cambridge School, nor Lawson, defend a conception of openness that sustains (or grounds) this observation. Lawson presents what can reasonably be taken as corresponding to the Cambridge notion of openness, one that is not stated in terms of non-closure. Rather Lawson writes:

> According to the conception I defend social reality is open in a significant way. Patterns in events do occur. But where the phenomena being related are highly concrete (such as movements in actual prices, quantities of materials or outputs, and most of the other typical concerns of modern economic modellers), such patterns as are found, tend to take the form of *demi-regularities* or *demi-regs*, that is, of regularities that are not only highly restricted but also somewhat partial and unstable.
>
> (Lawson 2003: 79)

Here the conception of openness is not negative, but positive, in terms of the assortment of types of patterns that occur. However, while we can see the notion of an open system is not dualistic in the sense of defining the latter as merely not closed, it might still conceivably be misconstrued as dualistic if the category of open system disallowed *variations* of form.

The Cambridge Group does however allow for such variations. By analogy, we can think of a window as having many degrees of openness. The notion of openness defended by the Group is similarly one in which a specific domain of reality can assume any of numerous states of openness (characterized only in part by degrees of strictness of event patterns), but only one of closure (or two if we distinguish deterministic and stochastic closures, see Lawson 1997: 76). Again, as Lawson observes:

> The point that warrants emphasis is that just because universal constant conjunctions of the form "whenever event x then event y" are unlikely to be pervasive it does not follow that the only alternative is an inchoate random flux. These two possibilities – strict event regularities or a completely non-systematic flux – merely constitute the polar extremes of a potential continuum. Although the social world is open, certain mechanisms can dominate others over restricted regions of time-space, giving rise to rough-and-ready generalities or partial regularities, holding to such a degree that *prima facie* an explanation is called for.
>
> (Lawson 1994: 276)

The Cambridge notion is not dualistic either, in the sense of systems supporting only two types of event patterns. Having so far clarified the Cambridge definitions of open and closed systems, I address in the section below the worry that it may be insufficiently pluralist by way of methodological recommendations.

But before I do so, I want to discuss briefly how other scholars have contributed to, and worked with, the Cambridge School notions of openness and closure. Indeed, Lawson is not alone (as may seem from the quotes I have selected) in promoting their elaboration and their application. If features described are seen to vary across authors, they tend to represent not competing conceptions of closure, but rather assessments associated with, and typically sufficiency conditions, of a conception of closure held in common by the various contributors.

So, we find contributions to the Cambridge conception supplied by a range of heterodox economists, more or less associated, or somehow identifying, with the Cambridge position. These include Runde (1997), Fleetwood (1999), Northover (1999), Pratten (1996), Pinkstone (2002), Rotheim (2002), Downward (2003), Lewis (2004), Perona (2004), Bigo (2006),[4] and Lawson (2007). Some of these contributions work on clarifying the very notions of open and closed systems themselves, while others can best be noted for the application of the notions to specific domains in economics.

## Insufficiently pluralistic?

Of central importance to this chapter, is the seeming concern by some that the particular Cambridge conception of, and emphasis on, open and closed systems have the effect of polarizing methodological debate in economics, allegedly encouraging heterodox economists sympathetic to the Cambridge position to be overly dismissive of certain methodological approaches.

Typically, if a system is open in the sense described of not manifesting event regularities, then it will follow that certain methods will be unsuccessful for an analysis of the system. Put differently, the inherently open character of the (social) realm does not allow the engineering of closure conditions (unlike in the natural realm where controlled experiments are often feasible), so as to ensure the event regularities, which lend themselves to deductive analysis. The Cambridge Group assesses that making sense of the social world is possible, but (and I will return to this below) by other more productive means.

The Cambridge Group, as we saw above, notes that systems lie along a spectrum of possibilities where the *extremes* are either strict event regularities, or a complete non-systematic flux. If the Cambridge Group were to focus on only these extremes, finding all other states to be irrelevant to the study of the social realm, then it seems there would be a legitimate concern that the Group unduly restricts the range of possible methodologies it deems appropriate. Let me address this contention first (that the Cambridge theoretical orientation somehow encourages methodological polarization).

One of Mearman's central criticisms concerning the Cambridge School is indeed that it is too dichotomous in its methodological recommendations. In particular, according to Mearman, the School supposes that where a situation is regarded as open, methods that presuppose a closure are prohibited. Thus,

Mearman writes of the Cambridge analysis "rendering closed-systems methods totally impotent" (Mearman 2006: 63). Specifically:

> It is argued that the Cambridge school of [critical realism] in economics has tended to adopt a strategy of *rejection* of what shall be called here "closed-systems" methods, i.e., techniques which presuppose closure [...]. In contrast, this paper argues that a central tenet of an "open-systems methodology" is that it can still employ "closed-system methods," because the former will take seriously into account the weaknesses of the latter in open environments and employ them more cautiously and limitedly.
>
> (Mearman 2006: 68)

Actually, it may be that there are really two concerns being voiced here. One possible worry, the one just noted, is that the Group does not allow for variation in the choice of methods, strictly (and dichotomously) recommending one set of methods for closed systems, and insisting on another set specifically for open systems. This worry then lies especially in the failure by the Group to consider the (possible) appropriateness of methods that presuppose closures in studying open systems.

A second worry, implicitly voiced by Mearman, bears on the School's rhetorical (or presentational) orientation. The worry here seems to be that by defining open and closed systems in the way it does, the Cambridge Group creates a climate of intolerance. Specifically, it is perceived as dismissive of certain methods, and so as not being sufficiently inclusive in its orientation. Let me address this latter concern first.

The Group's orientation is specifically to avoid any recommendation that a method (or methodological orientation) be ruled out or insisted upon *a priori*. That is, the position is one that seeks to counter dogmatism. On such a count, it is held that mathematical-deductivist methods be retained (though not insisted upon), among the array of possible methods in the methodological toolkit, in case circumstances arise where they prove useful. This is clearly visible in the following passage:

> I am not at all suggesting that formalistic modeling methods should not exist among the battery of options available. My aim [...] is not to narrow down the range of methodological options by attempting to prohibit a particular method. Rather it is to widen the range of possibilities through criticizing the fact that, and manner in which, in many quarters at least, the particular method in question is currently and unthinkingly universalized.
>
> (Lawson 2003: 27)

Elsewhere (Bigo 2007), I too have defended such an orientation when seeking a deeper explanation for the seemingly pathological state of affairs of modern economics. The situation is one in which the mainstream entails that such methods be insisted upon to the exclusion of all others, when the same methods are recognized by some of its now more critical eminent proponents to be unrealistic and inadequate. The purpose of my critique is to try and move beyond the noted dogmatism, that is, beyond a situation in which all non-mathematical deductive methods are regarded as illegitimate in economics (Bigo 2007).

The Cambridge's School pessimism as to the usefulness of methods that presuppose closed systems to help illuminate political economy cannot be denied. The School's appraisal does not, however, in any sense impact on its pluralist orientation. It remains keen on, and actively encourages all approaches and forms of experimentation, and excludes none in the process (see Downward 2003).

But what about Mearman's first concern? Is the pessimism of the Group as to the appropriateness of mathematical deductive methods for the study of open systems ungrounded, unreflexively derived, so that it is unduly dismissive of these methods? In truth, there are several issues at stake here that need to be unpacked in order to clarify matters further.

First, according to the Cambridge approach, closures or closed systems do in fact have a place in the study of the social realm. In particular, the School considers them relevant and useful in the context of one of its key contributions: *contrast explanation.* This is a kind of explanation appropriate to phenomena that arise in a social world that is both open and complex. It focuses on situations that challenge our pre-existing beliefs, and typically cause us to be surprised that things are not as we expected. The question is then "why x rather than y?" (rather than "why x?").

Where, for example, we find people with very similar skills receiving different salaries, so that there seems no justification for the discrepancy. In such cases, we will find it useful to look for how persons receiving lower pay differ from those with higher pay. By taking the latter as the "control" group, we may find that persons with lower pay are, by contrast, women (as opposed to men), or black (as opposed to white), or of a different religion, and so on. By focusing on surprising contrasts, we can establish and explain how gender, race, looks, and so on, underpin unexpected differences in patterns, as we have come to know them.

In doing so, we take the objects to which the phenomena relate (say skilled persons) to have sufficient in common, that is, their *causal histories* to be sufficiently similar, to expect a shared pattern of outcomes to be manifest among them. And a significant variation in outcomes typically leads us to find there is a need to revise our prior understanding of things, and so to seek to uncover causal mechanisms that explain the surprising observations.

My point is that in pursuing contrast explanation, a regularity or closure of sorts is often taken for granted. We suppose in this specific example that "whenever a person's skill is x, they receive a salary of roughly y" (perhaps especially if they work for the same company). As indicated above, this sort of regularity is referred to by the Cambridge Group as a demi-regulariy, or a so called demi-reg. This kind of regularity is of no practical relevance to economic modeling, however. For modeling, the concern is only to seek to minimize the significance of breakdowns as irrelevant or "insignificant" to regularities sought. What is of interest to contrast explanation is the breakdown of closures, not their continuance (over space and time), even though a regularity of sorts is initially presupposed to get the explanatory process on its way.

Typically, in economic modeling events are seen to stand in *each other's* causal history (corresponding to the occurrence of closures of causal sequence), such as, say, consumption and income. Instead, for contrast explanation to get under way, similar outcomes are interesting when they can be seen to have *similar or shared* causal histories in particular contexts (corresponding to the occurrence of closures of concomitance). It follows from their shared histories that such outcomes can rightfully be compared when closures break down (see e.g., Lawson 2003, chapters 1, 2, and 4).

Put differently, the Cambridge Group is only initially concerned with the regularities in event patterns associated with closures of causal sequence, such as, say, status and pay. In other words, for surprise to occur, some expectation of regularity, of mechanism expected to be in play and manifest in outcomes, is presupposed. But it is a scenario contrary to expectations, and so surprising, that is, of particular interest. We see here that there is a place for closures of sorts, in the way the Group proposes that political economy be made sense of.

A second point of clarification as to the Cambridge stance on closed systems is that, for closures to warrant modeling and prediction, an event regularity of a stricter sort than is usually encountered in the social realm is sought both in the way of past occurrence and prediction. The Group has devoted considerable time and effort in examining how methods presupposing such closures might in fact prove useful to the study of social reality. And so, accordingly, in a move to embrace alternatives, the School certainly has not dismissed these methods out of hand. Indeed in *Economics and Reality*, Lawson does address the question at length having suggested (in the same book) that *"the single most important question facing the advocate of mainstream economics"* is how such models can help us understand reality despite being necessarily unrealistic in their construction (Lawson 1997: 109).

Lawson does investigate at some length the circumstances in which models that presuppose closed systems may be useful, for example, as potential temporary heuristic devices in the context of methods of successive approximation. This, Lawson observes, may in fact be so under two conditions: "(1) that the factors considered in 'isolation' be real causal factors, structures and/or transfactually acting mechanisms or tendencies; and (2) that the effects of the factors so considered in 'isolation' combine or interact mechanically" (Lawson 1997: 129). In such cases, the models may be used to generate a partial picture in the context of the method of theoretical isolation. Equally though, Lawson notes that these conditions are rarely if ever encountered in the social realm, so explaining why the methodology typically proves unsuccessful.

If the Cambridge Group is pessimistic in there being a relevant use for methods presupposing closures to advance our understanding of social matter, it is certainly not the case, I hope to have shown, that the Group constructs a rigid rhetoric, defines openness only negatively, does not itself use methods that pre-suppose closures of sorts, or does not actively examine the ways in which mode-ling might be useful after all. There is clearly no *a priori* stance defended that warrants casting the Group as insufficiently pluralist in its orientation.

## An actively pluralist orientation

It remains the case that the mainstream economics project is not in a healthy state, that eminent persons in this grouping recognize this to be so themselves. In other words, we start with a state of affairs that is the *a posteriori* failing of the deductivist approach in economics, combined with the imposition of these methods in the economics academy at large, a state that is remarkably anti-pluralist.[5]

Once more, the Cambridge Group supports the exploring of all possible explanatory approaches that seek to further our understanding of the social world. And the Group remains most interested in approaches that prove success-ful, including any mathematical deductive methods, in explaining economic phenomena.

I have thus far defended the Cambridge School and shown that if it is insuffi-ciently pluralist it is not because of its particular conceptualizations of open and closed systems, or due to the recommendations that follow from these. Let me now though briefly indicate how the School can in fact be seen to adopt an actively pluralist stance.

It is both because methods of mathematical deductivist modeling are more or less exclusively insisted upon in mainstream economics, and because the latter group dominates the economics academy, that the Cambridge School is con-cerned with identifying and clarifying the usefulness of these methods. And it is a major contention of the Cambridge School that an essential feature of these methods is that they presuppose closed systems. Thus the identification of closed systems in terms of events and their regularities is fundamentally a project to reinstate pluralism in modern economics. Central to this project is (1) an argu-ment to the effect that explanatory success seems most likely in conditions where the methods employed are appropriate to the nature of the object under study, and crucially (2) an insistence that all methods be allowed into the eco-nomics toolbox, that no method should be ruled out *a priori*, or absolutely. So while the worries Mearman voices appear to be ungrounded, the two tenants that are a key feature of the Cambridge project make the latter not only ontological, but in addition, inherently and decisively pluralist in its orientation.

## Other conceptions

Others, as noted earlier, are equally concerned with adopting a pluralist orienta-tion in the economics academy. Their starting point is not, however, open and closed systems, and the associated dominance of methods presupposing the ubiquity of the latter. Rather, others have become aware of the rise in debates on open and closed systems in the economics academy, a turn of events largely due to Lawson, and the further efforts of the Cambridge Group. They can be seen in this context to explore *possible* meanings assigned to such systems. In doing so, they draw on other literatures and explore their meaning in other disciplines.

There are indeed other ways of defining open and closed systems than the one adopted by the Cambridge School. For example, the important contribution of Chick and Dow (2005) also employs the categories of openness and closure. However, their orientation is not primarily motivated by a concern with mainstream economic methodology and its long standing insistence on mathematical deductive modeling. Clearly, we can reasonably expect there to be some motivation grounding the choice to define systems in a particular way. A number can be envisaged, some less arbitrary than others.

Specifically, when Chick uses the idea of closed systems thinking, she clearly has a different notion of closed systems in mind than the one advanced by the Group (Chick 2003). Her conception is more akin to a non-open-mindedness than anything specifically to do with event regularity. I have myself addressed the lack of open-mindedness associated with mainstream economists who can be seen to insist on deductivist methods (Bigo 2007). But in doing so, the conception of closure, as defended by the Cambridge School, is a key feature of my analysis, for it allows me to identify the distinguishing (methodological) feature of the community, before moving on to provide a psychological explanation for the insistence on these methods in the face of their recognized inadequacy (as indeed a form of closed-mindedness, but "closed" in a very different sense to the Cambridge conception).

In truth, the Cambridge Group does not need the current categories of open and closed systems to sustain its project. For the Group is, with a view to instilling greater pluralism in economics, especially concerned with pointing to a state of affairs characterized by a dominance of methods that presuppose event regularities of a particular sort, and that seek, in using these methods, to make predictions. The concern in all this is then to show that such an insistence is not only anti-pluralist, but that it is, in addition, ungrounded, because it is inconsistent with the nature of the object under study (specifically with the nature of political economy).

The difference between the Cambridge School in its conception of systems and other approaches does not lie in their respective degree of pluralism. Instead, the former is centrally concerned with challenging the dominance of inadequate methods, by way of explaining their inadequacy, and further to transform the anti-pluralist state of affairs. In doing so, the School seeks a dialectical resolution of what it understands and characterizes as a conflict in methodological approaches (whether in terms of particular method or in terms of diversity), between mainstream and heterodox economics. As such, the Cambridge Group is inherently dialectical in its orientation.

Other approaches seem less concerned with the resolution of specific problems or tensions, and more concerned with an exploration and broadening of the range of available conceptions of open and closed systems, as an endeavor in its own right. As such, they can be best described as being more analytical in their approach.

## Final comments

I have attempted to clarify the contributions of the Cambridge School in respect of open and closed systems, and where the literature has engaged with it, to dispel important misunderstandings. In particular, I have addressed and corrected Andrew Mearman's claim that the Cambridge School's use of these categories is non-pluralistic in that they only serve to polarize methodological research and debate.

More positively, I hope to have shown how the Cambridge Group has adopted a conception of open and closed systems that is actually specifically designed to counter the lack of pluralism in economics. I maintain this, not least because the Cambridge School's conception of systems stems from a concern to clarify the usefulness of methods that dominate the economics academy. What is more, the Group can be seen to actively engage in a most supportive and inclusive manner with a variety of approaches and subject matters concerned with the study of political economy (see for example, the contributions of Fleetwood 1999; Northover 1999; Lewis 2004; Perona 2004; or Lawson 2006).

The more significant difference between the Cambridge approach and the one preferred by the likes of Mearman, Dow, and Chick is not bound up with plural-ist orientations, or lack thereof. Instead, it seems the difference is largely one of *strategy*. That is, the latter seek to explore existing classifications of systems, and find ways of applying these to economics, whereas the Cambridge School's strategy is keenly motivated by a perceived need to counter the allegedly anti-pluralist stance and state of mainstream economics. In particular, it seeks to chal-lenge the dominance of, and insistence upon, the *a priori* use of one methodological approach only; that only mathematical methods be counted as "proper" economics. As such, the Cambridge School can be seen to hold fore-most in its concerns the achievement, or reinstatement, of pluralism in modern economics.

## Notes

1 See for example Mearman (2006).
2 See for example the references provided in Lawson (2003).
3 Though in the social realm the triggering of mechanisms or processes will typically not be optional.
4 In a recent contribution, I provide an in-depth clarification of what is meant by the Cambridge School's conceptions of open and closed systems, seeking to dispel persist-ing misunderstandings that prevail or may arise (Bigo 2006). This follows earlier con-tributions, such as by Pratten (1996), who takes the notions of closure and openness and applies them to Neo-Ricardian Economics and Post-Keynesianism by way of sys-tematizing their respective world views (or ontological presuppositions), where such views can further be seen to bear on their more substantive theorizing. Elsewhere, Rotheim (1998) also applies the notions to Post-Keynesian approaches in economics.

Openness, following the Cambridge conception, is especially relevant in that it closely relates to the Post-Keynesian notion of and preoccupation with uncertainty. So, in his contribution Rotheim uses the Cambridge conceptions to render more explicit presuppositions reflected in this particular school of thought. Not unrelatedly, Rotheim (2002) and Bigo (2007) draw on the same understanding of closure and openness, pointing out how the openness of the world can be anxiety provoking. Specifically, each after their own fashion argues that in attempting to understand the complexities of political economy, a defense mechanism to cope with anxiety may involve the misconceiving of open systems as closed, so drawing on methods that similarly presuppose closures. Still elsewhere, Perona (2004) uses the Cambridge notions of open and closed systems to better understand the concept of complexity in economics. In a book edited by Lewis (2004), various authors, including Lewis himself, explicitly draw on the Cambridge conception of open and closed systems in grounding their understanding of political economy. Lawson (2007) develops a theory of technology, in which artefacts are understood as produced through a process of isolation (in closed systems), while re-embedded for use or application in open systems.

5  The Cambridge group thus seeks to challenge the mainstream's insistence on methods that by many of its own prominent proponents have been portrayed as inadequate and unrealistic. Thus Nobel Memorial Prize winner in Economics, Milton Friedman (1999: 137) finds that "Economics has become increasingly an arcane branch of mathematics rather than dealing with real economic problems." Similarly, a second Nobel winner, Ronald Coase (1999: 2) writes that "Existing economics is a theoretical [meaning mathematical] system which floats in the air and which bears little relation to what happens in the real world." And a yet further Nobel winner, Wassily Leontief (1982: 104) complains that "Page after page of professional economic journals are filled with mathematical formulas" [and that these lead us from] "entirely arbitrary assumptions to precisely stated but irrelevant theoretical conclusions"; that mathematical methods are everywhere employed in economics, "without being able to advance, in any perceptible way, a systematic understanding of the structure and the operations of a real economic system." In summing up this situation, Mark Blaug (1997: 3) has reason to formulate matters starkly: "Modern economics is sick. Economics has increasingly become an intellectual game played for its own sake and not for its practical consequences for understanding the economic world. Economists have converted the subject into a sort of social mathematics in which analytical rigor is everything and practical relevance is nothing."

# References

Bigo, V. (2006) "Open and Closed Systems and the Cambridge School," *Review of Social Economy*, 64(4): 493–514.

—— (2007) "Why is Mainstream Economics So Mathematical: A Psychological Assessment," unpublished paper, Cambridge University.

Blaug, M. (1997) "Ugly Currents in Modern Economics," *Options Politiques*, September: 3–8.

Chick, V. (2003) "The Future is Open: On Open-System Theorizing in Economics," paper presented at conference on Economics for the Future, Cambridge University.

Chick, V. and Dow, S. (2005) "The Meaning of Open Systems," *Journal of Economic Methodology*, 12 (3): 363–381.

Coase, R. (1999) "Interview with Ronald Coase," *Newsletter of the International Society for New Institutional Economics*, 2 (1): 3–10.

Downward, P.M. (ed.) (2003) *Applied Economics and the Critical Realist Critique*, London: Routledge.

Fleetwood, S. (ed.) (1999) *Critical Realism in Economics: Development and Debate*, London: Routledge.

Friedman, M. (1999) "Conversation with Milton Friedman," in Snowdon, B. and Vane, H. (eds) *Conversations with Leading Economists: Interpreting Modern Macroeconomics*, 124–144, Cheltenham: Edward Elgar.

Lawson, C. (2007) "Social Constructivism, Critical Realism and Technology," unpublished paper, University of Cambridge.

Lawson, T. (1994) "A Realist Theory for Economics," in R. Backhouse (ed.) *New Directions in Economic Methodology*, 257–285, London: Routledge.

—— (1997) *Economics and Reality*, London: Routledge.

—— (2003) *Reorienting Economics*, London: Routledge.

—— (2006) "The Nature of Heterodox Economics," *Cambridge Journal of Economics*, 30(2): 483–507.

Leontief, W. (1982) "Letter," *Science*, 217: 104–107.

Lewis, P. (2004) "Transforming Economics? On Heterodox Economics and the Ontological Turn in Economic Methodology," in P. Lewis (ed.) *Transforming Economics: Perspectives on the Critical Realist Project*, 1–32, London: Routledge.

Mearman, A. (2005) "Sheila Dow's Concept of Dualism: Clarification, Criticism and Development," *Cambridge Journal of Economics*, 29(4): 619–634.

—— (2006) "Critical Realism in Economics and Open Systems Ontology: A Critique," *Review of Social Economy*, 64(1): 47–75.

Northover, P. (1999) "Evolutionary Growth Theory and Forms of Realism," *Cambridge Journal of Economics*, 23(1): 36–63.

Perona, E. (2004) "The Confused State of Complexity in Economics: An Ontological Explanation," paper presented at the Facultad de Ciencias Economicas, Universidad Nacional de Cordoba.

Pinkstone, B. (2002) "Persistent Demi-Regs and Robust Tendencies: Critical Realism and the Singer–Prebisch Thesis," *Cambridge Journal of Economics*, 26: 561–583.

Pratten, S (1996) "The 'Closure' Assumption as a First Step: Neo-Ricardian Economics and Post-Keynesianism," *Review of Social Economy*, 54(4): 423–443.

Rotheim, R. (ed.) (1998) *New Keynesian Economics/Post Keynesian Alternatives*, London: Routledge.

—— (2002) "Timeful Theories, Timeful Economists," in P. Arestis, M. Desai, and S. Dow (eds.) *Methodology, Microeconomics and Keynes*, 62–72, London: Routledge.

Runde, J. (1997) "Abstraction, Idealization and Economic Theory," in P. Arestis, G. Palma, and M. Sawyer (eds.) *Markets, Unemployment and Economic Policy: Essays in Honor of Geoff Harcourt*, Vol. 2, 16–29, London: Routledge.

# Part II

# Pluralism and real-world economies

# 9 America beyond capitalism
## The Pluralist Commonwealth

*Gar Alperovitz*

Is it possible to conceive in serious and practical terms an "America beyond Capitalism" (*ABC*)? The following presents a summation of the pluralist systemic argument of my recent book of this title, with an elaboration of certain key points related to larger system goals and outcomes as well as to problems of political-economic context and possibility (Alperovitz 2006a).[1] Just below the surface level of media attention, theorists, policy makers, and informed citizens have been generating an extraordinary range of new ideas in recent decades. It is possible to bring together critical elements of the evolving foundational thinking, and project and extend others, to define the underlying structural building blocks of a democratic political-economic system "model" that is different in fundamental ways from both traditional capitalism and socialism.[2]

*ABC* holds that we face a long-term (and unusually structured) systemic crisis, not simply a political crisis. From any serious historical perspective the long-term trends are ominous: there is now massive evidence that for decades Americans have been steadily becoming *less* equal, *less* free, and *less* the masters of their own fate. Although we may experience momentary periods of important renewal, *ABC* argues that the emerging era is one in which truly fundamental values – equality, liberty, meaningful democracy, ecological sustainability – are all likely to be increasingly thwarted by real-world trends. Given the emerging constraints on traditional politics, it suggests, both serious liberal reform and genuine conservatism are likely to falter. In addition to growing social and economic pain, given the failing long-term trends related to equality, liberty, and democratic capacity, it holds that we are beginning to enter a sustained period in which the classic elements of a legitimation crisis appear to be slowly coming to the fore.

One of the critical points to grasp is that the American labor movement has long been in the process not simply of decline, but of radical decline. This, along with America's unusual racial and ethnic divisions, is a key reason why the book judges (after allowing for certain definable exceptions like health care) that most progressive social-democratic proposals based on European precedents are unlikely to be achieved in more than marginal ways in the United States. Although I would welcome whatever can be done, *ABC* argues that the traditional hope of reforming capitalism in general following the best liberal welfare state and corporatist precedents is not likely to be realized.

The book's central argument also rests on the judgment that we face a crisis which is not easily described in conventional or classic terms: The system may not be capable of fundamental reform; but it also unlikely to collapse. What we are already beginning to experience, *ABC* suggests, is a process of slow decay, one in which reform achieves sporadic gains, but the long-term trends of growing inequality, economic dislocation, failing democratic accountability, deepening poverty, ecological degradation, greater invasions of liberty (and growing imprisonment, especially of minorities) continue to slowly and quietly challenge belief in the capacities and moral integrity of the overall system and its governing elites. Surveys demonstrate that whereas 40 years ago three out of four believed the government does what the citizens wish, now roughly three out of four believe it does what the rich, the corporations, and the special interests urge.

It is quite possible, *ABC* suggests, that a sustained process of occasional gain, large-order stalemate, and failing belief will simply mean the continuation of long-term decay: Rome declined. Period. That there might also be other possibilities is the central thesis of the book.

## A Pluralist Commonwealth

The central question at the heart of *ABC* is whether it is feasible even in theory to develop an institutional architecture that allows for true democratic control of the political-economy. The book answers in the affirmative, but stresses that the problem is far more challenging than is commonly understood. Among other things it points out that the two main traditional capitalist strategies for controlling corporate behavior – anti-trust and various forms of regulation – are both deeply compromised: The attempt to use the former is almost a forgotten relic of history. And repeated studies of "regulatory capture" have shown that various forms of regulation are commonly narrowed, and often redirected, by the powerful corporate interests they seek to control. In socialist systems, many studies also demonstrate that in practice powerful institutional economic actors commonly dominate planning and other policy mechanisms.

What long-term structural arrangements might in principle be capable of achieving and sustaining the key values? *ABC* accepts the traditional socialist argument that democratic control ultimately will require some form of social ownership of significant industry. But this is hardly sufficient: The first question is "what form?" The second and third are: "What else would be required?" And: "Are there any real-world experiences which suggest the practicality and feasibility of a new approach?"

*ABC* argues that what is actually happening "on the ground" in a number of key areas involves the build-up of a mosaic of entirely different institutions that suggest the direction of new answers – and, further, a process which at this stage of development is both peaceful and evolutionary. At the heart of the emerging model is the principle that ownership of the nation's wealth must ultimately be shifted, institutionally, to benefit the vast majority – and in ways which draw upon and extend what is already happening in diverse areas.

The fact is literally thousands of real-world efforts that illuminate how alternative wealth-holding principles can work in practice have developed in communities throughout the nation over the last several decades. The range of social or common ownership models suggest a pluralist vision which may ultimately nurture greater diversity, decentralization, and democratic control of crucial economic institutions and processes. It might accordingly be called a "Pluralist Commonwealth."

*ABC* also holds that larger-scale industry will ultimately require new institutional forms. Here it also proposes a diverse and pluralist institutional model. In some areas, traditional public ownership will be appropriate. In Medicare and Medicaid we already have a nationalized partial health insurance system, and this is ultimately likely to be expanded. European experience provides numerous other practical public ownership precedents to draw upon and it underscores the obvious fact that private U.S. corporate control is not the only practical economic option.

*ABC* (23–27, 70–80) further suggests that in connection with a number of large industries the most appropriate structure of ownership is something close to that suggested by Nobel Laureate James Meade some time ago and a variation suggested by John Roemer more recently. In the first instance this involves establishing some form of national "Public Trust" or other agency which would own major controlling interests (ultimately perhaps nearly all stock) in very large corporations. Within a new public investment framework different groups of investment managers would compete with each other in managing chunks of the public portfolio (as investment managers commonly do today in both private and public pension fund investing). Larger ecological and other non-economic criteria for investment would be set by government trustees, in a manner analogous to the kinds of criteria that are imposed today in California by the California Public Employees' Retirement System (CalPERS).

Such strategies, though modest and flawed in their current limited range of demands, have demonstrated a growing capacity to bring together economic efficiency and larger political goals. They also maintain the market mechanism and competition. Critical from the perspective of longer term democratic control are the possibility they suggest for a system of public accountability and transparency – and the accrual of major portions of profits to the public.[3] Precedents also exist in the way the Swedish and Norwegian governments organize a substantial share of their present holdings. "Sovereign fund" investment management by other nations owning large shares of U.S. corporations suggests additional possible precedents.

*ABC* argues that for many industries there is no way around something like the Public Trust form of social ownership as a first approximation. However, it suggests that such a mechanism alone – a partial analog for large industry to some "market socialist" models – would hardly be adequate to achieve democratic accountability. The power of large enterprises – and of the market – would likely continue to substantially dominate even a fully realized system of public ownership of this kind.

Countering this power requires the *systematic* development of local democratic experience, along with its precondition: community economic stability. *ABC* gives great emphasis to the strategic arguments of earlier theorists like de Tocqueville and John Stuart Mill, and of modern theorists like Jane Mansbridge, Steven Elkin, and Benjamin Barber, who hold that over the long haul only if a strong and participatory version of democratic experience is nurtured at the local level can there ever be a strong and participatory capacity for democratic control in the nation at large.

Partly to achieve such objectives – but for much larger reasons as well – the model stresses the need to steadily develop new local ownership institutions, especially worker-owned and other community-benefiting firms. Most important are enterprises that are practical, anchored locally, and which either alter inequality directly or use profits for public or quasi-public purposes (or both). Employee-owned firms, co-ops, neighborhood-owned corporations, and a wide range of municipal and social enterprises, along with municipal and state investing agencies, are among the key locally based institutions of the "Pluralist Commonwealth" articulated in *ABC*.

## An emerging new mosaic

*ABC* spends a great deal of time on the issue of practicality. As noted, it emphasizes that key elements suggesting some of the outlines of what a new system would ultimately require are already discernable in American practice – if one takes the time to look. *ABC* provides information on the nearly 10,000 employee-owned firms now operating in the United States, on co-ops (more than 130 million members), on neighborhood corporations (4,600), and on numerous quasi-public land trusts and municipal businesses (including 2,000 public electric utilities), etc. It suggests that these and related efforts, including state and municipal investment strategies, already provide a practical basis for building toward an expanding decentralized, socially owned, public and quasi-public sector, and – along with public pension fund management – for learning the principles and practicalities of larger public efforts which might build upon these as time goes on. The quiet development of a mosaic of entirely different institutions suggests the possibility of an evolutionary process which, if extended and refined, points in the direction of a pluralist model organized around the principle that ownership of the nation's wealth must ultimately be shifted, institutionally, to benefit the vast majority.

### *Worker-owned firms*

That individuals work harder, better, and with greater enthusiasm when they have a direct interest in the outcome is self-evident. The obvious question is: why aren't large numbers of businesses organized on this principle? The answer is: roughly 10,000 are. Indeed, 11.2 million Americans now work in firms that are partly or wholly owned by the employees, three million more than are members of unions in the private sector (Bureau of Labor Statistics 2008, Table 3; National Center for Employee Ownership 2008).

Appleton (Co.) in Appleton, Wisconsin (a world leader in specialty paper production) became employee-owned when the company was put up for sale by Arjo Wiggins Appleton, the multinational corporation which owned it – and the 3,300 employees decided they had just as much right to buy it as anyone else (Appleton Ideas 2006; Dresang 2001). Reflexite, an optics company based in New Avon, Connecticut, became employee-owned in 1985 after 3M made a strong bid for the company and the founding owners, loyal to their workers and the town, chose to sell to the employees instead (Case 1992). W.L. Gore – the maker of Gore-Tex apparel – has been owned, since 1974, by (currently 8,000) worker-owners in 45 locations around the world (W.L. Gore and Associates, 2008).

Although there are 300–500 traditional worker co-ops, most worker-owned businesses are organized through "Employee Stock Ownership Plans" (ESOPs). Technically an ESOP involves a "Trust" which receives and holds stock in a given corporation on behalf of its employees. What is positive about this mechanism is that it offers major tax benefits for the creation of large numbers of worker-owned firms – especially when an original owner retires and decides to sell to the employees. What is negative is that although there are exceptions, in the main the ESOP form is not at this stage organized democratically.

Several considerations suggest, however, that greater democratic control of ESOPs is likely to develop: First, many ESOP companies – more than 25 percent according to one report (Wirtz 2007) – are already majority-owned by workers. Of these, the National Center for Employee Ownership estimates 40 percent already pass voting rights through to plan participants. Second, as workers accumulate stock their ownership stake tends to increase. Annual ESOP Association member surveys indicate that in 1982 only 20 percent of ESOP Association member companies were majority ESOP-owned companies; by 2000, that figure was 68 percent (Democracy Collaborative 2005: 59).

It is conceivable that as more and more ESOPs become majority-owned, workers will simply ignore the fact that some have little power. On the other hand, the more likely probability – as *Business Week* observed in 1991 – is that ultimately workers "who own a significant share of their companies will want a voice in corporate governance." In Ohio a survey completed in the mid-1990s found that employee ownership was becoming more democratic over time, with three times as many closely held companies passing through full voting rights to ESOP participants as had occurred in a previous 1985–86 survey (*Business Week* 1991; Logue and Yates 2001).

## Municipal enterprises

An extraordinary range of local municipal efforts embodying Pluralist Commonwealth wealth-related principles also exist. One of the most important areas of activity is land development. As early as 1970 the city of Boston embarked on a joint venture with the Rouse Company to develop the Fanueil Hall Marketplace (a downtown retail complex). Boston kept the property under municipal ownership. One study estimates that in the project's first decade the city took in 40 percent more revenue than it would have collected through conventional property tax (Frieden and Sagalyn 1989: 169). Entrepreneurial "participating lease" arrangements for the use of public property are now common. Alhambra, California, for instance, earns approximately $1 million a year in rent revenues from a six-acre holding it leases to commercial tenants (Williamson *et al.* 2002: 158).

A fast-growing arena of new activity involves Internet and related services. In Glasgow, Kentucky the municipally owned utility offers residents electricity, cable, telephone services, and high speed Internet access – all at costs lower than private competitors. The city also has access to an "intranet" which links local government, businesses, libraries, schools, and neighbors (Glasgow Electric Plant Board 2007). Tacoma, Washington's broadband network "Click!" also offers individuals and private companies Internet and cable service; as does Cedar Falls, Iowa (Cedar Falls Utilities 2008; Click! Network 2007). More than 700 public power utilities have equipped their communities with such networks (American Public Power Association 2008).

Municipalities have also been active venture capital investors, retaining publicly owned stock in businesses that hold promise for the city's economy. A survey conducted in 1996 found more than a third of responding city governments reported venture capital efforts of one kind or another (Clarke and Gaile 1998: 72, 79–86). During the 1990s the publicly owned New York Power Authority and two private companies formed a joint investment pool of $60 million which yielded $175 million at the end of the first five years of operation. (Brodoff Communications 2000). Many smaller cities have created local venture funds that make investments in the $500,000 to $2 million range (Loague 2004; Clarke and Gaile 1998: 84).

Municipally owned sports teams are also widespread. Communities which own (or have owned) minor league baseball teams include Indianapolis, Indiana; Rochester, New York; Franklin County (Columbus), Ohio; Lucus County (Toledo), Ohio; Harrisburg, Pennsylvania; Lackawanna County (Scranton), Pennsylvania; and Visalia, California (Mahtesian 1996: 42–45; Imbroscio 1998: 239–240). At the major league level, the Green Bay Packers are owned by a nonprofit corporation whose stock-holders are mainly city residents.

Other areas of innovation include health services and environmental management. Denver Health is a municipal enterprise which has transformed itself from an insolvent city agency ($39 million in debt in 1992) to a competitive, quasi-public health-care system ($54 million cash reserves in 1997) delivering over $2.1 billion in care for the uninsured over the last ten years (Moore 1997; Denver Health 2008). Denver Health operates a satellite system of eight primary care centers and 12 school-based clinics and employs some 4,000 Denver area residents (Denver Health 2008; Nuzum *et al.* 2007).

Hundreds of municipalities also generate revenues through land-fill gas recovery operations which turn the greenhouse gas methane (a by-product of waste storage) into energy. Riverview, Michigan, one of the largest such recovery operations, illustrates the trend. Riverview's sale of gas for power production helps produce enough electricity to continuously power over 5,000 homes. Royalties covered initial costs of the effort in the first two years of operation and now add to the city's cash flows (DTE Energy Company 2007; EPA 2007).

## Building community: neighborhoods and nonprofits with a mission

The neighborhood-based Community Development Corporation (CDC) combines the community-serving mission of a nonprofit organization with the wealth-building and ownership capacities of an economic enterprise. The CDC is a hybrid self-help entity that operates at both the community-building level and the economic level, and exhibits micro-level applications of Pluralist Commonwealth principles.

The Bedford-Stuyvesant Restoration Corporation (BSRC) – a CDC developed in the 1960s with the bipartisan support of then Senators Robert F. Kennedy and Jacob Javits – helped set the terms of reference for an institution which can now be found in thousands of communities: In its initial 15 years of operation BSRC developed some 3,000 units of residential and commercial property and provided start-up capital and other assistance to more than 125 local businesses, maintaining thereafter a revolving loan fund. The CDC also launched a major commercial development (Restoration Plaza) – including a 214-seat theater, retail attractions, and office space – as well as a property management company, and a construction firm (Pratt Center 1994).

Another leading example is New Community Corporation (NCC) in Newark, New Jersey – a CDC which employs 2,300 neighborhood residents and generates roughly $200 million in economic activity each year. Profits help support day-care and after-school programs, a nursing home, and four medical day-care centers for seniors (Rusch 2001: 5; Guinan 2003). NCC also runs a Youth Automotive Training Center; young people who complete its courses are guaranteed jobs offering $20,000-plus starting salaries (Rusch 2001).

Since the 1960s 4,600 neighborhood-based CDCs have come into being in American communities. Most are not nearly as large and sophisticated as the leaders, but all employ wealth-related principles to serve "small publics" in geographically defined areas. The assets they commonly develop center above all on housing, but many also own retail firms and, in several cases, larger businesses (National Congress for Community Economic Development 1999: 3; Sirianni and Friedland 2001: 59).

Other nonprofit organizations have picked up on the underlying principles of development (Emerson 2003; Massarsky and Beinhacker 2002). A leading example is Pioneer Human Services (PHS), in Seattle, Washington. Initially established with donations and grants, PHS is now almost entirely self-supporting. PHS provides drug- and alcohol-free housing, employment, job training, counseling, and education to recovering alcoholics and drug addicts. Its annual operating budget of nearly $60 million is 99 percent supported by fees for services or sales of products. PHS's various social enterprises employ nearly 1,000 people and include a light metal fabricator employing theoretically unemployable people, which manufactures parts for Boeing and other customers; a Food Buying Service which distributes food to other non-profit organizations; and two restaurants (Pioneer Human Services 2005; Dubb 2006).

A *Chronicle of Philanthropy* study estimates that over $60 billion was earned from business activities by the 14,000 largest nonprofits in 1998. Income from fees, charges, and related business activities are estimated in other studies to have grown from 13 percent of nonprofit social service organization revenues in 1977 to 43 percent in 1996 (Lipman and Schwinn 2001; Salamon 1999: 177; Strom 2002).

### State and national innovators

A number of larger efforts based on Pluralist Commonwealth principles have also emerged in recent years, especially at the state level. Particularly interesting are a group of sophisticated developments that point in the direction of practical – even dramatic – applications of the most radical and far-reaching system-wide Commonwealth strategies.

Historically several states have had considerable experience with significant scale efforts. For instance, the state-owned Bank of North Dakota – founded in 1919 – currently manages nearly $2 billion in assets (Bank of North Dakota 2003, 2001: 3). The Wisconsin State Life Insurance Fund has assets of over $75 million and has coverage in force totaling over $200 million (Wisconsin Legislative Audit Bureau 2002; Williamson *et al.* 2002: 154). More recent developments include venture capital initiatives in more than half the states which involve direct public investment and ownership in companies by state agencies (Heard and Sibert 2000: 48–49). A typical example is Maryland's Enterprise Investment Fund, which provides promising high-tech start-ups with up to $500,000 in capital in exchange for the state receiving equity shares and a guarantee from the firm that it will continue to operate in Maryland for at least five years.

At the Federal level, public ownership of stock in specific corporations is also a long-established (if little discussed!) tradition. In the post-9–11 airline bailout, for instance, the Bush Administration demanded a ten-year option to purchase a third of America West's stock at $3 per share in exchange for Federal loan guarantees (Kesmodel 2002; Wong 2003). Similarly, in 1980 as part of a $1.5 billion loan guarantee for the Chrysler Corporation the government received 14.4 million warrants (representing 10 to 15 percent of Chrysler stock). Again, in 1984, the government through the FDIC took a controlling ownership position (over 80 percent) in connection with the $8-billion bailout of Continental Illinois Bank. Other precedents can be traced back to World War II (Reich and Donahue 1985: 178, 186, 254–257).[4]

We may add to this list the long experience with public ownership the federal Tennessee Valley Authority and port authorities have throughout the nation. (Williamson *et al.* 2002: 158).

Perhaps of greatest significance – and suggestive of future possibilities – are federal, state, and municipal public employee retirement system boards. Prior to the 2008–2009 stock market collapse, these institutions controlled roughly $3 trillion in total assets (Barrett and Greene 2007). At the national level the Federal Reserve Board manages a pension fund of this kind, and more than 2 million Federal employees are involved in a similar public pension program which owns and manages over $200 billion (Financial Markets Center 2000: 1–9; Thrift Savings Plan 2008; U.S. Census Bureau 2003: table 521). Critically, many public pension funds have begun to explore new ways to use their ownership position for public purposes. For instance, in California CalPERS directly invested $8.3 billion in the state's economy in 2006 (Lifsher 2007). CalPERS also emphasizes information disclosure and the independence of boards of directors – and it enforces transparency, environmental performance, and other standards in many of its international investments (California Public Employees Retirement System 2008; Nesbitt 2001).

The state of Alabama also actively pursues Pluralist Commonwealth-related strategies. Retirement Systems of Alabama (RSA) – which manages the state employee and teachers' pension system – has invested in numerous local Alabama industries, in some cases also helping create worker-owned firms (Williamson *et al.* 2002: 182). An even more suggestive effort is the Alaska Permanent Fund which invests a significant portion of revenues derived from oil development on behalf of citizens of the state. In 2000, a high payout year, each individual state resident, as a matter of right, received dividends of just under $2,000 (almost $10,000 for a couple with three children) (Alaska Permanent Fund Corporation 2008).

CalPERS, RSA, and related efforts offer precedents for using public ownership strategies to achieve greater public oversight of corporate practices, and to help achieve state and community economic goals. The Alaska Permanent Fund takes us one step further: It is an on-the-ground operating system which demonstrates the feasibility of the kinds of far-reaching Public Trust proposals which might ultimately be advanced at the national level. Although each approach differs in specifics – and are at this stage incomplete – all are based on the principle that capital can and should be accumulated and managed in socially accountable ways.

It is also important to note that many of these emerging ownership-altering forms of wealth have demonstrated a capacity to develop much broader political support than most realize. Though they have progressive redistributive and community-building impact, *at the local level* they are rarely divisive. Because of their practical problem-solving capabilities they are often supported by independents and even moderate Republicans – a fact that also suggests political possibilities for splitting traditional conservative political groupings. Many "community-wealth" initiatives also resonate with new ecologically serious approaches to "the commons," and to the larger principles of sustainability.

## An evolving, reconstructive perspective on the future

*ABC* argues that ultimately there cannot be effective democracy – hence, control of major economic actors – unless inequality is altered in fundamental ways. It points out that for many years attempts to achieve significant positive improvement via traditional tax-and-spend strategies have been largely blocked; the main battle has involved attempts to reverse Bush era tax reductions. Changing the ownership of capital to benefit both workers and (local, state, and national) publics is important for distributional reasons as well as to negate the power associated with private corporate ownership. None of the existing models, of course, are adequate at this stage of development. The question is whether over time they might provide precedents for – and a basis upon which to build – more fully realized efforts.

Other longer term requirements include major "populist" forms of taxation which challenge the top 1–3 percent of elites who also own most of the nation's investment capital – in part for distributive reasons, in part to sharpen issues of capital ownership. *ABC* reviews various income and wealth taxation proposals aimed at complementing the social ownership strategy and radically altering the distribution of income and wealth. *ABC* also points to several little noticed state efforts which have shown that taxation of elites can be popular (169–181).

Reallocating capital and income in the direction suggested by the model is critical, ultimately, to re-allocating time free from the pressure of long work hours. This in turn is also the key to nourishing a citizenry with sufficient time to participate meaningfully in democracy – and thereby control any large order political-economic system (including the Pluralist Commonwealth). Time not hedged in by necessity of work is also a fundamental long-term condition of liberty, and of allowing the individual to make truly free choices (28–34). Finally, greater free time is one of the strategic keys to altering traditional male–female work–family roles (197–213).[5]

This overview of the various Pluralist Commonwealth elements is best understood as a sketch of the "structural girders" of an alternative system – i.e., the underlying institutional power arrangements of the political economy. *ABC* does not deal directly with the problem of economic planning, or more precisely, the relationship of planning and market. The main reason is related to the book's central argument about power and democracy: Any planning system will be compromised, the book holds, unless it deals explicitly with how to constrain the power of large economic institutions. All too many discussions of planning simply ignore underlying questions of institutional power. *ABC* urges that local democratization, decentralization, and time are *necessary* conditions of large-order system-wide democratization in general and planning in particular. It urges attention to *these* problems as a first priority.

On the other hand, it is clear that the development of a planning system is necessary in any fully realized political-economy. Such a system would likely also draw upon and use market arrangements in certain sectors. The most intriguing questions are: (1) how various sectors (e.g., health, energy, education, perhaps transportation, etc.) might be dealt with in evolutionary sequence; and (2) how technological progress might permit greater free time. Structures and processes in these and other areas might be expected to evolve as increasing priority is given to issues of planning, of individual fulfillment, and ultimately of a cooperative and community-serving culture. The title of the book was carefully chosen; it is about a stage of development we might reasonably term America *"Beyond Capitalism"* – not (yet) about a possibly more radically expansive America that might be built upon the foundations which currently evolving efforts establish.

Given the book's analysis of the dead-ends now facing most traditional strategies, a truly central question, *ABC* stresses, is whether Americans can achieve a practical and common-sense understanding of the traditional socialist principle that some form of social, public, or quasi-public ownership of capital is both necessary and possible. In the absence of this understanding, it holds, we cannot expect to move beyond the difficulties now facing traditional social democratic politics in many countries, and progressive efforts in the United States. *How* to achieve widespread public understanding of the importance of changing the ownership of capital to other social, economic, and planning goals is a key question – one that has hardly been broached by progressive theorists and activists. If changing the ownership of capital is important, then precisely *how* is this idea to be demonstrated and conveyed to large numbers of Americans in everyday life?

*ABC* returns again to practical experience to answer this question. It emphasizes the need to expand on real-world forms that embody social ownership principles. Without the development of such principles and "knowledge" in day-to-day experience, *ABC* argues, it is difficult to imagine further progress towards larger forms, or to a politics which builds on this principle. Most Americans have been taught to think of social ownership as inherently inefficient, undemocratic, even tyrannical. In the near term, the various practical efforts the book reports upon may be as important for what they teach about possibilities as what they accomplish in altering major trends. In this sense they are both precedents and instruments of popular education which help teach the practicality and common-sense nature of new principles. They may also slowly help build and nourish a larger community-building and more cooperative culture.

*ABC* stresses that the fiscal crisis, on the one hand, and globalization, on the other, are forcing ever greater attention to neighborhood, municipal, and other forms of enterprise which produce income flows for services – and to employee-owned firms and other institutions which anchor jobs in local communities threatened by global trade disruption. Not only are such efforts already politically viable; over time, there are reasons to believe they could become major (viable) large-order political responses to these two ever-increasing challenges. The new forms introduce into everyday life a set of political-economic principles, and they also help solve pressing immediate problems – thereby expanding political support. In this respect, again, the book's emphasis is on the next major step "beyond," not (yet) what might ultimately be achieved building forward on the basis of the emerging phase of development.[6]

Other aspects of *ABC*'s "phasing" and developmental understanding of long-term change which point in the direction of a larger vision include an emphasis on state and regional initiatives – especially as Congressional deadlocks continue both to frustrate efforts at reform, and to drive policy down to state and local decision, a condition that may persist even with a Democratic president and Congress, given the ability of 41 Senators to block most legislation through fili-buster tactics. Regional-level policy development in the direction of the larger model suggested by *ABC* is also already occurring in areas like New England, and in regional-scale states like California.[7]

*ABC* concludes with an assessment of longer term opportunities for building the political and social support needed for any serious strategy. Possibilities for future change building beneath the seemingly quiescent surface are suggested by the Civil Rights, Feminist, Environmental movements – and also by the development from a once very marginal position of modern Conservatism. All began to take form at a time when there were few reasons to believe they might achieve serious momentum. A quietly building grass-roots politics of movement-building is already evident in many parts of the country, and – as various global and domestic problems continue to multiply – a more tumultuous, ardent, and energized era of change could ultimately give new power to a serious longer term pluralist vision.

The concluding argument is straightforward (234–237):

> The first decades of the 21st century are likely to open the way to a serious debate about these and other systemic questions – and, further, that real world conditions during the coming period are likely to offer possibilities for establishing substantial foundations for a longer term systemic trans-formation thereafter.
>
> The prospects for near term change are obviously not great – especially when such change is conceived in traditional terms. Indeed, although there may be an occasional important "progressive" electoral success, there is every reason to believe that most of the underlying trends will continue their decaying downward course.
>
> On the other hand, fundamental to the analysis presented in the preceding pages is the observation that for precisely such reasons we are likely to see an intensified process of much deeper probing, much more serious political analysis, and much more fundamental institutional exploration and develop-ment. We have also noted that there are important signs of change in the tra-ditional "laboratories" of democratic process…
>
> Few predicted either the 1960s or the conservative revolution which fol-lowed. Major eruptions and political realignments are the rule, not the exception in American history. Large numbers of working Americans, blacks and Hispanics who will become a majority as the century develops, senior citizens (and those who will shortly become seniors), women who seek practical ways to achieve thorough-going gender equality, liberals and conservatives alike who value family and community, environmentalists who cannot secure protections either for endangered goals or sustainable

growth along current lines of development – all are finding it increasingly difficult to realize their objectives through traditional means.

None of this is to predict the inevitability of major positive change. On the other hand, history suggests that those who assume that nothing fundamental can ever change have repeatedly been wrong. It is appropriate – even urgent – that we clarify the principles and content of what might ultimately become the basis of a serious pluralist vision. Finally, of course, most of the immediate institutional and policy efforts which could help lay groundwork for (possible) longer term change would be useful to undertake no matter what – especially given the decaying failures of traditional approaches.

## Notes

1  Certain aspects of the discussion of public enterprise and of planning go beyond *ABC* and reflect subsequent research. My thanks to David Ferris and Steve Dubb for their help in preparing sources and other materials used in this chapter.
2  See Part I of *America beyond Capitalism*, which brings together several key theoretical discussions and provides references to the growing literature.
3  For a more extended discussion, see Part I of *ABC* (and the summary on pp. 233–234).
4  The Chrysler bailout legislation also required Chrysler to create an ESOP. See Logue and Yates (2001: 85).
5  *ABC* also stresses the importance of economic security, smaller scale governance, local community support, some degree of independent entrepreneurial possibility, and intermediate units of political power. All, I argue, would ultimately be required to round out an institutional and systemic capacity to meaningfully sustain liberty.
6  Socialists may also find of some interest in this regard various reports of Marx's view that a different non-revolutionary path to fundamental change might be feasible in the United States, Britain, and possibly the Netherlands. See Avineri (1969: 215–216).
7  In Alperovitz (2007 and 2006b), I note how developments at the state and local level during the 1920s became precursors of major national New Deal policies and how important new regional ideas have evolved in recent years.

## References

Alaska Permanent Fund Corporation (2008) "Permanent Fund Dividend Program." Available at www.apfc.org/alaska/dividendprgrm.cfm?s=4 (accessed May 15, 2008).
Alperovitz, G. (2007) "California Split," *New York Times*, February 10: A15.
—— (2006a) *American beyond Capitalism: Reclaiming Our Wealth, Our Liberty and Our Democracy*, Hoboken, NJ: John Wiley & Sons, Inc.
—— (2006b) "Another World Is Possible," *Mother Jones*, January/February: 66–69, 77.
American Public Power Association (2008) *Quick Summaries of Major Issues*, Washington, DC: APPA. Available at http://appanet.org/pressroom/index.cfm?ItemNumber=17 992&navItemNumber=21052 (accessed February 25, 2008).
Appleton Ideas (2006) "All About Appleton." Available at www.appletonideas.com/ Appleton/jsps/ourcompany.do?langId=-1&catalogId=239327&storeId=139327 (accessed February 25, 2008).
Avineri, S. (1969) *The Social and Political Thought of Karl Marx*, Crawley, UK: Cambridge University Press (Bookprint Limited).

Bank of North Dakota (2003) "Annual Report, 2002," Bismarck, ND: Bank of North Dakota. Available at www.banknd.com/pdf/BND2002AnnualReport.pdf (accessed May 15, 2008).

—— (2001) "Annual Report, 2000," Bismarck, ND: Bank of North Dakota. Available at www.banknd.com/pdf/BND_ANNUAL_REPORT_2000.pdf (accessed May 15, 2008).

Barrett, K. and Greene, R. (2007) "The $3 Trillion Challenge," *Governing*, 21 (1): 26–32. Available at www.governing.com/articles/0710pension.htm (accessed June 17, 2008).

Brodoff Communications (2000) *"Giuliani Administration to Reinvest in Successful High-Tech Venture Capital Fund*, New York, NY: Brodoff, July 18. Available at www.brodoff.com/pressreleases_08.htm (accessed June 17, 2008).

Bureau of Labor Statistics (2008) "Union Members in 2007." Available at www.bls.gov/news.release/History/union2.txt (accessed February 25, 2008).

*Business Week* (1991) "The Real Strengths of Employee Ownership," July 15: 156.

California Public Employees Retirement System (2008) "Facts at a Glance: Corporate Governance" (June 2008), Available at www.calpers.ca.gov/eip-docs/about/facts/corpgov.pdf (accessed June 12, 2008).

Case, J. (1992) "E.O.Y. 1992: Collective Effort," *Inc.*, 14(1): 32.

Cedar Falls Utilities (2008) "About the Communications Utility." Available at www.cfunet.net/commun/index.htm (accessed June 12, 2008).

Clarke, S. and Gaile, G. (1998) *The Work of Cities*, Minneapolis: University of Minnesota Press.

Click! Network (2007) "About Us." Available at www.click-network.com/AboutUs/tabid/88/Default.aspx (accessed June 12, 2008).

Democracy Collaborative (2005) *Building Wealth: The New Asset-Based Approach to Solving Social and Economic Problems*, Washington DC: The Aspen Institute.

Denver Health (2008) "About Denver Health." Available at www.denverhealth.org/portal/AboutDenverHealth/DenverHealthOverview/tabid/267/Default.aspx (accessed June 12, 2008).

Dresang, J. (2001) "It's A Gamble on Paper," *Milwaukee Journal Sentinel*, November 11: 1D.

DTE Energy Company (2007) "DTE Biomass – Success Stories." Available at www.dtebe.com/stories/index.html (accessed June 17, 2008).

Dubb, S. (2006) Interview of Mike Burns, CEO, Pioneer Human Services, March 9, College Park, MD: Democracy Collaborative.

Emerson, J. (2003) "Total Foundation Asset Management: Exploring Elements of Engagement within Philanthropic Practice," Stanford Graduate School of Business Research Paper No. 1803 (February). Available at https://gsbapps.stanford.edu/researchpapers/library/RP1803.pdf (accessed June 17, 2008).

EPA (2007) "Landfill Methane Outreach Program – City of Riverview." Available at www.epa.gov/landfill/res/riverview.htm (accessed June 17, 2008).

Financial Markets Center (2000) "Uncivil Service: Pension Rebellion Stirs the Fed," *FOMC Alert*, 4(5): 1–9.

Frieden, B. and Sagalyn, L. (1989) *Downtown, Inc.*, Cambridge: MIT Press.

Glasgow Electric Plant Board (2007) "FAQ." Available at www.glasgowepb.net/faq.html (accessed June 17, 2008).

Guinan, J. (2003) Interview of Mary Abernathy of New Community Corporation, August 26, Washington, DC: National Center for Economic and Security Alternatives.

Heard, R. and Sibert, J. (2000) *Growing New Businesses with Seed and Venture Capital: State Experiences and Options*, Washington, DC: National Governors Association.

Imbroscio, D. (1998) "Reformulating Urban Regime Theory: The Division of Labor between State and Market Reconsidered," *Journal of Urban Affairs*, 20 (3): 239–240.

Kesmodel, D. (2002) "United Holds Loan Talks With Feds," *Rocky Mountain News*, April 13: C1.

Lifsher, M. (2007) "Study Touts CalPERS' Benefit to Economy," *Los Angeles Times*, September 19.

Lipman, H. and Schwinn, E. (2001) "Nonprofit Groups Reap Billions in Tax-Free Income Annually," *Chronicle of Philanthropy*, October 18: 25–27.

Loague, D. (2004) "Enterprising Capital: Bringing the Knowledge-Based Economy Home," *Economic Development America*, Spring: 16–18.

Logue, J. and Yates, J. (2001) *The Real World of Employee Ownership*, Ithaca, NY: ILR Press.

Mahtesian, C. (1996) "Memo to the Cities: If You Can't Bribe the Owner, Maybe You Can Buy the Team," *Governing*, 9(6): 42–45.

Massarsky, C. and Beinhacker, S. (2002) "Enterprising Nonprofits: Revenue Generation in the Nonprofit Sector," Yale School of Management – The Goldman Sachs Foundation Partnership on Nonprofit Ventures. Available at www.ventures.yale.edu/docs/Enterprising_Nonprofits.pdf (accessed May 12, 2008).

Moore, J.D. (1997) "Denver Role Model," *Modern Healthcare*, 27(15): 68.

National Center for Employee Ownership (2008) "A Statistical Profile of Employee Ownership." Available at www.nceo.org/library/eo_stat.html (accessed February 25, 2008).

National Congress for Community Economic Development (NCCED) (1999) *Coming of Age – Trends and Achievements of Community-Based Development Organizations*, Washington, DC: NCCED.

Nesbitt, S. (2001) "The 'CalPERS Effect' on Targeted Company Share Prices," *Directorship*, 27(5): 1–3.

Nuzum, R., McCarthy, D., Gauthier, A., and Beck C. (2007) *Denver Health: A High-Performance Public Health System*, New York, NY: The Commonwealth Fund.

Pioneer Human Services (2005) *2004 Annual Report*, Seattle, WA: Pioneer Human Services.

Pratt Center for Community Development (1994) "Bedford Stuyvesant Restoration Corporation (BSRC), Brooklyn, NY," *Community Development Corporation (CDC) Oral History Project*, Brooklyn, NY: Pratt Institute. Available at www.prattcenter.net/cdc-bsrc.php (accessed June 11, 2008).

Reich, R. and Donahue, J. (1985) *New Deals: The Chrysler Revival and the American System*, New York: Times Books.

Rusch, K. (2001) *The Emerging New Society*, College Park, MD: The Democracy Collaborative.

Salamon, L. (1999) *America's Nonprofit Sector: A Primer*, Second edition, New York: The Foundation Center.

Sirianni, C. and Friedland, L. (2001) *Civic Innovation in America*, Berkeley: University of California Press.

Strom, S. (2002) "Nonprofit Groups Reach for Profits on the Side," *The New York Times*, March 17: 1, 32.

Thrift Savings Plan (2008) *Thrift Savings Plan Highlights*, January–February. Available at www.tsp.gov/forms/highlights/high08a.pdf (accessed June 17, 2008).

U.S. Census Bureau (2003) *2002 Statistical Abstract of the United States*, Washington, DC: U.S. Bureau of the Census.

Williamson, T., Imbroscio, D., and Alperovitz, G. (2002) *Making a Place for Community: Local Democracy in a Global Era*, New York: Routledge.

Wirtz, R. (2007) "Employee Ownership: Economic Miracle or ESOPs Fable?" *The Region* (June), Minneapolis: Federal Reserve Bank of Minneapolis.

Wisconsin Legislative Audit Bureau (2002) "An Audit of the State Life Insurance Fund," Report 02–18 (November). Available at www.legis.state.wi.us/lab/PastReportsByDate.htm (accessed May 15, 2008).

W.L. Gore and Associates (2008). "About Gore." Available at www.gore.com/en_xx/aboutus/index.html (accessed February 25, 2008).

Wong, W. (2003) "US Airways Makes Cuts and Leave Bankruptcy," *The New York Times*, April 1: C3.

# 10 From competition and greed to equitable cooperation

## What does a pluralist economics have to offer?

*Robin Hahnel*

If I could add a second subtitle to my recent book, *Economic Justice and Democracy: From Competition to Cooperation* (Hahnel 2005), it would be *"Speaking Truth to Ourselves."* The truth is that we did not do well in the twentieth century. By "we" I mean all who seek economic justice, economic democracy, and environmental preservation – both those of us who hope to eventually replace capitalism with a different system of economic cooperation to achieve those goals, and also those who accept a system dominated by corporations and driven my market forces, but seek to make it more humane. All of us – progressive activists and academics alike – have failed miserably over the past quarter century. While there was notable progress during the middle third of the twentieth century, it now appears that those few decades may have been an anomaly, not the trend we once so innocently presumed could be relied upon to continue.

The truth is that after three decades of defeats, the progressive economic movement is arguably worse off at the beginning of the twenty-first century than it was at the beginning of the twentieth. Moreover, we have hastened many of our own defeats through misconceptions about capitalism, lack of clarity about what economic justice and economic democracy require, ill-conceived programs and strategies, and seriously flawed visions of more desirable alternatives. This chapter addresses three areas in which we need to shed debilitating misconceptions and develop a better understanding, namely: (1) the nature of the epic struggle we are engaged in, (2) the necessity as well as the pitfalls of organizing for economic reforms within capitalism, and (3) the importance as well as the limitations of "pre-figurative" organizing.

## Understanding the nature of the struggle

The idea that capitalism contains *internal contradictions* which act as seeds for its own destruction is simply wrong and needs to be discarded once and for all. Encouraged by Marxist economists many twentieth-century activists sustained themselves emotionally and psychologically with false belief that capitalism's dynamism and technological creativity would prove to be its undoing as well as its strength. Marx's labor theory of value led him to believe that when capitalists substitute dead labor, i.e. capital, for living labor this would eventually produce a *tendency for the rate of profit to fall*. For over a hundred years some Marxist economists predicted that this tendency would eventually give rise to a system-threatening crisis once all the *counteracting tendencies* played themselves out, and many progressive activists wondered if every crisis that came along was "the big one." But in 1961 a Japanese political economist, Nobuo Okishio, published a theorem proving if the real wage remained constant any labor-saving, capital-using technical change that lowered production costs would raise, not lower the rate of profit in the long run. In other words, labor-saving, capital-using technical change does nothing, in and of itself, to depress the rate of profit in capitalism.

Marx also predicted *crises due to underconsumption*, as competition drives individual capitalists to reduce wages of their employees and increase their accumulation out of profits, thereby increasing overall production at a pace he suggested would eventually outstrip aggregate consumption demand. Paul Baran and Paul Sweezy revived this theory as a centerpiece of the "monopoly capital" school of Marxism in the 1960s (Baran 1957; Sweezy 1966). But once again, more rigorous theoretical modeling has shown that there is no inherent tendency within capitalism to generate an ever-widening gap between all that can be produced and the demand necessary to purchase it. Macroeconomic models of growth and distribution pioneered by Donald Harris, Stephen Marglin, Lance Taylor, and others over the past three decades have moved us beyond underconsumption crisis literature that was less rigorous and more conjectural (see Harris 1978; Marglin 1984; Taylor 2004). In its totality the newer literature demonstrates conclusively that *at a theoretical level*, the relationship between aggregate demand and supply is no more or less problematic in the long run than it is in the short run.

Of course many heterodox schools never subscribed to these "deterministic" theories of capitalist crisis in the first place, and most Marxists who once did have reformulated their theories as possibilities rather than inevitabilities. Moreover, since crises do occur in capitalist economies all the time, and since mainstream economic theory goes to great lengths to disguise and ignore their possibility, it is useful for heterodox economists to remind everyone that there is always danger of crisis in the financial sector, that there is no guarantee that desirable levels of aggregate demand will materialize spontaneously, and that sectoral imbalances frequently occur. Post Keynesian economists, for instance, have focused much needed attention on problems that arise when disequilibrating forces within and between markets render mainstream theories and models that assume markets reach their equilibria irrelevant.

But explaining why crises are possible in a market system driven by competition and greed, and demonstrating how government policies can reduce the likelihood and severity of crises can all be done in a straightforward manner without any of the mysterious innuendo associated with analyzing capitalism as a system "plagued by internal contradictions." Similarly, explaining why a system centered on a conflict of interest between employers and employees over how to divide the net product of the labor of the latter induces the former to go on investment strikes whenever workers win wage increases causing a *profit squeeze* need not be dressed up in the language of a "fundamental contradiction." And finally, explaining why neoliberal capitalism is likely to be more inequitable, less sustainable, and more inefficient than social democratic capitalism can all be done without recourse to complicated theories of "social structures of accumulation" which depart from an unwarranted assumption that capitalists will always seek to replace a structure whose rate of accumulation is lower with one whose rate is higher.[1] In short, there is still an air of mystery and pretentiousness about much of heterodox economics that is unwarranted and renders valuable insights less accessible to activists in progressive economic movements.

If the "plagued by internal contradictions" conceptualization is unwarranted and unhelpful, what is a more accurate and useful understanding of capitalism? What is true about capitalism is that despite impressive technological advances that should dramatically improve our lives, *laissez faire* capitalism will not satisfy today's need for basic economic security for most of the Third World and a growing underclass in the advanced economies. What is true is that despite the fact that scientists are capable of devising technologies that would allow us to protect the natural environment, neoliberal global capitalism will unleash unthinkable environmental catastrophes within the next hundred years. What is true is that the new era of global, Robber Baron capitalism in which financial capital reigns virtually unrestrained will continue to cause financial crises that destroy the livelihoods of billions who live in developing economies, and increase the economic insecurity of the majority who live in developed economies. What is true about the present course of global capitalism is that it will doom most to struggle harder than their parents to meet their economic needs, while a tiny, privileged minority accumulates fabulous wealth at an accelerating rate.

What is also true is that even when capitalism is tamed by a full panoply of social democratic reforms – even when there is a social accord between labor and capital, the financial sector is subject to prudent regulation, aggregate demand is managed competently, sectoral imbalances are reduced, and funding is adequate to support a humane welfare safety net – capitalism still will not satisfy the desire for self-managed, meaningful work that an increasingly educated populace will demand, nor satisfy our longings for community, dignity, and economic justice. And while reforms within capitalism can slow the pace of environmental destruction, they will never render capitalism environmentally sustainable. In other words, not even a fully reformed capitalism can provide economic democracy, economic justice, and environmental sustainability.[2]

Nor, unfortunately, does capitalism nurture the seeds of its own replacement in ways many once believed it would. It does not generate a growing, homogeneous, working class whose economic activities lead them to see the advantages of seizing and managing the means of production themselves. Instead capitalism pits different segments of the working class against one another and teaches all whom it disenfranchises that they are incapable of making good decisions and should be thankful that their fortunes ride on the decisions of their betters.

Capitalism rationalizes exploitation, fosters commercial values and behaviors, and propagates alluring myths about its desirability and inevitability. A transition to the economics of equitable cooperation, however, requires dispelling myths about the virtues of free market capitalism, challenging the legitimacy of all forms of exploitation, rejecting commercial values to embrace human values, and developing efficient democratic and cooperative patterns of behavior. Since these positive behaviors are penalized rather than rewarded by market competition, capitalism creates more obstacles for those seeking to tame it or replace it than our twentieth-century forebears expected, and leaves more hard swimming against the current than they dared to believe.

During the second half of the second millennium A.D., the political sphere of social life witnessed an epic struggle between tyranny and freedom – followed by a continuing struggle between elite political rule versus democratic rule. There has been a similar struggle going on in the economic sphere of social life – a struggle between the economics of competition and greed and the economics of equitable cooperation. Beside the rapid technological changes that distinguish the capitalist era – many of which were, indeed, wonderful advances, even if some will prove less so with hindsight – people have struggled over *how* to organize divisions of labor that improve the efficacy of our economic sacrifices. On the one side we have seen institutions grow that seek to organize our increasingly specialized economic endeavors based on a system driven by competition, greed, and fear, along with ideologies that preach the necessity and advantages of doing so. On the other side we have seen resistance to this epic trend. We have seen struggles of different kinds and sizes against the ravages of competition and greed and the misery, inequity, wastefulness, and inefficiency it creates. We have seen intellectual critiques of its destructive dynamics. We have seen theories developed that insist there *is* another possibility – that the human species is not so socially feeble that we cannot organize a productive division of labor in a system of equitable cooperation. And we have seen not just "macro" projects attempting to replace the economics of competition and greed with the economics of equitable cooperation, we have witnessed hundreds of millions of "micro" attempts to do so as well.

This understanding of capitalism and the struggle we are engaged in suggests we see ourselves as engaged in a struggle that is centuries old – a tug of war between those who would further refine and consolidate the system of competition and greed that has been spreading its sway for almost five centuries, and those who oppose its spread and struggle to achieve a more equitable system of economic cooperation. Naturally those who pull for the economics of competition and greed are usually those who enjoy more of the benefits and less of the burdens it distributes, while those pulling for equitable cooperation are often victims of the system of competition and greed.

Not surprisingly, the rope has sometimes moved slowly in one direction and sometimes in the other over the past five hundred years, sometimes lurched quickly, and sometimes remained stuck for a time. Not surprisingly some strategies and tactics for pulling the rope have proven more critical and decisive than others at particular junctures. And we should really not be surprised to discover that every once in a while when we thought we had achieved a significant lurch in the direction of equitable cooperation, we later discovered that we had grossly deceived ourselves. In contrast, the conception of capitalism as a system plagued by internal contradictions provides very little guidance for progressive behavior that I can see, and may be counterproductive if people conclude that only a priesthood can delve the mysteries of capitalism and there is little for anyone to do except adopt the role of spectator.

Seeing ourselves in a centuries old tug of war between two different ways of organizing our collective economic endeavors not only provides a guide for behavior it affects expectations. It suggests that the transition from the economics of competition and greed to the economics of equitable cooperation will prove less abrupt and decisive than many of our forebears believed. This does not diminish the importance of replacing key institutional knots in the rope that favor those pulling for competition and greed with different institutional knots that give those pulling for equitable cooperation stronger grips. It does not imply that some priorities are more strategic than others. The struggle is not only about pulling hard. Success also hinges on untying old knots that aid our opponents, and whenever opportunities arise, tying new knots that make our tugs more effective.

So how should those seeking to replace the economics of competition and greed with the economics of equitable cooperation proceed? What can we do differently to succeed where our twentieth-century predecessors failed? The question is not "reform" or "revolution." For the foreseeable future in the advanced economies the question is how to combine more effective reform organizing with building more successful experiments in equitable cooperation in the midst of capitalism.

## Reform organizing

If progressives do not throw ourselves body and soul into reform work we will never overcome our present isolation and nothing will be accomplished. At least for the foreseeable future most victims of capitalism will seek redress through various reform campaigns fighting to ameliorate the damage capitalism causes, and these victims have every right to consider us AWOL if we do not work to make reform campaigns as successful as possible. Moreover, there are no magical "non-reformist reforms." If reforms are successful they *will* make capitalism less harmful to some extent, and if this means successful reform struggles prolong the life of capitalism this is something anti-capitalists must simply learn to accept.

We must work in campaigns to tame finance capital that has literally hijacked the real economy and created a world where the tail is now waging the dog. We need to press for full-employment macroeconomic policies not only because they eliminate macroeconomic inefficiencies but also because they strengthen the bargaining power of labor versus capital and diminish opposition to affirmative action programs as well. We must fight to re-instate welfare programs, struggle for progressive tax reform and living wages, fight for single-payer healthcare, and we must participate in community development initiatives and anti-sprawl campaigns. Most importantly, until we have rebuilt the labor, consumer, and environmental movements, and built powerful new anti-corporate, anti-globalization, and poor people's movements as well, progressive economic change will remain impossible. Particularly in the United States most of the heavy lifting for the foreseeable future must be done to build different economic reform movements. Heterodox economists need to remember this as well, if only for the selfish reason that the future of heterodox economics rides on the fortunes of these economic reform movements.

However, working in reform movements does not mean we must abandon, or downplay our politics. When we work in the labor movement we must teach not only that profit income is unfair, but that the salaries of highly paid professionals are unfair as well when they are many times higher than the wages of ordinary workers who work just as hard and often harder. In short, we must insist that the labor movement live up to its billing and become the hammer for justice in capitalism. When we work in the anti-corporate movement we must never tire of emphasizing that corporations and their unprecedented power are the major problem in the world today. We must make clear that every concession corporations make is because it is rung out of them by activists who convince them that the anti-corporate movement will inflict greater losses on their bottom line if they persist in their anti-social and environmentally destructive behavior than if they accede to our demands. When we work on campaigns for higher pollution taxes to modify incentives for profit-maximizing corporations in the market system we must also make clear that production for profit and market forces are the worst enemies of the environment, and that the environment will never be adequately protected until those economic institutions are replaced. While we work to protect consumers from price gouging and defective products we should point out how the market system promotes excessive individual consumption at the expense of social consumption and leisure. And finally, even while anti-globalization activists work to stop the spread of destructive corporate-sponsored, neoliberal globalization, we must explain how a different kind of globalization from below can improve people's lives rather than destroy their livelihoods.

As people with economic expertise who share the values of activists in these movements, heterodox economists can be much more helpful than we have been, not only in helping organizers formulate proposals and demands, but also in framing the lessons these campaigns seek to teach all who they reach. Finally, it is also important for activists and economists supporting them to make clear that reform victories can only be partial and temporary as long as economic power is unequally dispersed and economic decisions are based on private gain and market competition. Otherwise, reform efforts give way to disillusionment when victories prove partial and erode over time.

Here in the United States, until these economic reform movements have attracted more supporters, until all these reform movements have become more politically powerful, and until these reform movements are more clear about what they are fighting for and how to go about it, the goal of replacing capitalism with a system of equitable cooperation will remain beyond our reach. But it is foolish to continue to ignore predictable pitfalls of reform organizing, and long past time to devise strategies to overcome them.

1 Reform work can lead people to accept outcomes that are unacceptable. Even the most successful reform struggles invariably settle for less than they fought for. This means reform work pressures us to water down what we consider to be fair or democratic to coincide with what we had to settle for.

2 While management procedures and pay structures in reform organizations and movements are seldom as undemocratic and unfair as they are in capitalist firms, they are rarely shining examples of participatory democracy and fair pay. Therefore, those who make successful careers in reform organizations often enjoy unfair advantages that weaken their personal commitment to full economic justice and democracy.

3 Reform work has historically led even those who initially understood that capitalism must be replaced to achieve full economic justice and democracy to renounce that belief in what Michael Harrington called the Great Social Democratic Compromise. In his words: "Social democrats settled for a situation in which they would regulate and tax capitalism but not challenge it in any fundamental way" (Harrington 1989: 105).

But Harrington did not appreciate the full consequences of the compromise. It is one thing to say: We are committed to democracy above all else. Therefore we promise that as long as a majority of the population does not want to replace capitalism we have no intentions of trying to do so. It is quite another to say: Despite our best efforts we have failed at this time to convince a majority of the population that capitalism is fundamentally incompatible with economic justice, economic democracy, and environmental sustainability. Therefore we will cease to challenge the legitimacy of the capitalist system and confine our efforts to reforming it. The first promise is a simple, unwavering commitment to always respect and abide by the will of the majority. The second promise bars any who make it from continuing to argue that private enterprise and markets are incompatible with economic justice and democracy, or campaigning for the replacement of capitalism with a system more compatible with economic justice and democracy. By accepting capitalism in a "strategic compromise" twentieth-century social democrats accepted the ideology that justifies capitalism as well.

With so much reform work to be done over the decades ahead, how can we inoculate ourselves to avoid the fate of our social democratic predecessors who began the twentieth century dedicated to replacing capitalism only to end the century as apologists for the system of competition and greed whose pernicious effects they worked to ameliorate? Besides working for reforms in ways that lead to demands for further progress, and besides working in ways that strengthen progressive movements and progressive voices within reform movements, I believe the answer lies in combining reform work with building imperfect experiments in equitable cooperation.

## Pre-figurative organizing

The culture of capitalism is firmly rooted among citizens of the advanced economies. Where can the culture of equitable cooperation grow in modern capitalism? During the twentieth century one of the most successful strategies of national liberation movements in Asia, Latin America, and Africa was to create "liberated territories" where they began to build the new society while simultaneously fighting guerrilla wars to overthrow pro-capitalist governments subservient to imperial interests. At the risk of overgeneralizing, the more people who lived in liberated territories, and the longer national liberation movements experimented with new social institutions and programs in zones under their control, the more successful these movements proved to be, at least initially, in advancing the cause of equitable cooperation after taking power nationally.

The lesson for those of us living in "the center" is that living experiments in equitable cooperation are of great importance. They provide palpable evidence that a better world is possible – which is crucial to combating widespread pessimism to the contrary. They are an invaluable testing ground for ideas about how to achieve equitable cooperation – some of which are in sore need of testing. Living experiments in equitable cooperation also begin the process of creating new norms of behavior and expectations among broader segments of the population beyond a core of anti-capitalist activists. Experiments in equitable cooperation provide opportunities for activists in reform campaigns suffering from "burn out" to rejuvenate themselves instead of drifting back into alienated lives within the capitalist mainstream. And finally, readily available opportunities to live according to the norms of equitable cooperation should reduce pressures on leaders and advisors of reform movements to "sell out" for personal gain.

Twenty-first century activists in advanced economies will have to seek different ways to achieve what twentieth-century Third World national liberation movements sometimes accomplished in their liberated territories. However, failure to find ways within advanced capitalist economies to build and sustain non-capitalist networks capable of accommodating the growing numbers we hope to draw to the economics of equitable cooperation can prove just as damaging to our cause as failure to wage successful economic reform campaigns and build mass economic reform movements. Fortunately, even in the United States there are more experiments in equitable cooperation involving more people than is commonly known.

### *Local currency systems*

Activists working in local currency systems like Ithaca Hours and Time Dollars point out that local regions often remain in recession even when the national economy picks up, and that national and global financial markets often siphon savings out of poor communities to invest them elsewhere. Advocates for local currencies are also correct when they sense that we can arrange a division of labor among ourselves that is fairer than the one capitalism arranges for us. On the other hand, local currency activists sometimes espouse crackpot theories about money and become overly enthusiastic about what their local currency systems can and cannot accomplish. Local currency systems are useful to the extent that they reduce local unemployment, reward people for their labor more fairly than capitalist labor markets, and help people understand that they can – and should – manage their own division of labor equitably. Local currency systems are counterproductive when participants deceive themselves about how much can be accomplished and see nothing wrong with allowing the laws of supply and demand to determine the terms of their labor exchanges. A little economic literacy taught by heterodox economists who share the values of participants could go a long way to strengthen local currency experiments.

### Producer cooperatives

Activists who work tirelessly to promote the growth of worker-ownership in capitalism should *not* expect their efforts to succeed in replacing capitalism incrementally. The vision of reversing who hires whom – instead of capital hiring labor, labor hires capital – by slowly expanding the employee-owned sector of modern capitalist economies is a utopian pipe dream. The deck is stacked against worker-owned firms, making it very difficult for them to survive, particularly in modern capitalist economies dominated by large multinational firms. And when forced to compete against capitalist firms in a market environment, even the most idealistic worker-owners find it difficult to retain their commitment to decision making according to human values. In short, incrementally increasing the number of worker-owned firms is *not* a feasible transition strategy from the economics of competition and greed to the economics of equitable cooperation.

However, this is not to say that creating employee-owned firms cannot be an important *part* of a feasible transition strategy. They afford workers important opportunities to participate in economic decision making unavailable to them in capitalist firms. They train workers to make decisions collectively, together with their co-workers. When they compete successfully against capitalist firms, worker-owned firms challenge the myth that workers cannot govern themselves effectively, and therefore require bosses to decide what they should do and compel them to do it. So the more worker-owned firms there are, and the more successful they are, the stronger the movement for equitable cooperation will become. Heterodox economists who share the values of cooperativists can help them understand how market pressures undermine their commitment to cooperative values so they are better prepared to resist those pressures.

### Consumer cooperatives

Nobody knows how many consumer cooperatives there are in the United States. A survey in the early 1990s counted more than 40,000, and consumer cooperatives have expanded rapidly since then. The problem is not so much lack of consumer cooperatives, but (1) failure to cultivate cooperative principles and practices within the consumer cooperatives that already exist, and (2) failure to develop cooperative relations between producer and consumer cooperatives, leaving individual cooperatives to interact instead with capitalist firms through the marketplace. We need to expand self-management practices and develop more equitable wage structures in consumer cooperatives. We need to devise more creative procedures to help members participate in consumer cooperatives without heavy burdens on their time. We need to develop ways to take advantage of the energy of dedicated staff without the staff usurping member control over cooperative policy. The University of Wisconsin Center for Cooperatives is a positive example of a productive collaboration between heterodox, academic economists and progressive activists. However, there is a great deal more educational work heterodox economists who understand how pressure from the bottom line can undermine cooperative principles could do with consumer cooperatives.

### Egalitarian and sustainable intentional communities

Besides religious communities like the Amish, the Mennonites, the Hutterites, and the Bruderhoff who all live outside the capitalist mainstream to varying degrees, there are close to a thousand secular "intentional communities" in the United States where individuals and families live in ways that are self-consciously different from capitalist life styles. Some of these communities concentrate on living in ways that are environmentally sustainable, including pioneering new environmentally friendly technologies. Others are primarily concerned with building egalitarian relationships. Many intentional communities try to do both, and practice democratic decision making in various forms as well.

The Fellowship for Intentional Community (FIC) serves as both a membership organization for over 200 communities, and as a clearinghouse for information on more than 700 communities appearing in the FIC encyclopedic publication: *Communities Directory: A Comprehensive Guide to Intentional Communities and Cooperative Living* (Fellowship for Intentional Community 2007). In 1976 more than a dozen communities formed the Federation of Egalitarian Communities (FEC) to promote egalitarian life styles. Communities in the FEC cooperate on publications, conferences, and recruitment, engage in labor exchanges and skill sharing, and provide joint healthcare coverage. The FEC now has members and affiliate communities spread across North America, ranging in size and emphasis from small agricultural homesteads, to village-like communities with over a hundred members, to urban group houses.

The stated aim of these egalitarian communities is "not only to help each other, but to help more people discover the advantages of a communal alternative and to promote the evolution of a more egalitarian world" (Federation of Egalitarian Communities, 2008). Each of the communities in the federation holds its land, labor, income, and other resources in common, and uses a form of decision making in which members have an equal opportunity to participate, either through consensus, direct vote, or right of appeal or overrule. The number of intentional communities in the United States committed to living in environmentally sustainable and egalitarian ways is truly impressive, as is the longevity and size of some of the communities. Unfortunately, these communities are virtually unknown to most Americans, including most who think of themselves as progressive. Overcoming this unfortunate "disconnect" is an important priority since intentional communities are both valuable sources of information about how well our visions of alternatives to capitalism work in practice, and opportunities to practice what we preach.

There is no point in putting any particular experiment in equitable cooperation on a pedestal and blinding oneself to its limitations. It is also important not to focus exclusively on the limitations of a particular experiment and fail to recognize important ways in which it advances the cause of equitable cooperation. If heterodox economists would study and work with these communities, they could help overcome both these mistakes. The glass will always be part full and part empty. All real-world experiments in equitable cooperation in capitalist economies will not only be imperfect because human efforts are always imperfect; more importantly, they will be imperfect because they must survive within a capitalist economy and are subject to the serious limitations and pressures this entails. It is important to evaluate how successfully any particular experiment advances the cause of equitable cooperation and to resist pressures emanating from the capitalist economy to compromise cooperative principles at the expense of commercial values – and heterodox economists could help make these evaluations. But there is little point in either pretending experiments are flawless or vilifying those struggling to create something better.

What is called for is to nurture and improve experiments that already exist, to build new ones that can reach out to people who continue to live in their traditional communities, and eventually to link experiments in cooperation together to form a visible alternative to capitalism in its midst. This is not a familiar intellectual orientation to most members of heterodox schools of economic thought. Our dominant instinct is to criticize – mainstream methodologies, theories, and analyses, and to a lesser extent existing institutions. Helping design new, cooperative economic institutions and procedures is not our intellectual forte, nor are many of us inclined to participate personally in these experiments since this would challenge our class privileges. But if we want to become more useful participants in the struggle to advance the cause of equitable economic cooperation, we need to stretch ourselves more in this direction. Expanding and integrating experiments in equitable cooperation to offer opportunities to more and more people whose experiences in reform movements convince them they want to live by cooperative not competitive principles will become ever more important as time goes on.

## Reform and pre-figurative organizing are complements, not substitutes

Reforms alone cannot achieve equitable cooperation because as long as the institutions of private enterprise and markets are left in place to reinforce anti-social behavior based on greed and fear, progress toward equitable cooperation will be limited, and the danger of retrogression will be ever present. Moreover, reform campaigns undermine their leaders' commitment to full economic justice and democracy in a number of ways, and do little to demonstrate that equitable cooperation is possible, or establish new norms and expectations.

On the other hand, concentrating exclusively on organizing alternative economic institutions within capitalist economies also cannot be successful. First and foremost, exclusive focus on building alternatives to capitalism is too isolating. Until the non-capitalist sector is large, the livelihoods of most people will depend on winning reforms in the capitalist sector, and therefore that is where most people will become engaged. But concentrating exclusively on experiments in equitable cooperation will also not work because the rules of capitalism put alternative institutions at a disadvantage compared with capitalist firms they must compete against, and because market forces drive non-capitalist institutions to abandon cooperative principles. Unlike liberated territories in Third World countries, in the advanced economies we will have to build our experiments in equitable cooperation inside our capitalist economies. So our experiments will always be fully exposed to competitive pressures and the culture of capitalism. Maintaining cooperative principles in alternative experiments under these conditions requires high levels of political commitment, which it is reasonable to expect from activists committed to building "a new world," but not reasonable to expect from everyone.

Therefore, neither concentrating exclusively on reforms, nor focusing only on building alternatives within capitalism are roads that lead to success. Only in combination will reform campaigns and imperfect experiments in equitable cooperation successfully challenge the economics of competition and greed in the decades ahead. Exclusive reliance on either form of organizing is a dead end. Campaigns to reform capitalism and building pre-figurative institutions within capitalism are both integral parts of a successful strategy to accomplish in this century what we failed to accomplish in the past century – namely, making this century the last that is dominated by the economics of competition and greed.

## Academics and activists

Heterodox economists should not think of ourselves as the "grand theorists" of economic transformation because we possess special knowledge about the inner contradictions of capitalism. Nor should we stand aloof from the struggle waged between those who defend the economics of competition and greed and those who fight for the economics of equitable cooperation.

Whereas members of some heterodox schools have forthrightly championed the cause of the victims of capitalism – workers, minorities, women, or the environment – others have sought to avoid taking moral stands and distanced themselves from the epic struggle being waged. For example, while the Neo-Ricardian theory of wage, price, and profit determination is technically superior to the Marxian labor theory of value, the refusal of Sraffa and many of his followers to draw moral conclusions about whether or not capitalist profits are unfair has rendered their theory less useful to those fighting for economic justice in capitalism than the logically flawed, but morally centered Marxist theory they sought to replace. Similarly, while the reluctance of most institutionalists to endorse twentieth-century socialism as a worthy institutional embodiment of the economics of equitable cooperation is understandable, it is lamentable that only "radical" institutionalists have been willing to denounce capitalism as the institutional antithesis of equitable cooperation. Finally, when Post-Keynesians focus exclusively on inefficiencies in laissez-faire capitalism and remain silent regarding questions of economic justice and democracy it renders their work less relevant to progressive economic campaigns to tame finance and promote full employment than it might be. Too often there has been a tendency to hide behind analysis and avoid moral issues in the work of academic heterodox economists. Moral issues should be central to the work lives of heterodox economists, not consigned to our lives as private citizens.

Heterodox economists should begin by heeding the Hippocratic ethic, "First, do no harm." We must stop disseminating illusions about self-destructive, internal contradictions of capitalism that mislead progressive activists about the nature of the struggle they are waging.[3] We must stop obfuscating insights with unnecessarily obscure language and formalisms that are inaccessible to all but a few who spend years studying for the "priesthood" in a particular heterodox economic "faith." Any economic "discovery" that cannot be explained in plain English to a non-economist is more likely to be nonsense than insight. We need to help progressive activists speak directly with the goddess of economics rather than interpose ourselves as an inaccessible priesthood through whom all communication must flow. And finally, we must stop discouraging activists seeking to build experiments in equitable cooperation from believing this is humanly possible. Paying careful attention to the incentives different economic institutions generate is not the same as insisting that human beings can only be motivated by greed and fear, or that institutions cannot be fashioned that promote solidarity and mutual concern rather than egotism and enmity.

Second, we should realize that the future of heterodox economics hinges more on what side we take in the epic economic struggle of our age, and what subjects we consider worthy of study, than on what methodology we deploy. The mainstream of our profession is increasingly united in its support for the necessity and virtues of the economics of competition and greed and the institutions of free enterprise and free markets in particular, and increasingly prone to dismiss the claims of the victims of capitalism. If heterodox economics is to have a future it will be because we forthrightly challenge these mainstream trends, not because we limit ourselves to challenging mainstream methodology.

Third, we should be more willing to apply our skills to tasks where economic reform campaigns and pre-figurative experiments require our help. Some Post-Keynesian, Structuralist, and Institutionalist economists have set a positive example by helping the UNDP and progressive governments in Third World countries develop alternative macroeconomic policies and development strategies to the destructive neoliberal policies peddled by the IMF and World Bank. But there is not a single reform campaign being waged today that does not suffer for lack of better economic analysis and professional help in formulating demands and responding to concessions. Campaigns to raise taxes on pollutants and subsidize sustainable energy could profit greatly from empirical studies about the prevalence and magnitude of externalities in the price system. Simulation studies of markets where some actors interpret price changes as signals of what direction the market price is headed could bolster the efforts of those combating the ravages of neoliberal capital liberalization. But neither is a major subject of doctoral dissertations in any of our heterodox graduate programs. Because ecological economists have focused so heavily on big picture analysis and had little to say about the pros and cons of different policy alternatives, organizations in the environmental movement have until recently had nowhere to turn for useful advice from progressive-minded economists.[4] There is also not a single experiment in equitable cooperation whose enthusiasts do not labor under serious misconceptions about how their hopes are likely to run afoul of predictable economic forces.

Those organizing producer and consumer cooperatives, local exchange and trading systems, experiments in participatory budgeting, and those trying to devise ways for people to commit to egalitarian living arrangements without joining a full-scale intentional community could all use more help from progressive economists than we have been willing to offer. I know academics are not rewarded for this kind of work. Instead we are rewarded for "research" that consists largely of empirical tests of theories of little consequence and dressing up ideas in specialized language. And I know that if untenured heterodox academics fail to publish in "reputable" journals they will lose their positions in academia from which to challenge mainstream economic myths. But why cannot more *tenured* heterodox economists who are willing to defy mainstream ideology also defy mainstream research agendas? Mainstream economists are virtually useless to those working in different parts of the movement for equitable cooperation because they do not share their values and generally oppose the reforms and projects they work for. Heterodox economists on the other hand are generally sympathetic to the values and projects of those working in progressive economic movements and should have useful advice to offer.

Finally, there is one task non-economists fighting for equitable cooperation are particularly ill-suited for: thinking clearly about systemic alternatives to capitalism. Heterodox economists could greatly improve the quality of discussion concerning alternatives to capitalism if more would join this debate. Analyzing the pros and cons of different versions of market socialism, different versions of democratic planning, and different versions of community-based economics is greatly facilitated by professional training in economics – provided one has not swallowed the mainstream myth that capitalism is the end of economic history. At present there are more activists and academics from other disciplines playing prominent roles in this important area than there are professional economists. While it is helpful to draw on insights from personal experience and the disciplines of philosophy, sociology, and political science when thinking about alternatives to capitalism, in essence the task is to design and analyze *alternative economic systems*, and professional economists bring some useful expertise to this project others are lacking.

## Notes

1  Social Structures of Accumulation theory and World Systems theory are an improvement over earlier, deterministic crisis theories. And some contributors criticize others who substitute teleological presumptions for matter-of-fact, causal reasoning. For example see Wolfson and Kotz (forthcoming). What I am criticizing is a lingering tendency to overmystify analysis and render it more obscure than needs be.
2  I do not expect these claims to be taken on faith. For the full argument, see Hahnel (2007) and parts one and two of Hahnel (2005).
3  The insistence of the founders of ecological economics that a thorough understanding of the second law of thermodynamics is prerequisite to understanding why global capitalism is destroying the biosphere is a poignant reminder that modern heterodox schools are still capable of scientistic obfuscation, which in this case is actually completely irrelevant. See Daly and Farley (2003).
4  Economics for Equity and the Environment is a small think tank of progressive environmental economists recently established to try to fill this gaping vacuum. www.e3network.org.

## References

Baran, P. (1957) *The Political Economy of Growth*, New York: Monthly Review Press.
Daly, H. and Farley, J. (2003) *Ecological Economics: Principles and Applications*, Washington, DC: Island Press.
Federation of Egalitarian Communities (2008) "What is the FEC?" Available at www.thefec.org/node/253 (accessed August 13, 2008).
Fellowship for Intentional Community (2007) "Communities Directory 2007," Rutledge, MO: Fellowship for Intentional Community.
Hahnel, R. (2005) *Economic Justice and Democracy: From Competition to Cooperation*, New York: Routledge.
—— (2007) "The Case against Markets," *Journal of Economic Issues*, 41(4): 1139–1159.
Harrington, M. (1989) *Socialism: Past and Future*, New York: Little, Brown & Co.
Harris, D. (1978) *Capital Accumulation and Distribution*, Stanford: Stanford University Press.
Marglin, S. (1984) *Growth, Distribution and Prices*, Cambridge: Harvard University Press.
Sweezy, P. (1966) *Monopoly Capital*, New York: Monthly Review Press.
Taylor, L. (2004) *Reconstructing Macroeconomics: Structuralist Proposals and Critiques of the Mainstream*, Cambridge: Harvard University Press.
Wolfson, M. and Kotz, D. (forthcoming) "A Re-conceptualization of SSA Theory," in T. McDonough, D. Kotz, and M. Reich (eds) *Understanding Contemporary Capitalism: Social Structure of Accumulation Theory for the Twenty-First Century*, Cambridge, UK: Cambridge University Press.

# 11  Growth, development, and quality of life

## A pluralist approach

*Daphne T. Greenwood and Richard P.F. Holt*

### Introduction

If growth means higher incomes, does higher quality of life always follow? Does development mean improvement in the standard of living? Standard neoclassical growth theory (Solow 1956; Lucas 1988; Maddison 1991) equates economic growth with economic development, implicitly assuming that growth brings improved quality of life or standard of living (Brinkman 1995). But this assumption is changing. Along with scholarly work in economics (Daly 1993; Norgaard 1994) there seems to be a growing popular movement for differentiating economic growth from development that is sustainable and improves people's quality of life.

The United Nations Human Development Index (HDI) and goals for sustainable development along with alternative measures like the Genuine Progress Index (GPI) for the United States (Talberth *et al.* 2006) are based on sustainability of development and production that improves quality of life. Many communities in industrialized countries are also developing locally based indicators of sustainability or quality of life to supplement traditional economic measures (Wismer 1999; Greenwood 2004). All of these measures reflect an increased recognition that improvement in people's lives depends on more than just raising national income. We believe this stems from two primary factors. One is the growing realization that economic prosperity depends on environmental and social sustainability. Another is the desire for balancing economic well-being with other aspects of human welfare such as health, culture, and human relationships.[1]

Economic development, in our view, means a broad based and sustainable increase in the standard of living. It is not equivalent to undifferentiated growth in output and income. Economic growth may not be broad based or sustainable, and may not include elements of quality of life beyond income. In this chapter, we lay the foundations for a pluralist approach to economic development incorporating quality of life and sustainability in ways the neoclassical model has not. It draws from ecological, feminist, institutionalist, and post-Keynesian approaches. We first turn briefly to neoclassical theory and its assumptions and methodology.

# Growth and development from a neoclassical perspective

## *Neoclassical and endogenous growth theory*

Neoclassical economics has historically been focused on explaining short run microeconomic patterns (such as how prices are determined) rather than dynamic models explaining growth and change over time. However, Robert Solow (1956) developed a simple growth model where economic growth follows a steady-state path. It has a production function with constant returns to scale and diminishing marginal productivity of labor and capital determined by the growth rates of labor and technology. These are determined exogenously.

One of the major limitations of the "Solow growth model" is having exogenous technological development. Endogenous growth theory (Romer 1986, 1994; Pack 1994) allows an increasing variety or quality of machinery and strong external economies from investment in new capital, which can eliminate diminishing returns. But the "new growth theory" model is still focused on technology, capital, and labor. It does not include natural resources as a separate, and potentially limiting, factor of production. In both models, (1) technological change can create a substitute for any resource (Nordhaus and Tobin 1972); (2) market pricing can achieve efficient allocation of all resources (Coase 1960); and (3) allocation of resources over time is handled by the discount rate. For example, Solow, in his 1974 Richard Ely lecture to the American Economic Association, said "the world, can, in effect, get along without natural resources" (Solow 1974: 11).

In addition to viewing natural capital as less important, traditional neoclassical theory posits a tradeoff between equality and growth (Panizza 2002; Partridge 2005, 2006) based on the need for incentives. At least in the short run, growth cannot lead to broadly based development, although over time the benefits of growth should trickle down. The new growth theory is silent on inequality. However, there is at least some empirical evidence that intercountry differences in growth rates are not helped by more inequality and that the reverse may even be true (Aghion *et al.* 1999). This empirical evidence lends support to our view that other social and economic variables (reflecting the distribution of power, income, and wealth) need to be captured in a pluralistic model of economic growth. We now look at the neoclassical view of economic development and quality of life issues.

## *Economic development in the neoclassical model*

Economic development is equivalent to economic growth in the neoclassical model. Both are measured through changes in gross domestic product (GDP). Since private manufactured capital plays such a central role in the neoclassical growth process, policies to promote economic development (i.e. growth) support the expansion of capital. This means minimizing barriers to its free flow and lowering or eliminating the taxation of capital so as to increase market output

(Meier and Seers 1984). In this model, there is little mention of other types of capital (natural, human, or social) that we believe are critical for true economic development.

Issues about the sustainability, composition, or distribution of growth are expected to be resolved over time through market mechanisms (World Bank 1991). If a resource such as oil is scarce this will be reflected in higher current and expected future market prices for oil. Profit-seeking firms will substitute other resources in its place. And utility-maximizing consumers will choose more attractively priced products that minimize use of the scarce resource. The market determines both allocation and distribution. There is no mention of power or social factors influencing outcomes in the neoclassical model. In the more liberal interpretation, distribution of growth between public and private goods, for example, is left to a democratic political system (Taylor 1983; Sundrum 1990). Income or wealth distribution issues not resolved to the public's satisfaction through markets can be offset through tax policy or public expenditures (Stiglitz 2000).

### *Quality of life in the neoclassical model*

Per capita income growth, producing more goods and services per person, is the most commonly used indicator of welfare and improvements in living because of its consistency with assumptions of neoclassical welfare theory like non-satiation and exchange theory (Earl 1995). But since the 1960s there have been questions about equating increased production of goods and services with increased consumer welfare. The primary concerns have been with (1) use of non-renewable resources and its impact on future production and (2) the impact that growth has on social and environmental systems, urbanization, and local communities (Zolatas 1981).

However, we know that neither industrialized nor developing countries rank in the same order on health and education indicators as they do on per capita income (Slottje 1991). Income differences between regions of a country are equally unreliable as indicators of quality of life differences, especially if they are unadjusted for variation in cost-of-living.

The neoclassical approach to quality of life or amenity differences between cities or regions has been quite limited. Movement from a location with higher average income to one with lower average income is viewed as evidence of a conscious tradeoff between income and other quality of life factors (Roback 1982; Berger *et al.* 1987; Blomquist *et al.* 1988; Greenwood 1989; Kahn 1995; Power 1996). However, since the neoclassical approach does not deal with differences in power, it cannot address the question of who is able to exercise the choice to be mobile or has sufficient information to make an informed choice. And it says nothing about how to increase quality of life beyond moving somewhere else to get it.

In addition to using income to measure well-being, neoclassical economics does not recognize the aesthetic component of quality of life in public and non-market arenas. Thomas Power writes that income growth is often, pitted against the largely "social" or "aesthetic" concerns of those who would pursue their vague notions about the "quality of life" the suggestion being that subjective judgments about quality are somehow noneconomic ... [but] economic activity is now and always has been centered on the pursuit of qualities we judge to be attractive and, therefore, important.

(Power 1996: 11–12)

These are some examples of why the neoclassical model is not well equipped to deal with the full gamut of quality of life issues. It has similar problems with sustainability.

### Sustainability in the neoclassical model

The classic definition comes from the U.N.'s 1987 Bruntland Commission: "Sustainable development is development which meets the needs of the present without compromising the ability of future generations to meet their own needs." This means producing and consuming in ways that preserve capital stocks necessary for producing a comparable standard of living in the future.

Neoclassical economists like Solow (1992, 1994) address this with a "weak" definition of sustainable development, ensuring that natural resource depletion is matched by commensurate increases in manufactured capital. Where there are externalities neoclassical economists call for taxes, tradable emission permits, etc. to reflect the true costs of resource use in the private sector. But while Coasian solutions such as market incentives can increase social efficiency of certain resource uses and reduce some kinds of pollution, it is clear they are not suited for large-scale problems where the parties have trouble coming together (Stiglitz 2000). Significant long-term damage at low discount rates is unlikely to have a present value high enough to affect current decisions about feasibility (Daly 1977; Norgaard 1989). Less extreme outcomes at high discount rates appear even less compelling in the neoclassical model.

Since issues of distribution and power are not part of the neoclassical model, control of resources by one group to the exclusion (or damage) of another cannot be dealt with unless the group at risk of damage has sufficient political or economic power to influence resource use. DeGregori (1974: 55–6) writes that the mythology of free choice in free markets creates a situation in which we accept activities that take place within the "market" that would be condemned if carried on elsewhere. He quotes Ayres "poisoning one's wife is a mortal sin, whereas poisoning thousands of people by selling adulterated food or drugs is a mere business misadventure." This can readily be extended to the long-term sustainability problems we face today, in which the people being "poisoned" are those in future generations and have no power to influence decisions today.

We believe a pluralistic approach to economic growth and development can emphasize differentiation between growth and development, incorporating "strong" sustainability (lack of substitutability for some resources) and quality of life issues in ways the neoclassical model cannot. In the next section we begin to lay the foundations of a pluralist approach.

## The roots of a pluralistic approach

We build our core ideas from alternative approaches to neoclassical economics, using just a sampling of the rich literature in these areas owing to the limits of a single chapter. Several approaches (ecological, feminist, and post-Keynesians) are considered relatively new schools. Others (institutionalist and Marxist) have a long history of dissent from classical and neoclassical thought. In this chapter, we review their contributions to a pluralistic approach to economic development, beginning with the institutionalists.[2]

Many institutionalists (including Ayres 1962; Galbraith 1969, 1996; Myrdal 1973) have seen economic growth as necessary, but not sufficient for economic development. Development is more than growth. It indicates that an ongoing (evolutionary) process has been established that will continue to raise standards of living for a broad spectrum of the population over time.

Philip Klein (1974: 801) writes that neoclassical economics emphasizes growth rather than progress for the same reasons "the traditional emphasis in statics is on allocation rather than valuation. Progress involves valuation through time, while growth involves simply increase in whatever it is the economy happens to be doing." Gunnar Myrdal, similarly, saw development as

> the upward movement of the whole social system ... not only production, distribution of the produce, and modes of production are involved but also levels of livings, institutions, attitudes, and policies.
>
> (1973: 190)

From Veblen's perspective, new "states of mind" accompany changing knowledge and technology with economic development, requiring fundamental changes in institutions, including long-established patterns of thought or ways of doing things (Veblen 1922 [1914], Veblen 1961 [1919]).

John Kenneth Galbraith identified the fixation with economic growth (vs. development) in an already affluent society with the power of corporations to set the agenda for society:

> Growth, being a paramount purpose of the society, nothing naturally enough is allowed to stand in its way. That includes its ... diverse effect, on the environment, on air, water, the tranquility of urban life, the beauty of the countryside.
>
> (Galbraith 1974: 286)

*The Affluent Society* describes "private wealth and public squalor" and extends Veblen's theory of "conspicuous consumption" and critique of marginal utility (Galbraith 1969; Veblen 1899, 1961). Galbraith went on to lay the foundations for a theory of quality of life in developed nations. Many of his observations have been further developed by Power (1996), Sen (1993), Allardt (1993) and others, but have been ignored by most mainstream economists (Greenwood and Holt 2007).

Ecological economists such as Georgescu-Roegen, Boulding, and Daly focus on natural resources as constraints on growth. The classical and neoclassical "free gifts of nature" have become "natural capital." No expenditure of human effort was required to create natural resources, so they appear "free" in the traditional economic context. But they can be depleted like any capital stock. And unlike most, they may not be renewable. Ecological economists have also emphasized that nature is more than resource inputs. It includes the life-giving elements of the biosphere in which we live. We are much more likely to develop substitutes for resource inputs than for these. These insights of ecological economists about sustainability of development are important.

However, we believe a pluralistic approach to growth, development, and quality of life must also emphasize that the level of natural capital is not static. While there is a nonreplaceable and essential life-giving envelope of atmosphere, the quantity of resource inputs into the production process depends heavily on technology and consumer preferences. The dynamic relation between the physical, biological, and institutional environment is unpredictable in many ways, due in part to human behavior.

And just as humans influence the level of available natural capital, their behavior is inextricably intertwined with other forms of capital. A pluralistic approach should explore the social relationships surrounding natural and human capital as well as manufactured (or physical) capital. By social relationships we mean both the forces which created the capital as well as the laws or customs surrounding how their benefits are allocated. To quote Veblen on the former:

> Productive goods are facts of human knowledge, skill, and predilection ... and it as such that they enter into the process of industrial development.... The changes that take place in the mechanical contrivances are an expression of changes in the human factor.
>
> (1961: 71)

Veblen also saw private manufactured capital differently than the classical or neoclassical economists. Capital is, he argued, "a pecuniary fact, not a mechanical one ... as a physical aggregate, capital does not appreciably decrease through business disasters, but ... [t]here is a destruction of values and a shifting, perhaps a loss of ownership" (1961: 197–8). He understood the productivity of capital assets to be a joint productivity:

> All tangible assets owe their productivity and their value to the immaterial industrial expedients which they embody or their ownership enables their owner to engross. These ... are necessarily a product of the community's

experience ... and can be transmitted only in the keeping of the community at large.

(1961: 347–8)

In other words, capital represents an asset value, i.e. a legally recognized right to capture an income stream or flow of services, rather than a productive entity in the technological sense. A machine may still retain its productive capability, but if there is no longer demand for its product the financial value is gone. Once again, the productive value derives from the process of transmission of community experience.

We see the important divisions between types of capital differently than is explained in most of the economics literature. Whether physical manufactured capital, natural, or human capital there exist two key categories: (1) private vs. common ownership; and (2) the extent to which rights of ownership and use are limited by the necessity to consider effects on others.

Physical or manufactured capital can be privately owned business capital or publicly owned infrastructure. Whether privately or publicly owned it may generate positive and negative externalities outside the realm of ownership. What we call "public" infrastructure is actually owned by one level of government but often has effects on other jurisdictions. Natural capital can also be privately owned, by an individual, business enterprise, or unit of government. Or as in the case of the oceans and the earth's atmosphere it can be part of "the commons." In either case, its use can generate externalities that are economic, aesthetic, or health effects on current or future populations.

Human capital has traditionally been used to refer to the privately owned element of human knowledge. But the publicly owned component makes up what is sometimes called "intellectual capital" or "social capital." Positive and negative externalities result from privately owned human capital (an individual's ability as a surgeon or marksman, for example). In contrast, intellectual and social capital exist solely in the public domain, much like the elements of natural capital we call "the commons." Intellectual property laws represent an effort to lay claim to portions of intellectual capital where technologically and legally possible to do so, rather than leaving them in the commons.

Sustainable development depends on all these capital stocks. Growing populations, affluence, and greater knowledge of ecological limits have put many more limits on their use than in the past. Whether physical manufactured capital, natural capital, or human/intellectual/social capital, our understanding of how it relates to sustainable development must change.

The role of people in expansion, enrichment, or depletion of *any* of these kinds of capital is critical. People are the source of knowledge and its application as superior techniques in agriculture, technological improvement of manufactured capital, and expansion of what functions as an economic resource within nature. It is the institutions people develop that facilitate or limit the applications of knowledge for human – economic and social – development. Investment in formal education is not enough to support human, intellectual or social capital.

Non-market inputs from family and society are critically important for early childhood and adolescence. The level of public discourse and civility (Putnam 2000; Gore 2007) and the resilience and adaptability of social institutions, customs, and support systems also depend on much more than market forces. The social imbalance identified by Galbraith (1969, 1996) applies to all types of human capital as well as to public infrastructure. A pluralist model of economic development should address these areas in ways the traditional model has neglected.

This brings us to the emphasis of feminist economists on new ways of defining economics. Julie Nelson writes,

> One can think of economics as the study of humans in interaction with the world which supports us – of economics as the study of organization of the processes which *provision* life.
>
> (2001: 296; our emphasis)

Aslaksen, Flaatten, and Koren (1999) also expand the traditional economic model of agency from "self-interest bordering on greed and destructive behavior to one that combines self-interest with responsibility for the common good."

Flynn (1999) calls for a less theoretical and more data- and experience-based approach to quality of life. But measures like the United Nations Sustainable Development Indicators are not favored by O'Hara (1999) who sees in them an overreliance on "expert systems and unchallenged epistemological assumptions." She calls for more participatory research design to arrive at social preferences, involving discourse between individuals as citizens rather than the aggregations of individually expressed preferences from surveys. Feminist economists are echoing Klein and other institutionalists in disagreeing with the accepted neoclassical social welfare function in many ways.

Complexity rather than reducibility is also emphasized by feminist economists (O'Hara 1999) and further developed in post-Keynesian economics, the fourth pillar of a pluralistic theory of growth, development and quality of life. Post-Keynesians emphasize realism and organicism. Path dependency and irreversibility – in stark contrast to Walrasian neoclassical economics – acknowledge that "history matters." The past influences subsequent outcomes (Holt and Setterfield 1999; Holt 2007). This line of thinking mirrors the ecological economist Georgescu-Roegen (1971) who writes in his discussion of entropy and the economic process that we move strictly from the present to the future and not vice versa.

Another area in which post-Keynesian economics contributes to a pluralistic approach is with uncertainty and bounded rationality. Barkley Rosser, Jr. (1999, 2005) builds on the work of Herbert Simon and Georgescu-Roegen on complex dynamics that imply lack of predictability for the future to study system sustainability. Marc Lavoie (2009) approaches consumer theory from a post-Keynesian perspective in ways that are often concerned with quality of life and sustainable development. He argues that needs are hierarchical (basic needs vs. "wants") and that preferences are not formed independently, in ways similar to some of feminist economics.

In sum, there are many strengths and commonalities among major heterodox traditions that lend themselves to a pluralist model of growth, development, and quality of life. However, the task to which we now turn is to lay a solid beginning upon which others may build and add.

## A pluralistic approach to growth, development, and quality of life

As discussed above, institutionalists were first to emphasize the fundamental difference between economic growth and economic development. Ecological economists have highlighted the difference between natural resources and other forms of capital, based in part on the difficulty of substitution for certain parts of our environment. Feminist economists have introduced provisioning vs. choice as the central problem of economies issues, along with the importance of non-market production and the existence of interdependent utility functions. They have joined institutionalists and neo-Marxists, in putting power and social relationships back into the economic equation. Post-Keynesian models have formalized the effects of uncertainty and path dependency useful in ways of dealing with sustainability issues if extended to natural capital. Their focus on mathematical models speaks the same language as many neoclassical economists but brings in new values such as distribution as well as growth.

A pluralistic approach to sustainability of development and the relationship of quality of life to economic growth can arise from all of these. It must be focused on realism, irreversible (historical) time, and the existence of uncertainty. Externalities must be recognized as frequently recurring problems rather than occasional exceptions to the normal case where market forces correctly allocate costs and benefits. A pluralist model must deal with the roles of power and culture in individual choices and public decisions. It should recognize joint determinations of productivity from several sources of capital (including the human and the natural) rather than attributing so much to private manufactured capital. Last, but certainly not least, justice, equality, and opportunity must be recognized as important ends in themselves as well as means to economic growth and development. We believe that in all these aspects the heterodox schools mentioned are in general agreement.

However, we recognize major issues of contention. For example, while institutionalists and ecological economists both use biological rather than mechanistic metaphors for the operation of an economy, they have very different views of technology and economic development. Both deserve further exploration as a pluralistic synthesis is explored (Greenwood and Holt 2008). And for institutionalists and post-Keynesians, the ideas of sustainability and natural capital bring back the view of supply constraints that dominated the classical literature. Despite this, we believe the contribution of ecological economists in acknowledging the differences between natural and manufactured capital and weak and strong sustainability are very important insights that must be integrated into a pluralistic approach.

We see six important facets to a pluralist approach:

1   A pluralist approach must differentiate between economic growth and economic development and recognize the need for development to be sustainable, broadly based, and equitable. Sen and Dreze have made this point for developing nations (1996). True development requires more attention to the composition and distribution of output.

2   A pluralist approach must account for uncertainty, full life-cycle costs of all activities, and irreversibility of historical time so that development is sustainable for future generations. It must recognize the natural environment, the economy, and society as inextricably interrelated, harking back to the closed system of "Spaceship Earth" (Boulding 1966) which includes natural capital and waste. A shift to systems analysis may be required – at least on a macroeconomic level – as a pluralist model moves from a mechanistic to a biological approach. The traditional circular flow model of interrelationships and flows in the market economy must be extended to include environment and society. As Daly (1977) pointed out, using only the circular flow model to understand the economy is like trying to understand an animal in terms of its circulatory tract without recognizing that it is connected to the larger world by a digestive tract on both ends. That is a metaphor that should not be forgotten!

3   A pluralist approach must include aspects of quality of life or standard of living outside market income measures, including both the expansion of human capabilities and the recognition of aesthetic values. This requires addressing issues of culture and gender, incorporating human values that are non-economic such as love, relationship, justice, equality, and opportunity (Sen 1987; Folbre 2001). Basic assumptions about "economic man" such as independent utility functions and the centrality of choice vs. provisioning (Nelson 1993) must be addressed.

    The aesthetic component of value in public goods has been explored by Power (1996). He makes a compelling case that humans at various levels of affluence and throughout history have valued the aesthetic, paying a price to experience it in their private consumption. He calls for the extension of these aesthetic values to the arena of wild species and open lands. But we argue it is important to further extend discussion of aesthetic values into many areas of individual and public life, including our public spaces and built environment, the quality of education and of public discourse.

    The discrepancy between increases in happiness and increases in GDP has been documented in Easterlin (2002) and may be related to all these issues, as well as to a mismatch between public and private goods. It was Galbraith (1969) who first described the dilemma of "private affluence and public squalor" where society fails to address other needs that are part of a good quality of life and cannot be met by higher private income. Neglect of public infrastructure and the quality of the environment came, he felt, from a fixation on private manufactured capital (1996).

4    A pluralist approach must address all forms of capital necessary to the life-process and avoid this fixation on private capital, addressing the power rela-tionships in society that support this bias. Development requires sustaining the capital needed to continue producing quality of life, which is larger than GDP. Natural capital, human capital, public infrastructure, and institutions (or social capital) are all necessary to produce this. Within the stock of natural capital, sustainable development must differentiate between resources that are renewable and nonrenewable as well as those for which technology/human knowledge may develop substitutes and those where it cannot.

The term "social capital" has been used by many social scientists and a few economists (Bowles and Gintis 2002) to describe the positive role of institu-tions, including the legal system, adherence to values such as honesty, and the level of civic participation. However, institutions can be negative factors in economic development (Ayres 1962; Greenwood and Holt 2008). If the term social capital is going to be used Schmid (2002) and Robison, Schmid, and Siles (2002) have pointed out that it needs to be more clearly defined (see also Durlauf 2000 for a further critique). This is another area a pluralist approach to growth, development, and quality of life should explore.

5    A pluralist approach must recognize the importance of power in economic relationships. Galbraith saw the power of producers to create "wants" when a society has already met basic needs for most members (and could easily do so for others). He did not oppose economic growth itself but rather the definition of growth (rather than development) as the "paramount purpose of the society" (1974: 286). He also recognized the problems growth can create. Galbraith advocated using the democratic process to control harm associated with growth. We believe the use and development of local indic-ators is needed to extend the nature of civic discourse and support participa-tion in the democratic process.

6    Finally, *pace* Galbraith (1969), a pluralist approach must develop measures beyond GDP to provide purpose and direction to society. We applaud the realization of this necessity by feminist economists (Wismer 1999; Flynn 1999) and ecological economists such as Norgaard (1988). Our benchmarks for "how we are doing" are still the measures we chose over half a century ago, despite increased recognition today of the importance of nonrenewable natural resources and public infrastructure. We need more than that. A plu-ralist economics should be in the forefront of developing and implementing these measures – measures which match both its values and its understand-ing of the processes of sustainable economic development.

There is broader public support today than in the past for protecting the envir-onment, ensuring that basic needs are met for all, and for valuing the aesthetic. But until we systematically collect numbers on a subject – sustainability, quality of life, changes in other stocks of capital, or any other – it is unlikely to be treated as a high priority. Businesses, governments, and individuals all tend to pay most attention to what is measured.

To measure progress in the standard of living (or quality of life), social and environmental variables outside the market economy must be included, as well as economic measures that capture distribution of income, affordability of housing, and access to health care. The measures we use now to monitor our economy reflect only market production and consumption, and focus almost exclusively on investment in private capital and incentives to support that. Alternative measures such as the Genuine Progress Index (Talberth *et al.* 2006) and comprehensive community indicators are needed for a pluralistic approach (Wismer 1999; Greenwood 2004).

## Final thoughts

Sustainability of development and quality of life are increasingly pressing con-cerns in the public arena. They are also fundamental economic concerns. And these concerns are not reserved for non-industrialized or developing nations. Focusing economic development in industrialized nations on quality of life and sustainability is one of the central tasks facing economists in the twenty-first century. There is a clear need for an alternative to the neoclassical model's focus on private manufactured capital and its faith in consumer sovereignty and market adjustment mechanisms. These have limited the ability of economists to deal with issues of growth, development, and quality of life.

We end this chapter with several examples of how pluralist thinking has already been used in the real world to deal with problems associated with eco-nomic growth, quality of life and sustainability:

- The World Bank, under the leadership of former chief economist Joseph Stiglitz, now measures "true national savings" which subtracts depletion of natural resources.
- The United Nations, following the pioneering works of Sen and others, pub-lishes a Human Development Index (HDI) for countries that averages per capita GDP with life expectancy, adult literacy, and school enrollment ratios. This helps to account for differences in income and wealth distribu-tion and composition of public spending between nations.
- The Genuine Progress Index (GPI) developed at *Redefining Progress*, with Richard Norgaard on the Board of Directors, begins with the GDP but includes estimates of household work and environmental services, as well as subtracting the costs of crime, lost leisure time, and decay in the stock of environmental resources. While GDP trends were upward from 1950 to the present the GPI increased much more slowly through the mid-1970s and has declined since 1980 (Cobb 2000; Talberth *et al.* 2006).
- The U.S. Commerce Department now computes expenditures on environ-mental cleanup that can be subtracted from GDP.

- Increasingly, communities are establishing their own indicators of sustainability and/or quality of life (see especially Jacksonville Quality of Life Indicators 2007; Sustainable Seattle 1998).

In a world where economics appears threatening or irrelevant to the underlying concerns of many people, we believe there is a real need for a pluralistic model of growth and development that incorporates sustainability and quality of life. We see its foundations in work done over the years by institutionalists, feminist, post-Keynesian, and ecological economists, and other heterodox groups that are not represented here. Our attempt is but a beginning to which we hope many others will contribute.

## Notes

1  Popular movements for sustainability or quality of life often occur outside economics and have some hostility to economic ideas. We believe that this can be traced to a view of economics that is identified with the neoclassical paradigm and is perceived as supporting whatever kind of growth in output that market forces call for based on "consumer sovereignty."
2  Though we do not discuss in detail the Marxist approach we recognize its important contribution to including the development of human potential in quality of life. This is very much grounded in Marx's emphasis on the evolution and growth of human nature to its full potential.

## References

Aghion, P., Caroli, E., and Garcia-Penalosa, C. (1999) "Inequality and Economic Growth: The Perspective of the New Growth Theories," *Journal of Economic Literature*, 37 (4): 1615–60.

Allardt, E. (1993) "Having, Loving, and Being: An Alternative to the Swedish Model of Welfare Research," in M. Nussbaum and A. Sen (eds) *The Quality of Life*, 88–94, Oxford: Clarendon Press.

Aslaksen, I., Flaatten, A., and Koren, C. (1999) "Introduction: Quality of Life Indicators," *Feminist Economics*, 5(2): 79–82.

Ayres, C.E. (1962) [1944] *The Theory of Economic Progress: A Study of the Fundamentals of Economic Development and Cultural Change*, 2nd edition, New York: Schocken Books.

Berger, M., Blomquist, G., and Waldner, W. (1987) "A Revealed Preference Ranking of Quality of Life for Metropolitan Areas," *Social Science Quarterly*, 68 (4): 761–78.

Blomquist, G., Berger, M., and Hoehn, J. (1988) "New Estimates of Quality of Life in Urban Areas," *American Economic Review*, 78(1): 89–107.

Boulding, K. (1966) "The Economics of the Coming Spaceship Earth," in H. Jarrett (ed.) *Environmental Quality in a Growing Economy*, 3–14, Baltimore: Johns Hopkins University Press.

Bowles, S. and Gintis, H. (2002) "Social Capital and Community Governance," *Economic Journal*, 112(483): 419–36.

Brinkman, R. (1995) "Economic Growth vs. Economic Development: Toward a Conceptual Clarification," *Journal of Economic Issues*, 29(4): 1171–88.

Bruntland, G. (1987) *Our Common Future: Report of the World Commission on Environment and Development*, Oxford: Oxford University Press.

Coase, R. (1960) "The Problem of Social Cost," *Journal of Law and Economics*, 3: 1–44.

Cobb, C. (2000) *Measurement Tools and the Quality of Life*, San Francisco: Redefining Progress.

Daly, H. (1977) *Steady State Economics*, San Francisco: W. H. Freeman and Co.

—— (1993) "Sustainable Growth: An Impossibility Theorem," in H. Daly and K. Townsend (eds), *Valuing the Earth: Economics, Ecology, and Ethics*, 267–73, Cambridge: MIT Press.

DeGregori, T. (1974) "Power and Illusion in the Marketplace: Institutions and Technology," *Journal of Economic Issues* 8(4): 759–70.

Durlauf, S. (2000) "Bowling Alone: A Review Essay," *Journal of Economic Behavior and Organization*, 47(3): 259–73.

Earl, P. (1995) *Microeconomics for Business and Marketing*, Northampton, MA: Edward Elgar.

Easterlin, R. (2002) *Happiness in Economics*, Northampton, MA: Edward Elgar.

Flynn, P. (1999) "Contributions Feminist Economics Can Make to the Quality of Life Movement," *Feminist Economics*, 5(2): 133–7.

Folbre, N. (2001) *The Invisible Heart: Economics and Family Values*, New York: The New Press.

Galbraith, J. (1969) [1958] *The Affluent Society*, 2nd edition, revised, Boston: Houghton Mifflin.

—— (1974) *Economics and the Public Purpose*, Boston: Houghton Mifflin.

—— (1996) *The Good Society*, Boston: Houghton Mifflin.

Georgescu-Roegen, N. (1971) *The Entropy Law and the Economic Process*, Cambridge: Harvard University Press.

Gore, A. (2007) *The Assault on Reason*, New York: Penguin Press.

Greenwood, D. (2004) "Measuring Quality of Life with Local Indicators," in E. Wolff (ed.) *What Has Happened to the Quality of Life In the Advanced Industrialized Nations?* 334–74, Northampton: Levy Economics Institute and Edward Elgar Press.

Greenwood, D. and Holt, R.P.F. (2007) "John Kenneth Galbraith and Quality of Life," Unpublished manuscript.

—— (2008) "Institutional and Ecological Economics: The Role of Technology and Institutions in Economic Development, *Journal of Economic Issues*, 42 (June): 445–52.

Greenwood, M. (1989) "Jobs vs. Amenities in the Analysis of Metropolitan Migration," *Journal of Urban Economics*, 25: 1–16.

Holt, R.P.F. (2007) "What is Post Keynesian Economics?" in M. Forstater, G. Mongiovi, and S. Pressman (eds). *Post Keynesian Macroeconomics: Essays in Honor of Ingrid Rima*, 89–107, London: Routledge.

Holt, R.P.F. and Setterfield, M. (1999) "Time," in P.A. O'Hara (ed.), *Encyclopedia of Political Economy*, 1158–61, London: Routledge.

Jacksonville Community Council (2007) "Quality of Life in Jacksonville: Indicators for Progress," Jacksonville, Florida. Available at www.jcci.org/statistics/qualityoflife.aspx (accessed April 17, 2008).

Kahn, M. (1995) "A Revealed Preference Approach to Ranking City Quality of Life," *Journal of Urban Economics*, 38: 221–35.

Klein, P.A. (1974) "Economics: Allocation or Valuation?" *Journal of Economic Issues*, 8(4): 785–813.

Lavoie, M. (2009) "Post-Keynesian Consumer Choice Theory for the Economics of

Sustainable Forest Management," in R.P.F. Holt, C. Spash, and S. Pressman (eds), *Post Keynesian and Ecological Economics: Confronting Environmental Issues*, Aldershot: Edward Elgar.

Lucas, R.E. (1988) "On the Mechanics of Economic Development," *Journal of Monetary Economics*, 22: 3–42.

Maddison, A. (1991) *Dynamic Forces in Capitalist Development*, Oxford: Oxford University Press.

Meier, G. and Seers, D. (eds) (1984) *Pioneers in Development*, Oxford: Oxford University Press.

Myrdal, G. (1973) " 'Growth' and 'Development'," in *Against the Stream: Critical Essays in Economics*, 182–96, New York: Pantheon Books.

Nelson, J. (1993) "Gender and Economic Ideologies," *Review of Social Economy*, 51(3): 287–301.

—— (2001) "Feminist Economics: Objective, Activist, *and* Postmodern?" in S. Cullenberg, J. Amariglio, and D. Ruccio (eds) *Postmodernism, Economics, and Knowledge*, 286–304, London: Routledge.

Nordhaus, W. and Tobin, J. (1972) "Is Growth Obsolete?" in *Economic Growth: 50th Anniversary Colloquium V*, National Bureau of Economic Research, New York: Columbia University Press.

Norgaard, R. (1988) "Sustainable Development: A Co-evolutionary View," *Futures*, volume 20: 606–20.

—— (1989) "The Case for Methodological Pluralism," *Ecological Economics*, 1: 37–57.

—— (1994) *Development Betrayed: The End of Progress and a Coevolutionary Revisioning of the Future*, London: Routledge.

O'Hara, S.U. (1999) "Economic, Ecology, and Quality of Life: Who Evaluates?" *Feminist Economics*, 5(2): 83–9.

Pack, H. (1994) "Endogenous Growth Theory: Intellectual Appeal and Empirical Shortcomings," *Journal of Economic Perspectives*, 8(1): 55–72.

Panizza, U. (2002) "Income Inequality and Economic Growth: Evidence from American Data," *Journal of Economic Growth*, 7(1): 25–41.

Partridge, M. (2005) "Does Income Distribution Affect U.S. State Economic Growth?" *Journal of Regional Science*, 45(2): 363–94.

—— (2006) "The Relationship between Inequality and Labor Market Performance: Evidence from U.S. States," *Journal of Labor Research*, 27(1): 1–20.

Power, T. (1996) *Environmental Protection and Economic Well-Being: The Economic Pursuit of Quality*, 2nd edition, Armonk, NY: M.E. Sharpe.

Putman, R. (2000) *Bowling Alone: the Collapse and Revival of American Community*, New York: Simon and Schuster.

Roback, J. (1982) "Wages, Rents, and the Quality of Life," *Journal of Political Economy*, 90: 1257–78.

Robison, L., Schmid, A., and Siles, M. (2002) "Is Social Capital Really Capital?" *Review of Social Economy*, 60(1): 1–21.

Romer, P. (1986) "Increasing Returns and Long-Run Growth," *Journal of Political Economy*, 94(5): 1002–37.

—— (1994) "The Origins of Endogenous Growth," *Journal of Economic Perspectives*, 8(1): 3–22.

Rosser, Jr., J.B. (1999) "On the Complexities of Complex Economic Dynamics," *Journal of Economic Perspectives*, 13(4): 169–92.

—— (2005) "Complexities of Dynamic Forestry Management Policies," in S. Kant and

R.A. Berry (eds) *Economics, Natural Resources, and Sustainability: Economics of Sustainable Forest Management*, 191–200, Dordrecht: Springer.

Schmid, A. (2002) "Using Motive to Distinguish Social Capital from Its Outputs," *Journal of Economic Issues*, 36(3): 747–68.

Sen, A. (1987) *On Ethics and Economics*, Oxford: Basil Blackwell.

—— (1993) "Capability and Well-Being," in M. Nussbaum and A. Sen (eds) *The Quality of Life*, 30–53, Oxford: Clarendon Press.

Sen, A. and Dreze, J. (1996) *India: Economic Development and Social Opportunity*, Oxford: Oxford University.

Slottje, D. (1991) "Measuring the Quality of Life across Countries," *Review of Economics and Statistics*, 73 (4): 684–93.

Solow, R. (1956) "A Contribution to the Theory of Economic Growth," *Quarterly Journal of Economics*, 70 (1): 65–94.

—— (1974) "The Economics of Resources or the Resources of Economics," *American Economic Review*, 64(2): 1–14.

—— (1992) "An Almost Practical Step toward Sustainability," *Resources for the Future*, Washington, DC.

—— (1994) "Perspectives on Growth Theory," *Journal of Economic Perspectives*, 8(1): 45–54.

Stiglitz, J. (2000) *Economics of the Public Sector*, 3rd edition, New York: W.W. Norton.

Sundrum, R.M. (1990) *Economic Growth in Theory and Practice*, London: Macmillan.

Sustainable Seattle (1998) "Indicators of Sustainable Community.," Available at www.sustainableseattle.org/Programs/RegionalIndicators/1998IndicatorsRpt.pdf (accessed April 17, 2008).

Talberth, J., Cobb C., and Slattery, N. (2006) "The Genuine Progress Index 2006: A Tool for Sustainable Development," San Francisco: Redefining Progress. Available at www.rprogress.org/publications/2007/GPI%202006.pdf (accessed March 24, 2008).

Taylor, L. (1983) *Structuralist Macroeconomics: Applicable Models for the Third World*, New York: Basic Books.

Veblen, T. (1899) *The Theory of the Leisure Class: An Economic Study in the Evolution of Institutions*, New York: The Macmillan Company.

—— (1961) [1919] "On the Nature of Capital," in *The Place of Science in Modern Civilization*, 324–86, New York: Russell and Russell. Originally printed in the *Quarterly Journal of Economics*, 22(1) (1908).

—— (1922) [1914] *The Instinct of Workmanship and the State of the Industrial Arts*, New York: B.W. Huebsch.

Wismer, S. (1999) "From the Ground Up: Quality of Life Indicators and Sustainable Community Development," *Feminist Economics*, 5(2): 109–14.

World Bank (1991) *Pacific Island Economies: Towards Higher Growth in the 1990s*, Washington, DC: World Bank Publications.

Zolatas, X. (1981) *Economic Growth and Declining Social Welfare*, New York: New York University Press.

# 12 Beyond the status quo, in the world and in the discipline

## The comments of an Austrian economist

*Emily Chamlee-Wright*

I am pleased to have this opportunity to comment on the three foregoing chapters by Gar Alperovitz, Robin Hahnel, and Daphne Greenwood and Richard Holt. As I understand my role, it is to serve as a provocateur rather than a standard discussant. In order to serve in this capacity I have made the bold assumption that the editors of this volume knew what they were doing when they invited an Austrian economist, someone who has devoted her career to thinking about and advocating for the market order, to comment on two contributions that explicitly advocate replacing markets with some other system of social coordination (Alperovitz and Hahnel) and a third which seeks to dethrone market indicators as the *sine qua non* of development. The editors assured me that indeed they did know what they were doing. So, without apology, the following comments are offered from the perspective of the Austrian School.

I have two clusters of questions that I invite readers of this volume to consider in their future discussions, thinking, and writing. But to make sense of these questions, I first need to put a frame around them.

Each of the three preceding chapters expresses a deep dissatisfaction with the status quo, which is characterized by intolerable asymmetries of political, economic, and social power and looming environmental disaster. Each chapter also points to an impoverished intellectual toolkit as at least part of the problem, with mainstream economic understanding failing to provide the language or intellectual tools needed to think about alternative routes away from the status quo. In keeping with the Austrian tradition (see Hayek 1978a) I share with the authors these same deep dissatisfactions and agree that a new course is required (both in the world and in our theoretical perspectives) if we are to obtain the common good. When considering how best to move away from the political-economic status quo we face in the world – and here I am responding primarily to Alperovitz and Hahnel – the principal question is *which* path or set of paths we ought to take? When considering how best to rethink the discipline of economics so that it is competent to foster a fuller understanding of human systems beyond the narrowly economic – and here I am responding primarily to Greenwood and Holt – the question is which intellectual traditions might help in the endeavor of moving beyond the intellectual status quo of mainstream analysis.

I shall consider first the question of how best to move away from the political-

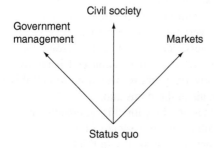

Civil society

Government
management

Markets

Status quo

*Figure 12.1* Potential paths to the common good.

economic status quo we face in the world. It seems to me that there are three possible pathways before us: (1) government restraint that reigns in markets, (2) civil society that allows for experimentation with alternative social arrangements, and (3) markets (Figure 12.1). It is important for me to say that I view the path of the market as a trajectory *away* from the status quo, as what I have in mind are radically de-politicized markets in which the winners and losers are not pre-ordained. I do not think that this is a path we are currently on, at least not at the highest levels of corporate power.

If our authors and the reader will forgive the broad brush strokes here, both Alperovitz and Hahnel advocate some combination of the first two paths – a good deal of government restraint on corporate power, and a great deal of experimentation within civil society, including experiments in common ownership such as employee-owned firms, neighborhood-owned corporations, decentralized democratic control over municipal and social enterprises (Alperovitz), and local currency systems, producer cooperatives, consumer cooperatives, and egalitarian and sustainable intentional communities (Hahnel). Both Alperovitz and Hahnel argue that if pursued systematically, the combination of these two paths would lead to an alternative system of social coordination that moves us beyond the market order.

An Austrian view begins with the same dissatisfaction with the status quo. But instead of advocating a combined path of civil society and government restraint, Austrians would advocate a combined path of civil society and de-politicized markets.

My first cluster of questions, then, is which approach offers the best potential for a radically democratic society – a combined path of government restraint and civil society or a combined path of markets and civil society? Which course offers the greatest potential for not only widespread wealth but widespread well-being – and not just for us, but across the globe?

This question seems to have fallen out of fashion since 1989 – you know, since the end of history and all. It is an abomination, I believe, if after all the intellectual effort and all the human suffering, the lesson we glean from the fall of the Soviet Empire is that the status quo is the best we are ever going to get.

In engaging this question of which course gets us to the common good, I encourage us to get beyond the quips, "oh you're just naive if you think that markets could ever be de-politicized – end of conversation." Or, for our part, "you're just naive if you think that government can be trusted to serve anyone other than the power elite – end of conversation." Don't get me wrong, these are important points of critique, but if we let the conversation end here, we play right into the hands of our common adversary: those who want to call this the end of the road; those who want to remain at the status quo.

The second cluster of questions has to do with this interesting common ground between us – this middle ground of civil society. I invite a pluralist conversation around the question, "what is the best way to think about this voluntary sphere of human interaction?"

Again, if you will forgive the broad brush strokes, both Alperovitz and Hahnel portray civil society as an arena in which human creativity flourishes, an arena in which we can experiment with new social, economic, and political arrangements. I think I am safe in assuming that both also see the market as potentially threatening to this sphere of human engagement – inappropriately intruding upon civic space by transforming communal relationships into commercial relationships. If this characterization is accurate, it is reasonable to suggest that government restraint aligns well with civil society, as government can help in blunting the intrusive effects of the market mechanism where it does not belong.

An Austrian view of civil society would agree that civil society is an arena in which human creativity flourishes; an arena in which we can experiment with new social, economic, and political arrangements. But an Austrian view would emphasize that it is the *voluntary* character of this sphere of human interaction that gives it its creative force. The discovery that unfolds within civil society is born of civic freedom and therefore more naturally aligns with the market order, not government restraint. Yes, I agree that markets can be an intrusive force, but my sense is that generally we can trust the robustness of civil society to resist and counter with non-market solutions where market intrusions are not welcome.

In this pluralistic conversation about civil society, I encourage us not to overly romanticize the concept in either our theoretical or empirical analysis. Civil society is certainly not devoid of power dynamics. But this common ground of civil society *is* worthy of our mutual attention as it is a context in which we can talk productively about the common good. On the one hand, scholars on the radical Left do not trust corporate power to offer a way toward the common good. And as I said, there is good reason to be suspicious of this power. Austrians, on the other hand, do not trust the state to offer a way toward the common good. And given the track record of state power in the twentieth and now twenty-first centuries, I think the skeptics are justified in *our* suspicions. But we ought not let our respective concerns keep us from moving the conversation beyond the status quo. Let us begin *our* conversation in this sphere of voluntary interaction we call civil society and see how far this path takes us.

As Greenwood and Holt's chapter suggests, a crucial step in advancing such a conversation is for us to critically examine the ways in which the intellectual tools and rhetorical styles of our discipline have shaped this conversation in the past. As an Austrian economist, I could not agree more. As Lavoie and I argue elsewhere (Lavoie and Chamlee-Wright 2000), our discipline has rendered itself relatively incompetent on questions of culture, power, and non-market social coordination via the narrow formalism of mainstream economic theory, the emphasis on aggregation in mainstream empirical analysis, and the exclusion of qualitative methodologies from standard economic training and practice.

Greenwood and Holt wisely point to institutional, feminist, post-Keynesian, and environmental economics as providing the intellectual tools we need to expand our conversation. I would suggest, however, that classical liberal scholars in general and Austrians in particular have been engaged in this conversation for a good long time and have much to contribute. Adam Smith's *Theory of Moral Sentiments* marks the classical liberal tradition as one that takes seriously the ways in which the market order and the moral order intertwine with one another into a complex interdependent human system. In their quest to point out the limiting nature of the neoclassical frame, and their efforts to ask questions that are relevant to the human condition Greenwood and Holt could not find a better ally than Austrian economist F.A. Hayek (1973, 1978b, 1984, 1988). Contemporary Austrians have carried on this tradition in the areas of comparative economic systems (Boettke 1990, 1993), economic development (Chamlee-Wright 1997; Storr 2004; Beaulier and Subrick 2006), post-war and post-disaster reconstruction (Coyne 2008; Sobel and Leeson 2007), and the study of social capital (Chamlee-Wright 2008).

Critiques of the political-economic status quo in the world and the intellectual status quo in the discipline have been at the center of Austrian economics discourse since its origins. Given this long and continuing intellectual history, it would seem prudent for a pluralist conversation aimed at expanding the economic discourse beyond the formalism, aggregation, and quantitative emphasis characteristic of the mainstream discourse, to include classic and contemporary Austrian scholarship as part of that conversation. Further, given the long history Austrians have had in promoting individual liberty as the pathway to human flourishing, such a voice is critical in any serious conversation about advancing human well-being.

# References

Beaulier, S. and Subrick, J.R. (2006) "Poverty Traps and the Robust Political Economy of Development Assistance," *Review of Austrian Economics*, 19 (2–3): 217–226.
Boettke, P. (1990) *The Political Economy of Soviet Socialism*, New York: Kluwer.
—— (1993) *Why Perestroika Failed*, London: Routledge.
Chamlee-Wright, E. (1997) *The Cultural Foundations of Economic Development: Urban Female Entrepreneurship in Ghana*, London: Routledge.
—— (2008) "The Structure of Social Capital: An Austrian Perspective on Its Nature and Development," *Review of Political Economy*, 20 (1): 41–58.

Coyne, C. (2008) *After War: The Political Economy of Exporting Democracy*, Stanford: Stanford University Press.

Hayek, F.A. (1973) *Law, Legislation and Liberty, Volume I: Rules and Order*, Chicago: University of Chicago Press.

—— (1978a) "Why I am not a Conservative," in *The Constitution of Liberty*, Chicago: University of Chicago Press.

—— (1978b) *The Constitution of Liberty*, Chicago: University of Chicago Press.

—— (1984) *Individualism and Economic Order*, Chicago: University of Chicago Press.

—— (1988) *The Fatal Conceit: The Errors of Socialism*, Chicago: University of Chicago Press.

Lavoie, D. and Chamlee-Wright, E. (2000) *Culture and Enterprise*, London: Routledge.

Sobel, R.S., and Leeson, P.T. (2007) "The Use of Knowledge in Natural-Disaster Relief Management," *The Independent Review*, 11 (4): 519–532.

Storr, V. (2004) *Enterprising Slaves and Master Pirates: Understanding Economic Life in the Bahamas*, New York: Peter Lang.

# 13 Hayek and Lefebvre on market space and extra-catallactic relationships

*Virgil Henry Storr*

## Introduction

This chapter explores some surprising and underappreciated commonalities between F.A. Hayek and Henri Lefebvre's writings on the market. The hope is that a richer conception of the market might result – i.e. one that corrects for Lefebvre's "anti-market bias" and Hayek's "abstractness" – by facilitating an exchange between these two thinkers. Along with Ludwig von Mises, F.A. Hayek is one of the two most significant figures in the Austrian school of eco-nomics. His reach, however, extends beyond Austrian economics. He has also made significant contributions to political theory and jurisprudence and has influenced complexity theory and psychology. Lefebvre is an important Marxian philosopher and sociologist who has critically explored dialectal materialism, alienation, the political aspects of everyday life, and most famously, the produc-tion of social space. He has been quite influential in urban studies, geography, philosophy, musicology, and applied sociology.

At first blush, we would expect a Marxian like Lefebvre and an Austrian like Hayek to have little in common. Marxists are strong critics of capitalism. They have consistently highlighted the dehumanizing and exploitive aspects of a socio-economic system based on private ownership of the means of production and the unrestrained rule of chaotic and impersonal market forces. Capitalism, for them, is a "vampire," attacking and disfiguring human souls as it expands into every quarter of our lives and ultimately every sphere of the globe in its never ending quest for more peoples and more territories to exploit. Its survival is contingent on its ability to conscript new victims and its *modus operandi* is to obscure and distort the relationships that individuals have with their labor product, their labor, themselves, and each other.

Austrians, on the other hand, have an altogether different view of capitalism. For Austrians, private ownership of the means of production, the defining feature of capitalism, is simply necessary for rational economic calculation. Without it, they argue, there is no rivalry between firms over resources, and so prices which reflect relative scarcities do not emerge. Absent meaningful prices and there can be no profit and loss accounting and so no rational economic calculation. In addition to pointing out the calculation problems that a socialist state would have to overcome, Austrians have also focused on the knowledge and incentive problems that socialist states would suffer. Rather than speaking to the potentially alienating nature of economic relationships under capitalism, Austrians have instead focused on the potential of markets to promote peaceful dealings between individuals, even between strangers.

Although these differences between Marxists and Austrians seem quite stark, however, there are a number of similarities between (at least some) Austrian and Marxian approaches. Sciabarra (1995), for instance, has argued that one can find dialectical sensibilities and strong indictments of utopian thinking in both schools. Likewise, Fleetwood (1997) has argued that Austrians and Marxists have similar methodological and philosophical perspectives. Lavoie (1983), Hong (2000), and Tomass (2001) have, similarly, highlighted a number of commonalities in Marxian and Austrian theories of money.

Despite having almost opposite attitudes toward the capitalist system, Hayek and Lefebvre have a great deal in common. They, for instance, shared the same philosophical enemies. Both objected to scientism and the hubris of central planners and social engineers (Hayek 1979; Lefebvre 2003a, 2003b). They also had similar conceptions of the market order. Both stressed that the market is a social space (in the language of Lefebvre) or a spontaneous order (in the language of Hayek) that is produced by the (inter-)actions of individuals competing against and cooperating with each other. Similarly, they had a similar blind spot when it came to the market. Neither paid any attention to the socially beneficial extra-catallactic relationships that can and do develop in capitalist markets.

A number of meaningful social relationships, however, are buttressed by markets and could not develop if markets did not exist. Paying attention to these beneficial extra-catallactic relationships is critical for at least two reasons (Storr 2008). First, economists of all stripes have been criticized by sociologists, anthropologists, and others for having too narrow a conception of the market. Although heterodox economists like Austrians and Marxists inarguably have richer conceptions of the market than their brethren in the mainstream, broadening their discussions of the market to include an appreciation for extra-catallactic relationships should lead to a better understanding of the various roles that the market plays in everyday social life. Second, recognizing that extra-catallactic interactions can occur in capitalist markets should improve their understanding of the relationship between the market and the community. It is commonplace to think of the market and the community as separate, antagonistic spheres where the growth of one means the decline of the other (Gudeman 2001) or to conceive of the market as being embedded in community and supported by social networks (Granovetter 2004). Focusing on beneficial extra-catallactic relationships augments these formulations by emphasizing that the market and the community need not be thought of as separate, competing spheres and that communal relations are also embedded within the market.

Although it is not particularly surprising that the Marxist Lefebvre does not highlight these beneficial extra-catallactic relationships, it is somewhat surprising that Hayek ignored this additional "benefit" of markets (beyond efficiency and coordination). After all, recognizing that significant social relationships can actually develop between market participants in addition to or instead of the distorted relationships that Marx believes necessarily develop under capitalism is another important argument that Hayek could have used in his defense of markets against Marx, Lefebvre, and others. Hayek might have argued, for instance, that the market not only encourages us to treat strangers as if they were honorary friends (as the term catallaxy suggests and Seabright 2004 explicitly argued) but it is also a space where actual, deep friendships can and do develop.

Interestingly, it is Lefebvre's spatial theory rather than Hayek's spontaneous order approach that most readily accommodates a discussion of extra-catallactic relationships. Because there is so much connecting the two thinkers, I propose using Lefebvre's spatial theory to extend Hayek's spontaneous order thinking in a way that opens the door to a discussion of extra-catallactic relationships. The next section, thus, focuses on some of their important differences and, then, on some surprising similarities in their approaches. The following section discusses the importance of paying attention to beneficial extra-catallactic relationships and some possible objections to extending both Hayek and Lefebvre's discussions of the market to include them. The final section offers concluding remarks.

## Understandable differences, surprising similarities

Not surprisingly, the differences between Lefebvre and Hayek become readily apparent when their respective views of the market are brought to the fore. While Hayek highlights the marvel of the market order, Lefebvre focuses on the alienation and exploitation that occurs within market spaces. The market is a space of dominance in Lefebvre's schema, whereas it is an order that results from the interactions of rule following, but freely choosing and self-regarding individuals in Hayek's oeuvre.

The marvel of the market, according to Hayek, is that, through the price system, market participants are encouraged to behave in appropriate ways without anyone directing them to do so. To see this, consider how individuals are led to conserve more when a product that they are using becomes scarcer. When an item becomes scarcer its price rises and this movement in price is sufficient to signal to buyers that they need to conserve more. As Hayek (1948: 87) writes,

> in a case like that of a scarcity of one raw material, without an order being issued, without more than perhaps a handful of people knowing the cause, tens of thousands of people ... are made to use the material or its products more sparingly.

The price system works to communicate information about scarcity and abundance, the presence of complements and substitutes, and advances in technology throughout the society.

This orchestra, as it were, plays without a conductor. In fact, no would-be conductor could hope to direct this symphony because no single mind can possess the knowledge that would be necessary to get each musician, each market participant, to sound the right notes at the right moments. The market is "an order of such a degree of complexity (namely comprising elements of such numbers, diversity and variety of conditions) ... we could never master intellectually, or deliberately arrange [it]" (Hayek 1973: 41). This notion, that it is impossible to plan and subsequently control an order as complex as the market, is at the center of Hayek's critique of socialism (Lavoie 1985).

According to Hayek, considerable general benefits accrue to societies which rely on the spontaneous ordering forces of the market. As the extent of the market expands, we are increasingly able to take advantage of the division of labor and so, as a community, we become increasingly prosperous. Lefebvre would assert, however, that we have paid dearly for this progress. In capitalist society, what I am calling market space and what Lefebvre calls at different times the space of work, exchange, and consumption is a space of alienation, domination, and exploitation. According to Lefebvre, in order to grow, capitalism created and inhabited a particular kind of space, one that is both global and fragmented (Lefebvre 1991: 282). Global in that "it abolishes distinctions and differences" (ibid.: 355) and "its circulatory systems and networks may occupy space worldwide" (ibid.: 341). Fragmented and fractured because it "locates specificities, places or localities, both in order to control them and in order to make them negotiable" (ibid.: 282). Interestingly, as Lefebvre (ibid., 355) explains,

> it is not ... as though one had global (or conceived) space to one side and fragmented (or directly experienced) space to the other – rather as one might have an intact glass here and a broken glass or mirror over there. For [capitalist] space "is" whole and broken, global and fractured, at one and the same time.

For Hayek, the expansion of capitalist space means social progress (Hayek 1988: 6). Lefebvre, however, worries about the expansion of capitalist space into other social spaces. According to Lefebvre, capitalism's survival depends on the extension of capitalist space to "space in its entirety" (ibid.: 325). Households, towns, rural expanses, and even outer space, in short, all pre-existing space has been (or if not yet must be) gobbled up and transformed by the expansion of capitalism. Additionally, capitalism creates new global and fractured spaces through processes like urbanization and globalization. This production of new space and the occupation of all pre-existing space which accompanies the growth of the market are not benign processes. Rather, "the mobilization of space for the purposes of its production makes harsh demands" (ibid.: 336). Most significantly, it requires "the entirety of space [to] be endowed with *exchange value*," which is ultimately alienating (ibid.). Following Marx, Lefebvre noted that within capitalist spaces man's labor products become alien objects, foreign things, which have a power over him. His labor product belongs to another and so ultimately he belongs to another.

Market space is what Lefebvre calls "abstract space." Abstract space is not only a space of work, exchange, and consumption; it is also a space of political power and social control. It is "the space of accumulation (the accumulation of all wealth and resources: knowledge, technology, money, precious objects, works of art and symbols)" through a variety of means, some straightforward and some quite devious, some dexterous and some quite vicious (ibid.: 49).

According to Lefebvre, because capitalism requires a space where accumulation of money and power is the supreme function, abstract space becomes "the dominant form of space" in capitalist contexts. Because, in Lefebvre's view, capitalism requires a subjugated proletariat, abstract space is also necessarily a "space of dominance." It is a space "manipulated by authorities" who are prepared to use force when necessary to "shape," "socialize," and "crush" the users of space, to bring about conformance with the edicts of the owners of space, to reinforce the distance between members of different classes (ibid.: 285). The alienating and hegemonic nature of capitalist market space is central to Lefebvre's critique of capitalism. In fact, alienation is a central concept of all of Lefebvre's work from his writing on dialectical materialism where here casts Marx as primarily a theorist of alienation to his critique of everyday life and his discussion of the production of space (Elden 2004: 41).

Potentially, Lefebvre and Hayek's differences over the nature of market space and the market order can be dismissed as having much more to do with the ideological priors of these two thinkers than any serious differences in their approaches to studying social phenomena. After all, Lefebvre is an ardent Marxist and Hayek is a leading classical liberal. We would, thus, expect them to have different views of the market. If it is these differences in orientation that are behind their different conceptions of the market, then the differences in their conceptions of market space and the market order, respectively, need not point to some fundamental incompatibility between Lefebvre and Hayek's approaches; especially since there is so much to link Lefebvrean-style spatial theorizing and Hayekian-style spontaneous order thinking.

Lefebvre and Hayek, as noted above, shared the same philosophical enemies. As noted above, both were very critical of scientism, an ideology that was coming to dominate the social sciences at the time they were writing where the "habits of thought" developed in and appropriate for the natural sciences were coming to dominate the study of social phenomena (Hayek 1948: 78). According to Lefebvre, scientism and its variants (i.e. positivism and empiricism) simply cannot comprehend reality. As Lefebvre (2002: 194) writes, "those empiricists and positivists who merely want to observe [reality] are frequently satisfied … [to] hunt down little facts … the flimsier the observation, the narrower and more precise the comment they make … the happier they are." The scientistic approach leads only to minor and quite tenuous insights about very small bits of social world; "they [only] discover a portion of reality" (ibid.) that might not stand up to even the "most cursory analysis" (Lefebvre 1991: 311). Nevertheless, hubris typically goes hand in hand with scientism. "The scientistic … view," Hayek (1979: 24) states, "is not an unprejudiced but a very prejudiced approach which, before it has considered its subject, claims to know what is the most appropriate way of studying it." The everyday experiences of individuals and the knowledge of particular circumstances of time and place which Lefebvre and Hayek thought all important are demeaned by scientism. Knowledge arrived at through any method other than the pre-prescribed "scientific method" of "deliberate experimentation" is thought to be inferior (Hayek 1979: 24; Lefebvre 1976: 61).

The hubris of scientism which leads positivists and empiricists to assume that they can know the appropriate way to study a phenomenon before considering it is also behind the spirit of social engineering and central planning which has similarly annoyed both Hayek and Lefebvre. Both thinkers emphasized the futility of trying to control social processes that were ultimately spontaneous and stressed the negative unintended consequences of efforts to do so. They have both had choice words for the "engineers," "planners," "technocrats," and "urbanists" who have "grandiose visions" of "remaking society." For Hayek (1988), as stated earlier, the constructivist assumption that human reason can direct complex social processes which no human mind can comprehend in totality let alone direct is not only an error but a potentially disastrous one that has led to totalitarianism and threatened us all with serfdom. Lefebvre, similarly, railed against constructivist planners, noting their inability to predict all of the potential consequences of their actions. Lefebvre has further described technocratic planning as a myth. Planners, architects, and urbanists, Lefebvre (2003a) notes, can at best pretend to quantify everything, control everything, predict everything and at worst produce repressive spaces instead of the urban utopias they imagine. An urban planner, Lefebvre (ibid.) notes, may zone for a certain kind of space (commercial space), an architect may design a particular kind of space (an office building), a construction company may build a certain kind of space (a two storey concrete structure), but the way that space is ultimately experienced is not the result of intentional design. The activities that (re-)produce that social space cannot be centrally planned.

In addition to sharing the same intellectual foes, Lefebvre and Hayek also articulate similar conceptions of the social world. Hayek's spontaneous order approach has much in common with Lefebvre's spatial theory. First, both spontaneous social orders and social spaces, as conceived by Hayek and Lefebvre respectively, are the result of purposeful human action but not the product of intelligent design. In fact, spontaneous social orders and social spaces are not only the site where social activity takes place they are also the unintended product of social activity. As Lefebvre (1991: 26) writes, "(social) space is a (social) product." And, as Hayek (1973: 37) writes, a spontaneous order is "the product of the action of many men but not the result of human design." Additionally, the orders and spaces that emerge as a result of the "unintended" actions of individuals are profoundly affected by context. Culture, the law, the structure of the means of production and the nexus of social relationships in which actors are embedded, influence and constrain human action and shape the kinds of orders and spaces which surface.

Both Lefebvre and Hayek, as noted earlier, also ignore the possibility that commercial relationships can grow into beneficial social bonds. Again, it is the Marxist Lefebvre and not classical liberal Hayek whose framework most readily accommodates a consideration of the benefits of the market. Hayek's approach, because it remains abstract, obscures certain aspects of the market, both the potential existence of alienation and the potential for beneficial extra-catallactic relationships to develop between market participants. Lefebvre's approach, because he forces a focus on both the activities that create social space as well as the activities that occur within social space, does not suffer from the sort of blinders that limits Hayek's method. By blinders, I mean simply to describe the tendency in Hayekian spontaneous orders studies to focus primarily on the rules of the game and the properties of the resulting order to the exclusion of other activities that are made possible by the existence of the order being studied. Moreover, Lefebvre's focus on alienation to the exclusion of other aspects of market space is not dictated by his conception of social space. Indeed, Lefebvre (2002: 206–215) opens the door to this kind of move by conceding that capitalist markets can under some circumstances be simultaneously alienating and disalienating.

This is not to suggest that Hayek does not appreciate that the market order facilitates all manner of social practices and that market participants are motivated by different and often incommensurable ends. In fact, Hayek believed that an important feature of the market order is that it allows individuals with different purposes and beliefs to peacefully coexist and to mutually benefit each other without forcing them to agree or even be aware of each other's aims and worldviews. But, Hayek was not concerned with the particularities of the various social processes that are made possible by markets. The emphasis is simply not on the specifics of this or that beneficial social process that is facilitated by the market order. Instead, Hayek's case for the market order rests on it being the only viable economic system that can facilitate these various processes without requiring agreement between market participants on their potential or actual benefits (Hayek 1988: 7). He is, thus, principally concerned with the rules that lead to a well-functioning market order and the consequences of interfering in this wealth-generating game. Alienation like inequality, exploitation, and all of the other complaints that Marx, Lefebvre, and others have leveled against capitalism are largely irrelevant because they are symptoms of our only viable option for maintaining our civilization, namely, the market order.

Because Lefebvre (1991: 73) understands social space as a space that is "itself the outcome of past actions" and which "permits fresh actions to occur," his spatial theory pushes us to look at the various social activities which produce a particular space and which take place within that space. According to Lefebvre, particular social spaces encourage certain social practices and proscribe others. We imbue particular spaces with certain meanings and so we use particular spaces in certain ways. We reserve and set apart particular spaces for particular activities. Similarly, certain social relations and kinds of social relations are sustained and are sustainable in particular spaces. A neighborhood church, for instance, is a social space that is produced and assigned potentially disparate (socially constructed) meanings by its architects and construction workers, its priests and parishioners, members of its broader faith community located around the globe and non-parishioners living in the community that it serves. Additionally, the neighborhood church is a space where we work, worship, find fellowship, volunteer, receive alms, and feel the presence of God.

The space of the market is likewise a social space. Viewing the market in this way brings several questions to the surface: What is the exact nature of this space? How is it produced? Which types of actions are possible and difficult, which are promoted and proscribed in the market? What kinds of relationships are encouraged and discouraged in the space of the market? What is the relationship between market space and other social spaces? Although Lefebvre has stressed the alienation that attends life in abstract space, his encouragement that we look to the various uses of space and the various spatial activities which produce space opens the door for the discussion of other social processes that occur within the market. Rather than remaining abstract, as does Hayek's discussion of the market order, Lefebvre's encourages us to look more closely at concrete everyday lived experience in the market under capitalism. One of the processes that can and does occur in the space of the market, and one that is typically overlooked, is the formation of significant beneficial extra-catallactic relationships between market participants.

A focus on the positive social bonds that can develop between participants is important for at least two reasons. First, it can lead to a more balanced view of market space than is found in Lefebvre. It can to a certain extent correct for his anti-market bias. Laborers in capitalist society need not be estranged from one another, beneficial extra-catallactic relationships can and do develop between coworkers which at the very least mitigate and possibly overturn the supposed alienating aspects of market space. Second, a focus on positive extra-catallactic bonds can push us towards a richer conception of the market order than is found in Hayek. Because his focus is elsewhere, whether workers in the market order are more likely to become alienated from their co-workers or to form close associations with one another is a question that Hayek ignores. This makes him needlessly vulnerable to attacks by those who contend that the growth of the market order is at the expense of social structures like communities, families, and friendships.

## On extra-catallactic relationships

The social capital literature is full of discussions of the economic significance of social networks (i.e. non-catallactic relationships that form outside the market). Where social capital is high, societies are said to more prosperous (Putnam 2000). Social networks are important enablers of economic development, innovation, and collaboration and can be an important resource for individuals as they pursue their economic goals (Coleman 2000). Social networks can also be an important economic salve by reducing transaction costs and improving economic efficiency. The reverse, however, is also true and is often overlooked. Social networks, to use Weber's terminology, are both economically significant and economically conditioned.

That deep social bonds can develop between market participants is an important feature of the market. A number of meaningful conversations happen in markets. Conversations that express more than bid–ask, conversations that are not just bartering and negotiations, conversations between socially bonded market participants concerned with more than simply making a deal happen frequently between market participants. Moreover, many beneficial social relationships are buttressed by markets and would not exist if markets did not exist. As the reach of the market continues to expand (as advocates and critics alike predict), its affect on community becomes an increasingly important question to address. Are the market and community really separate, competing spheres as some believe? Does the rise of one really mean the death of the other? Is it possible to think of the market as promoting community or must we think only in terms of the market estranging workers from their employers, customers, one another, and themselves? Are meaningful, positive friendships between coworkers possible? If we consider the possibility of extra-catallactic relationships then the market–community dualism so prevalent in modern economic and social thought might be overcome.

The market can serve as an incubator for several types of extra-catallactic relationships (Storr 2008). Family businesses, for instance, are quite widespread and can serve the income, fulfillment, and identity needs of family members and cement the natural bonds that exist between them (Kepner 1991). Similarly, master–apprentice and mentor relationships, typical in several trades and professions, can sometimes grow into close friendships or father–son, mother–daughter type relationships. As Kram (1983: 614) suggests, mentorship relationship fulfills a number of "psychosocial functions including role modeling, acceptance-and-confirmation, counseling, and friendship." Principal–client, seller–buyer relationships can also grow into deep friendships like those between lawyers and their clients, hairdressers and their customers, and retailers and their shoppers. As Price and Arnould (1999: 50) suggest, "commercial friendships, similar to other friendships, involve affection, intimacy, social support, loyalty, and reciprocal gift giving." Additionally, office romance is a common phenomenon. Love matches, flirting, dating, and sexual interactions that have nothing to do with harassment or improper motives are prevalent in the contemporary workplace (Williams *et al.* 1999). Work spaces can also serve as a screening mechanism for selecting appropriate mates. As Price *et al.* (1996: 12) note, since firms tend to select people who fit within their corporate culture, "organizations ... function as filters resulting in attitudinally similar employees which may, in turn, increase the potential for romantic initiations."

Not surprisingly, deep friendships can also develop between coworkers. Marx (1992) has also acknowledged this and has described the bonds that can develop between factory workers. Although much of the research on workplace friendships has focused on whether or not they contribute to productivity and worker morale, there exists a significant body of literature that discusses the nature of these relationships. Henderson and Argyle (1985), for instance, explain that three types of social relationships develop between coworkers: coworkers can become mere acquaintances, work friends, and social friends who frequently interact outside of the workplace. Although work acquaintances are probably the more common occurrence, social friendships between coworkers do occur with some frequency. As Bridge and Baxter (1992: 200) write, "for many adults who work outside the home, friendships frequently evolve from existing role relationships in places of employment and are maintained within those organizational settings." Berman, West, and Richter (2002) have similarly described the key proprieties of workplace friendships and have stressed how workplaces can facilitate friendships. As they write, "workplaces often have features that may facilitate friendship making. Workplaces are sites where people meet others, including co-workers, clients, members of other departments or organizations, and supervisors" (ibid.: 219).

The view of market space that comes into focus once these extra-catallactic relationships are highlighted does not look at all like the space of brutality, of exploitation, of alienation, which Lefebvre describes. Instead, the importance of markets as spaces where social friendships develop and are encouraged becomes evident. Highlighting these relationships also reinforces Hayek's claims that the market order plays a critical role in both our economic and non-economic dealings with others by providing a concrete example that escaped Hayek (1978: 113). In addition to its material wealth-enhancing properties, the market order is also seen to be potentially socially enhancing.

Admittedly, several objections might be raised to my extending Lefebvre and Hayek's description of the market in a direction that focuses on the beneficial extra-catallactic relationships that develop in the market. First, the focus here has been on extra-catallactic relationships that are welfare enhancing. No attention has been paid to extra-catallactic relationships that (re)produce class antagonisms or that lead to power, status, and income inequalities. Relationships of this sort are, of course, not foreign to Lefebvre. In fact, it is because of Lefebvre's insistence that we confront extra-catallactic relationships conditioned by exploitation and alienation that it is possible to extend his analysis to consider social relationships which develop in market space that are potentially beneficial. Additionally, extending Hayek's discussion and defense of markets to include considerations of the socially beneficial aspects of extra-catallactic relationships opens the door to a discussion of the various ways that they might also be socially harmful. Acknowledging that welfare-enhancing relationships may evolve is both an answer to market critics who assert that the growth of the market is at the expense of community, family, and friendships and an implicit acceptance of the validity of challenges along these lines. It remains an empirical question, then, as to whether or not the extra-catallactic relationships which do develop in markets are mostly socially beneficial.

A second potential objection to extending discussions of market space to include extra-catallactic relationships might be that similar relationships are apt to form wherever individuals spend large portions of time with one another. To be sure, similar friendships have formed between inmates, soldiers, congregants, classmates, workers in Soviet firms, and people in all sorts of social settings. Again, it is important to highlight the existence of these relationships within capitalist market settings because it has been argued that the market necessarily distorts and stands in the way of man's connection with his fellow man and that the market and community are necessarily in contention with one another. Even if the majority of commercial relationships are not deep social friendships that some commercial friendships have developed into deep connections undermines those arguments. Similarly, that friendships, romantic relationships, and family ties can be deepened within market contexts suggests that the space of the market is also a space of community. At the very least, it makes for a more balanced account. Whatever else it may be, the space of the market is also a social space where meaningful social relationships develop.

## Conclusion

The market is at the core of economic life but is all but ignored by economic theorists. Prominent sociologists like Lie (1997) and Swedberg (1994) have also criticized economists for lacking a full theory of the market, one that describes it as a rich social structure. As Lie (1997: 342) writes, "the market, it turns out, is the hollow core at the heart of economics." What is needed is an economic theory that treats the market as a "social phenomenon in its own right" (Swedberg 1994: 255). Both Hayek and Lefebvre have rich conceptions of the market. Both Hayek and Lefebvre, however, stop short of highlighting the meaningful conversations that can occur in markets and the social friendships that can grow out of market relationships. Combining the strengths of their approaches to understanding social phenomena can, arguably, overcome this important gap in their discussions of the market. Hayek becomes more concrete and Lefebvre becomes less one sided.

By embracing pluralism, this chapter ultimately suggests the benefits of both intellectual specialization and exchange. Austrian and Marxian approaches to understand the market are similar enough projects to make trade between them possible. Yet, they are distinct enough that trade between them is likely to be profitable. This has already proven true. The calculation debate, for instance, helped Austrians and Marxian economists alike improve their understanding of the market process, the role of prices, property, etc., as well as, the potential of market socialism and worker cooperatives (Lavoie 1985; Burczak 2006). Arguably, a pluralistic approach can be beneficial when looking at extra-catallactic relationships, especially since the empirical questions that need to be answered would benefit from the interdisciplinary bent of Marxian analysis (Muga 1990) and the Austrian insistence on treating individuals as being simultaneously embedded in the market, the society, and the polity and not merely materially or socially determined (Boettke and Storr 2002).

Does the market on balance distort and stunt relationships or incubate and make possible new and different types of relationships? Which kinds of relationships are likely to survive the growth of the market and which are likely to wither away? Are some markets better able to promote beneficial extra-catallactic relationships than others? To seriously explore these questions is to invite a pluralistic approach.

## References

Berman, E.M., West, J.P., and Richter, M.N. (2002) "Workplace Relations: Friendship Patterns and Consequences (According to Managers)," *Public Administration Review*, 62 (2): 217–230.

Boettke, P.J. and Storr, V.H. (2002) "Post Classical Political Economy: Polity, Society and Economy in Weber, Mises and Hayek," *American Journal of Economics and Sociology*, 61 (1): 161–191.

Bridge, K. and Baxter, L.A. (1992) "Blended Relationships: Friends as Work Associates," *Western Journal of Communication*, 56: 200–225.

Burczak, T.A. (2006) *Socialism after Hayek*, Ann Arbor: University of Michigan Press.

Coleman, J.S. (2000) "Social Capital in the Creation of Human Capital," in P. Dasgupta and I. Serageldin (eds.) *Social Capital: A Multifaceted Perspective*, 13–39, Washington, DC: World Bank.

Elden, S. (2004) *Understanding Henri Lefebvre: Theory and the Possible*, New York: Continuum.

Fleetwood, S. (1997) "Critical Realism: Marx and Hayek," in T. Keizer and Zijp (eds.) *Austrian Economics in Debate*, 127–150, New York: Routledge.

Granovetter, M. (2004) "Economic Action and Social Structure: The Problem of Embeddedness," in F. Dobbin (ed.) *The New Economic Sociology: A Reader*, 245–273, Princeton: Princeton University Press.

Gudeman, S. (2001) *The Anthropology of Economy*, Malden, MA: Blackwell Publishers.

Hayek, F.A. (1948) *Individualism and Economic Order*, Chicago: University of Chicago Press.

—— (1973) *Law, Legislation and Liberty: Volume I*, Chicago: University of Chicago Press.

—— (1978) *Law, Legislation and Liberty: Volume II*, Chicago: University of Chicago Press.

—— (1979) *The Counter-Revolution of Science: Studies in the Abuse of Reason*, Indianapolis, IN: Liberty Fund.

—— (1988) *The Fatal Conceit: The Errors of Socialism*, Chicago: University of Chicago Press.

Henderson, M. and Argyle, M. (1985) "Social Support by Four Categories of Work Colleagues: Relationships between Activities, Stress, and Satisfaction," *Journal of Occupational Behavior*, 6: 229–239.

Hong, H. (2000) "Marx and Menger on Value: As Many Similarities as Differences," *Cambridge Journal of Economics*, 24: 87–105.

Kepner, E. (1991) "The Family and the Firm: A Co-Evolutionary Perspective," *Family Business Review*, 4 (4): 445–461.

Kram, K.E. (1983) "Phases of the Mentor Relationship," *The Academy of Management Journal*, 26 (4): 608–625.

Lavoie, D. (1983) "Some Strengths in Marx's Disequilibrium Theory of Money," *Cambridge Journal of Economics*, 7 (1): 55–58.

—— (1985) *National Economic Planning: What is Left?*, Cambridge, MA: Ballinger.

Lefebvre, H. (1976) *The Survival of Capitalism*, London: Allison & Busby.
—— (1991) *The Production of Space*, Malden, MA: Blackwell Publishing.
—— (2002) *Critique of Everyday Life, Volume II: Foundations for a Sociology of the Everyday*, London: Verso.
—— (2003a) *The Urban Revolution*, Minneapolis: University of Minnesota Press.
—— (2003b) "Beyond Structuralism," in S. Elden, E. Lebas, and E. Kofman (eds.) *Henri Lefebvre: Key Writings*, 37–41, New York: Continuum.
Lie, J. (1997) "Sociology of Markets," *Annual Review of Sociology*, 23: 341–360.
Marx, K. (1992) *Capital: Volume I: A Critique of Political Economy*, New York: Penguin.
Muga, D.A. (1990). "The Marxist Problematic as a Model Interdisciplinary Approach to Ethnic Studies," *Journal of Ethnic Studies*, 17(4): 53–80.
Pierce, C.A., Byrne, D., and Aguinis, H. (1996) "Attraction in Organizations: A Model of Workplace Romance," *Journal of Organizational Behavior*, 17(1): 5–32.
Price, L.L. and Arnould, E.J. (1999) "Commercial Friendships: Service Provider-Client Relationships in Context," *Journal of Marketing*, 63(4): 38–56.
Putnam, R.D. (2000) *Bowling Alone: The Collapse and Revival of American Community*, New York: Simon & Schuster.
Sciabarra, C.M. (1995) *Marx, Hayek and Utopia*, Albany, NY: State University of New York Press.
Seabright, P. (2004) *The Company of Strangers: A Natural History of Economic Life*, Princeton, NJ: Princeton University Press.
Storr, V. (2008) "The Market as a Social Space: On the Meaningful Extra-Economic Conversations that Can Occur in Markets," *Review of Austrian Economics*, 21 (2 and 3): 135–150.
Swedberg, R. (1994) "Markets as Social Structures," in N. Smelser and R. Swedberg (eds.) *The Handbook of Economic Sociology*, Princeton, NJ: Princeton University Press.
Tomass, M. (2001) "Incommensurability of Economic Paradigms: A Case Study of the Monetary Theories of Mises and Marx," *Review of Political Economy*, 13 (2): 221–243.
Williams, C.L., Giuffre, P.A., and Dellinger, K. (1999) "Sexuality in the Workplace: Organizational Control, Sexual Harassment, and the Pursuit of Pleasure," *Annual Review of Sociology*, 25: 73–93.

# 14 The plural economy of gifts and markets

*Ioana Negru*

## Introduction

Economists' theories and histories of market exchange are increasingly attuned to the behavioral and institutional complexity of markets. Yet the pervasive phenomenon of gift (Godbout 1998) continues to receive relatively little attention from economists. This chapter outlines an integrated view of market and gift processes, viewing the modern economy as a gift–market nexus. This vision flows from a pluralistic, poly-institutional notion of economy, as distinct from the mono-institutional, market-centered conceptions which continue to be employed by even the most sophisticated institutionalist economists (North 1990; Hodgson 2001).

Markets have always exhibited a wider economic and social role than that prescribed by the conventional view of markets as simply exchange mechanisms. By looking at markets as institutions, it is possible to connect our thinking about markets with other institutions (such as gift) that are observed in contemporary economies. Economists, anthropologists, and historians have been inclined to pose the spheres of market and gift in complete opposition. This juxtaposition leads to, or derives from, the conventional linear image of historical development in which market relations systematically displace gift relations (Hicks 1969, Polyani 1944 [1957]). The present chapter challenges this conventional view.

## *Homo economicus* and pro-social behavior

Norms and rules are examples of institutions with varying degrees of permanence. While specific versions prevail at a given point in time, they also evolve and change historically. Gift is such an example. "To give" implies to transfer or to deliver voluntarily to another person something over which you have control or property rights. We define gift as a transfer motivated by altruism. The magic of gift is altered once there is an expectation of returning the gift. Accordingly, a *gift* may be thought of as a transfer, either material or non-material, between individuals, from an individual to a group, from a group to an individual, or from a group to another group.

Conventionally, gift-giving actions have been embodied in a form of social exchange theory. In anthropology, the traditional theory of gift can be traced to Malinowski ([1922] 1961). Gifts have long served the useful function of reducing uncertainty in important social interactions. Malinowski's contribution was further developed by Mauss ([1925] 1966), who asserts that gifts are not used to exchange goods and services but form the underpinnings of alliances that are broader in essence. Such alliances contribute to social cohesion and, of course, are not devoid of economic significance. Mauss (1966) claims that gift-giving was used to open a social relationship, to accumulate prestige, and to overwhelm rivals, while Homans (1961) suggests that gift-giving was also used to create trust, cohesion, and social capital. From this perspective, gift is a type of social exchange that is distinct from market exchanges since it is power and custom, rather than utility maximization, that is the driver in social relationships. Equally, for Bourdieu (1977), gift is a mechanism that converts economic capital into social capital. Gift thus has both an economic and a broader social dimension to it.

Gift-giving, in these societies, appears to be a form of social interaction not unlike contemporary market exchanges. This conception of gift as constituting weak forms of altruism clearly resonates with the axioms of self-interest, instrumental rationality, and utility-maximization that predominate within conventional forms of economic analysis. The concept of exchange is clearly differentiated in economic exchange and symbolic or social exchange (Malinowski 1961; Levi-Strauss [1949] 1969; Ekeh 1974) echoing the dichotomous relationship between gift and markets. Despite delineating the two spheres, it seems also that the duality of gift, or the co-existence of generosity and self-interest that motivates gift-giving, is the leitmotif of the traditional view advanced in sociology and anthropology. Thus, the motivations for gift-giving are conflated even by Mauss himself who presents gift as a symbolic form of reciprocity. Indeed, it is important to distinguish between a *pure gift*, which implies no expectation of reciprocity (or *quid pro quo*), and an *impure gift* that is given in anticipation of return. This raises interesting questions about the motivations of individuals and whether economics might have a contribution to make to our understanding of gift-giving.

Within economic theory, there is a long tradition of assuming that human behavior is inherently selfish. This is manifest in conventional economists' preoccupation with individual optimizing behavior. One argument for retaining self-interest as the behavioral baseline in economic analysis derives from Adam Smith's concept of the invisible hand: the claim that social resource allocation can best be achieved via competitive interactions among self-interested individuals (Collard 1978). Theorems on efficiency and Pareto-optimality are based on denying any role to altruistic goals or preferences.

Yet contemporary game theory has shown a wide range of circumstances in which competitive markets do not yield optimal allocations. Even where the invisible hand mechanism can be proven to operate successfully, this does not fully negate the role of gift in allocating certain resources. An efficient market also requires cooperative behavior and trust. According to Collard (1978), altruism (i.e. as a principle of action represents regard for others) creates a need for socially cooperative actions and facilitates voluntary social cooperation.

Non-selfishness (based on love or Kantian duty) can help in generating a cooperative solution and also foster redistribution. However, non-selfish preferences are not sufficient to generate spontaneous redistribution, and the fostering of altruism and gift has to be institutionalized through the state (Collard 1978).

Not all economists are convinced that economic analysis would be advanced by including gift-giving and altruism as part of our understanding of a market-based system. Becker (1981), for instance, has argued that altruism can be present in families or households, but is not a market characteristic. However, since members of the family maximize the utility of the *oikos* (the household), altruism is nothing but self-interest. Even when economists apply the concept of gift such as Akerlof (1984), who essentially adopts a Maussian model of gift exchange to examine the relationship between workers and firms as part of the process of wage determination in the labor market, his analysis closely resembles a form of reciprocity rather than gift (in the sense used here). In the neoclassical approach espoused by Akerlof (1984), there is no advantage to pay a higher wage than the market-clearing wage. In a gift economy, which functions on norms related to gift, there is the perception that benefits may occur by paying a higher wage. Sellers may accept lower prices or buyers may agree to pay higher prices in order to maintain a *relationship*.

Recent studies in economics have revisited the self-interest axiom. Studies such as charitable giving and intergenerational transfers (e.g. Andreoni 1989, 1990), voting (e.g. Mueller 1989, 1997), and voluntary tax-paying (Meier 2006) have convincingly argued that such actions cannot only be explained by using the selfishness paradigm. The reciprocity model gained status especially in experimental economics and the theory of games (Kolm 1984, 2000; Fehr and Schmidt 1999; Fehr and Gächter 2000). Meier (2006), who has made some valuable contributions to the theory of pro-social behavior (i.e. behavior that systematically deviates from self-interest), has argued that despite previous findings, contributions to public goods are possible without government intervention, and institutions need to be designed to foster and encourage pro-social behavior. For a pro-social behavior, the institutional environment in which people decide to contribute time and money to public goods is crucial and can influence intrinsic motivation to behave pro-socially. Meier (2006: 135 and 138) concludes:

> The good news is that the prospect of people behaving pro-socially does not look so gloomy as is often predicted by economic theory. People deviate systematically from the self-interest hypothesis by contributing money and time to public goods. The bad news is that they not always do so. In certain situations, people are not willing to contribute to a good cause and hence the public good is not provided in a socially optimal amount.

and

> The good news that people behave pro-socially is bad news for orthodox economists, who are reluctant to accept that standard economic theory is limited and sometimes purely wrong in predicting behavior.

Finally, in the absence of a coherent theory of gift, gift-giving has recently re-emerged in economic theory under different forms ranging from altruistic and non-selfish preferences to reciprocity, pure and impure altruism, charity and philanthropy, and cooperative and pro-social behavior. The outcome of such a development is the fragmented and counter-productive presence of different facets of gift within different theories: the economics of altruism, the economics of philanthropy, grant economics, economics of reciprocity. Social scientists have been skeptical about the ability of economists to understand adequately gift transactions in a conventional methodological framework (e.g. Cheal 1988; Monroe 1996). Paraphrasing Sen (1985), perhaps the time is ripe for building a robust theory of gift in economics.

## Coexistence of markets and gift: the gift–market nexus

On an evolutionary and historical scale, it can probably be argued that in the practice of gift-giving, as rooted in custom and traditions, we can find the origins of barter, exchange of goods, and subsequently the exchange of commodities (e.g. goods produced for market and trade processes). Conventionally, we have encountered the distinction between gift and market in the form of gift–commodity dichotomy as the basis for a non-market versus market-based system. *Gift* as a metaphor for a social, symbolic form of exchange embodying non-market, personal relations has been contrasted with *commodities* as a symbol of economic exchange and impersonal market relations. For Gregory (1982), gift and commodity are essentially two different forms of property. Commodities are *alienable* in the sense that all rights are given up when they are exchanged for other commodities while gifts are *inalienable* and create the obligation of counter-gift (i.e. a return). Gregory's analysis of gift however does not prove very useful in the context of a modern interpretation of gift when the importance of exclusive property rights for the actual act of giving or donation is essential (Cheal 1988).

The difference between gift and market has also been envisaged as a difference between subjective and objective values in exchange, as a promise versus contract, as implicit versus explicit *quid pro quo*, and so on. Reciprocity, too, seems to underpin the distinction between commodities and a pure gift. Market exchanges and reciprocal gifts both incorporate reciprocal transfers with intended consequences, but there is an implied notion of "exchange of equivalents" and "balance" in the latter, which is not necessarily the case in the giving of reciprocal gifts. In a Maussian interpretation, gifts often prove to be agonistic forms of social interaction. Even when the "magic" of gift seems to be altered, "to reciprocate is totally different from 'to receive' of mercantile exchange; the latter is accumulative, in essence, retentionist; we exchange to possess more, to accumulate. It represents a different logic" (Godbout 1998: 181). A gift creates the feeling of bonding as a basis for a social system of relationships while commodity exchange does not. Finally, for Bourdieu (1977, 1979), the gift brings a symbolic negation of calculability and economic rationality. The defining characteristic of gift is the time separation and the lack of simultaneity between gift and counter-gift.

The social sciences literature has accustomed us to a view that economic development represents a departure from community norms and values. Such norms and customs (e.g. gift) are in opposition to the markets that developed once the *impersonal* relations of exchange, production, and distribution replaced the *personal* relations or networks amongst identifiable agents. In most social sciences, including economics, the usual practice has been to present gift-economy as an economic system that has been replaced (and partially destroyed) by the development of capitalism as an economic system based on self-regulated, interconnected markets. The central question has therefore become whether development really destroys social capital, personal relations and networks, the moral codes in society, and so on. Thompson (1971) and Zelizer (1979) have responded positively to this question: markets have indeed replaced moral aspects with the emergence of capitalism. This discussion of the boundaries of the market has been extremely important for economists in demarcating what is inside and outside the realm of economic inquiry. But the presentation of gift as an economic system has contributed to the hard acceptance of a prominent role for gift in modern societies. Economists such as Peroux (1963) and Kolm (1984), and even Mauss (1966) himself conceptualized gift as an economic system. In contrast, and in line with the argument advanced in this chapter on the development of economic systems, very few economists have argued against viewing gift-systems as an alternative to market-systems. A notable exception is Mirowski (2001) who, rather than offering the two systems as alternatives, seeks to connect them with a theory of value.

Scholars have equally been drawn toward what we term the linear model of economic development advanced by economic historians such as Polanyi and Hicks. These two major works investigating the emergence of markets (Polanyi 1957 and Hicks 1969) have considered whether norms and markets are two rival institutions that operate as substitutes for each other within the economic development process. This perspective on the emergence and historical development of markets represents an important contribution to the economics literature because they have emphasized the importance of the institutional context for the development of markets.

Polanyi and Hicks place in historical opposition pre-modern societies based on *exchanges* governed by *norms, customs, and gifts*, and modern market-based societies governed by the *laws of demand and supply*. By constructing such a dichotomous view that identifies markets with economic principles, and non-market based systems with social relations, they have perpetuated a problematic divide between these modes of production and distribution. A similar distinction with Polanyi is made by Kreitner (2001) and also by Sahlins (1972), whose work has been deeply influenced by Polanyi's thought. In discussing the differences between the contractual economy and the gift-based economy, Kreitner (2001) acknowledges that the differences are to be found in the creation and accumulation of wealth (in the case of a market system) and the redistribution of wealth (for a gift-based economy). Moreover, in discussing the evolution of the contractual economy, Kreitner (2001: 1951) suggests that "the rejection of status and gift-exchange ... are part of a re-imagination of the market as a distinct sphere of activity." The institutional nature of markets contradicts any division of social spaces into spheres of calculability or non-calculability. After all, markets are built upon different norms, belief systems, and values with a diversity of cultural and historical dimensions – as is equally the case of gift as an institution.

The Polanyian pattern of transformation has since been much debated and disputed. It has been claimed (see Dalton 1969) that Polanyi developed his model with reference to research conducted on early European societies where a variety of non-market elements still exist and contribute to their development and growth. For instance, the transition experience has shown clearly that the emergence of market institutions has coexisted with norms such as gift, bribe, and other types of informal institutions (Negru and Ungurean 2001, 2002). This, it has been argued, gives the Polanyian model limited applicability for developing countries. Other scholars have found evidence against the Polanyian claim that markets only began to play an important part in society from the eighteenth and nineteenth centuries (e.g. Silver 1983; Anderson and Latham 1986, who identify elements of trade and market exchange in antiquity, the early Middle Ages, and pre-modern Africa.) This position is further supported by Boardman *et al.* (1990: 127, 133, 204, and 219) who identify that the Greeks had highly specialized trade, forms of protectionism, regulation of consumption, and financial institutions that regulated exchange and the market in the fifth century.

A whole literature on the importance of community and informal support that helped the development of market and contractual relations mushroomed. Greif (2001), for example, advocates an alternative understanding of the role of *communities* in complementing markets and economic development. Communities, along with the state and the market, were compliant in the enforcement of contracts and property rights. Greif (2001: 5) states:

> Perhaps more important than the above theoretical argument, the experience of pre-modern Europe indicates the important complementarity between communities and markets in the process of development. Indeed, a particular system of inter-community contract enforcement based on intra-community contract enforcement supported market expansion in Europe.

Thus Greif (2001) calls attention to the importance of other entities such as communities in providing support for the coordination of individual agents within the sphere of markets.

The perceived decline of informal support that occurred during the shift from medieval to modern society has been scrutinized by Krausman Ben-Amos (2000) amongst others. Research on philanthropy and charity has shown that both in England and Continental Europe, the volume of bequests and voluntary contributions to institutions and poor relief schemes has provided informal support at least from the sixteenth century onward (Krausman Ben-Amos 2000; Slack

1988; Archer 1991; Cavallo 1995). Informal support went beyond the material giving and provided emotional and social support as well. Krausman Ben-Amos (2000: 336) concludes her interesting study:

> Informal support based on personal, often face-to-face interactions remained viable throughout the sixteenth and seventeenth centuries. Its precise dimensions are difficult to quantify, and some types of informal support are hard to document at all ... It permeated a wide range of social, economic, and human exchanges: family life, labor, markets, leisure activities, migration. Not all interactions in these contexts entailed gift exchange, but the varied forms of personal help, the emergence of new forms of informal support even as older types declined, the infiltration of these types of support into the more formal, anonymous market and urban transactions – all suggest how vigorous informal support remained.

What is important for the present argument is that historical evidence shows that informal support continued after the development of markets, and complemented the formal, state support of the development of trade and exchange. All of these arguments cast doubt on attempts to clearly identify historical phases with specific economic systems. The idea that there is a specific phase of primitive accumulation which marked the transition from feudalism to capitalism is perhaps too linear. Economic systems are characterized by diversity and residues of previous systems (e.g. Perelman 2000, for an account of self-provisioning in capitalism).

Another issue that might explain the view of the narrow applicability of gift-giving theories to the modern world emerges in relation to the predominant focus of anthropology. Gift transactions have been studied mostly in primitive societies, thus ignoring the need for similar investigations in modern societies. Unfortunately, gift-giving has not been seen as a significant social phenomenon in the study of modern societies (even within sociological theory, see Cheal 1988). Anthropology, sociology, and even economic history have contributed to a dichotomization of primitive and modern spheres of economic and social activities that conclude that gift-giving somehow belongs to a pre-modern society that cannot usefully inform our daily lives. There are some notable exceptions, such as Bleshaw (1965) and Mauss (1966) who directed our attention toward the importance of studying archaic societies to improve our understanding of modern society. Although Levi-Strauss (1969) and Mauss (1966) both believed that gift-giving involved different social aspects, and was of far more importance in archaic societies than in our own, they did assert the relevance of gift for understanding modern society. Levi-Strauss (1969), for example, has drawn parallels between the gift in Melanesian and Polynesian societies, i.e. potlatch, and the Christmas gift norms in modern societies that both are underlined by a desire for power, prestige, and reciprocity. Mauss (1966) interpreted the modern system of social security as an example of gift-giving. Titmuss (1970: 224) emphasized that the role of giving, gifts, and altruism is even more important in complex, large-scale societies than was suggested by sociology or economic anthropology. It is very possible that such developments have influenced the incompatibility perspective between gift and markets.

What has been less discussed within the literature is the persistence of non-market forms of transfers and exchanges into modern times. The historical evidence on the previous coexistence of gifts and markets forms a sound basis for disputing a linear transformation of economic systems. Different forms of exchange such as reciprocity, redistribution, and market exchange have been present (although in a different guise to those existing within modern society) in pre-modern economies. In modern times, the persistence of non-market exchanges suggests that the potential coexistence of markets and gift is not simply a historical relic. For example, reciprocity and gift-giving have been identified as important components within the workplace (e.g. Akerlof 1984). The current systems of organ and blood donation based upon altruistic acts have supplanted the failed market mechanisms previously put in place to regulate the allocation of these scarce resources (Titmuss 1970: 205). Forms of gift-giving in the modern world are examples of cooperation that sit alongside market and state provision of benefits to society. Gift transfers are to be found in organ donations, charity and philanthropic contributions, bequests and so on. What makes gift to be modern is the *voluntary* character of these personal relationships (Godbout 1998) that can decide what is left at the level of individual and what can market and state do in terms of provision of public goods. Despite modernity refusing to accept the existence of a freely, disinterested given gift, the coexistence of market and gift can be seen as contribution to social order and social harmony. As Elster points out (1989: 287) "altruism, envy, social norms and self-interest all contribute, in complex, interacting ways to order, stability and cooperation."

## Institutional pluralism

Political economy as constructed by Smith and others perceives selfish behavior via the mechanism of the market as the process by which social harmony emerges within societies. Meier (2006) however argues that pro-social behavior also contributes to social harmony. This position appears to set up the conventional oppositional or incommensurable dichotomy between markets and gifts that exists within conventional economics. Markets based upon self-interested forms of exchange are constructed as the central arena within which economic activity emerges and takes place. Meier however contends that it is more important to examine the institutional context within which pro-social behavior emerges and is fostered. If we conceive of markets and gift as being the product of the institutional context from which they spring, then this places institutions such as values and norms as the central loci of economic activity, rather than the market. The economy becomes a multi-faceted mixture of economic and social institutions for which a pluralistic outlook is required both in terms of accepting the importance of different institutions and for coping with the diversity that prevails. Perhaps the solution rests on examining gifts and markets as complex inter-related institutions rather than opposing economic systems, i.e. as complementary components within the same economic system.

The co-existence of markets and gifts of different forms within different economic systems requires recognition of the complexity of economic systems and the varying degrees of importance that should be attached to markets and other institutions such as gift in seeking to understand different economies. It is both the complexity and uniqueness of the interaction between different institutions (including market and gifts) within individual economic systems that requires recognition. In some situations, therefore, certain institutions will prevail at the expense of others in terms of their relative importance. The key message here is that the mix of institutions is more important than the individual institutions themselves: economic analysis therefore needs to examine the institutional factors that give rise to the specific mix of forms of gifts and markets within different economic systems.

Economic diversity, or plurality, should be a theme common to any discussions on past and current economic systems. Diversity occurs over time and space and different institutional arrangements create distinct market logics. The institutional settings, the State, the market, and other socio-economic institutions complement and influence one another in creating different national economic processes. The kind of diversity that is relevant here is not reducible to a unique, universal model of development. Take the case of China: it is commonly viewed as an economy and society that is striving toward a system led by the market. Yet China has particular forms of institutionalized behavior, both formal and informal, such as the network of gift or *guanxi*. These institutional arrangements are not deviations from a universal market norm, but deserve to be analyzed in their own right. These variations in the elements that comprise economic and social systems are relevant in explaining and re-emphasizing the importance of path-dependence, change, historical specificity, and so on. These elements of diversity have been viewed as temporary residues and non-essential traits of transition phases from one development stage to another. What we would like to argue is that diversity should be perceived as a permanent attribute of economic and social development over time. Norms, institutions, and rules emerge, develop, change, and breakdown continuously. Our investigation of economic systems should not be limited and the role and place of gift in modern economic systems should be acknowledged.

If economic reality informs us of an alternative conception of the relationship between gift-giving and markets to that which is posited within conventional economic theory, then there is evidently a need for the adoption of a more pluralist approach to the analysis of economic systems and development. In this chapter we have explored what we term as *institutional* or *systemic pluralism*, i.e. the coexistence of a plurality of elements such as forms of gift and markets that are the outcome of different institutional arrangements. Through a discussion of the nature of gift, and the argument that gift does not necessarily exist outside the confines of the market, we have advanced a form of systemic analysis that is pluralist in its approach. Thus, institutional pluralism represents the mechanism for embracing institutional complexity and the non-universality of economic systems.

## Acknowledgment

The author wishes to express her gratitude to Robert Garnett for his comments on a previous version of this chapter.

## References

Akerlof, G.A. (1984) *An Economic Theorist's Book of Tales*, Cambridge: Cambridge University Press.

Anderson, B.L. and Latham, A.J.H. (eds) (1986) *The Market in History*, London: Croom Helm.

Andreoni, J. (1989) "Giving With Impure Altruism: Applications to Charity and Ricardian Equivalence," *Journal of Political Economy*, 97 (6): 1447–1458.

—— (1990) "Impure Altruism and Donations to Public Goods: A Theory of Warm-Glow Giving," *Journal of Political Economy*, 97(3): 1147–1158.

Archer, I.W. (1991) *The Pursuit of Stability: Social Relations in Elizabethan London*, Cambridge: Cambridge University Press.

Becker, G. (1981) *A Treatise on the Family*, Cambridge: Harvard University Press.

Bleshaw, C. (1965) *Traditional Exchange and Modern Markets*, Englewood Cliffs: Prentice Hall.

Boardman, J., Griffin, J., and M. Oswyn (1990) *The Oxford History of the Classical World*, Oxford: Oxford University Press.

Bourdieu, P. (1977) *Outline of a Theory of Practice*, Cambridge: Cambridge University Press.

—— (1979) *Algeria 1960*, Cambridge: Cambridge University Press.

Cavallo, S. (1995) *Charity and Power in Early Modern Italy: Benefactors and Their Motives in Turin, 1541–1789*, Cambridge: Cambridge University Press.

Cheal, D. (1988) *The Gift Economy*, London: Routledge.

Collard, D. (1978) *Altruism and Economy: A Study in Non-Selfish Economics*, Oxford: Martin Robertson.

Dalton, G. (1969) "Theoretical Issues in Economic Anthropology," *Current Anthropology*, 10 (1): 63–102.

Elster, J. (1989) *The Cement of Society: A Study of Social Order*, Cambridge: Cambridge University Press.

Ekeh, P. (1974) *Social Exchange Theory*, London: Heinemann.

Fehr, E. and Schmidt, K.M. (1999) "A Theory of Fairness, Competition and Cooperation," *Quarterly Journal of Economics*, 114: 817–868.

Fehr, E. and Gächter, S. (2000) "Fairness and Retaliation: The Economics of Reciprocity," *Journal of Economic Perspectives*, 14 (3): 159–181.

Godbout, J.T. (1998) *The World of the Gift*, Montreal: McGill-Queen's University Press.

Gregory, C.A. (1982) *Gifts and Commodities*, London Academic Press.

Greif, A. (2001) "Impersonal Exchange and the Origins of Market: From Community Responsibility System to Individual Legal Responsibility in Pre-Modern Europe," in M. Aoki and Y. Hayami (eds.) *Communities and Markets* in *Economic Development*, 3–42, Oxford: Oxford University Press.

Hicks, J. (1969) *A Theory Of Economic History*, Oxford: Oxford University Press.

Hodgson, G.M. (2001) *How Economics Forgot History: The Problem of Historical Specificity in Social Science*, London: Routledge.

Homans, G.C. (1961) *Social Behavior: Its Elementary Form*, London: Routledge and Kegan Paul.

Kolm, S.C. (1984) *La Bonne Économie. La Reciprocité Générale*, Paris: Presses Universitaires de France.

—— (2000) "The Theory of Reciprocity, Giving and Altruism," in L.A. Gerard-Varet, S.C. Kolm, and M. Ythier (eds.) *The Economics of Reciprocity, Giving and Altruism*, 1–44, Houndmills: Macmillan Press.

Krausman Ben-Amos, I. (2000) "Gifts and Favors: Informal Support in Early Modern England," *The Journal of Modern History*, 72 (2): 295–338.

Kreitner, R. (2001) "The Gift Beyond the Grave: Revisiting the Question of Consideration," *Columbia Law Review*, 101 (8): 1876–1957.

Levi-Strauss, C. ([1949] 1969) *The Elementary Structures Of Kinship*, London: Eyre and Spottiswoode.

Meier, S. (2006) *The Economics of Non-Selfish Behavior*, Cheltenham: Edward Elgar.

Malinowski, B. ([1922] 1961) *Argonauts of the Western Pacific*, New York: Dutton.

Mauss, M. ([1925] 1966) *The Gift: Forms and Functions of Exchange in Archaic Societies*, London: Routledge and Kegan Paul.

Mirowski, P. (2001) "Refusing the Gift," in S. Cullenberg, J. Amariglio, and D.F. Ruccio (eds.) *Postmodernism, Economics, and Knowledge*, 431–458, London: Routledge.

Monroe, K.R. (1996) *The Heart of Altruism: Perceptions of a Common Humanity*, Princeton: Princeton University Press.

Mueller, D.C. (1989) *Public Choice*, Cambridge: Cambridge University Press.

—— (1997) *Perspectives on Public Choice: A Handbook*, Cambridge: Cambridge University Press.

Negru, I. and Ungurean, S. (2001) "Corruption in Transition Economies," *Journal of Georgian Academy of Sciences*, Economic Series, 9 (1–2): 56–63.

—— (2002) "Axiology and Corruption in Transition Economies – Case Study: Romania," Paper presented at the 53rd Conference of the International Atlantic Economic Society, Paris.

North, D.C. (1990) *Institutions, Institutional Change and Economic Performance*, Cambridge: Cambridge University Press.

Perelman, M. (2000) *The Invention of Capitalism: Classical Political Economy and the Secret History of Primitive Accumulation*, Durham, NC: Duke University Press.

Peroux, F. (1963) *Économie et Société. Contrainte, Échange et Don*, Paris: Presses Universitaires de France.

Polanyi, K. ([1944] 1957) *The Great Transformation*, Boston: Beacon Press.

Sahlins, M. (1972) *Stone Age Economics*, Chicago: Aldine.

Sen, A. (1985) "The Moral Standing of the Market," *Social Philosophy and Policy*, 2 (2): 1–19.

Silver, M. (1983) "Karl Polanyi and Markets in the Ancient Near East: The Challenge of the Evidence," *The Journal of Economic History*, 43 (4): 795–829.

Slack, P. (1988) *Poverty and Policy in Early Modern England*, London: Longman.

Titmuss, R.M. (1970) *The Gift Relationship*, London: George Allen.

Thompson, E.P. (1971) "The Moral Economy of the English Crowd in the Eighteenth Century," *Past and Present*, 50: 76–136.

Zelizer, V.R. (1979) *Morals and Markets*, New York: Columbia University Press.

# 15 Communities and local exchange networks

## An Aristotelian view

*Philip Kozel*

## Introduction

Eric Helleiner notes that "beginning in the early 1980s, citizens in countries across the world, from Australia and Japan to Canada and Britain, have created hundreds of local currencies" (2002: 255–6). Local Exchange Trading Systems (LETS) are even more pervasive, with thousands in existence today all around the world. Local currencies and LETS comprise what I refer to as local exchange networks, where members buy/sell services and material goods either by utilizing local scrip or via electronic credits/debits. These networks vary widely in scale and scope, but a common objective behind them involves building a more self-reliant local economy and a "communitarian sense of identity" (Helleiner 2002: 257). Despite their prevalence and rapid growth, very little economic scholarship has emerged on these phenomena and what has emerged tends to dismiss them as either responses to market failures (Adaman and Madra 2002) or epiphenomenal utopian responses to global capital (Odekon 2006).

One rationale for this treatment resides in how most economic frameworks are ill equipped to make sense of the "ethics of communal reciprocity" underpinning these market-based networks. How trading relations can facilitate community building and a collective ethic/identity is not something the mainstream of economics or its critics usually consider. Celebrants of the marketplace today treat exchange as essentially the product of self-interested actions of individuals who give little thought to collective values and ethics (Kozel 2006). On the other hand, Colin Macleod notes that "In traditional left-wing critiques, the market has been characterized as the enemy of equality on various grounds: it generates exploitation; it creates alienation; it is hostile to genuine freedom; and it is corrosive to bonds of community" (1998: 1). Critics and celebrants of market activity profoundly disagree about what exactly exchange relations entail, but both envision market activity as essentially antithetical to community (for better or worse). Local exchange networks around the world beg to differ.

In what follows, I first explore Aristotle's economic writings and how he argued market activity can serve to build solidarity while promoting individual and communal well-being. I then analyze the workings of, and motivations behind, local exchange networks to flesh out their attempt to humanize the marketplace. This section focuses on how these movements strive to change the social relations surrounding the marketplace to promote specific goals and outcomes. I then consider a range of criticisms directed at these movements, from both the left and right, and conclude by highlighting how the Aristotelian perspective developed here reaches across the left/right divide.

## Aristotle and the marketplace

At first pass it may seem odd to turn to an ancient scholar to help understand contemporary social movements predicated upon humanizing the marketplace, especially one not widely noted for his economic views. Aristotle's writings on the economy certainly were not voluminous; book one of *The Politics* and chapter five of the *Nicomachean Ethics* contain most of his work on the subject. Nonetheless, in these brief passages Aristotle produced a nuanced understanding of market activity and its possibilities to bring the individual pursuit of the good life into harmony with the good life of the community. Aristotle's concern for community, like his mentor Plato, arose in part due to the great political and economic upheaval associated with the 30-year Peloponnesian War. Thucydides (1982), in his famous contemporary history of the era, argued that during and after the Peloponnesian War, *areté* (the aggregate of qualities such as valor and virtue that make up good character) and proper statesmanship – key facets of a just, cohesive community – became increasingly supplanted by individualistic self-seeking behavior with disastrous social consequences. Aristotle turned his intellectual prowess toward discovering the root causes of the decay of Athenian democracy and society during this period and suggesting ways to thwart them.

Aristotle's *The Politics* discussed the exchange of commodities in relation to the provisioning of households. Aristotle's *Nicomachean Ethics* in contrast evaluated exchange relations alongside a range of other social relations to explore how it might help or hinder social cohesion and virtue. The modern difficulty in interpreting Aristotle's theory of exchange arises in part because examinations of the relationship between communal solidarity and market activity have all but disappeared from economic literature. Contemporary economists (Finley 1970; Kauder 1953; Lowry 1987a, 1987b) tend to focus on Aristotle's discussion of the proper ratio (e.g., prices) for exchange and, in fact, much of the debate surrounding Aristotle's economic writing concerns the value-form he employed to determine the proper ratio of exchange.[1] Aristotle's price theory is, however, tangential to his primary rationale for exploring market activity in the first place, e.g., its linkages with communal and individual well-being.

Aristotle's introductory note on *oikonomia* (household management) in *The Politics* states: "Since every *polis* consists of households, it is essential to begin with household-management" (1253b). Aristotle began his economic analysis of *oikonomia* by asking the following:

> Is the acquisition of goods the same as household-management, or a part of it, or a subsidiary to it? And if it is subsidiary, is it so in the same way as

shuttle-making is subsidiary to weaving, or as bronze-founding is to the making of statues?

(*The Politics* 1256a)

Household management cannot be simply equated with the acquisition of goods (*chrematistike*), however, "because it is the task of the one to provide, the other to use" (*The Politics* 1256a). Nonetheless, acquiring goods via exchange did play a role within household management and the provisioning of needs because it helped re-establish "nature's own equilibrium of self-sufficiency" (*The Politics* 1257a). Aristotle in effect argued exchange could help rectify the imbalances of nature, for if one household finds itself with an excess of wine and another of grain, the exchange of surpluses can ensure both have the necessities of life (Lowry 1987a: 191, 197). These exchanges also help form communal bonds of reciprocity – a key feature of a just community.

Aristotle saw, however, another use for exchange – garnering profit – and worried about this for a number of reasons. Aristotle believed that using exchange simply for individual gain undermines communal solidarity because profits come at the expense of others in the community – an activity he saw as "the source of quarrels and accusations" (1131a). Aristotle also argued that seeking profits entailed a breakdown in the community structure by corrupting the people involved. To clarify this issue, Aristotle employed his notion of the good life. Aristotle considered the good life to be the ultimate goal of human happiness – "[t]he kind of life needed for perfect happiness is something fixed and given, being somehow dictated by men's very nature" (Saunders 1981: 37). The good life implies the pursuit of many activities, with the end goal or complete end (*teleios*) being the happiness obtained from fulfilling them within a socially cohesive community (Van Staveren 1999: 66–8).

All human pursuits serve ideally for Aristotle as a means toward *teleios*. The *techne* of doctoring, for example, concerns ensuring health, that of military leadership, victory, and that of acquiring goods, household provisioning. People pursuing any *techne* beyond its (limited) end not only violates its express purpose, but can be individually and social detrimental. Someone who pursues good health to an extreme, for example, may experience hypochondria or other obsessions that undermine their own well-being. Furthermore, the single-minded pursuit of one activity leads to a neglect of the other arts required for a cohesive community. The art of household provisioning and its relationship to the good life received special attention from Aristotle and are key for the discussion here.

The good life requires basic needs fulfillment, "for neither life itself nor the good life is possible without a certain minimum supply of the necessities" (*The Politics* 1253b23). Aristotle maintained, however, that people's unlimited desire for life coupled with the possibility of acquiring wealth in monetary forms occasionally led to the desire for unlimited wealth. Yet, he argued acting upon this desire resulted in disastrous social and individual consequences. Household accumulation above its immediate, discrete needs wastes social wealth and undermines community, because an excess in one household implies a deficiency of wealth in another.[2] Furthermore, Aristotle argued profit-driven exchange channeled people's energy toward a limitless end (wealth) and in doing so, crowded out other arts necessary for individual and communal well-being: "Acquisition beyond the necessary amount is a diversion of the citizen's capacities from the sphere of *polis* life" (Lewis 1978: 73).[3]

People leading a good life participate in social and political activities, while those obsessed with amassing wealth for "pleasures of the body" forsake them in their pursuit of gain. The social and political activities undertaken by these obsessed members of society become transformed into a means to acquire wealth; politics becomes analogous to the modern concept of rent-seeking, which for Aristotle meant empire and war. Furthermore, society itself becomes fragmented into self-seeking individuals with little concern for the well-being of the community as a whole. A society of self-seeking individuals of course comprises the foundational point of analysis for mainstream economic thought, which explains why collective actions or cooperative behavior emerged as an anomaly for mainstream economic thought.[4] Aristotle began from exactly the opposite theoretical standpoint, however, where communal solidarity and involvement were the norm.

Aristotle's belief that market activity can play a valuable role in building community helps explain why he did not condemn exchange *en toto*, but this stance produced a conundrum in his analysis: how to ensure market activity facilitated rather than undermined his ideal of the communal and individual good life. William Kern (1983) and Lewis (1978) argued Aristotle solved the problem by appealing to reason and education in the moral virtues. I agree with Kern and Lewis that Aristotle (like Plato) saw a role for educating the population to help combat self-centered greed – what Aristotle called a "type of wickedness" (*Nicomachean Ethics* 1130a25). Yet, others such as Pack (1985) and Lowry (1987a) argue that reducing self-centered behavior to an individual flaw or perversion misses how Aristotle also focused on the social relations inducing such behavior. Aristotle sought more than education to thwart the unnatural form of exchange and this is reflected in the concrete actions the Athenian state *did* take to (re)shape the marketplace, such as "public regulation to assure reasonable prices and profits while protecting flows of stables, such as corn (grain), upon which the people depended" (Lowry 1987a: 236). The regulation did not curtail market transactions, but instituted price controls "so as not to impinge deleteriously upon the proper functioning of the *oikonomia* of the household and state" (Lowry 1987a: 238). The conclusion drawn from Aristotle's analysis is clear: both moral suasion and the proper institutional structure are necessary to ensure the marketplace fulfills its proper role in ensuring communal and individual well-being.

## Local exchange networks and community

Local exchange networks employ either the use of a local currency or electronic credits in the non-profit systems known as LETS. These networks vary widely in scale and scope, but a common objective behind them parallels Aristotle's desire to promote individual and communal well-being via trade relations. In one of the few formal surveys undertaken of LETS members, Colin Williams, Theresa Aldridge, and Jane Tooke, note that 74.3 percent join for community-building reasons (2003: 159); a finding consistent with Eric Helleiner's (2002) work on local-currency movements. The modern concern about the loss of community by the participants in local exchange network arises, perhaps ironically at first pass, due to the perceived impact of today's market relations upon people's lives.

Like Aristotle, however, participants in local exchange networks do not condemn or condone market activity in the abstract, but seek to reconstruct the social arrangements surrounding the marketplace itself to produce outcomes they desire. The activists promoting the use of local payment systems maintain their use, coupled with grass-roots education in community values, facilitates communal solidarity and a more self-reliant local economy suited to fulfill the individual needs of the participants.[5] The ideal outcomes embraced by backers of these networks may have roots in an admixture of green philosophy and sustainable economic development as presented in E.F. Schumacher's *Small is Beautiful: Economics as if People Mattered* (1973), but they approach the marketplace in a very Aristotelian manner. One major difference between Aristotelian-inspired policy and these networks has to do with how they design collectively managed local payments systems instead of employing price controls or other top-down administrative actions.

Paul Glover founded Ithaca HOURs, a local currency in Ithaca, New York, which is now a prototype for local currency movements, and he maintains the use of local currency enables communal solidarity because using it "promote[s] the expression of values such as service, fairness, fellowship, and cooperation, rather than greed, privilege, and self-seeking" (1994: 2). For Glover, the use of national currencies promotes anonymous, *quid pro quo* transactions, where individuals seek simply the best prices for products and interact only long enough to establish a contract. How local payment networks promote greater sense of communal solidarity and individual well-being flows directly from how they function.

Local currencies, for instance, are inconvertible and bound by a specific geographical area; holders of a local scrip must spend it on locally available goods and services provided by other participating members. The use of scrip therefore necessitates repeated interactions amongst those involved, helping to promote an awareness and knowledge of the participating individuals and reinforcing bonds of community. Personal relationships fostered through the use of local payment networks therefore extend beyond *quid pro quo* interactions and possess positive externalities contributing to communal cohesion. Helleiner notes advocates of local currency networks report that people who "opt in" often provide as reasons an increased "sense of belonging" and/or a desire to be involved in "community building" (2002: 266). The slogan embossed on Ithaca HOURs – We're Making a Community while Making a Living – reflects this desire to promote the communal and individual good life.

Local currencies mediate transactions just like national scrip; Robert Swann and Susan Witt note that a "local currency may be dollar-denominated or measured in chickens or hours or cordwood, as long as people know they can spend that chicken cash, that cordwood note" (1995: 7). Paul Krugman illustrated how local scrip functions in his study of a 1970s babysitting co-op (1999). Coupons were issued among members of the co-op that entitled the bearer to one hour of baby-sitting. The more than 100 members earned additional baby-sitting scrip by tending the babies of fellow members and were given lists of fellow members. Employing baby-sitting scrip allowed the co-op members to know and trust each other through repeated interaction, helping to form bonds of trust and a greater awareness of each other as resources. Although Krugman uses the co-op to demonstrate the concept of a liquidity trap, for members eventually began to hoard baby-sitting scrip for rainy days, local currencies today go far beyond such specific usage.

Ithaca HOURs, for instance, in the city of Ithaca, New York are in wide circulation for a variety of uses. Members receive the newsletter *HOUR Town* which contains all in the area who will accept HOURs and this actually rivals the local yellow pages in size. *HOUR Town* lists more than a 1000 merchants, craftspeople, daycare providers, restaurants, and even credit unions for which Ithaca HOURs are acceptable means of payment (Glover 2000). Each HOUR is currently worth approximately 10 US dollars, which constitutes the going hourly wage rate in the Ithaca area, and HOURs come in several denominations (halfHOUR, quarterHOUR, etc). The HOURs system generates the revenues necessary to cover the costs of printing and maintaining the currency through the sale of ads in the directory, by the repayment of HOUR loans in dollars, and by keeping about 5 percent of new currency issued for operating expenses (Glover 2001).

LETS are similar to local currencies but they function by allowing members to buy/sell services and material goods via electronic credits (often called LETS credits) within a system overseen by a LETS committee or Board of Directors. James Taris, a prominent LETS activist, defines them as "local community trading groups where members exchange their goods and services with each other in a spirit of harmony and a genuine desire to help each other" (2003: 1). New members typically pay a small registration fee, which both covers the operating costs and effectively gives them a permit to use or expend LETS credits. Members provide an initial list of needs alongside services or goods they are willing to provide and continually update their list. Members can run LETS deficits, which also allows these payment systems to function as an informal credit systems. In Australia, where LETS are widespread, several people have even constructed housing using LETS credits instead of a bank mortgage (Wikipedia 2007). Some local currencies like Ithaca HOURs also serve as a source of credit; the organizers of HOURs, for example, provide zero-interest loans to individuals for a range of purposes. The local currency in Magdeburg, Germany, the Urstromtaler, even has an on-line banking system where individuals can take out loans (BBC 2007).

Besides providing access to credit, local exchange networks also help finance a range of community-related activities. The Ithaca HOURs network, for example, issues 14 percent of new Ithaca HOURs as community grants which have gone toward more than 60 local organizations. These grants go toward providing "modest start-up payments to businesses and individuals who provide published backing for HOURs by agreeing to be listed in HOUR town" (Glover 2001). Businesses and individuals which agree to accept HOURs are initially given a goodwill grant of HOURs, allowing them to purchase goods and services from other members of the network. This practice allows participating businesses to lower their initial start-up costs by using HOURs to purchase local goods and services; a practice which in turn facilitates building relationships with other participating members. In line with the philanthropic, communal ethic underpinning these movements, many professionals and businesses charge a lesser amount of local scrip or LETS credits for goods and services than their dollar equivalent, effectively giving a discount to those using them.

Local exchange networks may also stimulate regional economic development and the fulfillment of household needs in other ways as well. Purchasing commodities and services from national or even regional chain stores often means dollars (e.g., profits) leave the area, but local scrip and LETS credits stay put; this implies these networks promote local economic activity in ways national currency cannot. Local exchange networks have in fact both demand and supply side effects for the participating area. Regarding demand, the regionally bounded nature of local scrip and LETS potentially creates a near infinite local multiplier.[6] The circulation of local currency and LETS also gives the participants in the community more purchasing power in national scrip since they may earn and spend local currency and LETS credits for many of their needs. Ron Shaffer examines how local currencies also stimulate the supply side of the local economy writing that "people who have limited cash income might have more to offer if the local economy valued something other than that which we exchange for cash, e.g., hours, product or service" (1998). Local currencies and LETS thereby help stimulate local skills which are often forgotten and abandoned.

Local exchange networks are regional by definition and design but their proponents stress the global implications of their use. Taking the phrase "think globally, act locally" to heart, Glover envisions a global economy populated by regional payment networks. National and supernational currencies would serve primarily to link "a planet of such communities" (2001: 2). Local exchange networks may be integrated within the prevailing national and global marketplace, but they nonetheless help strike a better balance between local and global market integration. These networks seek to transform what Sen (2002), an economist who has pioneered bringing Aristotelian concepts and ethics into contemporary economic development theory, calls the "enabling conditions" of the marketplace, both locally and globally, to produce the specific results they desire. Promoters of local exchange systems share a nuanced understanding of market activity, for like Aristotle, they recognize that exchange relations entail radically different outcomes depending upon their social context. This insight, coupled with their desire to foster a communal and an individual good life, comprises the basic philosophic foundation and rationale for the proliferation of local currency and LETS movements in today's economic landscape.

## Critics of local exchange networks

The popularity and rapid growth of local exchange networks today demonstrates their popular appeal, but they have been subject to a wide range of criticisms. It is often pointed out, for example, how these networks suffer from all the problems typical of voluntary, community-based organizations. Many local exchange networks have been spearheaded by a small group of activists who become overworked and burn out. Forbes recently (2006) ran a story about the demise of the Brooklyn, N.Y., Brooklyn Greenbacks in 2001 because the organizers basically ran out of steam. Many of these problems have been overcome, however, with surviving networks actively sharing organization tips and even start-up manuals for new networks. Local trading systems have a strong tradition of learning by doing while overcoming obstacles, and have produced impressive and growing knowledge bases for new groups to learn from. Hence, while this criticism has some merit, the problems cited were more pervasive with the "pioneer" movements a decade or so back.

Free market optimists such as Hayek (1991) possess three more theoretical concerns about local exchange networks. First, they argue that the rules behind, and usage of, local exchange networks violate personal liberty and freedom – presumed key features of commercial life today. What these optimists seem to have in mind here, however, are mining towns in the nineteenth and early twentieth century which used company scrip. Company scrip could only be spent at the company's store and took many forms – "pasteboards, coupon books, paper bills called shinplasters, brass checks, and metal discs with holes through them like Turkish piasters" (Korson 1965: 72). Companies provided employees with scrip typically as an advance on their wages or in the form of loans, for which the chronic layoffs, part-time work, and low wages created a fertile environment. George Korson also notes "Miners resented the company store for three reasons: prices were much higher than those charged by independent retail stores, their grocery and supply bills were checked off their earnings even before they received their pay, and trading was compulsory" (1965: 72). Historians point out that not all companies used local scrip to create local fiefdoms (see for example Duke 2003), but nonetheless, the communities established via company scrip often served to exacerbate local power dynamics.

Market optimists also dismiss the ethical philosophical concerns voiced by participants in local exchange networks, deeming it retrogressive. The market system as a whole is championed precisely because the anonymous transactions it engenders serve to promote community among strangers. Localism (LETS "buy-local" initiatives for example) is condemned therefore because it both coerces people to detach themselves from the vigorous and evolving system of commercial life today and makes strangers enemies rather than friends. The coexistence of local exchange networks alongside the "traditional" marketplace points out a fundamental error of lumping today's local exchange networks with company scrip and undermines the ethical argument as well.

Besides the fact that the mere existence of a local exchange system does not imply any specific economic or social outcomes – these are determined by the social/institutional context within which they are located – local exchange networks are not designed to control the workforce or enforce the prices for buying/ selling commodities. Local exchange networks work from the bottom up, not like top-down price controls or company scrip, and people today enter into local exchange networks voluntarily, implying if anything, more freedoms rather than less. Local exchange networks do not function as a substitute for a more traditional market, but rather as a complement; the co-existence of market forms therefore undermines the localism argument as well.

Market optimists also argue that local exchange networks, along with "buy-local" campaigns, impede rather than foster economic growth and social welfare. For market optimists, attempts to direct or humanize the marketplace in effect produce sub-optimal levels of growth and inefficient outcomes by shackling Smith's invisible hand. As Sen (1999, 2002) notes, however, the marketplace is always dependent upon a host of enabling conditions, such as ownership patterns and social opportunities, and outcomes depend on these conditions. Local exchange networks, from this perspective, should not be seen as distorting the marketplace, but rather instituting a new set of conditions more conducive to producing optimal communal and individual outcomes. In fact, even if one could empirically demonstrate that local exchange networks resulted in lower levels of economic growth, this in itself would be beside the point. Local exchange participants simply employ a different (Aristotelian) rubric to evaluate economic outcomes, where wealth is a means to an end, not an end in itself.

A third line of criticism, which deserves detailed attention due to its prevalence on the left, dismisses local exchange networks as populist or utopian for failing to challenge the structure of capitalism in general. Odekon, for example, argues these movements present themselves as an alternative to neoliberalism (i.e., the establishment of a Polanyian "one big market") "but often fail to realize that neoliberalism is a class-based ideological movement that has systematically marginalized labor and rendered capital victorious in its struggle against labor, at home and abroad" (2006: 420). Basically, these critics dismiss local exchange initiatives for not presenting a systemic alternative to capitalism as a whole.

The flaw in this criticism resides in how these critics commonly portray capitalism (or today, neoliberalism) as a monolith – an all-powerful hegemonic structure – which in turn needs another all-powerful structure to challenge it. J.K. Gibson-Graham provocatively rejects this line of thinking, for example, "the tendency to constitute 'the' economy as a singular capitalist system or space rather than as a zone of cohabitation and contestation among multiple economic forms" (2006: xxi). Gibson-Graham instead envisions today's economic space as already populated with alternative economies easily overlooked by the myopic "monolithic" gaze. Making these alternatives visible serves as an alternative politics in itself as it works to challenge the "all powerful," demoralizing vision of capitalism and allow, in their words, "an ever-replenishing sense of room to move, air to breath, and space and time to act" (2006: xxxiii; also 1996).

The importance of local exchange networks for the left goes beyond stimulating economic activity, for these networks foster alternative ways to view economic life that extends far beyond simple trading relations. Although predicated upon exchange relations, they help produce ways of thinking about economic activity that extends much further than simply distribution. Regarding production, local currency and LETS networks can and do challenge normal (e.g., capitalist) production processes. First, these alternative exchange systems explicitly foster individual and household production and thereby provide income opportunities without the sale of their labor-power to capitalist enterprises. Second, local trading systems can facilitate non-capitalist production directly by targeting worker/producer cooperatives with their start-up grants and LETS credits. Third, these trading systems enable people to find needed items and services produced via non-capitalist forms of production. For these three reasons, Kojin Karatani (2003) touts LETS as uniquely positioned to support anti-capitalist struggles within the broader capitalist economy.

Local exchange networks also challenge capitalist social relations by facilitating an alternative economic ethic based on community and needs fulfillment – a concrete manifestation of what Gibson-Graham calls a "politics of economic possibility." Such a politics "rests on an enlarged space of decision and a vision that the world is not governed by some abstract, commanding force or global form of sovereignty" (2006: xxxiii). The burgeoning local exchange movement embodies a new way of approaching economic life based on communal values and ethics and highlighting the goals and accomplishments of these systems works to provide a refreshing antidote to the right's "end of history" narrative and the pessimism on the left regarding neoliberal globalization.

## Conclusion

> Aristotle's economic writing was an attempt to harness and discipline the exchange process; it was an attempt to solve the problem of using the exchange process without being dominated by it. The problem remains.
>
> (Lewis 1978: 89)

The perceived conflict between the marketplace and community has been, and remains, a staple of right- and left-wing social and economic thought. The market optimists on the right maintain attempts to build community via "restrictions" on market activity are counterproductive and ethically retrogressive. Marxists and others on the left argue market activity, by its very nature, undermines communal solidarity and accordingly view local exchange networks as utopian. The ability to go beyond entrenched positions on the left and right is one of the virtues of pluralism in economic theory and philosophy. The Aristotelian analysis presented here gives us a framework to understand both the motivations behind local exchange networks and how they actively reconstruct market relations to foster individual and collective well-being.

## Notes

1 The controversy initiated by Joseph Schumpeter over whether or not Aristotle or other Ancient Greeks such as Xenophon in his *Ways and Means* produced a systemic analysis of economic activity (a theory of prices) or simply dispensed "pompous common sense" (Schumpeter 1954: 57) is rooted in which value-form Aristotle employed. Marginalist theorists (Kauder 1953; Soudek 1952) read Aristotle as expressing a nascent version of a subjective theory of value. Karl Marx argued, however, that Aristotle was the "first to analyze the value-form, like so many other forms of thought, society, and nature" (1990: 151) and maintained he was groping toward a labor theory of value, even though the prevalence of slave-based production in Ancient Greece undermined his efforts; see also de Ste. Croix (1981).
2 Van Staveren (1999) provides a lucid and detailed study of the importance of excess and deficiency in Aristotle's notion of justice; see especially chapter 7.
3 Champlin and Knoedler (2004) make a similar argument, linking a Polanyian "disembedded" economy with a decline in public interest.
4 It should be noted, however, that some recent research on cooperative behavior has emerged lately (see, for example, Kolm and Ythier 2006, and Meier 2006) that challenges equating economic rationality with self-centered, maximizing behavior.
5 As mentioned above, these movements are not homogeneous. Many of these movements, especially local currencies, began as attempts to stimulate the local economy rather than build communal solidarity per se. It was quickly discovered, however, that the two often go hand in hand.
6 The multiplier refers to the total impact of some initial spending and is predicated on the notion that every expenditure is an income for another party. The size of the multiplier depends on how much of the income a party received is in turn spent to provide an income for someone else.

## References

Adaman, F. and Madra, Y. (2002) "Theorizing the 'Third Sphere': A Critique of the Persistence of the Economistic Fallacy," *Journal of Economic Issues*, 36 (4): 1045–78.

Aristotle (1985) *Nicomachean Ethics*, trans. T. Irwin, Indianapolis: Hackett Publishing Company.

—— (1982) *The Politics*, trans. T.A. Sinclair, Bungay, Suffolk: Penguin Books.

British Broadcasting Corporation (2007) *Germans Take Pride in Local Money*. Available at http://news.bbc.co.uk/2/hi/europe/6333063.stm (accessed April 2007).

Champlin, D. and Knoedler, J. (2004) "Embedded Economics, Democracy, and the Public Interest," *Journal of Economics Issues*, 38 (4): 893–907.

de Ste. Croix, G.E.M. (1981) *The Class Struggle in the Ancient Greek World: From the Archaic Age to the Arab Conquests*, Ithaca: Cornell University Press.

Duke, J. (2003) *Tennessee Coal Mining, Railroading, and Logging*, Paducah, KY: Turner Publishing Company.

Finley, M.I. (1970) "Aristotle and Economic Analysis," *Past and Present*, 47: 3–25.

Forbes (2006) *Funny Money*. Available at www.forbes.com/2006/02/11/local-currencies-ithaca_cz_el_money06_0214local.html (accessed August 2006).

Gibson-Graham, J.K. (1996) *The End of Capitalism (As We Knew It)*, Maldon, MA: Blackwell Publishers.

—— (2006) *A Postcapitalist Politics*, Minneapolis: University of Minnesota Press.

Glover, P. (1994) *New Money for Healthy Communities*, Tucson: Thomas H. Greco Jr.

—— (2000) "A History of Ithaca HOURs," *Hour Town*, January.

—— (2001) "Instead of War: Localizing while Globalizing with Community Paper Money," *Ithaca Community News*, October.

Hayek, F.A. (1991) *The Fatal Conceit: The Errors of Socialism*, W.W. Bartley, III (ed.), Chicago: University of Chicago Press.

Helleiner, E. (2002) "Think Globally, Transact Locally: The Local Currency Movement and Green Political Economy," in T. Princen, M. Maniates, and K. Conca (eds.) *Confronting Consumption*, 255–73, Cambridge: MIT Press.

Karatani, K. (2003) *Transcrique: On Kant and Marx*, trans. S. Kohso, Cambridge: MIT Press.

Kauder, F. (1953) "Genesis of the Marginal Utility Theory, From Aristotle to the End of the Eighteenth Century," *Economic Journal*, 63: 638–50.

Kern, W. (1983). "Returning to the Aristotelian Paradigm: Daly and Schumacher," *History of Political Economy*, 15(4): 501–12.

Kolm, S. and Ythier, J. (eds) (2006) *The Handbook of the Economics of Giving, Altruism and Reciprocity*, volumes 1 and 2, New York: North-Holland Press.

Korson, G. (1965) *Coal Dust on the Fiddle*, Hatboro, PA: Folklore Associates.

Kozel, P. (2006) *Market Sense: Toward a New Economics of Markets and Society*, New York: Routledge.

Krugman, P. (1999) *The Return of Depression Economics*, New York: Norton.

Lewis, T.J. (1978) "Acquisition and Anxiety: Aristotle's Case against the Market," *Canadian Journal of Economics*, 11: 69–90.

Lowry, S.T. (1987a). *The Archaeology of Economic Ideas: The Classical Greek Tradition*, Durham: Duke University Press.

—— (1987b) "The Greek Heritage in Economic Thought," in S.T. Lowry (ed.) *Pre-Classical Economic Thought*, Boston: Kluwer Academic Publishers.

Macleod, C. (1998) *Liberalism, Justice, and Markets: A Critique of Liberal Equality*, Oxford: Clarendon Press.

Marx, K. (1990) *Capital, Volume I*, New York: Penguin.

Meier, E. (2006) *The Economics of Non-Selfish Behavior: Decisions to Contribute Money to Public Goods*, Northampton, MA: Edward Elgar.

Odekon, M. (2006) "Globalization under Interrogation," *Rethinking Marxism*, 18(3): 415–32.

Pack, S. (1985) "Aristotle and the Problem of Insatiable Desires: A Comment on Kern's Interpretation of Aristotle, With a Reply by William S. Kern," *History of Political Economy*, 17(3), Fall: 391–3.

Saunders, T.J. (1981) "Reviser's Introduction to *The Politics*, by Aristotle," Bungay, Suffolk: Richard Clay (The Chaucer Press).

Schumacher, E.F. (1973) *Small Is Beautiful: Economics as if People Mattered*, New York: Harper and Row.

Schumpeter, J. (1954) *History of Economic Analysis*, E.B Schumpeter (ed.), New York: Oxford University Press.

Sen, A. (2002) "How to Judge Globalism," *The American Prospect*, 13 (1): A2–A6.

—— (1999) *Development as Freedom*, New York: Anchor Books.

Shaffer, R. (1998) "Local Currency and Low-Income Communities and Families," *University of Wisconsin – Extension Center for Community Economic Development Community Economics Newsletter*, No. 256.

Soudek, J. (1952) "Aristotle's Theory of Exchange: An Inquiry into the Origin of Economic Analysis," *Proceedings of the American Philosophical Society*, 96 (1): 45–75.

Swann, R. and Witt, S. (1995) *Local Currencies: Catalysts for Sustainable Regional Economies*. Available at www.schumachersociety.org/currencypiece.html (accessed February 2005).

Taris, J. (2003) "LETS Changed My Life," originally published in *New Community Quarterly*, May. Available at www.lets-linkup.com/080-All%20About%20LETS.htm (accessed August 2006).

Thucydides. (1982) *The Peloponnesian War*. (The Crawley Translation). New York: Modern Library.

Van Staveren, I. (1999) *Caring for Economics: An Aristotelian Perspective*, CW Delft: Eburon.

Wikipedia (2007) "Local Trading Systems." Available at http://en.wikipedia.org/wiki/Local_Exchange_Trading_Systems (accessed May 2007).

Williams, C., Aldridge, T., and Tooke, J. (2003) "Alternative Exchange Spaces," in A. Leyshon, R. Lee, and C. Williams (eds.) *Alternative Economic Spaces*, California: Sage Publications.

# Part III

# Pluralism and economics education

# 16 Promoting a pluralist agenda in undergraduate economics education

*KimMarie McGoldrick*

## Introduction

Although outlets dedicated to research in economics education have existed since the establishment of the *Journal of Economic Education* in 1969,[1] its content has remained almost exclusively mainstream regardless of whether such research discusses course content or pedagogical practices. Despite the lack of a dedicated outlet for heterodox approaches to economics education, it takes little effort to locate a significant (and growing) body of work appearing throughout heterodox journals and in edited volumes. In light of literature critical of the status quo, one might find it surprising that there has been little change in either content or pedagogical practices over the decades for which this information has been gathered. For example, the lecture mode still dominates despite scores of active learning exercises described throughout the literature (Becker and Watts 2007) and the principles textbook has deviated little from the Samuelsonian model of the 1950s in spite of significant changes in the economics it is purported to introduce (Colander 2005a, 2006). Despite this apparent inertia, I remain optimistic about the future of pluralism in economics education, and in the forthcoming pages I describe what I see as an opportunity to expand economics education in a way that is consistent with a pluralistic perspective.

Any call for change must be accompanied by discipline-wide conversations, lest change be relegated to the margins. The lack of communication between heterodox and mainstream economics educators is readily apparent in reviews of either mainstream pedagogical journals or competing heterodox outlets in which the status quo is routinely criticized. Rarely are leaders in economics education on the other side of the aisle invited to participate in these conversations. As a result, voices calling for change speak in languages that are both exclusionary and isolating, whether one considers research across the array of heterodox paradigms or in comparison with the mainstream, and their impact is relegated to participants who are already engaged in this work or are predisposed to alternative perspectives.

The goal of this chapter is to provide an alternative approach for promoting pluralism in undergraduate economics education, one that is motivated by conversations covering broad educational goals, focusing on desired student outcomes rather than classroom inputs. I begin by describing my view of this pluralistic agenda and why change is needed. To highlight the difference between my approach and previous reform attempts, I provide a brief categorization of past heterodox efforts, arguing that their minimal impact is due, in part, to the isolationist tendencies of this work. Emerging trends in higher education toward liberal education and outcomes-based assessment are then described, providing a motivation for advocating pluralism through focusing conversations on desired student outcomes. In conclusion, I offer a number of recommendations consistent with this alternative approach.

## Promoting pluralism, promoting conversation

Promoting pluralism in economics education requires a change in the status quo: the single paradigm, single delivery approach. To motivate this change, we must formulate learning goals associated with the undergraduate economics major. Including all perspectives in this conversation will provide credibility to the process. Yet a simple identification of expected outcomes is meaningless, providing no incentive for the professoriate to change, if outcomes are not measurable. It is only when the gap between stated goals and measured achievements is revealed that incentives emerge to motivate a shift away from the status quo.

The extent to which undergraduate economics is devoid of pluralism is readily documented. While the discipline is populated with a diverse set of viewpoints, the majority of undergraduate students are never exposed to perspectives beyond mainstream economics. For example, while "forty-four percent of undergraduate students enrolled at four-year colleges and universities take at least one economics course" (Salemi and Siegfried 1999: 355), evidence suggests that exposure to nonmainstream ideas has been "systematically weeded out of most principles texts" (Knoedler and Underwood 2003: 706). Furthermore the lecture mode overwhelmingly dominates pedagogical practices across economics courses at all levels and across all institution types (Becker and Watts 2007).

Insights into why learning outcomes is the key component of the pluralistic agenda appear sporadically throughout the literature. Consider, for example, how the presentation of economics as a settled science professed from the lectern limits the development of one universally accepted educational goal: enhancing critical thinking skills. Borg and Borg (2001) argue that teaching "the economic way of thinking" is reflective of analytical thinking, a necessary but not sufficient condition for critical thinking. Using Perry's framework for intellectual development as their basis for defining critical thinking, they describe how the reliance on a single perspective can limit students to the stage of dualism, where all questions are viewed in black and white with decidedly right and wrong answers (ibid.: 20). While they argue that alternative perspectives provided through interdisciplinary teaching can move students to higher stages of cognitive development (multiplicity, contextual relativism, and contextually appropriate decisions), the argument also holds for the multi-paradigm approach. Knoedler and Underwood (2003) employ this line of reasoning to argue for a multi-paradigmatic approach to principles of economics, but because they provide no evidence of learning gains there is little incentive for this type of course to be fully developed or widely adopted.

The exposure to multiple perspectives is a necessary but not sufficient component in developing critical thinking skills; it also requires pedagogical practices that move instructors beyond "sage-on-the-stage." "Many researchers have concluded that lectures are effective for only a small proportion of today's U.S. college students and that, even for those students, active learning environments provide more effective education" (Aerni *et al.* 1999: 31). Alternatively, experiential pedagogies provide "an opportunity to engage students in the learning process by problematizing mainstream economics" (Banks *et al.* 2005: 348). Well designed activities not only enhance learning, they also encourage students to raise questions regarding the accuracy of a single perspective in describing real-world phenomena.

Although focus on educational inputs into the learning process generates multiple paths for achieving a more pluralistic economics education (Aerni *et al.* 1999), no single path has been worn sufficiently to have much impact because this process misses opportunities to engage more participants in reform efforts and create incentives for change. While it is clear that this lack of conversation is a result of *both* the mainstream and heterodox isolationist tendencies, the following describes heterodox isolation, providing insight into a more productive pathway for change.

Previous calls for change can be loosely characterized by their use of rigorous critique, introduction of alternative theory, or promotion of unique premises and methods.[2] The practice of rigorous critique suggests defining and categorizing concerns with existing pedagogical practices or content. Research in this vein focuses primarily on the principles textbook, discussing the treatment of race, ethnicity, and gender, the use of lists, laws, and standards, and the lack of acknowledgment that economics includes value judgments. Providing examples of how to teach specific nonstandard concepts, redesign entire courses, and change curriculum are analogous to developing alternative theories. New applications of pedagogical techniques and criticisms of a proficiencies approach to skill development[3] provide examples of attempts to demonstrate uniqueness. Table 16.1 provides a truncated listing and brief description of notable examples for each of these categories.[4]

This wide range of foci for reform exists, in part, because there is no consistently agreed upon outcome and thus no focused process for achieving pluralism in economics education. Outlining criticisms without sufficiently grounding them in well documented learning gains fails to provide incentives that promote change, even if the intended audience agrees with such criticisms. Alternatively, the pluralistic agenda should exploit a gap in the literature, stated succinctly in the early 1990s and thereafter reiterated (Becker 1997; Walstad 2001): "outputs from learning economics need to be defined, measured, and investigated so that a fuller range of benefits from studying economics can be incorporated into decisions about courses and degree programs" (Becker *et al.* 1991: 241). An

*Table 16.1* Calls for change in economics education

| Rigorous critique: Defining and categorizing fault with existing pedagogical practices or texts | |
|---|---|
| Integrating race and gender requires that *current methodology, content, and pedagogy* be reconsidered | Bartlett and Feiner 1992 |
| Discusses *morality* of teaching a single perspective | Parvin 1992 |
| Critiques introductory textbooks including *methodology, rhetoric, and gender* as well as specific issues of *content* | Aslanbeigui and Naples 1996 |
| Demonstrates that *bias in treatment of race and gender* in texts results from neoclassical philosophical premises and equilibrium analysis | Feiner and Roberts 1990 |
| Existing practices in *pedagogy, content, methodology, and definition* limit students ability to appreciate how economics can be used to understand complex world | Lewis 1999 |
| Criticism of *lists and standards* as a narrow form of economic thinking generating less inclusive course content | Schneider and Shackelford 2001 |
| Criticism of *National Content Standards* on basis of scholarship and pedagogical practices | Lewis and McGoldrick 2001 |
| Summarizes post-autistic economics movement: student petition for more *realism* in economics teaching, less reliance on *mathematics* for its own sake, and less *dogmatic* reliance on mainstream viewpoints | Fullbrook 2003 |
| Describes importance of *teaching controversies* | Raveaud 2003 |
| Shows how uncritical and unexamined use of *perfect competition and equilibrium concepts* in introductory courses are misleading | Bernstein 2004 |
| Argues that *ethics* is an integral part of economics | Wilber 2004 |
| Argues that there are *no rules, laws, or dogmata* in economics, suggests the introduction of controversy as a way of bringing real economics into the classroom | Becker 2007 |

| Alternative theory: Entire courses using an alternative paradigm or examples of how to teach a specific concept | |
|---|---|
| Provides model for *curriculum and specific course* | Barone 1991 |
| Recommendations provided for *integrating controversies throughout curriculum* | Moseley *et al.* 1991 |
| Volume dedicated to *teaching the social economics way of thinking* including course examples | O'Boyle (ed.) 1999 |
| View of how pluralism might impact *curriculum and teaching* including a need for grounding in policy, historical, and cross-disciplinary | van Dalen 2003 |
| Expands mainstream presentation of principles to include *environmental, institutional, political, psychological, ethical, and social issues* | Goodwin *et al.* 2005 |

Table 16.1 Continued

| | |
|---|---|
| Theoretical and interdisciplinary pluralism introduced via *curricular* revision | Groenewegen 2007 |

*Uniqueness: Demonstrating the learning gains as a result of more open pedagogical techniques*

| | |
|---|---|
| *Critical thinking skills* facilitated by competing paradigms approach in introductory economics | Feiner and Roberts 1995 |
| Uses *feminist pedagogy* to show how the intersection of course content and learning environment can make the economics classroom more inclusive | Aerni *et al.* 1999 |
| Position papers, policy simulations, and *service-learning* are techniques used to promote the social economics way of thinking | Kasper 1999 |
| *Perry's framework* motivates how students may progress through (and gain from) the multi-paradigm approach | Earl 2000 |
| Challenges narrow and simplistic nature of *Hansen's proficiencies* as indicative of deeper unresolved questions about economics as a discipline | O'Donnell 2004 |
| Challenges superficial *critical thinking* that is purported to be communicated by the mainstream model | Nelson (2007) |

invitation for this research, however, does not ensure that the necessary conversations will also occur. The appropriate scaffolding for these conversations must also exist.

The teaching commons is "a conceptual space in which communities of educators committed to inquiry and innovation come together to exchange ideas about teaching and learning and use them to meet the challenges of educating students" (Huber and Hutchings 2007). As such, the commons acts as a public clearinghouse of examples. Because the commons is intended to be an exchange of ideas, it

> can include (at one end) studies with elaborate research designs and formal execution that go beyond a single classroom, program, or discipline, as well as (at the other end) quite modest efforts to document and reflect on one's teaching and share what one has learned.
>
> (Huber and Hutchings 2005: 4)

The scaffolding that this teaching commons provides begins with the process by which pedagogical practices are documented: through an organized framework, providing detailed descriptions of learning objectives and instructional environment in addition to the activity itself. The commons encourages others to join the conversation, providing a venue for contributions and reflections, including the challenging of and expanding on documented ideas about teaching and learning. Furthermore, increasing the awareness of nonstandard pedagogical practices and content in a common accessible location lowers the cost of adaptation and increases the probability of incorporating such methods.

## The role of higher education trends

Current pressures in higher education provide an environment which has the potential to foster change. Higher education is under scrutiny on (at least) two fronts, focusing on student outcomes: preparing the next generation for participation in the world (civic engagement) and ensuring that students are receiving a quality education in light of increasing higher education costs (assessment). A potential intersection across these fronts is the "liberal education" movement which identifies expected student learning outcomes and provides an impetus for targeted efforts to advance the pluralistic agenda in economics education.

Across the country, American colleges and universities are in the process of renewing civic commitment to their communities. This comes in response to criticisms that higher education has moved away from missions of educating students for citizenship and democracy (Astin 1994; Boyer 1996; Hirsch and Weber 1999). Increased civic engagement has the potential to rectify the current public displeasure through meaningful reconnections with the community. Students are challenged to combine course content with skills of civic engagement to address critical issues and problems in their communities. Civic engagement activities are argued to enhance political knowledge, critical thinking skills, communication skills, public problem-solving skills, civic judgment, creativity and imagination, community/coalition building, and organizational analysis (Battistoni 2002).

Criticisms contained in the highly publicized Spellings Report[5] (2006) are consistent with the growing public displeasure over what is seen as a lack of accountability of postsecondary institutions in ensuring that students have access to and complete their education, acquiring adequate skills for workforce participation. While the report focused on accessibility, affordability, and accountability, it is the issue of accountability which is most relevant for the present discussion of educational reform. The report claims that there are "disturbing signs that many students who do earn degrees have not actually mastered the reading, writing, and thinking skills we expect of college graduates" and it cites the lack of clear accountability mechanisms as a contributing factor (ibid.: x). Furthermore, the report encourages "institutions to make a commitment to embrace new pedagogies, curricula, and technologies to improve student learning" (ibid.: 4).

Liberal education is, one might argue, at the intersection of critiques generated by the civic engagement movement and the call for more rigorous assessment. While many definitions of liberal learning have been put forth, its common theme is aptly expressed by the Association of American Colleges and Universities (AAC&U 2007)[6]: a liberal education should involve more breath in the range of skills developed and topics covered and less depth than it currently does. They see liberal education as empowering students with broad knowledge and transferable skills.[7] It is an education that instills in students a strong sense of values, ethics, and commitment to civic engagement.

Although the liberal education movement is not new (it has been one focus of the AAC&U since its founding in 1915), renewed attention to these ideals is now fueled by prominent figures *within* educational institutions. For example, Derek Bok, former President of Harvard University, suggests majors "often become so focused on covering their field of knowledge that they neglect or even under-mine the teaching of good writing, critical thinking, and other important goals" (2006: 47). His arguments for reform in higher education focus on liberal educa-tion skills such as the ability to communicate, critical thinking, moral reasoning, preparing citizens, living with diversity, living in a more global society, develop-ing breath of interests, and preparing for work.

It is not hard to recognize the connection between skills associated with a liberal education and those of civic engagement, yet the connections to assess-ment are not nearly as transparent. Concurrent with calls for rededication to liberal education skills are efforts to systematically evaluate the degree to which students are prepared to participate in the world beyond college. The promotion of specific pedagogical strategies by advocates of the liberal education move-ment is based on empirical evidence indicating enhanced skill acquisition. Thus, assessment practices have already been established for these techniques in other disciplines and could be adapted for economics.[8]

The liberal education movement blends the focus on civic engagement skills and assessment outcomes, advocating that successful educational practices be more fully integrated across the disciplines. This is important because as noted in Siegfried *et al.* (1991), most of our students, even if they major in economics, are not likely to see themselves in jobs as economists after graduation. In their reflections on the relationship between the goals of the economics major and objectives of a liberal education, Colander and McGoldrick (2009: 614) argue that the major remains in precarious balance because of its need to service both a small group intending to further their education in graduate economics (for which technical, quantitative training is important) and the much larger constitu-ency which is focused on business and policy (for which a liberal-oriented edu-cation is more relevant). If research promoting pluralism in economics education were to focus on defining and measuring student learning outcomes, they would address outside pressures for increased pedagogical effectiveness in light of these dual roles for the major.

The AAC&U report on liberal learning outlines a number of pedagogical practices that have been shown to develop desired learning skills, including two that already have roots in economics: undergraduate research and service-learning.[9] Those who oversee undergraduate research opportunities generally agree that expected outcomes include "understanding a research problem in suf-ficient depth so as to be able to pose a question about it, determining what evid-ence is needed to solve the problem, and collecting data that will answer the question" (Kardash 2000: 191).

Undergraduate research experiences are consistent with liberal education ideals because "as a single experience it may facilitate empowered learning (including communication, problem solving, and teamwork), informed learning (allowing the student to study the natural and cultural world), and responsible learning (permitting the study of social problems and the self)" (Lopatto 2006: 22). The complex nature of the real world and conducting original research motivates students to employ multiple forms of argumentation and evidence. In economics, such opportunities promote evidence building and analytical reasoning that can move beyond the prevailing deductive form of reasoning to include inductive and warrant-based forms. New questions are likely to be raised as students are provided opportunities to choose issues to investigate. As a result, students are better prepared to participate in the world beyond college. Currently, undergraduate research opportunities occur throughout the curriculum, but significant projects are typically relegated to seniors or honors programs that serve a limited number of students (McGoldrick and Greenlaw 2008).

Service-learning is an experiential learning pedagogy that promotes deep learning because students integrate their study of a subject in the classroom with service activities in their communities. It is

> a strategy that builds character, spurs civic engagement, and applies content to abstract theories, allowing teachers to engage students as active participants in the learning process. Instead of simply asking students to open their textbooks, teachers using service-learning engage students in a critical thinking exercise to examine their world. Students are guided to connect their interests and moral leadership to solve a problem, serve a need, or be of service to others. Once a focus for service is identified, students may apply skills such as data collection, documentation, problem-solving, charting and graphing, and persuasive writing to test theories, develop surveys, analyze data, inform community decision-makers, and practice communication skills.
>
> (Pearson 2002: 6)

Students apply economic principles as they analyze issues within the context of the world in which they will ultimately participate, providing a natural link with liberal education skills as students learn to filter complexities of the real world. Furthermore, it is a pedagogical practice that can be developed in a wide range of courses, beginning with principles and continuing all the way through to senior seminar courses (McGoldrick and Ziegert 2002).

The pluralistic agenda in economics, however, does not encourage the introduction of pedagogical techniques simply for the sake of enhancing liberal education skills. Rather, these create an environment in which students evaluate existing economic models based on individual and collective life experiences, thereby critically assessing the applicability of these models to the world in which they live. "The result of this process is that students are actively engaged in the production of knowledge, as opposed to being the passive recipients of teacher imparted 'truth'" (Shackelford 1992: 571). McGoldrick (2002: 20) argues the following for service-learning experiences:

> if [students] have the opportunity to interact with those they serve, they may also realize that many of the factors contributing to people's predicaments are neither quantifiable in the neoclassical tradition nor consistent with the standard analysis in the text.

Significant undergraduate research opportunities also challenge students to apply and evaluate their understanding of economics. My own experience directing a senior research course suggests that student driven topics engender pluralistic perspectives because they typically employ interdisciplinary research (linking economics with sociology, political science, etc.) and their applications provide a basis for broadening theoretical perspectives (challenging assumptions and anomalies) (McGoldrick 2008).

Pressures on higher education provide the impetus to reconsider effective pedagogical practices throughout the disciplines, and economics is no exception. Building on practices which already have a foothold in economics creates an environment ripe for furthering the pluralistic agenda. Yet progress can be accelerated through more proactive efforts. In the final section of this chapter I provide some specific recommendations for advancing this cause.

## Recommendations for future efforts

Others have argued that significant transformations in what and how undergraduate economics is taught will not occur without changes in graduate education. Recommendations for changes at this level include, but are not limited to, the reintroduction of courses focused on history and institutions, de-emphasis on technical economic analysis, and greater application of economic ideas to public policy problems (Colander 1992, 2005b; Colander and Holmes 2007). Graduate students need training if we expect them to include content and use techniques that they are not likely to have exposure to throughout their own education. Even if such changes are instituted, however, a long lag is likely before such practices become commonplace, as changes only filter down as the newly educated generation of graduate students takes positions teaching in the undergraduate program. While I agree that changes are needed at the graduate level, the long lag suggests one should also consider actions that can be initiated now.

Promoting the pluralistic agenda in economics education necessitates refocusing efforts on identifying, developing, and assessing student outputs. Identifying skills expected of economics majors requires conversations by faculty across perspectives. Aligning these expectations with movements such as liberal education generates the impetus for promoting specific pedagogical techniques that encourage exposure to multiple perspectives. This entails moving away from traditional lectures and providing students with opportunities to practice the art of economics.[10] Examples of these pedagogical practices must be grounded in expected outcomes, detailed enough for easy adaption, and readily available. The key to ensuring their sustainability, however, requires documenting their impact in learning. Economics lags behind other disciplines in measuring student outcomes.[11] Thus, opportunities exist for those committed to promoting pluralism – lead the movement to define and assess student learning outcomes, demonstrating the extent to which exposure to multiple perspectives enhances skill acquisition. So the question that remains is: What specific actions would promote a process focused on student learning outcomes? I offer the following recommendations and rationales:

### *Develop a better understanding of instructor choice of pedagogical practices*

Despite a vast literature documenting active learning and other non-lecture techniques, the lecture mode still dominates. In order to bring about a change in behavior, one must go beyond the simple documentation of *what* techniques are employed in the classroom and investigate *why* these dominate. A better understanding of current behaviors provides a foundation for developing incentives and providing resources needed to promote change.

### *Develop evidence that non-lecture pedagogical practices enhance learning in economics*

The current push for greater assessment of learning is certain to trickle down to the level of the major. Yet, "[w]ith the exception of a few liberal arts colleges, little is done to assess the impact of the economics major on our students' intellectual development" (Siegfried *et al.* 1991: 214). Empirical evidence regarding the effectiveness of pedagogical practices in economics which support multiple perspectives (such as service-learning and undergraduate research) simply does not exist. A balance must be achieved, however, between the use of (often criticized) standardized tests of learning and alternative evidence such as anecdotal and argumentative prose. As others have argued "... modern mainstream economics is open to new approaches, as long as they demonstrate a careful understanding of the strengths of the recent orthodox approach and are pursued with a methodology acceptable to the mainstream" (Colander *et al.* 2004: 10). Assessment should focus on both content and skill development and be conducted using traditional (quantitative) methods and supplemented by qualitative approaches used in other disciplines. Enhancements shown through a critical evaluation of the learning associated with these techniques will provide the impetus for instructors to move away from lecture-based teaching.

### *Develop and promote the teaching commons*

Understanding why the lecture mode dominates and developing evidence of the impact of pedagogical techniques on student learning will not be effective, however, unless faculty members are engaged in related conversations. Currently, such conversations are limited to venues such as conferences where participation is not likely to reflect the wide range of perspectives held by the professorate. In order to avoid the isolationist tendency of past reform efforts, conversations must engage leaders in economics education within and across paradigms. The teaching commons provides a vehicle for such conversations. Consider, for example, a web-based pedagogical portal housing modules documenting specific pedagogical practices and courses.[12] Modules contain a library of examples grounded in research on learning coupled with guides for adaptation and implementation; reflecting efforts addressing the first two recommendations. This wealth of resources in a single location reduces the cost of developing, adopting, and implementing classroom practices that support pluralism in economics education. To ensure ongoing conversations regarding these practices, invitations to post reflections and additional examples would be extended to all who visit the site. Special invitations would also be extended to leaders in economics education representing various perspectives. Lest one consider this a far-fetched idea, both a multi-disciplinary and a Geoscience specific pedagogical portal currently exist and a National Science Foundation funded project, Starting Point: Teaching Economics, has launched a similar portal for economics (http://serc.carleton.edu/econ/index.html).

## *Empowering voices*

The power to encourage change necessitates that voices participating in the teaching commons are both heard and listened to. A movement is more likely to gain momentum when someone acts as its champion thus ensuring that evidence is internalized throughout the profession (Colander *et al.* 2004). Further, while it is not appropriate for either students or employers to dictate curriculum, understanding their current (dis)pleasures with acquired skills is an important perspective on skills acquired through the major. Students who state that economics does not provide enough real-world applications, and employers who suggest that economic students have excellent technical skills but few practical ones, will promote some to reconsider their courses, in terms of both content and pedagogical practices.

## Notes

1 Although the longevity and ranking of the *Journal of Economic Education* suggests it is the lead journal in the field, the introduction of the *International Review of Economics Education* in 2003, the *Australasian Journal of Economic Education* in 2004, and *Perspectives on Economic Education Research* (*PEER*) in 2005 has encroached on its monopoly position. (Other economics education journals have also existed, with lesser impacts, such as the *Japan Economic Education Journal*, established in 1982 and *Computers in Higher Education Economics Review*, established in 1987).
2 This characterization is based on the perspective of Garnett (2006) in a description of the methods that dissenting researchers used throughout the 1970s and 1980s in their attempts to overthrow (in the Kuhnian sense) the mainstream neoclassical model of the time.
3 The proficiencies approach to economics education was first introduced by Hansen (1986).
4 This characterization and provided examples are meant to be demonstrative rather than exhaustive and ultimately indicate the richness (depth and breadth) of work in this area.

5 This report (The Test of Leadership: Changing the Future of U.S. Higher Education, www.ed.gov/about/bdscomm/list/hiedfuture/reports/final-report.pdf) was commissioned by the Secretary of Education (M. Spellings) and completed by the Commission on the Future of Higher Education which was "charged with developing a comprehensive national strategy for postsecondary education that will meet the needs of America's diverse population and also address the economic and workforce needs of the country's future."

6 The AAC&U represents over 1000 colleges and universities and is the "only major higher education association whose sole focus is the quality of student learning in the college years" (AAC&U 2007: vii).

7 For a detailed description of each of these skills, see AAC&U (2007: 12).

8 Resources describing methods of assessment and developing related tools for the pedagogical methods described below include a monograph released by Portland State University (1998) and Bringle *et al.* (2004) (for the practice of service-learning) and Harrison (2006) (for a bibliography of articles on assessment in undergraduate research).

9 The full list of recommended practices includes first-year seminars and experiences, common intellectual experiences, learning communities, writing-intensive courses, collaborative assignments and projects, undergraduate research, diversity/global learning, service-learning/community-based learning, internships, and capstone courses and projects (AAC&U 2007: 53–54).

10 I use the term "art" to describe economics as opposed to science purposefully. As Colander (2001: 20) writes, "The art of economics is applied economics. It relates the lessons learned in positive economics to the normative goals determined in normative economics." Undergraduate students should be prepared to participate in the art of economics to be active citizens.

11 Other disciplines, such as physics, have developed a rich, cumulative knowledge base of effective teaching strategies and curricular resources grounded in the learning sciences, focused on conceptual knowledge, and empirically tested in the classroom.

12 It is important to note that this site (www.indiana.edu/~econed/online.htm) differs dramatically from the online version of the *Journal of Economic Education*, whose stated purpose is "to identify exemplary material for teaching and learning economics that is interactive or otherwise not conducive to traditional printed-page format. It provides a timely outlet for noncommercial work by economists and educators who are creating teaching materials *using innovative electronic technology*" (emphasis added).

## References

Aerni, A.L., Bartlett, R., Lewis, M., McGoldrick, K., and Shackelford, J. (1999) "Towards a Feminist Pedagogy in Economics," *Feminist Economics*, 5 (1): 29–44.

Aslanbeigui, N. and Naples, M. (1996) *Rethinking Economic Principles: Critical Essays on Introductory Textbooks*, Chicago: Irwin Press.

Association of American Colleges and Universities (2007) "College Learning for the New Global Century." Available at www.aacu.org/advocacy/leap/documents/Global-Century_final.pdf (accessed March 2, 2007).

Astin, A.W. (1994) "Higher Education and the Future of Democracy," Symposium conducted at the first Annual Allan M. Carter Symposium, University of California–Los Angeles, October 26.

Banks, N., Schneider, G., and Susman, P. (2005) "Paying the Bills is Not Just Theory: Service-Learning about a Living Wage," *Review of Radical Political Economics*, 37 (3): 346–356.

Barone, C.A. (1991) "Contending Perspectives: Curricular Reform in Economics," *Journal of Economic Education,* 22 (1): 15–26.

Bartlett, R.L. and Feiner, S.F. (1992) "Balancing the Economics Curriculum: Method, Content, and Pedagogy," *American Economic Review,* 82 (2): 559–564.

Battistoni, R.M. (2002) *Civic Engagement across the Curriculum: A Resource Book for Service Learning Faculty in All Disciplines,* Providence: Campus Compact.

Becker, W.E. (1997) "Teaching Economics to Undergraduates," *Journal of Economic Literature,* 35 (3): 1347–1373.

—— (2007) "Quit Lying and Address the Controversies: There are No Dogmata, Laws, Rules, or Standards in the Science of Economics," *American Economist,* 51 (1): 3–14.

Becker, W.E. and Watts, M. (2007) "A Little More Than Chalk and Talk: Results from a Third National Survey of Teaching Methods in Undergraduate Economics Courses," Available at http://mypage.iu.edu/~beckerw/working_papers.htm (accessed February 1, 2008).

Becker, W.E., Highsmith, R., Kennedy, P., and Walstad, W. (1991) "An Agenda for Research on Economic Education in Colleges and Universities," *Journal of Economic Education,* 22 (3): 241–250.

Bernstein, M.A. (2004) "The Pitfalls of Mainstream Economic Reasoning (and Teaching)," in E. Fullbrook (ed.) *A Guide to What's Wrong with Economics,* 33–40, London: Anthem Press.

Bok, D. (2006) *Our Underachieving Colleges: A Candid Look at How Much Students Learn and Why They Should be Learning More,* Princeton, NJ: Princeton University Press.

Borg, J.R. and Borg, M.P. (2001) "Teaching Critical Thinking in Interdisciplinary Economics Courses," *College Teaching,* 49 (1): 20–29.

Boyer, E.L. (1996) "The Scholarship of Engagement," *Journal of Public Service and Outreach,* 1 (1): 11–20.

Bringle, R., Phillips, M., and Hudson, M. (2004) *The Measure of Service-Learning: Research Scales to Assess Student Experiences,* Washington, DC: American Psychological Association.

Colander, D. (1992) "Reform of Undergraduate Economics Education," in D. Colander and R. Brenner (eds.) *Educating Economists,* 231–241, Ann Arbor: University of Michigan Press.

—— (2001) *The Lost Art of Economics,* Aldershot, UK: Edward Elgar Publishing.

—— (2005a) "What Economics Teach and What Economists Do," *Journal of Economic Education,* 36 (3): 249–260.

—— (2005b) *The Making of an Economist Redux,* Princeton, NJ: Princeton University Press.

—— (2006) "Caveat Lector: Living with the 15% Rule," in D. Colander (ed.), *The Stories Economists Tell: Essays on the Art of Teaching Economics,* 33–43, New York: McGraw-Hill.

Colander, D. and Holmes, J. (2009) "Gender and Graduate Economics Education in the U.S.," *Feminist Economics,* 13 (2): 93–116.

Colander, D. and McGoldrick, K. (2008) "The Economics Major as Part of Liberal Education". The Teagle Report.

Colander, D., Holt, R.P.F., and Rosser, J.B. (eds) (2004) *The Changing Face of Economics: Conversations with Cutting Edge Economists,* Ann Arbor: University of Michigan Press.

Earl, P.E. (2000) "Indeterminacy in the Economics Classroom," in P.E. Earl and S.F.

Frowen (eds) *Economics as an Art of Thought: Essays in Memory of G.L.S. Shackle*, 25–50, London: Routledge.

Feiner, S.F. and Roberts, B. (1990) "Hidden by the Invisible Hand: Neoclassical Economic Theory and the Textbook Treatment of Minorities and Women," *Gender and Society*, 4 (2): 159–181.

—— (1995) "Using Alternative Paradigms to Teach Race, Gender and Critical Thinking," *American Economic Review*, 85 (2): 367–371.

Fullbrook, E. (2003) "Introduction: A Brief History of the Post-Autistic Economics Movement," in E. Fullbrook (ed.) *The Crisis in Economics: The Post-Autistic Economics Movement: The First 600 Days*, 1–9, London: Routledge.

Garnett, R.F. (2006) "Paradigms and Pluralism in Heterodox Economics," *Review of Political Economy*, 18 (4): 521–546.

Goodwin, N., Nelson, J.A., Ackerman, F., and Weisskopf, T. (2005) *Microeconomics in Context*, New York: Houghton Mifflin Co.

Groenewegen, J. (ed.) (2007) *Teaching Pluralism in Economics*, Abingdon, UK: Edward Elgar Publishing.

Hansen, W.L. (1986) "What Knowledge is Most Worth Knowing for Economics Majors?" *American Economic Review*, 76 (2): 149–152.

Harrison, R. (2006) *The Assessment and Efficacy of Undergraduate Research*. Available at www.castl.ucf.edu/resources/CASTL%20Bibliography.pdf (accessed February 27, 2007).

Hirsch, W.Z. and Weber, L.E. (1999) *Challenges Facing Higher Education at the Millennium*, Phoenix: American Council on Education and Oryx Press.

Huber. M.T. and Hutchings, P. (2005) *The Advancement of Learning: Building the Teaching Commons*, Stanford, CT: Jossey-Bass.

—— (2007) *Building the Teaching Commons*, Carnegie Foundation for the Advancement of Teaching. Available at www.carnegiefoundation.org/perspectives/sub.asp?key=245&subkey=800 (accessed May 1, 2007).

Kardash, C.M. (2000) "Evaluation of an Undergraduate Research Experience: Perceptions of Undergraduate Interns and their Faculty Mentors," *Journal of Educational Psychology*, 92 (1): 191–201.

Kasper, S.D. (1999) "Teaching the Social Economics Way of Thinking in Money and Banking," in E.J. O'Boyle (ed.) *Teaching the Social Economics Way of Thinking*, 157–170, Lewiston: Edwin Mellen Press.

Knoedler, J.T. and Underwood, D.A. (2003) "Teaching the Principles of Economics: A Proposal for a Multi-Paradigmatic Approach," *Journal of Economic Issues*, 37 (September): 697–725.

Lewis, M. (1999) "Breaking down the Walls, Opening up the Field: Situating the Economics Classroom in the Site of Social Action," in A.L. Aerni and K. McGoldrick (eds) *Valuing Us All: Feminist Pedagogy in Economics*, 30–42, Ann Arbor: University of Michigan Press.

Lewis, M. and McGoldrick, K. (2001) "Moving beyond the Masculine Neoclassical Classroom," *Feminist Economics*, 7 (2): 91–103.

Lopatto, D. (2006) "Undergraduate Research as a Catalyst for Liberal Learning," *Peer Review*, 8 (1): 22–25.

McGoldrick, K. (2002) "Using the Theory of Service Learning as a Tool for Teaching Economic Theory," in McGoldrick, K. and A. Ziegert (eds) *Putting the Invisible Hand to Work: Concepts and Models of Service Learning in Economics*, 11–26, Ann Arbor: University of Michigan Press.

—— (2008) "Doing Economics: Enhancing Skills through a Process-Oriented Senior Research Course," *Journal of Economic Education*, 39 (4): 342–356.

McGoldrick, K. and Greenlaw, S. (2008) "Practicing What We Preach: Undergraduate Research Experiences in Economics," Unpublished paper, Department of Economics, University of Richmond.

McGoldrick, K. and Ziegert, A. (eds) (2002) *Putting the Invisible Hand to Work: Concepts and Models of Service Learning in Economics*, Ann Arbor: University of Michigan Press.

Moseley, F., Gunn, C., and Georges, C. (1991) "Emphasizing Controversy in the Economics Curriculum," *Journal of Economic Education*, 22 (3): 235–240.

Nelson, J. (2007) "Resources for Teaching Critical Thinking in – and about – Economics," *Newsletter of the Association for General and Liberal Studies*, 23 (2) (Winter): 5.

O'Boyle, E.J. (ed.) (1999) *Teaching the Social Economics Way of Thinking*, Lewiston: Edwin Mellen Press.

O'Donnell, R. (2004) "What Kind of Economics Graduates Do We Want? A Constructive Critique of Hansen's Proficiencies Approach," *Australasian Journal of Economics Education*, 1 (1): 41–60.

Parvin, M. (1992) "Is Teaching Neoclassical Economics as the Science of Economics Moral?" *Journal of Economic Education*, 23 (1): 65–78.

Pearson, S.S. (2002) *Finding Common Ground: Service Learning and Educational Reform: A Survey of 28 Leading School Reform Models*, Washington DC: American Youth Policy Forum.

Portland State University, Center for Academic Excellence (1998) *Assessing the Impact of Service-Learning: A Workbook of Strategies and Methods*, Portland, OR: Portland State University, Center for Academic Excellence.

Raveaud, G. (2003) "Teaching Economics through Controversies," in E. Fullbrook (ed.) *The Crisis in Economics: The Post-Autistic Economics Movement: The First 600 Days*, 62–69, London: Routledge.

Salemi, M. and Siegfried, J. (1999) "The State of Economic Education," *American Economic Review*, 89 (2): 355–361.

Schneider, G. and Shackelford, J. (2001) "Economics Standards and Lists: Proposed Antidotes for Feminist Economists," *Feminist Economics*, 7 (2): 77–89.

Shackelford, J. (1992) "Feminist Pedagogy: A Means for Bringing Critical Thinking, and Creativity to the Economics Classroom," *American Economic Review*, 82 (2): 570–560.

Siegfried, J., Bartlett, R.L., Hansen, W.L., Kelley, A.C., McCloskey, D.N., and Tietenberg, T.H. (1991) "The Status and Prospects of the Economics Major," *Journal of Economic Education*, 22 (3): 197–224.

Spellings Commission (2006) *A Test of Leadership: Charting the Future of U.S. Higher Education*. Available at www.ed.gov/about/bdscomm/list/hiedfuture/reports/final-report.pdf (accessed December 1, 2007).

van Dalen, H.P. (2003) "Pluralism in Economics: A Public Good or a Public Bad?" Tinbergen Institute Discussion Paper. Available at www.tinbergen.nl/discussionpapers/03034.pdf (accessed March 1, 2007).

Walstad, W. (2001) "Improving Assessment in University Economics," *Journal of Economic Education*, 32 (3): 281–294.

Wilber, C.K. (2004) "Teaching Economics as if Ethics Mattered," in E. Fullbrook (ed.) *A Guide to What's Wrong with Economics*, 147–157, London: Anthem Press.

# 17 The illusion of objectivity
## Implications for teaching economics

*Alison Butler*

> Economists seek to measure well-being, to learn how well-being may increase
> over time, and to evaluate the well-being of the rich and the poor.
> (American Economics Association 2007)

## Introduction

One of the first lessons learned by most economics students, and reinforced throughout their curriculum, is the distinction between positive and normative economics. Textbooks define positive analysis as "what is," while normative analysis is "what should be." Milton Friedman (1953: 4) states that "positive economics is in principle independent of any particular ethical position or normative judgments." He goes on to assert that "positive economics is, or can be, an 'objective' science" (ibid.). The idea that economics and positive economics are equivalent is central to the dominant paradigm in economics. Any analysis that incorporates ethics, values, or reflects a particular perspective is considered normative and not economic analysis.

In this chapter I argue the falsity of this dichotomy and its implications for economic education. I demonstrate how the unacknowledged bias that exists in the dominant paradigm creates an intellectually and demographically homogeneous curriculum, reinforced by the pedagogical methods chosen, with its implicit assumptions of shared cultural values and heteronormativity that ignore racial and gender differences among students.

The epistemological link between positive economics and scientific objectivity is not directly addressed in the standard textbook definition, but, as discussed in Albelda (1997), positive analysis is in fact a notion of objectivity that is assumed to be value-free. Feminists such as Blau (1981), Harding (1995), Nelson (1996), and Albelda (1997) examine how the assumption of positive economics functions to maintain the existing dominant paradigm and ignores the social, historical, gendered, and racial context within which these "objective truths" are determined. When mainstream economics addresses issues related to gender, sexual orientation, or people of color, they are generally treated as special topics rather than "categories of analysis" (Bartlett and Feiner 1992; Figart 2005).

Other economists have challenged the notion of economics as a value-free discipline, arguing that economics can never be completely distinct from ethics. Weston (1994) argues that acknowledging the existence of ethical values is not, in the fears of the positivists, a license to abandon critical scrutiny. Rather, by bringing those biases to the forefront economists can recognize the limitations of their analysis. For example, economists have been long concerned with the equity/efficiency tradeoff; yet, under the guise of objectivity, they tend to address only questions of efficiency. As Davis (2005) points out, the idea that efficiency, particularly Pareto efficiency, is value free ignores the moral philosophy underlying those concepts. In addition, the micro/macroeconomic distinction can also reflect different ethical considerations, as, among other things, the positivist microeconomic framework emphasizes individual responsibility while the macro/Keynesian framework stresses the social responsibility of the group (Best and Widmaier 2006).

Teaching economics as a positive science implies that the economic theory and analysis students learn are independent of the professor's perspective as well. However, the choice of curriculum and teaching methodology inevitably reflects the values of the professor. For example, when I first taught I was committed to teaching in the positivist tradition because of my experiences as a student. What I failed to realize was that, by choosing to spend a significant amount of class time analyzing the tax cuts of 2001 and 2003 rather than on the Keynesian Cross, I was privileging some topics over others. These decisions reflected my views on what was important for my students to learn. In doing so, I made normative choices about what they *should* learn while holding on to the façade of objectivity. Presumably faculty have the expertise to make these decisions; doing so, however, violates in principle and in spirit the tenet of objectivity, particularly since professors make significantly different curricular choices for the same course. Similarly, how students are evaluated reflects, at least in part, the priorities and values of the professor teaching the course.

Students also bring their own experiences, culture, race, and gender identity to the classroom. These students may have worldviews that conflict with the conception of the economic behavior taught in class. Their views, however, are given little credence in an environment where presumably there is only one correct way to understand economic behavior (Amariglio and Ruccio 1999).

As a result, my decision to write this chapter in the first person is intentional. My perspective as a teacher is shaped by many factors including my experiences as a student, my colleagues, being a woman in a predominantly male discipline, and growing up Jewish in a bi-racial household in the United States.[1] I share this information with my students because only by acknowledging our own standpoint can we hope to become more objective (Harding 1995). The examples used come from my own teaching experience and so have a U.S. macroeconomic perspective, although the ideas, I hope, are far more broadly applicable. One caveat: I realize that in writing this type of chapter I am guilty of making some of the same generalizations that I observe in the discipline. I recognize that not all women, students of color, or people from working class backgrounds respond the same, any more than white male students and faculty are guilty of the behavior discussed in the article, but space constraints prevent me from presenting a more finely nuanced argument throughout.

## Objectivity in economics

The fundamental behavioral assumptions of the dominant paradigm emphasize competition, individuality, and rationality. Mainstream economists apply the resulting framework to essentially all decisions. Gary Becker exemplified this approach, applying economics to all aspects of human behavior, including fertility decisions and other intrafamily activities.[2] He assumes a single utility function for the household, ignoring the role of differences in power and social pressures that exist between family members. The effect of this assumption is to privilege the behavior of some groups – those predictably captured in the operating assumptions for the household – over that of everyone else in the household, hardly a value-free notion. These assumptions and the results that follow reflect the world view of those who hold them. As discussed by Nelson (1995: 132), "Traditionally, male activities have taken center stage as subject matter, while models and methods have reflected a historically and psychologically masculine pattern of valuing autonomy and detachment over dependence and connection."

Positive economics reinforces the emphasis on a single paradigm, as "objective facts" cannot have explanations that are inconsistent with that paradigm. While competing perspectives on particular assumptions may be addressed, they do not challenge the objectivity of the discipline itself: New Keynesians and Neoclassical economists may have different assumptions about price stickiness, but the general paradigm within which they work is the same.[3]

Although ethics and values are not explicit in the mainstream framework, the idea that the assumptions and analysis are simply assumed to hold true for everyone is itself a normative point of view. Assumptions of universality are particularly problematic for the classroom environment. Under the guise of objectivity, the economics discipline perpetuates a curriculum that excludes a critical analysis of the fundamental assumptions and implications of the dominant paradigm. As a result, topics of particular importance to women and people of color are rarely addressed in the core curriculum, limiting the appeal of the discipline. Issues relating to gender or people of color are often relegated to special topics or only discussed in stereotypical or pejorative ways, for example, illegal immigrants, single mothers, or welfare recipients.[4] This problem is exacerbated by the limited discussion of gender and race in textbooks. According to Robson (2001), the percentage of pages in which gender and/or race was mentioned in a survey of Principles texts was only 3.5 percent. The contexts in which gender and race were raised, however, were not examined.

Simply raising these topics within a mainstream framework, not surprisingly, is found to have little effect in increasing the discipline's appeal, unless the professor raising those topics was female (Jenson and Owen 2001). Given that women constitute only 18.6 percent of the economics faculty in Ph.D. granting institutions and 28.9 percent at liberal arts schools (Lynch 2007), it is perhaps not surprising that Bollinger *et al.* (2006) found that women are more likely to have a more unfavorable view of economics *after* taking an economics course than before. Tellingly, little research has investigated the reasons for the lack of students of color, particularly African-, Hispanic-, and Native American students, in economics.

In addition, the assumption of universality assumes culture is irrelevant, which suggests that students and faculty share the same cultural norms; usually those of the teacher. Thus a professor who uses sports analogies for almost all of her examples alienates students who do not share her frame of reference. Similarly, a professor who speaks colloquially assumes students share a familiarity with a particular cultural and class background. This in turn affects which students succeed in the class and are likely to continue on in economics beyond the introductory level.

Even our terminology reflects the attempt of economists to remove humanity from the discipline. Who does the image of the "economic agent" represent? The individualistic values embedded in the dominant paradigm come out of a specifically European philosophical tradition that excludes people with other values. This approach teaches students to see the economy through the eyes of Western business and financial professionals: a well-functioning system to understand but not challenge if one wants to thrive in the marketplace. This reinforces the current demographics of the economics profession, which remain overwhelmingly male and white.

### *Acknowledging the role of perspective*

Removing the invisibility cloak from the frames of gender, race, and class provides a powerful challenge to the very notion of objectivity in the classroom. A white professor and white students who discuss race in terms of issues facing people of color ignore their own race; instead, race is defined in terms of the "other," while whiteness and the privilege it confers are unexplored and invisible. Students of color, on the other hand, do not have the same privilege and see whiteness whether or not the professor recognizes it (Maher and Tetreault 1997). If professors do not acknowledge their own point of view, students come to their own conclusions about what that perspective is. Faculty of color and women, particularly when discussing issues related to race and gender, are often assumed to have a particular point of view while a white male faculty member is perceived as neutral. For example, if I, as a white female faculty member, discuss gender and racial discrimination, I am (correctly) identified as a member of a group that has both been discriminated against and the biggest beneficiary of affirmative action (which my African-American students are generally quite aware of). That standpoint, however, is no less subjective than that of a white male colleague who, acknowledged or not, is a member of a group that has historically benefited from that discrimination. This in turn shapes students' view of what each of us is teaching.

If, as researchers and teachers, we accept that that illusion of objectivity is also relevant to the classroom, we can begin to create a richer learning environment that not only deepens students' understanding of economics, but teaches them how to contextualize economics within a greater world view.

## In the classroom

Professors also play a role, however unconscious or unacknowledged, in maintaining the dominant paradigm through not only their choice of content but also via pedagogy, content choice, and evaluation methods used. While the overall content of the core curriculum is fairly standardized across textbooks, professors emphasize different material, and a class rarely covers all the material provided in a textbook. In addition, each professor usually has some discretion over the content included and/or how to teach the material. For example, one macroeconomics professor might emphasize the negative effects of government spending, another professor the role of fiscal policy in reducing the costs of recessions, while a third might hardly talk about fiscal policy at all. Students come away from each of these courses with very different understandings of the desirability of using fiscal policy, having internalized the priorities of their professor without being aware of the beliefs underlying those views. More importantly for the purpose of this paper, each professor's choice reflects their own personal knowledge, experience, interpretations, and values, although students are required to accept the material as universally true.

### *Alternative curriculum*

Bartlett and Feiner (1992), Bartlett (1996a), and Rishi (1998) present alternative syllabi for creating a more inclusive one-semester introductory economics class using Peggy McIntosh's feminist approach to curricular transformation. Aerni (1999: 95) creates an alternative syllabus for a macroeconomics principles class emphasizing applicability and context. She argues that a professor should

> examine and revise the standards of one's own discipline, recognizing that standards have been set in most disciplines and across disciplines predominantly by white, European, wealthy men ... and that these standards have functioned, whether deliberately or not, partly to exclude women, blacks, and other groups and to exclude certain ideas.

Several excellent pluralistic anthologies offer alternative approaches to teaching economics, including Bartlett (1996a), which focuses on race and gender, and Aerni and McGoldrick (1999), which demonstrates ways to incorporate feminist pedagogy into the curriculum.

*Even definitions are subjective: what is GDP?*

In spite of the increased criticism of mainstream economics, the most frequently used textbooks still reflect the biases inherent in the dominant paradigm. The textbook treatment of gross domestic product (GDP), one of the first macro concepts students learn, exemplifies this approach.[5] Although GDP is presented as a "positive" definition, the way GDP is defined, measured, and used is hardly value free and provides an illustration of how economics textbooks discount certain activities and prioritize others. These choices reinforce the dominant paradigm at the expense of more inclusive or critical perspectives.

GDP is the most widely reported economic statistic, often used as a measure of "well-being" and the primary method used to compare the standard of living across countries. Criticisms regarding the measure and use of GDP in this manner are often ignored. GDP, according to the Bureau of Economic Analysis (BEA) (U.S. Department of Commerce 2007: 2) "is defined as the market value of the goods and services produced by labor and property located in the United States." The definition itself does not describe *how* to measure value or what activities should be included in production. For estimating purposes, however, value is defined as equivalent to prices, except when ."..prices do not fully reflect the value of a good or service or where services are provided without an actual exchange, the value ... may [then] be 'imputed' from similar market transactions" (U.S. Department of Commerce BEA 2007: 3). For example, the rental value of owner-occupied housing is currently included to ensure GDP is "invariant to institutional arrangements." Thus the actual calculation of GDP depends crucially on the assumptions regarding how value is determined, the institutional arrangements being considered, and which activities are considered "production."

The primary justification given by the BEA for excluding non-market production is that it has limited effect on the economy and could affect the usefulness of this statistic in understanding business cycle behavior. However, a recent report by the Panel to Study the Design of Nonmarket Accounts (Abraham and MacKie 2005: 1) argues the opposite, stating that "Failure to account for [non-market] activities may significantly distort policy makers' sense of economic trends." Clearly the decision of what to include reflects the activities, and sphere in which they are performed, thought to be worth valuing.

Economists working on national accounting issues for at least 40 years (e.g. Kendrick 1967) have discussed the intertwined issues of excluding non-market production and possible ways of redressing the data problem. Projects currently exist worldwide to include productive activities historically characterized as leisure, such as caring labor and other forms of household production, into measures of national output. This would also create more consistency in accounts across countries (see, for example, Jorgenson *et al.* 2006).

Interestingly, even the definition of GDP varies somewhat across textbooks. Most texts define GDP in terms of "market value" rather than prices (e.g. Mankiw 2006; McConnell and Brue 2005), which suggests that some goods and services included are not traded in the formal market since the value is not equated with price. Baumol and Blinder's text (2006) defines GDP in terms of "the sum of the money values." In addition, their definition specifies that goods and services be "sold on organized markets." This definition explicitly excludes household production, which is not sold in a marketplace. However it also excludes other imputed values in GDP, such as the rental value of owner-occupied housing, which is currently included in GDP.

The degree to which textbooks address important measurement problems and common misuses of GDP varies significantly. Some textbooks simply state the definition of GDP without any discussion of its limitations or its misuse as a measure of social welfare (e.g. Krugman and Wells 2006). Case and Fair (2007) and Mankiw (2006) discuss the limitations of GDP as a measure of social well-being, but do not address the choices made in calculating GDP. A few texts address the exclusion of non-market activities (McConnell and Brue 2005; Baumol and Blinder 2006). Only Colander (2006) presents methods to correct for these exclusions by discussing alternative measures of national output.

In spite of this clear distinction between the measurement of production and the conceptualization of productive activity, most textbooks treat them as equivalent. The distinction is illustrative as it reveals how economists define value, work, and leisure and what activities are considered "appropriate" for economic study. When someone moves from the formal labor market (that is, the taxpaying sector) into the informal one, GDP falls although work effort has not changed. Thus economically valued work only occurs in the formal marketplace. Estimates of the amount of production provided by caring labor range from 30–50 percent of GDP. In addition, Salary.com (2007) estimates the median replacement value of a full-time stay-at-home mother with two children at $138,095 in 2007. While one can disagree with any particular estimate, the economic value of these activities is considerable.

## Students' perceptions and GDP

In the same way that a professor's choice of content is contextual, students also filter the information provided through their own social, historical, gendered, and racial lens. For example, a student who defines work in the same way as the economics discipline is more likely to respond neutrally to the traditional presentation of GDP. On the other hand, those who define value in ways other than price and work in activities not included in GDP are likely to feel dissatisfied or invisible in the definition of economic activity even if they are unaware why.

Directly addressing these issues in class provides the opportunity to incorporate a more pluralistic view of economics. For instance, a student whose mother quit her job to take care of a family member is taught that his mother is no longer doing economically valuable work. This sends a particularly negative signal to women, who are most likely to take on the role of caregiver, about the values associated with choices they might make; that is, that caring labor is not "real work." This issue is exacerbated by the language economists use to describe this decision: the labor/leisure tradeoff. Thus any activity done outside the legal labor market must be considered some version of a leisure activity which by definition is not productive activity.

The exclusion of non-market production also has implications for how students relate to economics as well. I have taught students whose parents came to the United States illegally and worked as laborers or domestic workers.[6] Their parents may work extremely hard yet not only are they stigmatized for their illegal status but their work is also excluded from national production. For others, having family members who work illegally may be the result of the limited economic options available in their community or country. Not addressing the reasons for (and effect of) this exclusion can increase the sense of isolation for these students in the classroom.

The exclusion of some productive activities from GDP can create significant difficulties when trying to make comparisons across countries. For some countries, much of the production is informal, and different social policies may create different preferences for or constraints on working outside the home. The types of economic activity that are legal also differ across countries. For example, prostitution and gambling are not legal in many countries, and thus are counted in the GDP of some countries but not others.

Production that creates negative environmental externalities also has important race and class implications. Larry Summers, in his infamous World Bank memo in 1991, argued that wealthy countries should encourage the migration of "dirty industries" to poor countries: given that demand for a clean environment is highly income elastic, countries with low wages and low population densities are actually below their optimal levels of pollution. This argument, although morally repulsive to many, is consistent with economic logic and has clearly been used to discuss locational questions within wealthy countries. For example, race and low socioeconomic status remain highly correlated with the location of hazardous waste facilities in the United States (Bullard *et al.* 2007), something students from low-income communities already know.

The new text *Macroeconomics in Context* (Goodwin *et al.* 2009) provides an excellent illustration of how these issues can be integrated into a principles of macroeconomics course. By demonstrating alternative ways of valuing externalities and caring labor, it raises the conceptual and measurement issues associated with GDP and addresses the subjectivity that exists even in presumably objective definitions. This also creates an opportunity to discuss issues of class privilege, as the discussion of formal and informal work inevitably leads to a discussion of economic opportunity and labor market decisions. While these examples of students' response may seem extreme to some, GDP is just one of many instances during the semester where definitions, theory, and pedagogy privilege some views and experiences over others.

## Alternative pedagogy

As discussed by Aerni (1999) and others, changing the curriculum alone is insufficient. Without also changing the way students engage in the material, students remain passive participants in the classroom and are still likely to remain disengaged. Mainstream economic educators have long been concerned with changing the emphasis on "chalk and talk" yet economic classes remain overwhelmingly taught in lecture-style format (Becker and Watts 2001). One reason for maintaining the lecture format is the encyclopedic nature of an economics curriculum that seems to favor breadth over depth. That, too, is a disciplinary choice.

Research shows that African-, Hispanic-, and Native American students tend to learn best when collaborative learning and group activities are emphasized (Anderson and Adams 1992; Bartlett 1996a). However, in the traditional classroom, as Gay (2002: 114) observes,

> These students have been expected to divorce themselves from their cultures and learn according to European American, male cultural norms. This places them in double jeopardy – having to master the academic tasks while functioning under cultural conditions unnatural (and often unfamiliar) to them.

Women also face unique challenges in an economics class, particularly when "discussion" is actually question/answer. More than two-thirds of college men rate themselves as above average or in the highest 10 percent in terms of intellectual self-confidence, while less than 50 percent of women students do (Sax 2007). As a result, women students often underestimate their own understanding, while overestimating that of the more confident male students.[7] Similarly, research shows that the tone of women's voices tends to rise at the end of the sentence so their statements are often heard as uncertain by men, rather than as a way to leave room for further discussion. Women students generally perform better in cooperative learning situations, although one study (Jensen and Owen 2001) found that result only held true in classes where men did not dominate the class.

How we as teachers relate to students and how students relate to each other in the classroom can be as important as the choice of curriculum or pedagogy. Part of the conceit of objectivity in much of academia is that all students are treated equally. In economics, one of the justifications for multiple choice and mathematical questions in exams is that they are more objective, yet these privilege certain learning styles over others. A student who visits their professor when they are struggling is often better perceived and more likely to improve than a student who does not. A professor may assume the latter student did not want help because of a lack of commitment to the course (assuming a small enough class for the professor to notice), yet the difference may actually reflect their understanding of appropriate student behavior. I have been told by first-generation college students that they saw I was busy and so did not want to bother me with their problems, something I have rarely heard from students with upper-middle class backgrounds.

A key assumption in the dominant paradigm is that individuals are self-seeking; that idea is reinforced by the incentives in many classes. Students who answer quickly are often rewarded for their behavior, particularly when participation is part of the grade. Doing so ignores the real externalities that these students may create for other students, who may not be as quick to respond or as confident. Students have told me they do not feel like they have enough time to think and once they know someone else is going to answer, they stop trying. Without addressing this issue, these same students dominate in group work as well.

One important aspect of an inclusive classroom is that students need to understand that the classroom itself is a community and how they behave affects the learning of other students. When I have talked to students about "excessive participation" and explain how their participation is affecting others, they acknowledge it never occurred to them to be concerned with anyone else in the class. Several commented that they learned a lot by not talking!

Given the diversity of students and learning styles, multiple teaching and evaluation strategies should be used to provide all students with an equal opportunity to succeed. I find that if I discuss my reasons for my pedagogical choices with my students, I encounter far less resistance, and I can allow them to be part of the decision-making process.

## *Strategies for macroeconomics*

Macroeconomics presents a particular challenge to faculty who are trying to create a more diversified curriculum. Given that macroeconomics is traditionally defined as the study of the economy as a whole, issues of race and gender are theoretically not relevant categories of analysis. The very distinction between micro- and macroeconomics is itself an artificial one that leaves many important topics without a place in the curriculum (or the discipline itself). For example, while microeconomics may look at the distributional effects of a particular government policy, when fiscal or monetary policy is taught the possible distributional effects are not addressed. This leaves an odd cognitive dissonance when, for example, trying to evaluate the overall macroeconomic effects of the 2001 and 2003 tax cuts without addressing the distributional effects of the policies.

I believe it is important to have students think critically about perspective and bias in macroeconomics from the beginning, even at the principles level. I begin on the first day of Principles of Macroeconomics by asking students to think about how personal experiences, characteristics, and socioeconomic attributes such as race, gender, or related factors have shaped their political views, particularly as they relate to economic issues. I explain that since we are going to be examining issues that have policy implications, the more they are aware of what personal perspective they might bring to the analysis, the better able they might be to step back from those views.[8] Thus issues of positionality are raised from the very first class.

The first day of my Intermediate Macroeconomics class begins by writing all the assumptions they remember from their other economics classes on the board. The students then examine each one, discussing how realistic they think they are, the importance of that assumption in economic theory, and any racial, cultural, or gendered biases it contains. This raises the artificiality of the positive/

normative economics on the first day and shapes the discussion of theory and policy for the rest of the semester.

## Conclusion

The assumption of objectivity that underlies mainstream economics creates an artificial distinction between the practice of economics and the perspective of the practitioners. I argue that this distinction further creates a disciplinary and classroom bias that reflects the specific point of view of those working within the dominant paradigm, excluding alternative points of view; in particular those of women and other traditionally under-represented groups. Mainstream textbooks then reinforce the intellectual and cultural narrowness of the discipline. This silences alternative perspectives, alienating students for whom the curriculum does not reflect the realities of their lives.

One of the goals of pluralistic economics is to develop pedagogy that encourages a multiplicity of views, including those that challenge the dominant paradigm. To create a more demographically as well as intellectually inclusive profession, changes need to begin (although certainly not end) in the undergraduate classroom. If students remain invisible in the assumptions of the discipline, not only do they feel excluded from economics as a field, but the invisibility itself denigrates their own life experience. Without their challenging voices, the growth of the discipline remains limited. Historically, the study of caring labor and household production, outside of the Beckerian sense, did not occur until significant numbers of women entered the economics profession. Similarly, the understanding of race as a category of analysis has increased as the diversity in the profession has begun to increase. Still, economics lags far behind other social sciences. Many of the ideas that attract students to economics – such as issues of income inequality, concerns about discrimination, a desire to alleviate poverty, and interest in public policy – are not well served by the models and methods currently used. In addition, the mainstream framework does not reflect the experience of students who are raised in alternative family structures, those for whom the decision to work outside the home reflects more than the wage gained or lost, or the lives of students who experience discrimination and racism in their daily lives. These realities need a new, more inclusive pedagogy and economic theory that explains their experiences as well. By teaching students how to challenge the very ideas they are learning, students gain the critical skills necessary to challenge not only the prevailing paradigm in economics, but to bring new perspectives as well.

## Acknowledgments

The author would like to thank the participants of the ICAPE conference, Sandra Butler, and April Overstreet for helpful comments and Martha Starr, whose suggestions and insightful comments significantly improved this chapter. Most importantly, I would like to thank my students, without whom this paper could not have been written.

## Notes

1 I have tried to define my particular standpoint for the readers of this article; however, I discovered that my identity is not easily defined in a sentence.
2 See, for example, Becker (1960). The use of the term "fertility" in this context refers to the optimal choice of children, which is quite different from the way women describe fertility; that is, the ability to have children. In a genderless world, the ability to have the desired number of children is simply assumed.
3 Feminists, Institutionalists, Marxists, and others continue to challenge this paradigm. Their perspectives are rarely published in the primary journals of the profession or included in the curriculum.
4 I use the term "people of color" in this context to include African-American, Asian-American, Latino-American, and Native American.
5 Nugent (1997) and Shah (1996) provide alternative approaches to teaching GDP.
6 I realize that many illegal immigrants do not work as laborers or domestic workers; however, these jobs take place in the informal marketplace and therefore are not included in GDP.
7 See Niederle and Vesterlund (2005) for an analysis of gender and competition.
8 This is a simplified version of Harding's (1995) argument that acknowledging one's perspective increases the potential for objective analysis.

## References

Abraham, K. and MacKie, C. (2005) *Beyond the Market: Designing Nonmarket Accounts for the United States*, Washington, DC: National Academies Press.

American Economics Association (2007) "What is Economics?" Available at www.vanderbilt.edu/AEA/students/WhatIsEconomics.htm (accessed December 27, 2007).

Aerni, A.L. (1999) "What Do My Students Need to Know? Experiences with Developing a More Feminist 'Principles of Macroeconomics' Course," in A.L. Aerni and K. McGoldrick (eds.) *Valuing Us All: Feminist Pedagogy and Economics*, 86–96, Ann Arbor: University of Michigan Press.

Aerni, A.L. and McGoldrick, K. (eds) (1999) *Valuing Us All: Feminist Pedagogy and Economics*, Ann Arbor: University of Michigan Press.

Albelda, R. (1997) *Economics and Feminism: Disturbances in the Field*, New York: Twayne Publishers.

Amariglio, J. and Ruccio, D.F. (1999) "The Transgressive Knowledge of 'Ersatz' Economics," in R. Garnett (ed.) *What Do Economists Know?*, 19–36, New York: Routledge.

Anderson, J.A. and Adams, M. (1992) "Acknowledging the Learning Styles of Diverse Student Populations: Implications For Instructional Design," *New Directions for Teaching and Learning*, 49: 19–33.

Bartlett, R. (1996a) "Discovering Diversity in Introductory Economics," *Journal of Economic Perspectives*, 10 (2): 141–153.

Bartlett, R. (ed.) (1996b) *Introducing Race and Gender into Economics*, London: Routledge.

Bartlett, R. and Feiner, S.F. (1992) "Balancing the Economics Curriculum: Content, Method and Pedagogy," *American Economic Review*, 82 (2): 559–564.

Baumol, W.J. and Blinder, A.S. (2006) *Macroeconomics: Principles and Policy*, 10th edition, Cincinnati, OH: South-Western College Publishing.

Becker, G.S. (1960) "An Economic Analysis of Fertility," in National Bureau of Economic Research (ed.), *Demographic and Economic Change in Developed Countries*, 209–231, Princeton, NJ: Princeton University Press.

Becker, W.E. and Watts, M. (2001) "Teaching Economics at the Start of the 21st Century: Still Chalk-and-Talk," *American Economic Review*, 91 (2): 446–451.

Best, J. and Widmaier, W. (2006) "Micro- or Macro-Moralities? Economic Discourses and Policy Possibilities," *Review of International Political Economy*, 13 (4): 609–631.

Blau, F.D. (1981) "On the Role of Values in Feminist Scholarship," *Signs*, 6 (3): 538–540.

Bollinger, C.R. Hoyt, G.M., and McGoldrick, K. (2006) "Chicks Don't Dig it: Attitude and Performance in Principles of Economics Classes," unpublished paper.

Bullard, R.D., Mohai, P., Saha, R., and Wright, B. (2007) "Toxic Waste and Race at Twenty: 1987–2007. Grassroots Struggles to Dismantle Environmental Racism in the United States." Available at www.ucc.org/justice/pdfs/toxic20.pdf (accessed December 27, 2007).

Case, K.E. and Fair, R.C. (2007) *Principles of Macroeconomics*, 8th edition, Upper Saddle River, NJ: Pearson Prentice Hall.

Colander, D. (2006) *Macroeconomics*, 6th edition, New York: McGraw-Hill Irwin.

Davis, J.B. (2005) "Robbins, Textbooks, and the Extreme Value Neutrality View," *History of Political Economy*, 37 (2): 191–196.

Figart, D.M. (2005) "Gender as More than a Dummy Variable: Feminist Approaches to Discrimination," *Review of Social Economy*, 63 (3): 509–536.

Friedman, M. (1953) *Essays in Positive Economics*, Chicago: University of Chicago Press.

Gay, G. (2002) "Preparing for Culturally Responsive Teaching," *Journal of Teacher Education*, 53 (2): 106–116.

Goodwin, N., Nelson, J.A., and Harris, J. (2009) *Macroeconomics in Context*, Armonk, NY: M.E. Sharpe.

Harding, S. (1995) "Can Feminist Thought Make Economics More Objective?" *Feminist Economics* 1 (1): 7–32.

Jensen, E. and Owen, A.L. (2001) "Pedagogy, Gender, and Interest in Economics," *Journal of Economic Education*, 32 (4): 323–343.

Jorgenson, D.W., Landefeld, J.S., and Nordhaus, W.D.E. (2006) *A New Architecture for the U.S. National Accounts*, Chicago: University of Chicago Press.

Kendrick, J.W. (1967) "Studies in the National Income Accounts," *Forty-Seventh Annual Report of the National Bureau of Economic Research*, 9–15, New York: National Bureau of Economic Research.

Krugman, P. and Wells, R. (2006) *Macroeconomics*, New York: Worth Publishers.

Lynch, L. (2007) "2006 Report of the Committee on the Status of Women in the Economics Profession," *CSWEP Newsletter* (Winter): 3–8.

Maher, F.A. and Tetreault, M.K.T. (1997) "Learning In The Dark: How Assumptions of Whiteness Shape Classroom Knowledge," *Harvard Educational Review*, 67 (2): 321–350.

Mankiw, N.G. (2006) *Principles of Macroeconomics*, 4th edition, Cincinnati, OH: South-Western College Publications.

McConnell, C.C. and Brue, S.L. (2005) *Economics*, 16th edition, New York: McGraw-Hill Irwin.

Nelson, J.A. (1995) "Feminism and Economics," *Journal of Economic Perspectives*, 9 (2): 131–148.

—— (1996) *Feminism, Objectivity and Economics*, New York: Routledge.

Niederle, M. and Vesterlund, L. (2005) "Do Women Shy Away From Competition? Do Men Compete Too Much?" Working Paper No. 11474, Cambridge, MA: National Bureau of Economic Research.

Nugent, R. (1997) "Critique of National Accounting," in R. Bartlett (ed.) *Introducing Race and Gender Into Economics*, 125–136, New York: Routledge.

Rishi, M. (1998) "Curriculum Transformation at the Introductory Economic Level: Taking the First Steps," *Feminist Teacher*, 12 (2): 137–149.

Robson, D. (2001) "Women and Minorities in Economics Textbooks: Are They Being Adequately Represented?" *Journal of Economic Education*, 32 (2): 186–191.

Sax, L.J. (2007) "College Women Still Face Many Obstacles in Reaching Their Full Potential," *Chronicle of Higher Education*, 54 (5): B46.

Shah, S. (1996) "Gender in Introductory Economic Textbooks," in N. Aslanbeigui and M.I. Naples (eds) *Rethinking Economic Principles: Critical Essays on Introductory Textbooks*, 28–43, Chicago: Irwin.

Summers, L. (1991) "The Memo." Available at www.globalpolicy.org/socecon/envronmt/summers.htm (accessed February 11, 2008).

U.S. Department of Commerce, Bureau of Economic Analysis (2007) "An Introduction to the National Income and Product Accounts." Available at www.bea.gov/scb/pdf/national/nipa/methpap/mpi1_0907.pdf (accessed November 12, 2007).

Weston, S.C. (1994) "Toward a Better Understanding of the Positive/Normative Distinction in Economics," *Economics and Philosophy*, 10 (1): 1–17.

# 18 A pluralist teaching of economics
## Why and how

*Gilles Raveaud*

> I think the textbooks are a scandal. I think to expose young impressionable minds to this scholastic exercise as though it said something about the real world, is a scandal.... I don't know of any other science that purports to be talking about real world phenomena, where statements are regularly made that are blatantly contrary to fact.
>
> (Simon 1997: 397)

### What's wrong with economics teaching? The students' protests

In June 2000, a small group of French undergraduate students launched a protest that became known worldwide (Fullbrook 2003). Having decided to study economics in order to understand the world they live in, they had realized that they were not going to make it, despite the fact that they were students in prestigious French institutions, mainly the Ecole Normale Supérieure and the Université Paris 1 ("La Sorbonne"). They made their frustration public.

A graduate student at the time, I joined the group. At first, everything seemed so wrong that we did not really know how to articulate our protest. We invited Bernard Guerrien, a Sorbonne professor and a fine specialist of neoclassical economics, who told us that our concerns were shared (see the papers collected in Fullbrook 2004). With his intellectual support, we wrote an "open letter" addressed to our teachers.[1] The open letter raised three critiques. First, we denounced the fact that economists built up "imaginary worlds," i.e. unrealistic theories.[2] Second, we opposed the use of mathematics as "an end in itself."[3] Last, the open letter pleaded against the "dogmatism" of the curriculum, and for "pluralism." In fact, not so long ago, in France at least, undergraduate students were exposed very early on to different schools of economic thought. In most departments around the world, this is no longer the case (Blaug 1998). Most courses have the same gray color of neoclassical economics – even if modern textbooks use fancy colors to present it.

During private discussions with teachers that publicly opposed our petition, we were surprised to realize that quite a few of them would acknowledge the validity of our claim. So why did they oppose our protest? Here, social pressure and conformity, widespread diseases as they are within the academy, provide the first reason for this strange behavior. But there is a second reason: the appeal of mainstream economics. Here, I would like to focus on three aspects of main-stream economics which, among others, account for its appeal: its ideology, its scientific nature, and the formal flexibility of its language.

## Mainstream economics: ideology, science, and formal openness

A first strength of mainstream economics is its (implicit) ideology. Mainstream economics rests on the ideals of freedom, efficiency, and fairness. Neoclassical economics is about freedom: it describes an unlimited world within which indi-viduals operate with universal agency. It is the world on which the ideology of modernity rests (Marglin 2007). Second, mainstream economics is about effi-ciency. According to this view, markets, if not hampered, will deliver the great-est amounts of resources at the minimum costs. Last, mainstream theory is about justice: markets, when perfect, reward individuals according to their contribution to the well-being of all.

Mainstream economics thus has an extremely powerful appeal: it represents a world with the widest possible range of actions, which allows the best use of the resources available while at the same time ensuring that everyone gets what he or she deserves. Even if those results hold only under very specific conditions, and only if one subscribes to the version of equity here put forward, they do remain impressive.

But there is another, unrelated, ground on which it is possible to defend main-stream economics. It is its scientific nature. Mainstream economics is the grand theory of economics because it is the one which rests on the most general hypotheses, and which has produced the most general results. True, some remark that those results turn out to be negative more often that not.[4] But, like it or not, general equilibrium is the common language of modern economics.

There is more: this language is flexible enough to allow for critiques to be developed within its framework. As proponents of the mainstream argue, econo-mists like Joseph Stiglitz, George Akerlof, Lawrence Summers, or Gregory Mankiw have made a significant number of modifications to the mainstream while using its very instruments. It is possible within the framework of general equilibrium to show that asymmetries of information can be pervasive, that equi-libria can be suboptimal, that monetary policy can have lasting effects, and so on. The mainstream framework thus does offer some latitude for pluralism.

But, of course, this latitude is limited. The mainstream framework is not ade-quate for ideas such as holism, social classes, gender roles, uncertainty, solid-arity, or finite resources. Following Garnett (personal correspondence, 2007), we can qualify mainstream economics as a space of "ostensible pluralism," i.e. a space of nominal openness and pluralism that is in fact tightly confined, ideolog-ically and pedagogically. In fact, when it comes to introductory classes, this space boils down to a very simple – and thus powerful – representation: the supply and demand diagram.

## The (lethal?) weapon of the mainstream: the story of supply and demand

When it comes to teaching to undergraduates, mainstream economics strikes by its simplicity. The story told is a short and simple one. Let us imagine the market for apples. Consumers would like to buy apples, which producers are willing to supply. For consumers, the best is to get apples at the lowest possible price. On the contrary, producers would like to sell at the highest possible price. The quantities demanded and supplied are thus going to be inversely related to the price of apples. When the price is very low, consumers demand high quantities, but only a few producers are interested in supplying them. On the contrary, when the price is high, producers are willing to produce large quantities, but few buyers are interested in buying them.

Somewhere in between these two extremes, there is a price for which the quantities demanded are equal to the quantities supplied. Economists call this price the equilibrium price. A major claim of mainstream analysis is that, at the equilibrium price, *everybody is satisfied*. This is so despite the fact that not everybody participates in the exchange. It is easy to understand why the consumers who do get apples and the producers who sell them are satisfied. In fact, not only are these people satisfied, but several of them even enjoy a surplus: if I was ready to but apples at $5 a pound and they sell for only $3, I am enjoying a "consumer surplus." If, as a producer, I would have been able to produce apples at $4 a pound and they sell at $5, I am making an extra profit, called "producer surplus."

All market participants are then satisfied, and some of them are more than satisfied. But why is it that even the producers and consumers who, under other circumstances, would have participated in the exchange but who do not when the price is $5 are satisfied too? According to neoclassical economics, this is because they *prefer* not to. When apples sell at $5 a pound, producers who can sell apples only if their price is above $6 a pound prefer to put their productive resources (land, labor, capital) to other uses such as, for instance, growing pears. What about consumers who cannot afford apples at $5 a pound? The theory assumes that they prefer to devote their scare resources to other purchases (for instance, bread). Well, one may ask, what if they have no resources at all? In fact, neoclassical economics has no answer to this question.

The fact that, at the equilibrium price, everybody is satisfied – non-market participants included – and that some people even enjoy a surplus is the reason why, according to the neoclassical account, free markets deliver the highest possible collective satisfaction, or "social surplus." Also, the market ensures the most efficient use of the scarce resources. In effect, competition between producers ensures that apples are grown by the most efficient producers. On the other side, competition between buyers ensures that the good goes to those who prefer it most, i.e. those who are willing to pay most for it.

Of course, such reasoning is contrary to commonsense. It makes no room for the notion of need, nor does it explain or justify why some people enjoy higher incomes than other. The neoclassical story would hold only in a world where everybody would earn the same. It is only in such a world that the hypothesis that different willingness to pay reflects only different individual preferences would begin to make sense.[5] The question thus becomes: do we or do we not live in such a world? Or in one that is close enough to this representation?

According to mainstream economists, we do. In the mainstream view, social problems originate not from the pervasiveness and ruthlessness of markets, but rather from their absence, or their imperfection. A problem can persist for only one of two reasons: humans are interfering with the market, or the market is missing. For instance, if you let the labor market work freely, you will have no unemployment. Unemployment results only from human intervention – as the comparison between the United States and Europe is supposed to prove. Humans create harm when they fiddle with markets. They also do harm when they ban markets, as the shortage of organs shows. Thus, "many economists believe that there would be large benefits to allowing a free market for organs" (Mankiw 2004: 152). By giving an incentive to people with healthy organs to sell them, a free market would help to resolve the current shortage, and in the end, save lives.[6]

This last example shows that market thinking and promoting is intrinsically limitless. This is why it is necessary to discuss this view of the world.

## The necessity to debate markets

The case in favor of markets might sometimes seem overwhelming. But in fact, once one leaves the quiet realm of the academy, the picture changes dramatically. It is observable everywhere that markets can induce waste, can be unfair, and can displace more efficient ways of organizing life.

The typical example is health systems. Studies by the World Health Organization have shown that public health systems are *more efficient* than private ones (WHO 2000). For instance, when it comes to the "performance" of health systems, i.e. to how efficiently health systems translate money into health – measured by disability-adjusted life expectancy – the United States ranks ... 72nd. Countries not as rich as the United States but where health is mostly publicly provided, like Italy (3rd), France (4th), or Japan (9th) obtain much better results (WHO 2000, tables 9 and 10).

How come? According to the WHO, part of the result can be explained by the *fairness* of public health systems. When health is provided to all, people do not wait to see a practitioner: they are cured earlier, which is better for their health, and less costly to the system. Also, competition is costly for a number of reasons. First, competition takes place between private companies which, unlike public systems, have to pay dividends to their shareholders. These profits and dividends are, at the end of the day, paid by consumers. Second, competition induces important marketing and advertising costs – costs nonexistent with a public monopoly. Third, competition leads to redundant positions among the competing firms. Fourth, top wages are higher in private companies than in public institutions.

In total, the health care example shows that, in some cases at least, a public monopoly is more efficient than the market – and ensures access to cure for all. Against this, the reaction of mainstream economists is to point out the specificity of health care: while they may accept that in this case markets do not work very well, they would claim that this is an exception. Health care is a specific example, for sure. But what about other markets? Are not food, housing, education, transportation, and the media specific markets as well? Is it the case that perfect competition is always achievable, or desirable, in those markets? Are there so many real-world markets that match the textbook perfectly competitive case?

The point is not to give answers to those questions. It is to raise them – in class. Because what this discussion shows is the necessity to debate the relative merits of competition versus other modes of organization in a systematic manner. True, it is probably better to have competition than monopoly for most consumption goods. But in many other cases the advantages, and sometimes the very possibility, of competition might not be obvious. Of course, even within mainstream economics, public goods and externalities have long been classic cases in favor of public intervention in the economy. But the fact remains that, in introductory economic classes, the good referred to is what we could call the "no problem good," that is a good which is relatively homogeneous, that requires little capital to produce, that causes no externality, for which there are many producers, and to which consumers have accessible alternatives. It is no accident that Mankiw uses the example of pizza and cola again and again in his textbook. His message would be much harder to get across with health care.

My point is that the "no problem good" is a problem. It is not acceptable to do as if the perfectly competitive model was a good approximation of reality or as if it represented a desirable ideal. Both the relevance of the neoclassical model and its normative implications must be discussed. In fact, many elements which are presented as "natural" by mainstream economists vary in time and place, and can be subjected to collective decision. The pizza and cola example of Mankiw suggests that food is a "no problem good." But too much pizza and cola has made food become a health issue in the United States and many other countries. Public authorities, which have always tightly controlled the production of food, now also intervene on its distribution and advertising, and try to educate their population. What used to be a "no problem good" has become one which causes losses of individual well-being and which is at the source of massive negative externalities.

There are thus many ways to look at food, either as a "no problem let individuals decide" kind of good, or as a good that raises important social, economic, and ecological issues which require collective actions. The point of introductory economics classes is not to present solutions to these problems. It is to teach the students that those questions are political questions, which require political answers – the free market just being one of them.[7] This is the reason why we called for a serious revision of undergraduate education. For us, this education needs to be multidisciplinary and real-world oriented.

## A sensible undergraduate economics pedagogy

I think that introductory economics should start with the premises that we the teachers do not know – and that we have no failsafe recipes to offer. The argument is often made that you cannot afford to do this because this is an introductory class, and that if you do so, you are going to deter the students from your discipline or, at the very least, puzzle them. But I would argue that students need to be challenged, and that they can be challenged from the very beginning, because this is when their minds are the most flexible, when they are more open to discomforting views. Also, while students need to be reassured that their professors know better that they do, they also like to be puzzled. They are students, after all, not guinea pigs! Our role as teachers is not to give them ready-made answers. It is to provide them with the tools and opportunities they need in order to learn to think for themselves about the relative value of competing economic ideas, institutions, and policies in the face of genuine uncertainty about which one is "right."

In 2000 and 2001, we the French post-autistic group devised an undergraduate curriculum that, in our mind, matched this ideal. Our central idea was to ask the students to analyze concrete problems from different standpoints. The competing views would be assessed by students along two dimensions, empirical and normative. In effect, contrary to what some of our critics have said, we are in favor of a wide – but reasoned – use of data, and of its treatment via econometrics, as judgments on competing approaches and policies cannot dispense with the analysis of their quantitative impact. The second dimension is the normative one. The "welfare effects" of a given policy proposal cannot be left to passing remarks, or to advanced courses. This is why we proposed to add a political philosophy course to the curriculum.

In fact, for us, economics cannot be taught in isolation. We thus called for pluridisciplinarity, something non-existent in the French context where economics students, even undergraduate, do not have the time nor the possibility to study other subjects. To our surprise, the report written by the French Economist Jean-Paul Fitoussi (Fitoussi 2001) went even beyond our demands. Jean-Paul Fitoussi suggested that, in their first year, students be introduced to the main thinkers and principles in two other subjects, to be chosen among philosophy, sociology, law, history, political science, or psychology. Second, Fitoussi called for an "integrated" teaching of economics, that is one that combines economic theories with history of thought and economic policy.

Regarding pedagogy, we propose two major changes. The first one is to downplay significantly the role of textbooks. I know that textbooks play a central role in undergraduate education these days, especially in North America. But I cannot forget the immense pleasure I had as a student to be confronted with classic texts, in sections, from day one. Sections were organized by themes. For instance, on the question of consumption, we would read Marx as well as French sociologists like Baudrillard. Being faced head on with those deep reflections on the central concepts of economics has given me my strong inclination for economics. Let me insist on this: yes, if guided, students can, *in first year*, read Smith, Marx, Ricardo, Marshall, Keynes, Robbins, and the like. And many enjoy it.

But those readings have to be linked up with real-world issues. That is our second main proposed change. We propose to create thematic courses such as "Is there a tradeoff between equality and growth?", "For or against the WTO?", or "Public services or competition?" (ideally, the themes would be chosen with the students). Those courses would rely on sources like official reports from the OECD, the World Bank, the United Nations, governments, NGOs, papers from think tanks, and the like. Those reports combine economic analysis and normative judgments, and give recent data on major topics. In our view, they are an excellent way to train students in all the skills of an economist.

The pluralist approach advocated here combines data, economic reasoning, and political philosophy to address current issues. The point of this approach is to put debates and controversies everywhere. Organizing teaching around issues and debates is a great way to make economics engaging for students. It also corresponds to an idea of science we want to defend. And I claim that it is pedagogically feasible. Now, going into the specifics, how should we present these debates and controversies? Here, unfortunately, it seems that there is no choice but to organize them around ... mainstream economics.

## Teaching pluralism at Harvard: the "social analysis 72" experiment

In Steve Marglin's introductory course at Harvard, five critiques are studied. The first is what Marglin has labeled the "structural critique," which deals primarily with the internal limits of mainstream economics. This critique stresses the fact that what are regarded as "exceptions" by mainstream economists – externalities, market power, increasing returns in production, asymmetric information – are central features of real markets. In effect, extra profits always derive from some kind of market imperfection. If markets were what mainstream economics say they are, there would be no stimulus for extra profit, no investment, no capital, no ... capitalism.[8]

The second is the Keynesian critique. In the course, Keynes's analysis is presented as a critique of neoclassical economics. This diverges from conventional curricula, which present "macro" and "micro" courses as complementary, the macro course following the micro class. In fact, one of Keynes's crucial points was that the general state of the economy ("macro results") does not follow from individual decisions ("micro actions"). On the contrary, what is rational for the individual firm – diminishing its wage expenditures – may end as a catastrophic result – depression – for the economy as a whole.

The third critique is the distributional critique. A major flaw in mainstream economics is its complete disregard for poverty and inequality – even when they are so widespread that they threaten the very existence of society, as in the Great Depression or more recently in Russia or Argentina. To address the relation between efficiency and equity is, in most economists' terms, to discuss the "tradeoff" between these two goals. This is because, according to the mainstream view, inequalities are an incentive for people to work harder, invest more, and so on, which will lead to a larger pie. This is a strong argument. But, on the other hand, one can remark that developed countries are at the same time richer and much more equal then poor countries, and that, within rich nations, the Scandinavian countries are more efficient *and* more equal than most (Jackson 2000). Also, efficiency and equality can be promoted simultaneously, both through state interventions, such as in public education or health, or at the micro level, when trust between workers and management favors productivity. So there are a number of empirical and theoretical arguments against the idea of an inescapable tradeoff between equity and efficiency.

The last two critiques addressed in Marglin's course are the ecological and the "foundational" critique. The ecological critique deals with the irreversible effects of human economic activity on the environment. Mainstream economics is unable to address the issues of resources depletion, because it postulates a world of unlimited resources. In fact, as Cambridge (U.K.) professor Tony Lawson has put it, mainstream economics is a "closed system" (Lawson 1997). That is, mainstream economics is a purely logical world, a world which cannot be disrupted from the outside – including by the disappearing natural environment. For mainstream economics, nature is reduced to a good which can be traded like any other. On the contrary, ecological economists remind us that the economy is a subset of nature, not the other way round.

What Marglin has labeled the "foundational" critique tackles the anthropological dimension of markets. Here, the stress is on the fact that markets may impact negatively on communities, local cultures, and more generally, social ties. A case in point here are Indian workers who work in outsourced call centers in India for U.S. companies and who change their name, their accent, and progressively, their entire behavior, because of their interaction with U.S. customers. While the evaluation of these changes inevitably depends on the observer's point of view, this example shows that one cannot discuss the merits of free trade without questioning its effect on habits, customs, and ways of living.

In a sense, these two last critiques deal with the impact of the market on our "environment" – both natural and human. Mainstream economics is blind when it comes to the effects of the market on this environment simply because it takes the environment as given, unaffected by economic activities. Neoclassical economics cannot as such address the current depletion of resources, the destruction of communities, the desperate quest for material goods, and the expansion of greed. This is problematic as the development of mainstream economics and markets are linked. Sure, one did not have to wait for mainstream economists to invent markets. But many economists have played and continue to play an active role in promoting market-based solutions to the world's most pressing problems.[9]

All in all, Marglin's course includes a variety of views which allow the students to have a broader analysis of the issues at stake. The next step would be to apply these different views (and others, such as the feminist critique) to current issues. Indeed, this is where the thematic courses presented above would come in. But this would require an orientation of the entire Harvard economic department in that direction. Even if forecasts are always hard, I take the chance to say that I might not live long enough to see this happen. Neoclassical economics is likely to stay dominant for a number of years. It occupies the main role in most classes, including Marglin's. This is problematic.

## Should we begin with neoclassical economics?

In most economics departments, neoclassical economics occupies the vast majority of teaching time. I think that this is unfortunate. But this situation corresponds to the fact that neoclassical economics is the current language of the economic profession. It is also the language of many politicians and journalists. In short, neoclassical economics is "the language of power." Therefore, students (and citizens) have to know it – and to know it well. Also, one should not forget that Keynes and Marx presented their own work as, in Marx's words, "a critique of political economy." Thus, for all these reasons, I am afraid that, *in the current intellectual and political context*, there are just too many reasons to put neoclassical economics center stage, and to present other views as "critiques."

Still, one must be aware of the limits of this choice. First, this way of proceeding presents the mainstream view as "the way economists think." Also, this sequence may diminish the attractiveness of alternative theories. Marglin rightly points out that beginning with the mainstream has the advantage of introducing the students to the limits of neoclassical theory early on, which may raise their interest in alternative approaches. But I fear that students might find those heterodox views less convincing.

In effect, it may prove difficult to introduce the conflict-laden worlds of the Marxists, the deterministic world of the feminists, or the endangered world of ecological economists to students who have in mind a world of rational individuals with infinite agency operating in a limitless world. Indeed, power, gender, and nature cannot be represented on the supply and demand diagram. It thus requires an effort from the teacher to remind the students of the even greater arbitrariness and narrowness of this very diagram. Were theories presented the other way around, it is quite possible that the students' judgment on the relevance of each might be different.[10]

For instance, once one has started with neoclassical economics, the macroeconomic view of Keynes always has difficulties going through, because it is "ad hoc." But this resistance to Keynes does not take place when one begins with his theory. On the contrary, the typical circular flow diagram appeals a lot to students, who understand the flows of consumption, investment, and also the fact that the economy involves different kinds of actors, i.e. the state, firms, and households. The inherent disequilibrium in a market economy, the perils of finance, the relevance of economic policies – these themes all appeal to students. Once those have been introduced, students are shocked by the neoclassical view of the world, where there is no uncertainty, no disequilibrium, no state…

The same goes with Marx. I am always surprised to see how my students spontaneously share Marx's views on alienation at work. (I suppose this is in part because many of them have a firsthand knowledge of poor jobs, which I lack). Also, the notion of exploitation, or at least the idea that there is a basic conflict between employees and capitalists is also intuitive to many of them. Here again, the order of presentation matters a lot. If you begin your class with Marx, neoclassical economics tends to look ridiculously simplified and right-wing. But if you begin with neoclassical economics, Marx looks "lefty," and "political," "unscientific."

Those examples show the importance of the order of the course. I think this importance derives from the fact that the theory which is presented first sets the stage for "what economics is." Marx, Keynes, or Walras give very different definitions of economics. It is impossible to disentangle entirely the content of the theory from the definition of the discipline this theory entails. When the teacher presents the different theories, he/she also sends a message to his/her students about the nature of economics as a discipline. I suppose the best one can do is to be aware of it and, when teaching those different theories, to spend some time analyzing the author's conception of economics.

In any case, the order in which theories are presented matters less than the fact that several of them are presented. This is rarely done, despite the fact that tenured professors (and assistant professors in France, who get tenure immediately) have a considerable amount of nominal freedom in deciding what to teach. What each of us does with this freedom is our own responsibility.

## Conclusion: fear not our freedom

To quote again Herbert Simon, current introductory economics classes are a "scandal." For Simon, the scandal consists in presenting a theory of individual decision which has been proven wrong. For us, those classes are scandalous because they are unfaithful both to the very discipline of economics and to the real world. Current classes not only exclude Marx and Keynes. They also exclude the environment, poverty, large multinational companies, international institutions, financial markets, states, communities, and households.

This situation is unacceptable intellectually, biased politically, and plainly sad. When liberal education is all about being confronted with great works from great authors, engaging with pressing issues, and challenging oneself, the current mass indoctrination system is all about learning one textbook by heart, avoiding the real world, and following mainstream political leaders and the mass media. When what we hope to do as teachers is to challenge the conventional wisdom of our times, introductory economics classes forces it on the students.

Happily, a number of alternative textbooks have been published in the last few years[11] (Bowles *et al.* 2005; Colander 2004; Goodwin *et al.* 2004, 2009).

These textbooks present various critiques and alternatives to the mainstream. They offer a resource that is simply necessary in the current ideological fight. One can thus hope that the teaching of economics at the undergraduate level will soon become somewhat more pluralistic.

But resistance to change is impressive. I am still puzzled by the fears we heterodox economists often have. Far too often, we are afraid to introduce first-year students to classic texts; we are afraid to engage with real-world issues; we are reluctant to puzzle our students; we are terrified to look stupid in the eyes of our colleagues by admitting that we do not know. Those fears are so prevalent that we do not see them anymore. I think that those fears, more than mainstream economics, incredibly powerful as it is, are our worst enemy. Those fears prevent us from liberating ourselves, from liberating knowledge, from using the incredible freedom that academia grants so many of us. Let us use this freedom. Our students deserve it.

## Acknowledgment

Thanks to Robert Österbergh and Steve Marglin for their helpful remarks and suggestions on a previous version. Rob Garnett has provided invaluable advice and helped me improve this text very significantly.

## Notes

1 This text and others can be read on the website run by Edward Fullbrook, www.paecon.net.
2 A survey showed that, for the vast majority of Ph.D. students, the knowledge of empirical facts was not useful for their research (Davis 1997).
3 Although the open letter stated that we did not oppose the use of mathematics per se, many commentators focused on this point, engaging in epistemological debates only loosely related to our protest. One may wonder if some people did not use this "math controversy" just as a way not to answer our more important questions.
4 For a critique of the shortcomings of general equilibrium theory, read the debate Bernard Guerrien launched in the on-line *Post-Autistic Economic Review*.
5 In order to ensure the viability of general equilibrium, Arrow and Debreu had to make the hypothesis that each household has enough resources to participate in market exchange.
6 One may resist the creation of this market on moral grounds: with a market, only those who can pay can have an organ. But think of the current situation. As Professor Mankiw (2004: 152) puts it, "Now, most of us walk around with an extra organ that we don't really need, while some of our fellow citizens are dying to get one. Is that fair?"
7 To repeat: No theorem demonstrates that more markets or better markets lead to an unambiguous increase in social welfare.
8 The neoclassical perfectly competitive model is a model that corresponds best to small markets for fresh produces. In our postindustrial age, it is no accident that many examples used by the most popular textbooks come from agriculture.
9 Up to the point where entire institutions are shaped according to the requirements of mainstream economic theory, such as the World Trade Organization or the European Central Bank.

10 An interesting experiment would be to teach the same content to different groups of students, while changing the order of presentation, to evaluate the effect of this change on their evaluation of the merits of each theory.
11 See also the promising "economic conversation" convened by Arjo Klamer, Deirdre McCloskey, and Stephen Ziliak (forthcoming).

## References

Blaug, M. (1998) "Disturbing Currents in Modern Economics," *Challenge*, 41 (May–June): 11–34.

Bowles, S., Edwards, R., and Roosevelt, F. (2005) *Understanding Capitalism: Competition, Command, and Change*, 3rd edition, Oxford: Oxford University Press.

Colander, D. (2004) *Economics*, 5th edition, New York: McGraw-Hill.

Davis, W.L. (1997) "Economists' Perceptions of Their Own Research: A Survey of the Profession," *American Journal of Economics and Sociology*, 56 (2): 159–172.

Fitoussi, J.-P. (2001) *L'enseignement supérieur de l'économie en question*, Paris: Fayard.

Fullbrook, E. (ed.) (2003) *The Crisis in Economics. The Post-Autistic Economics Movement: The First 600 Days*, London: Routledge.

—— (ed.) (2004) *A Student's Guide to What's Wrong with Economics*, London: Anthem Press.

Goodwin, N., Nelson, J.A., Ackerman, F., and Weisskopf, T. (2004) *Microeconomics in Context*, 1st edition, Cincinnati, OH: South-Western College Publications.

Goodwin, N., Nelson, J.A., and Harris, J. (2009) *Macroeconomics in Context*, Armonk, NY: M.E. Sharpe.

Jackson, A. (2000) "Why We Don't Have to Choose between Social Justice and Economic Growth: The Myth of the Equity/Efficiency Trade-off," Canadian Council on Social Development Report. Available at www.ccsd.ca/pubs/2000/equity (accessed February 21, 2008).

Klamer, A., McCloskey, D., and Ziliak, S. (forthcoming) *The Economic Conversation*, London: Palgrave Macmillan.

Lawson, T. (1997) *Economics and Reality*, London: Routledge.

Mankiw, N.G. (2004) *Principles of Economics*, 3rd edition, Mason, OH: South Western College Publications.

Marglin, S. (2007) *The Dismal Science: How Thinking Like an Economist Undermines Community*, Cambridge, MA: Harvard University Press.

Simon H. (1997) *Models of Bounded Rationality, Vol. 3: Empirically Grounded Economic Reason*, Cambridge, MA: MIT Press.

WHO (2000) *The World Health Report 2000. Health Systems: Improving Performance*, Geneva. Available at www.who.int/whr/2000/en/index.html (accessed February 15, 2008).

# 19 Economic pluralism and skill formation

## Adding value to students, economies, and societies

*Rod O'Donnell*

## Introduction

This is an exciting time for economics, and hence for the teaching of economics. In recent decades, alternative approaches have proliferated, whether as new schools or as modernized versions of earlier schools. Depending on how they are counted, around 10 to 12 major schools (including neoclassicism) now confront anyone enquiring into the state of contemporary economic thought. The result has been a higher degree of intellectual ferment and a greater sense of the possibilities for the future. As elsewhere, the existence of difference opens, broadens, and deepens the mind. The understanding of any theory, framework, or methodology is always improved when its alternatives are explored. Even for neoclassical economics, the best way to improve students' comprehension is to provide them with exposure to other schools and their contrasting conceptions.

To introduce students to this stimulating environment, a 300 level course, "Contending Perspectives in Contemporary Economics," was recently introduced at an Australian university. Two primary objectives motivated its introduction. One was to bring students into contact with the current state of modern economics as a whole, on the grounds that it is important for economics graduates to have this knowledge and to be acquainted with the wide range of analytical tools available to them as economists. The second was to help develop skill sets that benefit students, employers, and society. The need for these skills is obvious, but most courses are so focused on content that they neglect to pay attention to skills formation, which is often a much more important determinant of success and satisfaction in students' later lives than further content knowledge.

In relation to skill formation, it is the central contention of this chapter that pluralist courses are inherently superior vehicles for inculcating a range of desirable skills (outlined below) compared with orthodox courses which are severely restricted in this area. The key reason why this advantage is inherent is that pluralism explores multiple frameworks, while orthodoxy is based on only one framework. Three points may be made by way of clarification. First, the argument is about *relative* abilities in promoting desirable human capital formation. No claim is entered that orthodoxy has no capacity whatsoever, the actual claim being that pluralism is capable of providing a wider range of skills and of taking more of these skills to higher levels. Second, to maximize this potential, pluralist courses need to be *well-designed*, that is, they should exploit their natural advantages by making skill formation a central objective rather than a mere by-product. In this context, skill formation is enhanced by the synergistic integration of course content, selected activities, and instructive fun. Third, in the economics education literature, it is notable that skills formation is quite infrequently discussed compared with content and technique issues, a point evident from a perusal of the *Journal of Economics Education* over the last decade, for example. However, this dearth of discussion is not altogether surprising if, as claimed here, the potential of orthodoxy is relatively limited in this area.

## A puzzle concerning skill formation

For some time, there have been calls in Australia and elsewhere for the development of important skills in graduates. One report, published in 2000 by an Australian Government department, found that the "skills employers consider to be *most* important in graduates" were:

- creativity and flair
- enthusiasm, and
- independent and critical thinking.

It also observed that significant skill deficiencies in new graduates existed in the areas of:

- creativity and flair ("the most important of the skills tested")
- oral business communication
- problem solving
- independent and critical thinking, and
- interpersonal skills.[1]

A more recent report, issued in 2006 by the Business Council of Australia (a peak employer lobby group), emphasized the importance of innovation in raising productivity and global competitiveness. In relation to education, it highlighted the need for the development, not only of strong technical skills in the workforce, but also of other significant skills including:

- communication
- teamwork
- problem solving
- creativity
- ongoing learning
- cultural understanding
- entrepreneurship, and
- leadership.

It also noted employer dissatisfaction with educational outcomes because graduates with sufficient of the latter skills were not being produced to meet the needs of business.[2]

Underpinning this report was a straightforward economic argument. Higher productivity and international competitiveness depend on innovation; innovation depends critically on particular forms of human capital; education and training systems have vital roles in creating human capital; current education systems are failing to develop the necessary forms of human capital to sufficient degrees; hence, education systems need to be improved if stronger innovative capacities, skills, and cultures are to be developed to promote economic growth.

Given the essential role of creativity in innovation, as well as its appearance in both reports, it is worthwhile examining the attributes that underpin this key capacity. The extensive literature on this complex notion indicates that the subtle mix of factors contributing to creativity includes the following:

- appreciation of holistic standpoints
- awareness of different viewpoints and approaches
- capacity to see things in new ways
- thinking outside the conventional framework
- openness to non-conformity
- courage to question received wisdom
- stimulating milieus
- free communication and discussion
- willingness to take risks, and
- playfulness.[3]

Three observations may be made at this point. The first is that innovation, in and of itself, is *necessarily disruptive of the status quo*, for its nature is to challenge, overthrow, or rearrange current views and practices. The parallelism with pluralism (in economics or elsewhere) needs no further elaboration.[4] Second, whether or not similar calls for graduate skill formation have been made by governments or interest groups in countries outside Australia, a little reflection shows that the inculcation of such skills as those listed above is clearly of value to *all* economies and societies. And third, the economic argument can be extended to other spheres. Improvements in any field – social programs, environmental sustainability, or scientific advance, for example – depend on innovation in one form or another, which means that virtually all members of society have an interest in developing skills that facilitate the creation of new ideas and ways of doing things. If we seek higher standards of living that are ecologically sustainable, for instance, we require innovation, creativity, and leadership in a wide range of areas. And if we want more individuals to display creativity, initiative, and openness to new ideas, we need to educate them in a manner that encourages the relevant skills as much as possible. This is one of those cases where what benefits business and the economy also provides benefits (of at least equal magnitudes) to individuals, non-business interests, and society as a whole.

The above considerations lead me to conclude, first, that the above skills are desirable and, second, that education systems should foster their acquisition. However, very little activity within education systems (in Australia at least and very probably in other countries) appears to be systematically directed towards this end. In economics, in particular, there seems to be very little interest in, or effort expended towards, the inculcation of these particular skills even though they are clearly of economic importance and, indeed, requested by interest groups closely associated with the economy.[5] Despite miniscule knowledge, I am prepared to wager that there are no economics courses anywhere in the world that consciously seek the development of this skill set.

This is the puzzle concerning skill formation. Why, despite calls for their development by influential groups (at least in Australia) and their obvious benefits to everyone, is so little effort being devoted (at least in economics) to the inculcation of these skills in graduates? Is it solely due to a lack of time, resources, interest, or motivation on the part of academics and administrators? This is likely to be part of the answer because most economics courses are, and have been, predominantly focused on content rather than skill formation. But if this were the only obstacle it could, in principle, be fixed relatively easily. Or are there other causes at deeper levels? Are there inherent impediments and limitations in orthodox courses which inhibit the promulgation of these skills? I shall contend that these deeper causes do exist and are the primary underlying reason why this skill set is underdeveloped in graduates (in economics at least).

My contention is twofold: (1) orthodoxy is intrinsically restricted in the type and level of the skills it can foster; and (2) pluralism possesses large natural advantages in this area, such that (well-designed) pluralist courses provide inherently superior platforms for skill formation. By "well-designed" in this context, I mean courses in which content and activities are synergistically combined to create environments conducive to developing *both* knowledge and desirable skills. However, before presenting arguments supporting the above propositions, it will be helpful to provide an example of such a course, namely, "Contending Perspectives in Contemporary Economics."[6]

## Course design, organization, and content

The general design principle that was adopted was full immersion of students in a skill-forming environment in the context of a discipline-based course. Rather than being left at the periphery, skill formation was placed at the center of the course alongside discipline content, these two core elements being encouraged to interact synergistically using well-chosen activities. In this manner, an environment was provided which modeled and demonstrated the relevant skills to students in various ways, and gave them opportunities to experience, practice, and reflect on them. The engine so formed, I suggest, provides a powerful means of assisting students toward the desired skill sets.

The course was nominated at the 300 level on the grounds that the more content students had covered, the better would be their understanding of alternative approaches. The prerequisites were either micro or macro at the 200 level, which meant that the earliest that students could enroll was midway through their second year.[7] Although desirable, the history of economic thought was not a prerequisite because the intention was to have a stand-alone treatment of contemporary thought. For the entire semester (13 weeks), the two lecture hours and one seminar hour per week were taken in blocks of three hours class time. The course motto was "Take an exciting intellectual and practical journey, and have fun on the way."

The lecture syllabus traversed eight schools of economic thought. Preceded by introductory remarks and a major economic game, the lectures on schools were followed by discussion of various methodological issues and implications for the economics discipline. The seminar syllabus consisted of a range of key activities which provided experiential learning as well as insights into conceptual and practical issues. *Both* the lectures and seminars contributed to human capital formation by encouraging the development of valuable skills. The weekly arrangement of lecture and seminar topics is outlined in Table 19.1.

Neoclassical economics received twice the time given to each of the other schools, all of which were given equal time. This is partly because students, although having been heavily exposed to orthodox economics, are rarely given an overview of neoclassicism as a whole, and partly because this school is the main target and departure point for heterodox schools.

There are obviously degrees of freedom in selecting the number and type of schools. In relation to number, it is a matter of deciding a suitable combination of breadth and depth; for a course relying on debates, however, even numbers are more convenient than odd ones. In relation to types, a subset of the available alternatives will most likely be chosen rather than an all-inclusive approach. Other courses may use different selections, but excluded schools can always be mentioned at relevant moments so that students know they exist and can pursue them independently.

*Table 19.1* Weekly lecture and seminar topics

| Week | Lecture topics | Seminar topics |
| --- | --- | --- |
| 1 | Introduction | Organization; Administration |
| 2 | Economic Game (Starpower) | |
| 3 | Neoclassical Economics | Mankiw Exercise |
| 4 | Neoclassical Economics | Mankiw Exercise |
| 5 | Post Keynesian Economics | Mankiw Exercise |
| 6 | Institutional Economics | Mankiw Exercise |
| 7 | Ecological Economics | Round table; Debate preparation |
| 8 | Radical Political Economy | Debate 1 |
| 9 | Austrian Economics | Debate 2 |
| 10 | Behavioral Economics | Debate 3 |
| 11 | Feminist Economics | Debate 4 |
| 12 | Methodological Issues | Game; Round table |
| 13 | Conclusion and Revision | Q&A; Feedback |

Because issues concerning methodology and philosophy of science emerge so strikingly during the course, the final lectures were given over to matters rarely discussed in Neoclassical courses, these including the scientificity of economics, the social science/natural science issue, the role of mathematics, criteria for rigor, the positive/normative distinction, theory testing, the construction of economic data, and the theory-dependence of facts.[8]

It is an important feature of the course that each student must belong to one of the eight schools of economic thought. Group-forming or "tribalizing" is done in the first seminar after students have listened to a survey of all the schools in the first lecture. Initially, choice of school can be voluntary, but guided reassignment by the lecturer may be required to produce roughly equal groups of two to four students. Belonging to a school assists skill formation in several ways, and deepens engagement with the material.

## Activities

As well as the conceptual material of the lectures, the course is organized around three activities that engage students in pedagogically effective ways – games, short presentations, and debates.

### *Games*

To pose fundamental questions and to set the scene for later discussions, the entire three hours of class time in the second week are devoted to playing Starpower, a powerful and instructive game developed in the 1960s. Its power comes from drawing players into the game, intellectually, morally, and emotionally. As a result, it is most important that thorough de-briefing and discussion takes place at the end for at least 30 minutes so that no one leaves with unfinished business.

It is a trading game in a society composed of individuals who are apparently equal, but who, after a short period, fall into three groups or classes (upper, middle, and lower). Movement between the groups is possible depending on trading success or failure, but inter-group mobility is usually not high. The game has an initial set of rules which are explained by the game supervisor but, at a certain point in the game, the supervisor announces that henceforth the rules will be made by the upper group. Players are also told at the start that the game is intended to simulate reality. The relevance of this message will not make an impression on players until later in the game, but the message is repeated at key points during play to allow students to envisage and express forms of non-acquiescent behavior such as negotiation, strikes, or even revolution. Such behavior requires leadership by one or more players. At a certain stage, the supervisor will judge that it is time to call an end to proceedings. Discussion and de-briefings then occur, with the supervisor ensuring that everyone says something about their feelings, and that students representing the lower class in particular are given adequate opportunity for this. The supervisor usually has one or two assistants to help manage the game.

The game challenges students' preconceptions about exchange and economic relationships, allowing them to learn more about the deeper structure of exchange and its non-economic foundations. Experientially, it drives home several important points – that exchange does not occur in a vacuum; that what lies behind exchange are sets of relations between agents which are ultimately based on power and/or morality; that rules (institutions) precede markets; that issues of politics and power concerning the content of rules and how they are decided are crucial to the outcomes of exchange; that exchange can lead to inequality, social injustice, and exploitation as well as to mutual benefit; and that rules generate structures which perpetuate themselves until they, and associated institutions, are changed (democratically or otherwise). Another important aspect of the game is that it allows players, individually or in groups, to exercise (and experience) both leadership and follower behavior.

While the long Starpower game is regarded as essential to the course, other shorter optional games may be included. One is the Marbles (or Nuts) game, outlined in Edney (1979), which can be played for about 20 minutes during a seminar toward the end of the course. The marbles simulate a self-reproducing but exhaustible natural resource, and the game neatly illustrates the difference between individual and collective rationality, and how politics (in the form of communication between players) can affect individual behavior and social outcomes.

### Presentations

Students also undertake a short presentation exercise. In the present case, this was based on the opening chapter of Mankiw's introductory textbook, *Principles of Economics*, which advances and briefly discusses "Ten Principles of Economics."[9] The aims of the exercise are to give students opportunities to hone their critical thinking skills and to display their communication skills for the first time.

Mankiw's principles are broadly familiar to students because of previous exposure to orthodox economics. But what students frequently do not realize is just how contestable, school-specific, and unsatisfactorily formulated they are. These features (familiarity and contestability) mean that Mankiw's principles provide excellent raw material for students to use in developing their critical faculties. They begin to think independently rather than just rely on authority, and to start to learn how to assess the strengths and weaknesses of certain ideas or propositions (and schools of thought), no matter how initially plausible they may seem or how "biblically" they are presented. The principles also provide an opportunity for exploring pretensions, rhetorical practices, and ideology. For not only are the above propositions poorly formulated, they are also principles of Neoclassical Economics rather than principles of economics in general.

The short presentations start in the seminar following the Starpower game, and continue for four weeks. To develop teamwork, presentations are done using the same groups as constitute the schools of thought, with each student having a turn in speaking. The exercise requires each group to select a different principle from Mankiw's list, to present a critical assessment of that principle for five minutes (based on Mankiw's discussion, their own reflections, and any other reading), and then to use their remarks to lead into a related topic that interests them (concerning the real world or economic analysis) for another five minutes. Students are encouraged to use transparencies or brief handouts, and are given a prior list or "dos" and "don'ts" for delivering good presentations. The class then discusses the content of the presentation and provides helpful feedback on presentation skills, having previously been informed on how to convey useful feedback (including negative reactions) to presenters in constructive ways.

### *Debates*

The debates also have intellectual and practical aims. The main intellectual aim is for students to be attached to a particular school for a period of time so that they can work their way into its framework and become aware of the nature and characteristics of that kind of thinking. The practical aims are the same as for the presentations (including the development of communication skills for employment situations where concise reports need to be delivered and questions answered), but extend beyond these in fostering *attitudinal* skills such as respect for different viewpoints and the ethics of good conversation. As this is their second opportunity to communicate with an audience, it is hoped that noticeable improvements have occurred.

   In the latter half of the seminar program, each school debates another school, the set of pairings used in the present case being:

- Neoclassical Economics vs Post Keynesian Economics
- Institutional Economics vs Ecological Economics
- Radical Political Economy vs Austrian Economics
- Behavioral Economics vs Feminist Economics.

Other oppositions can be used, but the best appear to be those with significant (or at least sufficient) contrast. The question debated can be common to all debates or different. In the present case, the following common questions were used:

1   Outline the strengths of your own school and the weaknesses of the other school.
2   Can you think of ways to adapt your school to make it more compatible with some of the views of the other school?[10]

   Timing during the debates was crucial, and an important part of the exercise. Each school was given about 12 minutes for delivery and four minutes for reply. General discussion followed, with adjudication of the debate by class vote. Feedback was also provided on presentation skills by class members and the lecturer at the end of the seminar. Students were expected to do their own research and to use presentation aids. The debates were quite lively, engaging, and entertaining events, for students often put their hearts and souls into their deliveries. Within two weeks of their debate, each student submitted a seminar paper (1500–2000 words) based on the question debated and including a substantial list of references. For the debates to be successful, students need to be well organized, exhibit good teamwork, and stick to time, these also being characteristics of good presentations in employment and other situations. Experience indicates that time is the issue that students find hardest to manage.[11]

## Why well-designed pluralist courses are inherently superior for desired skill formation

The core reason why pluralism has natural advantages regarding skill formation is because exposure to multiple frameworks provides a far superior environment for developing the desired skill set. By contrast, orthodoxy is inevitably limited because of its focus on only one framework (monism). As discussed below, it can only develop a few of the desired skills to high levels, a couple of important skills lie entirely beyond it, and the majority of skills can only be moderately or weakly inculcated.

The simplest way of demonstrating the superiority of pluralism over orthodoxy is to draw up a scorecard. In Table 19.2, the left-hand column lists the desired skills while the right-hand column scores the *ability* of pluralism and orthodoxy to deliver these skills. The first ten skills relate to those called for by government and business in Australia, while the second ten relate to creativity. Although much more could be said in relation to these rankings, discussion here is necessarily concise for space reasons.[12]

As regards creativity, pluralism is capable of engendering this attribute far more strongly than orthodoxy because it is far more closely associated with all of the creativity-related skills discussed below (skills 11 to 20). For the next three skills, pluralism is strong in its capacity to deliver while orthodoxy only has medium capacity. In the case of independent and critical thinking, nothing is off-limits in pluralism, whereas orthodoxy places boundaries on the exercise of this skill. Pluralism can enhance communication and presentation skills more effectively because the range and contrast of contestable issues are much larger, thus providing greater scope for argument and persuasion; orthodoxy can certainly inculcate this skill but only at moderate levels because genuine discussion and debate are restricted to issues internal to its framework.

Pluralism is also capable of fostering interpersonal skills more strongly because it embraces more belief systems and evaluation issues to be constructively negotiated between parties than orthodoxy; the contrast here is akin to that between a world of multiple belief systems and one with various sects of the same belief system. For skills 5, 6, and 7 (problem solving, teamwork, and ongoing learning) there seems to be little or no difference between pluralism and orthodoxy in their abilities to deliver these skills strongly. For the last three skills

*Table 19.2* Comparison of abilities of pluralism and orthodoxy to provide desired skills

| Skill | Ability to deliver | |
|---|---|---|
| | Pluralism | Orthodoxy |
| *Skills sought by government and business* | | |
| 1 Creativity | S | W |
| 2 Independent and critical thinking | S | M |
| 3 Communication and presentation skills | S | M |
| 4 Interpersonal skills | S | M |
| 5 Problem solving | S | S |
| 6 Teamwork | S | S |
| 7 Ongoing learning | S | S |
| 8 Enthusiasm | S | M/W |
| 9 Cultural understanding | S | M/W |
| 10 Leadership | S | M/W |
| *Skills related to creativity* | | |
| 11 Appreciation of holistic standpoints | S | A |
| 12 Thinking outside conventional framework | S | A |
| 13 Awareness of different viewpoints | S | W |
| 14 Capacity to see things in new ways | S | W |
| 15 Openness to non-conformity | S | W |
| 16 Courage to question received wisdom | S | W |
| 17 Stimulating milieus | S | M/W |
| 18 Free communication and discussion | S | M/W |
| 19 Willingness to take risks | S | M/W |
| 20 Playfulness | S | M/W |

Notes
A = absent, M = medium, S = strong, and W = weak.

in this set, orthodoxy can again contribute but not as strongly as pluralism. Enthusiasm is promoted more strongly by pluralism because of more stimulating intellectual environments, the contrasts of competing perspectives, and the greater scope for playfulness and self-development. Cultural understanding is more strongly enhanced because students are immersed in a multi-perspective world with the same things viewed from different standpoints in a manner similar to multiculturalism. And the ideas and practice of leadership are more effectively exposed through the Starpower game, as well as the debates where students can take leadership roles as representatives of their schools.

The capacity of pluralism to outperform orthodoxy is even more striking when we turn to the creativity-related skills. Skills 11 and 12 are essential parts of pluralism but are effectively absent from orthodoxy. Pluralism not only provides a holistic view of economics, but also a holistic view of orthodoxy itself, because wholes are best viewed from external vantage points. For the next four skills, pluralism outperforms orthodoxy by a very wide margin. All four are inherent to, and powerfully promoted by, pluralism but only weakly encouraged by orthodoxy because variety and difference are restricted by orthodoxy to positions within a single framework. The same considerations apply to the last four skills except that the gap is narrowed somewhat. Pluralism can provide far more stimulating intellectual *and* practical milieus for learning and discussion; communication is freer because there are no taboos on method or approach; risk-taking is showcased by the material and can be encouraged in presentations and debates; and playfulness is promoted strongly by the wider range of games that can be played, as well as the challenges of seeking accommodations between different ideas. Here well-chosen activities play important roles because they create more receptive and fertile environments for skill development.

The overall conclusion from the above scorecard is the strong dominance of pluralism over orthodoxy in relation to the full skill set. Pluralism is strong in all skills whereas orthodoxy is only strong in three, of medium, medium to weak, or weak ability in fifteen, and of no ability at all in two. Although I have tried to be fair in making the above judgments, I recognize that others may make different evaluations which could be more favorable to orthodoxy. Even so, it is impossible, I contend, to overturn the *overall* conclusion that pluralism is strongly superior to orthodoxy. This is because it is impossible for orthodoxy to equal pluralism on *all* these skills; the only question is how close or distant is its second placing.

If we are to find remedies for the skill formation puzzle noted earlier, innovation inside the classroom is required to foster innovation outside the classroom. Well-designed pluralist courses can play a significant part in this process because they are ideally suited to developing the relevant skills. The innovation proposed here is the synthesis of inherently suitable and receptive course material with instructive activities to provide an environment in which maximum skill formation is a primary objective. In the present case, all the desired skills are either modeled by the material under study, or illuminated in practical ways by the activities built into the course. One cannot participate in the course without being surrounded by, and engaging with, all these skills in diverse ways; students are fully immersed in an environment in which the skills are center-stage. Thus, by responding much more effectively to the calls for the desired skill sets, well-designed pluralist courses can, in this area, make greater contributions than orthodox courses to productivity, individual fulfillment, and social and international outcomes. For this reason alone, it is highly desirable for every standard economics program to have at least one such pluralist course.

One should not overlook the importance of instructive fun in this context. In principle, orthodox courses can include games, debates, and presentations, although this is fairly rare in practice. But the range and nature of such activities is heavily constrained. First, there will be a tendency not to choose games or exercises that seriously challenge the orthodox framework (as Starpower and the Mankiw exercise do, for instance) and hence to choose games or exercises that are supportive of orthodox discourse and do not trouble its foundations. Second, the scope for debates is restricted to debates between positions within a single school.[13] Both constraints reduce the possibility for instructive fun. By contrast, pluralist courses are never shackled in these ways. Games and exercises which challenge the presuppositions or foundations of any or all schools can be embraced, and debates can become much more engaging contests between whole schools or frameworks where strengths and weakness become more visible. There need be no fear of these activities conflicting with course content or violating any taboos – students can play with ideas unconstrained by prior methodological dicta.[14]

The benefits of an exposure to pluralism are that it becomes an exciting experience which generates mental stimulation and practical engagement. Students are "turned on" to economics rather than "turned off."[15] Orthodox courses can easily become humdrum and mechanical, repeating the same ideas in different contexts, applying the same techniques to different problems, and tending to become forms of mental gymnastics or calisthenics performed for their own sakes. Any deeper queries or puzzles about foundations, assumptions, or rationales are usually deflected without being seriously addressed. By contrast, pluralist courses embrace variety and diversity through focusing on alternative ways of seeing and analyzing. They present mind-opening, mind-broadening, and mind-deepening experiences, rather than mind-conforming experiences based on the repeated use of one set of conceptual tools. If J.K. Galbraith's (1975: 226–7) acerbic comment that "Economists are economical, among other things, of ideas; most make those of their graduate days do for a lifetime" is correct, we should surely make this set of ideas as large as possible.

## Student responses

"But is the course practical?" was a prior-to-enrollment question asked by vocationally minded students. Most definitely, was my reply. The course is not practical in the sense that it will just teach you new mathematical models or new quantitative techniques. It is practical in deeper and more important ways. You will become a better economist because you will have more than one perspective and more than one set of tools to use in your analyses. And it will expand and develop your skills in vital ways – skills which are both career-enhancing and personally fulfilling because they are valuable to employers, yourself, and society. So, although primarily about ideas, the course is, in fact, highly practical. It gives you knowledge and abilities you will not otherwise obtain if you just do further mainstream work.

In end-of-course discussion and confidential surveys, student feedback was universally positive about all aspects of the course – lectures, games, debates, and presentations. The level of enthusiasm was indicated by the widely shared view that every economics major should do the course. Other comments also indicated that deep learning had taken place – as one student put it, "you are required not just to learn about a school, but also to get inside it and defend it." There was strong appreciation of the explicit focus on key skill formation, particularly the presentation and communication aspects. Students very much liked the idea that their skills were being developed in a supportive environment, and even when debates and presentations went over time, they willingly stayed back rather than depart at the scheduled hour.

From the students' viewpoint, the main issues of concern centered on degrees of indecision and frustration. This stemmed from moving from the comfort of a "one school/single answer" world to the complexity of a "multiple school/different answers" environment. How to choose between schools? How to choose which analysis to use in addressing particular problems? How to choose between different conclusions regarding the same question? Such issues led to interesting exchanges at the end of the course. In essence, my response was to pose three questions:

1   If this is the actual nature of modern economics, should we not be aware of it so as to be better economists?
2   Is it not always better to be in a position of informed awareness about complexity rather than a state of ignorance, narrow-mindedness, or "fundamentalism"?
3   Is not exposure to multiple approaches a necessary part of desired skill formation?

I find it difficult to disagree with these propositions, even though they do not provide answers to the earlier questions about which schools or toolkits should be adopted in analyzing particular problems. All they do is provide intellectual support whilst one grapples with the issue of choice. As Cropley (1999: 635) has noted, creative individuals tolerate considerable ambiguity, this tolerance being "so highly developed that it does not involve simply tolerance for two alternatives (ambivalence) but a willingness to see that anything could be combined with anything else (omnivalence)."[16]

## Conclusion

Pluralist courses, by their very nature, are in a superior position to orthodox courses for the development of the desirable skill set outlined above. Orthodoxy is certainly capable of developing most (but not all) of these skills with varying degrees of success, but the very nature of orthodoxy (the single analytical framework) inhibits their fuller development. However, where orthodoxy restricts, pluralism liberates. A range of analytical frameworks combined with reinforcing activities provides a natural vehicle for driving desired skill formation to higher and more comprehensive levels within the time available. Teaching pluralist economics can thus make significant contributions to producing better graduates (including orthodox ones) by broadening and deepening intellectual reach, fostering creativity and innovation, and developing richer skill sets beneficial for students, economies, and societies.

Pluralism may be likened to foreign travel. It provides a journey across the whole globe in all its diversity and similarity, it promotes curiosity about other cultures, it offers numerous possibilities for further exploration (now or in the future), and it deepens understanding of one's own culture. At the end of the journey, the traveler is more sophisticated, more sensitive to alternative ways of seeing and doing, more self-aware, more acquainted with other societies as well as their own, and better equipped for work and for life. In short, well-designed pluralist courses greatly enrich all those involved in the journey.

## Acknowledgments

I would like to thank participants at the 2007 ICAPE conference for helpful remarks and criticism, especially Rob Garnett whose comments were very valuable. Length restrictions have necessarily curtailed discussion at certain points.

## Notes

1 Department of Education, Training and Youth Affairs (2000: *viii*, 14).
2 Business Council of Australia (2006: 14–15).
3 For pertinent discussion of many aspects of creativity, see Runco and Pritzker (1999).
4 The problem of managing innovation is an important issue which should not be neglected.
5 Attention has been paid, however, to the acquisition of certain proficiencies by students (Hansen 2001; O'Donnell 2004). Elsner (2007: 194), for example, has briefly noted how students in heterodox postgraduate programs can learn and acquire superior "strategic" competencies beneficial to their professional futures.
6 This is only one of a number of good designs for pluralist courses, not the only possible one. For an earlier example, see Barone (1991) which was one of the stimuli for the present course. While Barone's discussion focused mainly on intellectual benefits, the present course seeks to harvest intellectual *and* practical benefits.
7 The level at which to introduce a stand-alone pluralist course in an otherwise fairly orthodox undergraduate degree is an issue with pros and cons for each option.
8 The course thus reflects Raveaud's (2003) suggestion to teach economics through controversies, so making the subject more lively, relevant, and exciting.
9 See Mankiw (2006) chapter 1, or the same chapter in many other editions of this text.
10 Note that the second question shifts the focus toward greater inclusiveness by requiring students to reflect on any valuable elements in the opposing school.
11 Three other points deserve mention. (1) In the absence of a suitable text, no textbook was prescribed although Stilwell (2002) was recommended for general reading. (2) Assessment consisted of a final exam (70 percent), seminar paper (15 percent), and participation (15 percent). The final exam (three hours) contained long answer questions only, with three out of five questions to be answered – all questions covered at least two schools, and students had to pass the exam to pass the course. The seminar paper (1500–2000 words) was based on, and completed after, the compulsory debate. Participation covered lectures, seminars, and games (5 percent), and speaking in the debate (10 percent). (3) Class size raises organizational issues for seminar activities. The optimum number of students per school of thought is probably two to three with a maximum of four. With one instructor in one room over four weeks of seminar time, the upper limit on class size is thus 32. For larger classes, extra resources are required to supervise the debates and presentations in parallel sessions, one additional instructor and classroom being needed for each additional 32 students (or part thereof). Lectures may still be given to the whole class, but the seminar program will require the additional resources.
12 As we proceed through the list, readers may wish to test the extent to which their own (serious) judgments conform to, or diverge from, these rankings.

13 While Mankiw (2006) concludes his text with five debates over *macro*economic *policy*, these are fairly timid affairs conducted within the orthodox framework. The citadel of *micro*economic *theory* is left essentially untouched.

14 More fun can also be had by selecting some of the better economist jokes and putting them up before or during lectures; see Kuoppamäki (2001) for one collection.

15 This is important if enrollments in economics majors are to be sustained in the face of challenges from business, marketing, and other programs.

16 In relation to Earl's perceptive remarks on teaching pluralist economics (Earl 2000, 2002), students in the course displayed no resistance to being exposed to multiple perspectives (the nature of the course was clear from the start, and enrollment was optional), but they still had to commence (without necessarily completing) the challenging journey from dualism (the True/False framework of orthodoxy) to pluralism (multiple "truths," degrees of analytical freedom, open-minded commitment, and the importance of respectful argument).

## References

Barone, C.A. (1991) "Contending Perspectives: Curricular Reform in Economics," *Journal of Economic Education*, 22 (1): 15–26.

Business Council of Australia (2006) "New Concepts in Innovation: The Keys to a Growing Australia." Available at www.bca.com.au/Content.aspx?ContentID=100408 (accessed February 15, 2008).

Cropley, A.J. (1999) "Education," in M.A. Runco and S.R. Pritzker (eds.) *Encyclopedia of Creativity, Volume 1*, 629–42, San Diego: Academic Press.

Department of Education, Training and Youth Affairs (2000) "Employer Satisfaction with Graduate Skills," AC Neilson Research Report, Canberra: Australian Government. Available at www.dest.gov.au/sectors/higher_education/publications_resources/profiles/archives/employer_satisfaction_with_graduate_skills.htm (accessed February 15, 2008).

Earl, P.E. (2000) "Indeterminacy in the Economics Classroom," in P.E. Earl and S.F. Frowen (eds.) *Economics as an Art of Thought: Essays in Memory of G.L.S. Shackle*, 25–50, London: Routledge.

—— (2002) "The Perils of Pluralistic Teaching and How to Reduce Them," *Post-Autistic Economics Review*, issue 11, January 30, article 1.

Edney, J. (1979) "The Nuts Game: A Concise Commons Dilemma Analog," *Environmental Psychology and Non Verbal Behavior*, 3 (4): 252–4.

Elsner, W. (2007) "Heterodox Economics and its Integration in Pluralist Teaching: A German Case," in J. Groenewegen (ed.) *Teaching Pluralism in Economics*, 189–99, Cheltenham: Edward Elgar.

Galbraith, J.K. (1975) *Money: Whence it Came, Where it Went*, Boston: Houghton Mifflin.

Hansen, W.L. (2001) "Expected Proficiencies for Undergraduate Economics Majors," *Journal of Economic Education*, 32 (3): 231–42.

Kuoppamäki, P. (2001) "JokEc: Jokes about Economists and Economics." Available at http://netec.mcc.ac.uk/JokEc.html (accessed February 15, 2008).

Mankiw, N.G. (2006) *Principles of Economics*, 4th edition, Cengage Learning.

O'Donnell, R.M. (2004) "What Kind of Economic Graduates Do We Want? A Constructive Critique of Hansen's Proficiencies Approach," *Australasian Journal of Economics Education*, 1 (1): 41–60.

Raveaud, G. (2003) "Teaching Economics through Controversies," in E. Fullbrook (ed.)

*The Crisis in Economics: The Post-Autistic Economics Movement: The First 600 Days*, 62–9, London: Routledge.

Runco, M.A. and Pritzker, S.R. (eds.) (1999) *Encyclopedia of Creativity, Volumes I and II*, San Diego: Academic Press.

Stilwell, F. (2002) *Political Economy: The Contest of Economic Ideas*, Oxford: Oxford University Press.

# 20 A most peculiar success

## Constructing UADPhilEcon, a doctoral program in economics at the University of Athens[1]

*Yanis Varoufakis*

### A pluralist agenda for postgraduate economics

> [The] Azande see as well as we that the failure of their oracle to prophesy truly calls for explanation, but so entangled are they in mystical notions that they must make use of them to account for failure. The contradiction between experience and one mystical notion is explained by reference to other mystical notions.
>
> (Evans-Pritchard 1937: 388)

Mainstream economics is little different. Its success, like that of the Azande's priesthood, is due to its capacity to offer full (and fully mystical) explanations of its explanatory failures and, additionally, to maintain its position of monopoly on "economic witchcraft" by ensuring that only *its* disciples are listened to. To gain that accolade, the young must, courtesy of a suitably rigorous postgraduate education, first suppress their critical faculties and, subsequently, learn how to account for the mainstream theory's failures by appealing to the same mystical notions which failed in the first place.[2]

Pluralism is the best antidote for the mystification that has become functional to our profession. The primary aim of a pluralist education in economics ought to be simple: *Demystification!* It holds the greatest hope for emancipating the minds and souls of the young from the rituals of "scientific" superstition that are the staple diet of mainstream graduate programs in economics. It also promises to help economics (even mainstream economics!) overcome the deep crisis it has landed in as a result of two developments: (1) the exodus of market-oriented students to assorted business studies, and (2) the flight of the more intellectually inclined students to the rest of the humanities.

A humanist higher education in economics must strive for demystification in two ways: First, by shining the light of open-minded debate on the axiomatic foundations, and limitations, of mainstream economic theory. Students must be able to read the most obtuse and mystical models that the mainstream can throw at them. They must understand their language perfectly, without however becoming hostage to the mythological tales narrated in that language. Second, students must be allowed to acquire intimate knowledge of multiple competing modes of economic reasoning. Such an Archimedean perspective is essential for the defeat of the systematic ignorance that today takes the form of a mathematical religion, complete with its sacred texts, apocryphal notions, and rigid priesthoods.

## Mainstream economics must be taught at its highest level

A natural reaction to the state of contemporary economics is to wish for a syllabus which aims to shield students from the arid rituals of the current orthodoxy and, instead, help them approach the economic world as a system that has evolved historically. Would it not be delightful to design a program that sidesteps the countless hours of repetitive mathematical modeling whose end result is negative value added to our understanding of capitalism? Would it not send most of us into a frenzy of joy to be able to dismiss most of the orthodox curriculum, and its sad fixation with rational expectations that no rational person would ever entertain, competitive markets in which no competition ever occurs, models of development in which nothing of substance ever develops, theories of trade in which systemic trade deficits are assumed never to exist, econometric exercises which can never really distinguish between the competing theories, and so on? Of course it would.

And yet, doing that would be an appallingly bad idea. During the late 1980s and the 1990s I taught at an undergraduate program that did precisely that. *The Political Economy Program* at the University of Sydney was offered to students who wanted to understand contemporary capitalism but who did not want to go through the tortuous path designed for them by the mainstream Economics Department, before ending up with even less of a feel for capitalist dynamics than they had entered university with. Thus, an interesting experiment, lasting almost three decades, occurred with two economics degrees being offered at the same time and in the same faculty.

The intellectual superiority of the *Political Economy* degree over its mainstream economics counterpart was clear.[3] Students acquired a broad social science education, were introduced to all the important schools of thought (albeit somewhat epidermically), and delved in issues ranging from industrial relations and environmental economics to globalization and Far Eastern economic development. In short, the *Political Economy* graduates understood the world as well as one could after dedicating three to four years of one's life to a university education.

In sharp contrast, my standard economics students were confined to the usual unsavory diet of micro, macro, mathematics, econometrics, and the inevitable array of applications of the equi-marginal principle to anything and everything that moves (in a static, of course, way!). At the end of their degree, they were blissfully ignorant of the important economic problems afflicting the world they were about to enter. Technically excellent, they combined the philosophical background of a rather primitive computer with the historical understanding of an amnesiac.

And yet, it was the economics students that exuded the confidence which makes or breaks a career. The *Political Economy* students, although highly employable, lacked in confidence that which they possessed in educational and intellectual essence. Deep down, they did not really think of themselves as competent economists. The mere mention of Lagrange multipliers, fixed point theorems, and co-integration tests that their colleagues from across the corridor knew off the top of their heads, cowed them into a form of intellectual submission that was utterly at odds with their actual capacities. Meanwhile, the economics graduates had no qualms in pronouncing simplistic views and policy recommendations regarding issues that they were genuinely innocent of.

Even worse, after graduating, a small number of the *Political Economy* students enrolled in mainstream economics graduate programs and became neoclassical zealots. With the infinite pathos that is typical of the "born again," they espoused the orthodoxy with a ferocity and anti-pluralist fervor that turned them into the greatest enemies of the type of political economy which they had studied as undergraduates. Interestingly, these few cases, as I witnessed them, led to sad and unfulfilled academic careers, full of bitterness and devoid of any real intellectual excitement.

In short, *any attempt to build a curriculum which sidesteps the techniques of the mainstream is bound to backfire*, for two reasons: First, for practical reasons, economists need to speak the language of the dominant meta-narrative when attempting to undermine it. Mainstream economics is a web of beliefs and a set of language games (of a Wittgensteinian sort) which are used to couch all the arguments that contribute to the reproduction of society as we know it. In this sense, a study of capitalism which is separate from a study of this meta-narrative is both impossible and ineffective. Second, for purely psychological reasons, not understanding the orthodoxy better than the orthodox do exposes young minds to the danger that they will turn to the latter's soothing embrace as born again zealots.

There is another reason too for investing in the mainstream. "The great virtue of mathematical reasoning in economics" Frank Hahn once wrote,

> is that by its precise account of assumptions it becomes crystal clear that application to the 'real world' could be at best provisional ... the task we set ourselves after the last war, to deduce all that was required from a number of axioms, has almost been completed, and while not worthless has only made a small contribution to our understanding.[4]

An effective pluralist curriculum must therefore subject students to the highest forms of mainstream economics while simultaneously preventing the latter from taking over the spirit and direction of the curriculum. Such a combination of a neoclassical education and a pluralist disposition is becoming increasingly rare these days in the "first" world. Below I relate the experience of putting together such a program in the relative backwardness of the University of Athens, deducing from it that the "periphery" may prove a fertile breeding ground for pluralist economics.

# The making of UADPhilEcon: from the Greek Civil War to a pluralist doctoral program

The last sentence requires justification. Why is the periphery a good breeding ground for a pluralist doctoral program such as UADPhilEcon? My answer, drawn from the particular experience with UADPhilEcon, comes in two parts: (1) That a pluralist doctoral program such as UADPhilEcon could only have sprung out of a nineteenth-century university in the European periphery, and (2) that a traumatic recent history, which included a Civil War in which the Left was defeated totally, also played a decisive role.

The University of Athens, the oldest in the land, was founded concurrently with the modern Greek state and as part of the same nation-building exercise that followed Independence from the Ottoman Empire in the 1830s. This background helps generate a healthy student demand for UADPhilEcon places, but also a genuine willingness from academics belonging to other universities to contribute to our courses for a minimal fee. As for the University itself, it harbored sufficient ambition, under the weight of its own history, to look kindly at the prospect of an ambitious doctoral program. The fact that Greece's universities are still unaffected by the strictures of commercialization helped us sidestep the usual pressures (that manifest in newer institutions) to orient any new postgraduate program toward the amorphous market and its precise whims.

In short, innovative doctoral programs, like UADPhilEcon, could be built *tabula rasa* only at a traditional, well established, university that had not caught up with the times. Sometimes, especially in lean and uncertain times, and after society has lost much of the confidence it once had regarding its value system, a university that is "stuck" in the nineteenth century is a university far ahead of its times (without, naturally, either knowing it or wishing it)! Unlike in the United States, the United Kingdom, and other academically developed places, where a progressive doctoral program can be built only after the costly business of undoing some pre-existing program (together with its conventions, norms, and prejudices) is completed, the creation of UAPhilEcon was unimpeded by such burdens.[5] Putting together such a radically critical and overtly ambitious doctoral program in the stead of an existing mainstream one would require an institutional war that no pluralist either possesses the energy or the power to survive.

Turning now to the surprising claim that UADPhilEcon's existence owes much to the turbulent political history of Greece, it is useful to recall that contemporary Greece was shaped by a civil war that lasted, in its many guises, almost 40 years. It, effectively, started in the 1930s (with the establishment of a fascist regime in 1936),[6] continued unabated during the years of World War II and the Axis Occupation, took the form of armed conflict during the 1944–1949 period between the Left and the Anglo-American supported conservative forces, metamorphosed as a parliamentary dictatorship of the latter during the 1949–1963 era, showed signs of retreating between 1963 and 1965, only to return in its most tragicomic, but also brutal, form during the Colonels' dictatorship (1967–1974).

To put it bluntly, Greece's academics, including those who were born and/or raised abroad, grew up in a mental environment that precluded political disengagement. The Left and the Right produced intellectual output not just as a means to itself but, also, as ammunition to be utilized in the context of this gigantic clash. Musicians, poets, and academics "belonged," or were thought to belong, to one of the two sides. However, there was no symmetry between the two.

The Right controlled the State fully and utterly. To have had a play admitted onto one of the stages of the National Theatre one had to go through processes that any student of either Franco's or Stasi's practices should be intimately familiar with. None of this, of course, means that the Right's intellectuals lacked quality, integrity, or substance: only that they operated within a system that excluded forcefully their left-wing counterparts. The Left, on the other hand, labored under the long shadow of their 1949 military defeat and the subsequent purges (including executions, lengthy imprisonment, social and institutional exclusion). Stripped of all positions of power, leftists were free to invest in Gramscian intellectual projects which, by the beginning of the 1960s, brought the Left to a position of cultural hegemony.

The 1967–1974 dictatorship, in an ironic manner, strengthened further this hegemony, especially in view of the student uprising of 1973, a "delayed Greek May 1968,"[7] and ensured that the 1970s and 1980s, the renaissance years that followed the collapse of the post-civil war state, were dominated, in terms of discourse, by the defeated Left. As from the late 1970s, and especially the early 1980s (following the electoral victory of the Socialist party), leftist or left-leaning intellectuals began to enter the universities. Many formerly exiled professors, mostly of a left-wing disposition, were recalled from European and American universities.

Thus, the current generation of Greek academic economists grew up in a relatively peculiar intellectual and political milieu. Unlike in the United States, Canada, and in northern Europe, even right-wing economists matured in an environment that encouraged a serious engagement with the emancipatory ideas of a Left which, in contrast to eastern Europe, preserved its high moral ground as a result of having lost all coercive power in 1949 (when it became the victim of state oppression). A number of left-wing, highly intellectual students went abroad to study mathematical economics in the belief that they were following Voltaire's advice; namely, to understand the scriptures better than the priesthood who provided the irrational (and thus despised) Establishment with the necessary legitimacy.

Most of them eventually (by the 1990s) lost their leftist fervor but retained, at the very least, a deep-seeded sympathy for a critical approach to mainstream economics. As for their right-wing colleagues, they too retain an awareness that there is something philosophically controversial, historically inconvenient, and intellectually dishonest hiding behind the mainstream's equations. Greece being the European corner where the Cold War erupted, back in 1944, and ended so terribly late (in the mid-1970s), was a natural locus of an economics which still resonates with the Cold War's echoes.

Of course the Cold War played a crucial role in shaping economics world-wide. We tend to forget that in the 1920s and 1930s, the great questions tortur-ing the mind of the great economists were: Can efficiency be achieved without some form of Central Planning? Can capitalism survive its endogenously gen-erated crises? These questions could only be asked within a pluralist intellec-tual framework. Hayek strived to disprove Lange and Keynes had no shortage of neoclassical detractors. Economic theory was a battleground on which opposing armies of ideas clashed mercilessly on the basis of their arguments' strengths, rather than on the capacity of one side to pretend that the other simply did not exist.

The Cold War that followed World War II put paid to the intellectual honesty of the interwar period, eventually ending these debates forever, and not only through the efforts of the Rand Corporation and the like. Once the Vietnam War (and the renewed interest in radical social theory) was over, in 1975, and stagfla-tion led to the long march to oblivion of the post-war western social democratic experiment in the corridors of power, it was only a matter of time before a com-bination of rational expectations macroeconomics, game theory, and new politi-cal economy (i.e., politics as pure non-market exchanges) would render economics a politics-free (and thus highly conservative) discipline. The momen-tous events of the 1989–1991 period sealed things well and truly.

In Greece, by contrast, the Cold War, rather than putting on ice the great debates, rekindled them. Our political upheavals ended much later than their European or American equivalent (some would argue as late as in the 1980s). Our Cold War, it must be remembered, was not particularly cold, as it took the form of an initially red hot Civil War, followed by a period of political oppres-sion that kept the ashes of conflict glowing for much longer, causing young aca-demics to take a heated interest in the political economy behind economics, even while studying Arrow and Debreu's pristine theorems at some Anglo-Celtic or German university.

It is for these two reasons (first, the combination of tradition and relative backwardness typifying the University of Athens, and, second, because of an historically engendered shared appreciation of the political, philosophical, and socially contingent aspects of economics) that a doctoral program such as UAD-PhilEcon could get off the ground on the back of hard, mostly unpaid work put into its creation by enthusiastic colleagues with good mainstream credentials from some of the top universities in the United States, United Kingdom, France, and Germany; colleagues who felt the need to participate in a pluralist program such as the one described in the next section.

That willingness, to conclude, was not merely a type of accidental volunta-rism. It was, I submit, the product of the turbulent history of a small country ravaged by Civil War and caught up in the wake of a broader global power struggle, the Cold War, which had profound effects on almost every family, every village, and every cell of its extensive Diaspora. Economic theory, in this context, was not an end in itself but an attempt to study analytically the causes of all that had befallen us.

## UADPhilEcon: its philosophy and structure

*Philosophy*

For the reasons stated in the previous section, UADPhilEcon teaches the highest form of neoclassical economics most rigorously to all its incoming students; regardless, that is, of their individual preferences or plans. But, at the same time, it forces upon them a critical disposition which is at odds with the mainstream's practices. For instance, modules in political philosophy, economic history, and history of economic thought are compulsory.

Of course all good economics departments in the United States and the United Kingdom offer courses in the latter (especially economic history, law and economics, and to a lesser extent, philosophy). However, they do so in the same manner that military schools teach cadets good table manners, or that companies organize golfing weekends for their executives: they are treated as, at best, essential add-ons to the real business they are engaged in; either as a vital induction in etiquette or as pastimes which help rejuvenate the mind while the latter is taking a break.

In contrast, UADPhilEcon teaches history, political philosophy, and the history of ideas as an integral part of economic theory's central core: neoclassical, classical, Austrian, Ricardian, Marxist, and Keynesian, among others. The simple idea here is that economics is infected to the core with philosophically exciting concepts and historically contingent hypotheses that no one can properly understand in the absence of such a philosophical-*cum*-historical approach. In short, UADPhilEcon espoused early the following two mottos:

> [We] … should wish to see a world in which education aimed at mental freedom rather than at imprisoning the minds of the young in a rigid armor of dogma calculated to protect them through life against the shafts of impartial evidence. The world needs open hearts and open minds, and it is not through rigid systems, whether old or new, that these can be derived.
>
> (Russell 1957: vii)

> The study of economics does not seem to require any specialized gifts of an unusually high order. Is it not, intellectually regarded, a very easy subject compared with the higher branches of philosophy and pure science? Yet good, or even competent, economists are the rarest of birds. An easy subject at which very few excel! The paradox finds its explanation perhaps, in that the master-economist must possess a rare combination of gifts. He must reach a high standard in several different directions and must combine talents not often found together. He must be mathematician, historian, statesman, philosopher – in some degree. He must understand symbols and speak in words. He must contemplate the particular in terms of the general, and touch abstract and concrete in the same flight of thought. He must study the present in the light of the past for the purposes of the future. No part of

man's nature or his institutions must lie entirely outside his regard. He must be purposeful and disinterested in a simultaneous mood; as aloof and incorruptible as an artist.

(Keynes 1924: 321–322)

However, this is not the whole story. Although UADPhilEcon is pluralist from its inception, this choice is not only due to our normative beliefs. It is also a choice made on the basis of some clear evidence that *all* economics, including the mainstream, is in deep trouble – and that the pluralist avenue is the only one that has a chance of steering economics away from academic extinction.

Indeed, mainstream economics' troubles have the same causes as its fabulous success. The latter was built (since the 1870s) on the claim that it had expunged politics, philosophy, sociology, psychology, and history from its scientific theory of society. This was, indeed, a clever political strategy, as it helped the mainstream not only rid itself of the eccentrics, the radicals, and the downright inconvenient thinkers, but also helped it gain a great deal of influence both within universities (as perhaps the sole "respectable" social science) and the epicenters of real power (government and the corporations).

However, once it succeeded, what was left was a colorless and complicated economic theory, foundationally disconnected from economic reality, which could neither address the big issues (e.g., poverty or the choice of ecological strategy that is in the public interest) nor stir the passions amongst the young. Thus, over the past decade, passionate young intellectuals are voting with their feet, turning their back on economics degrees and heading for the rest of the humanities. As for the bulk of the student body, who try (in George Bernard Shaw's ironic words) are reasonable enough to aspire only to adapting themselves to our world (as opposed to doing the opposite), they are being lured away from economics by more "practical" competitors (e.g., marketing), with greater market value (and fewer demands on one's brain). Thus, economics departments are beginning to resemble magnificent cathedrals with a dwindling flock.

The only antidote to both the mainstream's intellectual totalitarianism and its unfolding decline is to delve into time-honored economic, political, and philosophical debates – to give the emotions another stir; to turn the spotlight on the politics and philosophy that lurk in the shadows of every neoclassical model, every co-integration, and every game-theoretic narrative. To this end, UADPhilEcon imposes the rest of the social sciences, history, and philosophy on its first-year students: first, to help them understand economics deeply, something that is otherwise impossible, and, second, to help save even neoclassicism from its own folly.

## Course structure

To put the above philosophy into practice, UADPhilEcon's stated objectives of (1) a solid education in mainstream economics at the highest theoretical and applied levels, and (2) a critical approach to mainstream economics which investigates carefully the historical, philosophical, and political foundations (as well as prejudices) of every major theory or model are served by the following two strategies: (1) an *ongoing dialogue between economics and the rest of the humanities, between mainstream and non-mainstream economic theories*, built into the courses from the very first to the very last lecture or seminar; and (2) an *emphasis on the discipline's original sources* (as opposed to textbook versions of them). For instance, we expect our *MPhil* graduates to have read, from the original, at least some of the classic texts by Smith, Ricardo, Marx, Keynes, Arrow, Debreu, Friedman, Hayek, and Sweezy.

The above are reflected in the curriculum in three ways. First, incoming students are exposed to a compulsory year-long course entitled *Economics as a Social Science* (Soc10). This course consists of three components: *Political Philosophy, Economic History*, and *History of Economic Thought*. It is taught in tandem with advanced microeconomics and advanced macroeconomics and engages the latter in a constant dialogue (e.g., on the nexus between Hobbes, Hume, Bentham, and utility theory). Second, in their second year, students choose at least one course per semester based on the systematic reading of classic texts (e.g., a semester-long reading course on *General Equilibrium, Game Theory and Social Choice*, or *Financial Economics*, or *Economic Philosophy*, or Keynes's *General Theory*, or Marx's *Capital*). Third, among the optional courses in the second year of coursework, students are offered the choice among courses in applied economics but also options with a social science orientation (e.g. History, Anthropology, or Political Economy).

In more detail, in their first year, students take four year-long compulsory courses (and no optional courses): *Advanced Microeconomics, Advanced Macroeconomics, Quantitative Methods* (consisting of mathematical analysis, an emphasis of topology, statistics, and econometrics), and *Economics as a Social Science* (which comprises three segments: political philosophy, economic history, and history of economic thought) (see Appendix). Importantly, all first-year courses, whilst subject to monthly assessment, are examined at one sitting at the end of the academic year (i.e., they are not divided into semesters). Thus, our students must revise *simultaneously* on diverse fields ranging from topology to Locke's and Hegel's philosophies and from Hicksian or Marxist growth theory to general equilibrium and game theory.

In the second year, and besides the standard *Research Methods* course which is compulsory to all, laissez-faire replaces the rigidity of the first year. Students choose freely from the following diverse menu of courses:

*A  General – Economic Theory*

**EcT201** – Seminal Texts on Philosophy and Economics
**EcT202** – Seminal Texts on General Equilibrium, Game Theory, and Social Choice
**EcT203** – Reading Keynes's General Theory and the Keynesians
**EcT204** – Seminal Texts on the Theory of Growth
**EcT205** – International Macroeconomics and Public Finance

**EcT206** – Marx's Economic Theory I
**EcT207** – Marx's Economic Theory II
**EcT208** – Comparative Economic Systems
**EcT209** – Technology, Growth, and Economic Change
**EcT210** – Development Economics and Industrial Dynamics
**EcT211** – The Theory of the Firm
**EcT212** – Structural Policies and the Management of Change
**EcT213** – International Trade
**EcT214** – Post Keynesian Economics
**EcT215** – The Political Economy of Globalizing Capital
**EcT216** – Feminist Economics

*B Finance*

**EcF201** – Seminal Texts on Financial Economics
**EcF202** – Banking and Firm Finance
**EcF203** – Financial Analysis
**EcF204** – Mathematical Models of Derivative Pricing

*C Applied Economics*

**EcA201** – Public Finance
**EcA202** – Industrial Organization
**EcA203** – Labor Economics
**EcA204** – Environmental Economics

*D Economic History*

**EcH201** – History of Firms and Entrepreneurship
**EcH202** – Greek Economic History I (nineteenth century to the interwar years)
**EcH203** – Greek Economic History II (interwar to date)
**EcH204** – History of Economic Development

*E Quantitative Methods*

**Q201** – Seminal Texts on the Theory of Statistics and Probability
**Q202** – Mathematical Programming
**Q203** – Control and Economics
**Q204** – Topics in Econometrics
**Q205** – Statistical Computing
**Q206** – Topology

## Conclusion

Why call UADPhilEcon a success? Some statistics follow in lieu of an answer: the batch of around 15 students who graduate each year with a Master of Philosophy in Economics (MPhilEcon), after two years of intensive coursework, typically have sat through 576 hours of lectures and seminars, and have been taught by 37 professors of whom seven come from abroad (the United States, United Kingdom, Germany, Belgium, Australia, or elsewhere) exclusively for the purposes of teaching at UADPhilEcon. Meanwhile, they have been exposed to around 52 diverse research seminars, taking in subjects from anthropology and philosophy to macrodynamics, game theory, and mathematical finance. Of those 52 seminar presenters, 22 are foreign academics. Finally, our students have already started publishing internationally both in the mainstream and in the heterodox journals.

One more datum that places the above into perspective: *UADPhilEcon charges not one dollar of fees to* any *of its students* (Greek or foreign). Pluralism not only works but is also produced and re-produced as a purely public good. No fees are charged and only a few external teachers get some paltry sums to cover for their per diem expenses while in Athens. Additionally, the program's administrators offer their labor for free. It is in this sense that, perhaps, the noun "success" in my title is not an inappropriate choice.

Why "most peculiar"? Because, as I wrote in the introduction, it was achieved almost accidentally at a university which would not have come readily to mind if a few years ago one had been asked to predict the place where a pluralist, and at the same time well organized and utterly rigorous, doctoral program in economics would emerge.

Our greatest source of hope for the future is our most peculiar student body. They make a conscious choice to forego a highly paying private sector career for the uncertain pleasures of a genuine intellectual engagement with economics. As for our greatest fear, it is that market norms will infect Greek society's attitude to education to the extent that they will extinguish the historically induced ethos which has hitherto motivated both our staff and students to think of education as a non-commodity of great value.

Does it matter whether a program like UADPhilEcon survives? Iris Murdoch once wrote that "it is the punishment of a false God to become unreal." This seems to be the unfolding fate of mainstream economics. Yes, it succeeded in becoming a cross between a religion with equations and the Queen of the Social Sciences. However, it ended up holding a poisoned scepter. With its success founded not on the truth status of its results but, instead, on the late twentieth-century historical and political triumph of the ideology of the market, its students are now abandoning it and its dominance is becoming increasingly irrelevant. Ironically, therefore, pluralist programs like UADPhilEcon may offer mainstream economics a lifeline whose necessity its practitioners are too unsophisticated to recognize.

# Appendix: the structure of first-year UADPhilEcon courses

## *Advanced microeconomic theory Ec10*

*Ec101 – Advanced microeconomic theory I (semester 1)*

- *Module 1 – Parametric Choice:* The rational choice model, expected utility theory and its discontents
- *Module 2 – Strategic Choice:* Theory of strategic choice, game theory (non-cooperative, static, dynamic, evolutionary games), models of imperfect competition
- *Module 3 – Social Choice:* Aggregation of preferences, social welfare functions, compensation principles, impossibility theorems

*Ec102 – Advanced microeconomic theory II (semester 2)*

- *Module 4 – Production Technologies:* Production functions, cost, technologies, duality, optimization under price taking, degrees of strategic competition
- *Module 5 – General Equilibrium Theory:* Brouwer's fixed point theorem, the 1st and 2nd fundamental theorems, the theorems of Arrow-Debreu
- *Module 6 – Market Failures, Market Power, and Regulation:* Contracts, incentives, bargaining, externalities, mechanism design

## *Advanced macroeconomic theory Ec11*

*Ec111 – Advanced macroeconomic theory I (semester 1)*

- *Module 1 – Open Economy Macroeconomics and the Economics of the European Monetary Union:* Monetary and fiscal policy in Hicks's neoclassical synthesis, money and inflation, interpretations of competing, interpretations of Keynes's effective demand, the Mundell-Fleming model and extensions, Euro-zone economics and lessons from Greece's entry into EMU
- *Module 2 – Business Cycles, Nominal Rigidities, and Macroeconomic Policy:* Flexible-price models with rational expectations, new-Keynesian economics, monopolistic competition, staggered wage and price setting, introduction to dynamic stochastic general equilibrium models with nominal rigidities, policy analysis in a new-Keynesian framework, monetary policy rules, optimal policy design
- *Module 3 – Growth and Cycles:* Classical-Marxian reproduction, growth and cycles, neoclassical growth theory, new versus old growth theories

*Ec112 – Advanced macroeconomic theory II (semester 2)*

- *Module 4 – Long Run Equilibrium in Goods, Money and Stocks:* Recursive macroeconomic theory, the equity premium puzzle, the behavior of stock prices, overlapping generation models
- *Module 5 – Aggregate Savings:* Expected and non-expected utility theories of savings, liquidity constraints, general equilibrium with incomplete markets, portfolio choice
- *Module 6 – Money and Capital Pricing:* Money and interest, capital asset pricing models, inter-temporal asset pricing contracts

## Quantitative methods Q10

*Q101 – Mathematical economics (semester 1)*

- *Module 1 –* Differential equations, phase diagrams, Liapunov's theorem
- *Module 2 –* Optimization: Unconstrained optimization, quadratic programming, Markowitz portfolio, constrained optimization, Karush-Tucker conditions
- *Module 3 –* Calculus of variations and optimal control: Lagrange-Euler lemma, the Maximum principle
- *Modules 4, 5, & 6 –* Topology, fixed point theorems, dynamic optimization, difference equations

*Q102 – Econometrics (semester 2)*

- *Module 7 – Statistical Inference:* Likelihood, ML estimators, testing, power functions, likelihood ratio, Wald's decomposition, Lagrange multiplier tests, confidence intervals, the generalized linear model (random variables, estimators, regression, maximum likelihood), least squares, mis-specification, non-linearities
- *Module 8 – Identification:* Model choice: heteroskedasticity, serial dependence, method of moments, correlation of regressors with errors, instrumental variables estimator, SURE estimators, Kroenecker products, efficient estimation, simultaneous equations
- *Module 9 – Applied Econometrics:* Dynamic models: empirical models as derived entities, statistical representation for systems, theory of reduction, linking economics and econometrics. Dynamic models of aggregate demand, money demand, consumption. Stationarity, integratedness, random walks, the distribution of the autoregressive coefficient. Cointegration. Empirical illustrations

**Economics as a social science Soc10**

*Soc101 – Political philosophy (first two modules, or eight weeks, of semester 1)*

- *Module 1 – The Anatomy of Liberalism I:* Introduction to political philosophy. Economics as a branch of the Enlightenment Project. Neoclassicism as an offshoot of Anglo-Celtic philosophy: From Aristotle to Hobbes, Hume, Locke, Bentham, ordinal utilitarianism, and Arrow's impossibility theorem. Then, on to Rawls, Nozick, and Hayek
- *Module 2 – Liberalism's Discontents:* Non-instrumental rationalities, Kant's categorical imperative, dialectical reasoning, feminist critiques: Rousseau, Marx, Carol Pateman. The rational choice model, empiricism, positivism, and the scientific status of economic theories

*Soc102 – Economic and social history (last four weeks of semester 1 and first four weeks of semester 2)*

- *Module 3 – The Transition to Capitalism:* The fifteenth–eighteenth-century period: Economic, social, and demographic traits of pre-industrial Europe. The rise of commercial capitalism. Pre-industrial and proto-industrial forms of production. Origins of the industrial revolution. The factory system and the growth of the proletariat. The liberal period 1850–1875. Laissez-faire in industry and the great Boom. Economic unification of the world. Social changes (city, industry, working class). Bourgeoisie and agriculture 1750–1875
- *Module 4 – Late Capitalism:* The 1875–1914 period. The great depression of 1875–1890. Protectionism, state regulation, imperialism. The second industrial revolution. Mass production and mass market. The scientific organization of labor (Taylorism-Fordism). The interwar period (1918–1940). The rise of U.S. economic domination. The economic reconstruction of Europe. The 1929 crisis. The 1950–1992 period: Post-war economic order. The decades of crisis 1973–1992: The rise of late globalization. The transition from competitive to oligopolistic capitalism. The rise of conglomerates. The Great Depression. The post-war world economic order.

*Soc103 – History of economic thought (last eight weeks of semester 2)*

- *Module 5 – Early and Classical Political Economy:* Mercantilism, the Physiocrats, early equilibrium concepts, classical political economy – Smith, Ricardo, and Marx. The marginalist revolution.
- *Module 6 – Twentieth-Century Debates:* Neoclassical value theory, the Keynes versus the (neo)classics controversies, the Cambridge controversies, the rise and fall of the rational expectations revolution, recent trends and debates.

## Notes

1 UADPhilEcon is an international doctoral program established by the Department of Economics at the University of Athens with a strong commitment to pluralism and to treating economics as a social science (see www.uadphilecon.gr). After two years of planning, UADPhilEcon opened its doors to the first cohort of students in October 2003. Since then approximately 25 students are admitted each October of which, on average, 15 graduate with a Master of Philosophy in Economics (MPhilEcon) at the end of two years of intensive coursework. Subsequently, they write a thesis whose successful defense leads them to the DPhilEcon. UADPhilEcon's students come from different walks of life, diverse educational backgrounds (economists, engineers, historians, mathematicians, and so on), age groups, and nationalities. Already, a series of high caliber research publications has started flowing out of UADPhilEcon students in areas as diverse as political economy, finance, economic philosophy, and game theory.

2 For instance, the notion of "natural" unemployment was conjured up in order to explain the failure of the market to engender full employment and of economics to explain that failure. Hundreds, if not thousands, of young, up and coming macroeconomists worked energetically for decades in order to compute the relevant NAIRUs. To no avail, of course.

3 My credentials as an impartial assessor, I submit, are rather good: I was appointed by the "real" economists as a game theorist but proved a part time defector, teaching courses in both degrees.

4 My work on game theory led me to the same conclusion. There is no better means of exposing the limitations of any attempt to explain society in terms of methodological individualism than a careful analysis of the logical impasses of its highest form: that is, of Game Theory. For an expansion upon this point see the Epilogue to Hargeaves-Heap and Varoufakis (2004).

5 There were of course countless other types of impediments; the bureaucracy of the Greek state being the first that comes, painfully, to mind.

6 If we wish, we could trace its roots further back, to the clash between the modernizing bourgeois elements of Greek society and an alliance between the landed lords and the Palace. That clash marked the first three decades of the twentieth century, at times taking the form of open warfare.

7 I borrow this term from Margaret Anagnostopoulou.

## References

Evans-Pritchard, E.E. (1937) *Witchcraft, Oracles and Magic among the Azande*, Oxford: Oxford University Press.

Hargeaves-Heap, S. and Varoufakis, Y. (2004) *Game Theory: A Critical Text*, London: Routledge.

Keynes, J.M. (1924) "Alfred Marshall, 1842–1924," *The Economic Journal*, 34 (September): 311–372.

Russell, B. (1957) *Why I Am Not a Christian*, P. Edwards (ed.), London: Allen & Unwin.

# Index

Abraham, K. 241
Adaman, F. 205
Adams, J. 3, 58
Adams, M. 244
Aerni, A.L. 223, 225, 240, 243
Aghion, P. 161
Akerlof, G.A. 196, 201
Albelda, R. 49, 236
Aldridge, T. 209
Allardt, E. 165
Allied Social Sciences Association
    (ASSA) 63, 64, 66, 68
Alperovitz, G. 8, 129, 141n7, 176, 177
altruism *see* pro-social behavior
Amariglio, J. 2, 236
*America Beyond Capitalism*: alternative
    system, "structural girders" for 138;
    American labor movement, decline of
    129; capital, social ownership of 139;
    democracy, and inequality 138;
    democratic political-economic system
    model, emergence of new 129;
    economic decay, process of 130; local
    enterprises 139; planning, and
    institutional power 138–9; political
    support, need for 140–1; state and
    regional initiatives 139; see also
    pluralist commonwealth
American Economics Association 44
*American Economic Review* 3
Anagnostopoulou, M. 292n7
Anderson, B.L. 199
Anderson, J.A. 244
Andreoni, J. 196
anti-pluralism: heterodox economics,
    dismissal of 20–1; Institutionalists 20;
    mainstream *versus* heterodox journals
    21–2; Marxist economists 20;
    responding to 31–2; state *versus*
    professional power 20

Archer, I.W. 200
Argyle, M. 190
Aristotle, and the marketplace: communal
    solidarity, and profit 207; household
    management 206; market activity, and
    community 208; *Nicomachean Ethics*
    206; Peloponnesian War 206; *The
    Politics* 206–8; price theory 206; *teleios*,
    human pursuits as means towards 206;
    unlimited wealth, desire for 207–8;
    well-being, communal and individual
    206
Arnould, E.J. 189
Arnsperger, C. 101
Aslaksen, I. 167
Aslanbeigui, N. 224
Association for Evolutionary Economics
    (AFEE) 24–5, 63, 64
Association for Institutionalist Thought
    (AFIT) 24–5
Association for Social Economics (ASE)
    24–5, 63, 64
associations, heterodox 23, 24–6, 28,
    29–30
Astin, A.W. 226
Austrian economics: civil society 177–8;
    common good, potential pathways to
    177; intellectual tools, influence of 179;
    and Marxist approach 181–2, 191–2;
    status quo, dissatisfaction with 176
Avineri, S. 141n6
Ayres, C.E. 50, 164, 170

Banks, N. 223
Baran, P. 146
Barker, D. 54
Barone, C.A. 224, 275n6
Barrett, K. 137
Bartlett, R. 4, 224, 236, 240
Battistoni, R. 226

Baumol, W.J. 242
Baxter, L.A. 190
Beaulier, S. 179
Becker, G. 196, 237, 244, 247n1
Becker, W.E. 4, 221, 222, 223, 224
Bedford-Stuyvesant Restoration
    Corporation (BSRC) 135
Beinhacker, S. 135
Berger, M. 161
Berman, E.M. 190
Bernstein, M.A. 224
Best, J. 236
Bigo, V. 117, 118–19, 122, 123n4
Blau, F.D. 236
Blaug, M. 123n5, 250
Bleshaw, C. 200
Blinder, A.S. 242
Blomquist, G. 161
Boardman, J. 199
Boettke, P.J. 4, 179, 191
Bok, D. 227
Bollinger, C.R. 239
Bourbaki school 101
Borg, J.R. 222
Borg, M.P. 222
Born, M. 88
Boulding, K. 169
Bourdieu, P. 195, 197
Bowles, S. 170, 259
Boyer, E.L. 226
Bridge, K. 190
Bringle, R. 232n8
Brue, S.L. 241
Bruntland Commission 163
Bruntland, G. 163
Buchanan, J.M. 5
Bullard, R.D. 243
Burczak, T.A. 191
Butler, A. 11

Caldwell, B. 80, 89
California Public Employees Retirement
    System (CalPERS) 137
Cambridge School: "ontological turn",
    114; strategy of 123; *see also* open and
    closed systems
*Cambridge Social Ontology Group*
    (CSOG) 114
capabilities approach 66–9
capital: human capital 165, 166; intellectual
    capital 166; manufactured capital 165–6;
    natural capital 165; social capital 166,
    170; social ownership of 139; sustainable
    development 163–4, 167, 166

capitalism: Austrian views of 181–2;
    competition and greed 145–8; crises in,
    explanations for 146–7; failure to
    challenge structure of 213; laissez faire
    capitalism 147–8; Marxist economics
    145–6, 181–2; moral issues 156–7;
    myths of desirability of 148
Case, C.E. 242
Cavallo, S. 200
Chamlee-Wright, E. 9, 179
Champlin, D. 215n2
Cheal, D. 197
Chick, V. 114, 122, 123
civic engagement movement 226, 227
civil society 177–8
Coase, R. 123n5, 161, 163
Cobb, C. 171
cognitive dissonance 94
Colander, D. 4, 6, 21, 37, 39, 42–3, 47n1,
    47n6, 221, 227, 229, 230, 231, 232n10,
    242, 259
Cold War: Greece, pluralism in 282–3;
    Kuhn's narrative 2
Coleman, J.S. 188
Collard, D. 195–6
Commons, J.R. 48, 49, 54
communication, inter-paradigmatic 37–8,
    41–2, 46, 75–8, 82–3
community *see* local exchange networks
Community Development Corporations
    (CDC) 135–6
competition and greed: academics, and
    activists 156–9; aggregate demand-
    supply relationship 146; anti-corporate
    movement 150; capitalism 145–8;
    consumer cooperatives 153–4, 158;
    counteracting tendencies 146;
    democracy, commitment to 151;
    economic failure, truth of 145; *versus*
    equitable cooperation 148–9; finance
    capital, taming 149; full-employment
    policies 149; intentional communities
    154, 158; internal contradictions 145–6;
    local currency systems 152–3; national
    liberation movements, learning from
    152; pitfalls of 150–1; politics,
    importance of 150; pre-figurative
    organizing 152–5; producer
    cooperatives 153, 158; rate of profit,
    tendency to fall 146; reform victories, as
    partial and temporary 150; reforms,
    organizing 149–51, 155–6;
    underconsumption, crises due to 146
consumer cooperatives 153–4, 158

convergence, among heterodox schools:
alternative view of 50–6; borrowed
ideas, potential of 57–8; choices
following 49–50, 58; feminist
economics 54, 55–6; inevitability of
51–3; Institutional economics 54, 55–6;
meaning of 48–9; new-original
institutional economics, dialogue
between 48–9, 58; ontological realism
57; opportunity 54–6; Post Keynesians
54; shared understanding 57
convergent *versus* divergent thinking 76–8
Coyne, C. 179
Craver, E. 1
Cropley, C.A. 274

Dalton, G. 199
Daly, H. 159n3, 160, 163, 169
Davidson, D. 97n4
Davidson, P. 83
Davis, J.B. 1, 4, 12, 236
Davis, W.L. 260n2
Dawkins, R. 51
DeGregori, T. 163
democracy, commitment to 151
Dennett, D. 51
Desai, M. 2
Dimand, M.A. 56
dissensus, causes of 92; cognition 89;
experiential diversity 89; ontology 89;
path dependence 89; pragmatism 89;
situatedness 89; underdetermination
88–9
diversity, handling: eclecticism,
impossibility of 95; implausibility 95;
inconsistency, loss of 94; individual/
aggregate distinction 91–2; isolationism
94–5; loss of scope 93–4; relativism 90;
skepticism 90; syncretism 90; warranted
choice, at individual level 93, 95–6
Dolan, E.G. 2
Dorfman, J. 56
Dow, S. 2, 3, 74, 81–4, 114, 122, 123
Downward, P.M. 117
dualism *see* open and closed systems
Dubb, S. 136

Earl, P.E. 4, 161, 225, 276n14
Easterlin, R. 169
Eastern Economics Association 44
*Economic Justice and Democracy*
(Hahnel) 145
Economics for Equity and the
Environment 159n4

Edney, J. 61, 268
education *see* graduate programs; skills
formation, and economic pluralism;
teaching, of pluralist economics;
undergraduate economics education
Eichner, A. 2, 54
Ekeh, P. 195
Elden, S. 185
Elsner, W. 275n5
Elster, J. 201
Emerson, J. 135
Employee Stock Ownership Plans (ESOP),
133
Erlich, B. 102
Evans-Pritchard, E.E. 278
evolutionary theory: convergent evolution
51–2; Darwinian approach 51; and
economics 53; ideational memes 52–3;
meme concept 51; warranted knowledge
53
extra-catallactic relationships 182–3, 187;
market as incubator for 189–90; social
networks, and economic development
188–9; workplace relationships 189–90

Fagg Foster, J. 50
Fair, R.C. 242
Farley, J. 159n3
Federation of Egalitarian Communities
(FEC) 154
Fehr, E. 196
Feiner, S. 4, 54, 224, 225, 236, 240
Fellowship for Intentional Community
(FIC) 154
feminist economics 12n1; convergence 54,
55–6; feminist perspective, omission of
61–3; inequality, as "natural", 62–3;
pluralistic approach, roots of 167; social
relationality 110–11
Ferber, M.A. 4
Ferris, D. 141n1
Festinger, L. 94
Fine, B. 101
Finley, M.I. 205
Fitoussi, J.-P. 253
Flaatten, A. 167
Fleetwood, S. 182
Flynn, P. 167, 170
Folbre, N. 169
Forbes 212
formalism 104–5, 106
Freeman, A. 80, 85n7
Friedland, L. 135
Friedman, M. 123n5, 236

full-employment policies 149
Fullbrook, E. 2, 3, 4, 12, 69, 101, 224, 250, 260n1
Fuller, S. 2

Gächter, S. 196
Galbraith, J.K. 54, 164–5, 167, 169–70, 273
Garnett, R. 2, 22, 80, 231n1, 251
Gay, G. 244
gender analysis 55–6
Genuine Progress Indicator (GPI) 160, 171
Georgescu-Roegen, N. 167
Gibson-Graham, J.-K. 5, 213–14
gifts and markets: anthropology, current focus of 200–1; community and informal support, literature of 199–200; economic development, linear model of 198–9; gift-commodity dichotomy 197; gift-market nexus 197–201; market boundaries 198; markets, social role of 194; pluralism, institutional 194–203; pro-social behavior 194–7, 201–2; reciprocity 197; transfer and exchange, non-market forms of 201
Gilman, C.P. 55, 56, 58
Gintis, H. 170
Glover, P. 209
Godbout, J.T. 194, 197
Goffman, E. 69
Goodwin, N. 224, 243, 259
Gore, A. 167
graduate programs 40–1
Granovetter, M. 182
Grapard, U. 54, 55
Greene, R. 137
Greenlaw, S. 228
Greenwood, D. 9, 160, 170, 176, 178–9
Gregory, C.A. 197
Greif, A. 199
Groenwegen, J. 225
Gudeman, S. 182
Guerrien, B. 250, 260n4

Hahn, F. 105
Hahnel, R. 8, 159n2, 176, 177
Hands, W. 69
Hansen, W.L. 231n2, 275n5
Haraway, D. 72n3
Harding, S. 236, 237, 247n8
Hargeaves-Heap, S. 4, 292n4
Harley, S. 21
Harrington, M. 151

Hayek, F. 10, 176, 179, 181–92, 212
Hayes, C. 22
Helleiner, E. 205, 209
Henderson, M. 190
heterodox approach, and mainstream economics: communication, need for multiple frames of 37–8, 41–2, 46; heterodox economists, by country 28, 31t; ideas, transference of 43–4; "inside-the-mainstream" heterodoxy 37, 41–2; Institutionalism 100–1; mainstream economics, compass of 30–40, 37–8; mainstream organizations, involvement in 44–5; marginalisation of 46; mathematical methods 44, 99–100, 101; methodology 45; need for change in 38–42; rhetoric of pluralism, failure of 36–7
Hicks, J. 194, 198–9
Hirsch, W.Z. 226
Hodgson, G.M. 3, 5 , 12, 32n8, 50, 62, 101, 194
Holcombe, R.G. 112n6
Holmes, J. 229
Holt, R.P.F. 9, 32n1, 47n6, 83, 165, 167, 170, 176, 178–9
Homans, G.C. 195
Hong, H. 182
Huber, M.T. 225
Human Development and Capabilities Association (HDCA) 68
Human Development Index (HDI) 160, 171
Hutchings, P. 225
Hutchinson, T.W. 1

inclusiveness: capabilities approach 66–9; organizations, impact of 70; scholarship, by women 69–70; social studies of science 69; sociolinguistic analysis 69–70
incommensurability, Kuhnean *see* Kuhnean incommensurability
Institutionalist economics 26, 27t 43, 54, 55–6, 100–1, 164–5
intentional communities 154, 158
inter-paradigmatic communication 37–8, 41–2, 46, 75–8, 82–3
International Association for Feminist Economics (IAFFE) 63, 64, 66, 68, 70, 71
International Confederation of Associations for Pluralism in Economics (ICAPE) 63, 103–4

International Confederation of Associations for the Reform of Economics (ICARE) 3
International Monetary Fund (IMF) 158
isolationism 94–5, 109–11

Jensen, E. 238, 244
Jorgenson, D.W. 241
*Journal of Economic Education* 221, 263
*Journal of Post Keynesian Economics* (JPKE) 24–5

Kahn, M. 161
Kant, I. 97n11
Karatani, K. 214
Kardash, C.M. 227
Kasper, S.D. 225
Kauder, F. 205, 215n1
Kellert, S.H. 5
Kendrick, J.W. 241
Kepner, E. 189
Kern, W. 208
Keynes, J.M. 54, 285
Keynesian economics 258–9
King, J.E. 4, 28, 32n8
Kitcher, P. 89, 95, 97n13
Klamer, A. 2, 21, 32n2, 261n11
Klasan, S. 61
Klein, P.A. 167
Kliman, A. 80, 85n7
Knoedler, J. 4, 215n2, 222
Knudsen, T. 50
Kolm, S. 196, 198, 215n2
Koppl, R. 5
Koren, C. 167
Korson, G. 212
Kotz, D. 159n1
Kozel, P. 10, 205
Kram, K.E. 189
Krausman Ben-Amos, I. 199, 200
Kregel, J. 2
Kreitner, R. 198, 199
Krugman, P. 210, 242
Kuhn, T.S. 2, 74–8
Kuhnean incommensurability: Babylonian mode of thought 74, 81, 82, 83; consideration of 81; external criticism, failure of 82; inter-paradigmatic communication 82; mainstream techniques, possible use of 83–4; pluralism, Dow's modified 81–4; science, Kuhn's vision of 74–8; utility of confrontations, Mill's vision of 78–81
Kuoppamäki, P. 276n14

Kurz, H. 93

Labov, W. 69
Latham, A.J.H. 199
Laudan, L. 97n12
Lavoie, D. 2, 179, 182, 184, 191
Lavoie, M. 54, 167
Lawson, T. 2, 8, 12, 22, 83, 99, 100, 101, 103, 110, 111, 116, 117, 118, 120, 123, 123n2, 123n4, 256
Lee, F.S. 3, 4, 6, 12, 21, 22, 24, 26, 27, 28, 30, 32n4, 54
Leeson, P.T. 179
Lefebvre, H. 10, 181–92
Leijonhufvud, A. 1
Leontief, W. 123n5
LETS *see* local currency systems
Levi-Strauss, C. 195, 200
Lewis, M. 32n8, 56, 224
Lewis, P. 117, 123, 123n4
Lewis, T.J. 208, 214
liberal education movement 226–7
Lie, J. 191
Lifsher, M. 137
Lipman, H. 136
Lipsey, R. 105
local currency systems 152–3; Ithaca HOURS, as prototype for 209–10, 211
local exchange networks: Aristotle, and the marketplace 206–8; capitalism, failure to challenge structure of 213; community building 208–9, 211; critics of 212–14; economic growth, impediment to 213; electronic credits 210; global implications of 211–12; individual liberty 212; local economic activity, promotion of 211; localism, criticism of 212–13
Logue, J. 133, 141n4
Longino, H. 65
Lopatto, D. 228
Lowry, S.T. 205, 207, 208
Lucas, R.E. 160
Lynch, L. 239

MacKie, C. 241
Macleod, C. 205
Maddison, A. 160
Madra, Y. 205
Maher, F.A. 239
Mäki, U. 2, 3, 22, 74
Mankiw, N.G. 241, 242, 253, 260n6, 268–9, 275n9, 276n13
Marglin, S. 146, 251, 256

markets *see* Aristotle, and the marketplace; gifts and markets; space, and extra-catallactic relationships

Marx, K. 189, 215n1

Marxist economics 26; and Austrian approach 181–2, 191–2; heterodox approaches, theoretical engagement between 27t; "monopoly capital" school 146; teaching, of pluralist economics 258, 259

Massarsky, C. 135

mathematics, and methodology 99–100, 101, 106, 111, 119, 121, 280

Mauss, M. 195, 198, 200

McCloskey, D.N. 1, 2, 3

McConnell, C.C. 241

McGoldrick, K. 4, 10, 224, 228, 229, 240

McIntosh, P. 240

Meade, J. 131

Mearman, A. 114, 116, 117–18, 121, 123, 123n1

Medema, S. 54

Meier, G. 161, 215n2

Meier, S. 196, 201

Mill, J.S. 4, 74, 78–81, 84

Mirowski, P. 2, 198

Monroe, K.R. 197

Morgan, M.S. 1

Moseley, F. 224

Mueller, D.C. 196

Muga, D.A. 191

Murdoch, I. 288

Myrdal, G. 164

Naples, M. 224

National Economic Association (NEA) 66, 68

national liberation movements, learning from 152

Negru, I. 10, 199

Nelson, J. 167, 169, 225, 236, 238

Nelson, R. 48

neoclassical model: quality of life 161–4; teaching, of pluralist economics 258–9

Nesbitt, S. 137

New Community Corporation (NCC) 135

*Nicomachean Ethics* (Aristotle) 206

Niederle, N. 247n7

Nordhaus, W. 161

Norgaard, R. 160, 163, 170, 171

North, D. 48, 194

Northover, P. 117, 123

Nugent, R. 247n5

Nussbaum, M. 66

Nuzum, R. 134

objectivity, illusion of: assumptions, challenging 245–6; in classroom 240–6; curriculum content 240; economics, as value-free 236–7; GDP, definitions and perceptions of 241–3; gender and race, as special topics 238–9; inclusive profession, developing 246; macroeconomics, strategies for 245–6; pedagogy, alternative 243–5; perspective, acknowledging role of 237, 239–40, 242–3; practice of economics *versus* practitioner perspective 246; professor, values of 237–8, 239; universality, assumptions of 238–9

O'Boyle, E.J. 224

Odekon, M. 205

O'Donnell, R. 11, 225, 275n5

O'Hara, S.U. 167

O'Hara, P.A. 28, 48

Okishio, N. 146

"ontological turn", 114

ontology 57, 89, 100, 107–8, 111; see also *Reorienting Economics*, replies to

open and closed systems: Cambridge School, dialectical orientation of 122; closure, definition of 115; closure conditions, intrinsic and extrinsic 115–16; contrast explanation 119–20; demi-regularity 119–20; mathematical deductivist methods 115, 119, 121; methodological recommendations, dichotomous nature of 117–19; open system, definition of 116; social reality, study of 120; systems, spectrum of 117; variations of form 116

Owen, A.L. 238, 244

Pack, H. 161

Pack, S. 208

Palermo, G. 28

Panizza, U. 161

Partridge, M. 161

Parvin, M. 224

Pearson, S.S. 228

pedagogy, alternative: collaborative learning, emphasis on 244; incentives, nature of 244–5; inclusiveness 245; interpersonal relationships 244; lecture-style formats, maintaining 244; women, and self-confidence 244

Perelman, M. 200

Perona, E. 117, 123, 123n4

Peroux, F. 198

Peterson, J. 32n8, 55

Pinkstone, B. 117
Pioneer Human Services (PHS) 135–6
pluralism, and integration in heterodox
 economics: academic rights 22;
 heterodox approaches, theoretical
 engagement between 26–8, 27;
 heterodox associations 23, 24–6;
 heterodox economics, pluralistic
 communities of 22–3; informal 23;
 professional integration 23–6;
 professional segregation 23; voluntary
 integration 23–4
pluralist commonwealth: *America Beyond
 Capitalism* (*ABC*) 130–2; California
 Public Employees Retirement System
 137; community, building 132, 135–6;
 democratic political-economic system,
 feasibility of 129; Employee Stock
 Ownership Plans 133; environmental
 management 134–5; health services 134;
 Internet services 134; land development
 133–4; local ownership institutions 132;
 municipal enterprises 133–5; political
 support 137; practicality, focus on 132;
 public employee retirement system
 boards 137; Public Trusts 131;
 regulatory capture, studies of 130;
 Retirement Systems of Alabama 137;
 social ownership models 130–1;
 sovereign fund investment management
 131; sports teams 134; state/national
 innovators 136–7; state-owned financial
 institutions 136; stock ownership,
 Federal level 136; venture capital
 investment 134; worker-owned firms
 132–3
Polanyi, L. 69, 72n4, 198–9
*Politics, The* (Aristotle) 206–8
Popper, K. 1, 77
Post-Autistic Economics (PAE) movement
 3, 11, 255
*Post-Autistic Economics Review* 30, 83,
 102
Post Keynesian economics 10, 24–5, 26,
 43, 54, 167–8
postgraduate education *see* UADPhilEcon,
 University of Athens
Power, T. 161–2, 165, 169
Pragmatism 56
Pratten, S. 117, 123n4
Pressman, S. 32n1
Price, L.L. 189
Pritzker, S.R. 275n3
pro-social behavior: gifts, pure *versus*

impure 194, 195; institutional context of
 201–2; markets, and gifts 195;
 reciprocity model 196; and self-interest
 201; self-interest *versus* altruism 195–7;
 social exchange theory, and gift-giving
 194–5
producer cooperatives 153, 158
Public Trusts 131
Putnam, R.D. 167, 188

quality of life, and growth and
 development: capital, forms of 165–6,
 170; ecological economists 165, 168;
 economic development 160, 161–2, 164,
 169; endogenous growth theory 161;
 feminist economists 167; GDP,
 measures beyond 170; heterodox
 schools, agreement/disagreement
 between 168–9; Institutionalist approach
 164–5, 168; neoclassical model 161–4;
 people, role of 166–7; post-Keynesian
 economics 167–8; power, in economic
 relationships 170; progress in standard
 of living, measures of 171; quality of
 life 162–3, 169–70; real world examples
 171–2; sustainability 163–4, 166;
 systems analysis, shift to 169

Randall Wray, L. 54
ranking systems 38–9, 45
Ranson, B. 50
Raveaud, G. 11, 224, 275n8
*Reorienting Economics*, replies to 99–101;
 Davis, J. 102–6; Garnett, R. 106–8; Van
 Bouwel, J. 109–11
Rescher, N. 89, 97n5
research, criteria for judging 39
Resnick, S.A. 2, 5
Retirement Systems of Alabama (RSA),
 137
Richardson, A.W. 1
Richter, M.N. 190
Rishi, M. 240
Roback, J. 161
Roberts, B. 224
Robinson, L. 170
Robson, D. 238
Roemer, J. 131
Romer, P. 161
Ropke, I. 28
Rosser, Jr. J.B. 47n6, 167
Rottheim, R. 117, 123n4
Ruccio, D.F. 2, 236
Runco, M.A. 275n3

Runde, J. 117
Russell, B. 284
Rutherford, M. 1

Sahlins, M. 198
Salamon, I. 136
Salemi, M. 222
Salvadori, N. 93
Samuels, W.J. 2, 54
Saunders, T.J. 207
Sax, L.J. 244
Schmid, A. 170
Schmidt, K.M. 196
Schneider, G. 224
Schumacher, E.F. 209
Schumpeter, J. 215n1
Schwinn, E. 136
Sciabarra, C.M. 182
science, Kuhn's vision of: convergent
    *versus* divergent thinking 76–8;
    extraordinary research 78; inter-
    paradigmatic communication 75–8,
    82–3; knowledge, growth of 76;
    pluralism, as defense of attitude 75–8;
    pluralism, as defense of plurality 74–5;
    utility of 76
scientific monism, postwar U.S. 1–2;
    crusading idealism 1–2; first- *versus*
    second-wave pluralism 2–3; monist
    *versus* pluralist ideals 4–5; paradigmatic
    alternatives 2; post-Kuhnean pluralism 3
Sebberson, D. 56
Seers, D. 161
Seigfried, C. 56
Sen, A. 5, 61, 62, 66, 165, 169, 197, 211,
    213
Sent, E.-M. 1, 4, 83
service-learning 228–9
Setterfield, M. 167
Shackelford, J. 224, 229
Shah, S. 247n5
Shapin, S. 89
Shaw, G.B. 285
Sherman, H. 49
Siegfried, J. 4, 222, 227, 230
Silver, M. 199
Simon, H. 167, 250, 259
Sirianni, C. 135
skills formation, and economic pluralism:
    activities 267–70, 272–3; ambiguity/
    choice, toleration of 274; course design/
    organization/content 265–7; course
    prerequisites 265–6; creativity 264, 270,
    271–2, 271t; debates 269–70, 272–3;

employers, skills required by 263–4;
    games 267–8, 272; government and
    business skills 270–1, 271t; innovation,
    fostering 264, 272; lecture syllabus
    266–7; perspectives, diversity of 262;
    pluralist courses, superiority of 262–3,
    265, 270–3; practicality 273;
    presentations 268–9, 272; skill
    formation, as central 265–7, 273; skills
    comparisons 270–3; student engagement
    273; student responses 273–4
Slack, P. 199
Slottje, D. 161
Smith, A. 179, 201
Sobel, R.S. 179
"social analysis 72" experiment, Harvard:
    critiques, study of 256–7; distributional
    critique 256–7; ecological critique 256;
    foundational critique 256; Keynesian
    critique 256; market, effect on
    environment 256; structural critique 256
social exchange theory, and gift-giving
    194–5
social ownership models 130–1
Social Structure of Accumulation theory
    159n1
Solow, R. 160, 161, 163
Soudek, J. 215n1
space, and extra-catallactic relationships
    (Hayek and Lefebvre): abstract space
    181, 185; anti-market bias 181; Austrian
    and Marxist approaches 181–2, 191–2;
    extra-catallactic relationships 182–3,
    187, 188–91; Hayak and Lefebvre,
    commonalities between 182–3; market
    order 183–4, 185, 187; market space
    183, 184–5; scientism 185; social
    engineering and central planning 186;
    social space 186–8; spatial theory 183
Spellings Report (2006) 226
Stanfield, J.R. 58
state/national innovators 136–7; California
    Public Employees Retirement System
    137; political support 137; public
    employee retirement system boards 137;
    Retirement Systems of Alabama 137;
    state-owned financial institutions 136;
    stock ownership, Federal level 136
Steedman, I. 2
Stiglitz, J. 161, 163, 171
Stilwell, F. 275n11
Storr, V. 10, 179, 182, 189, 191
Strassmann, D. 2, 6, 21, 69, 72n3, 72n4
Strom, S. 136

*Structure of Scientific Revolutions* (Kuhn) 2
Subrick, J.R. 179
Summers, L. 243
Sundrum, R.M. 161
Sustainable Development Indicators, UN 167
Swann, R. 210
Swedberg, R. 191
Sweezy, P. 146

Talberth, J. 171
Taris, J. 210
Taylor, L. 146, 161
teaching, of pluralist economics: current situation, as unacceptable 259; mainstream economics 251–2; markets, necessity to debate 253–5; neoclassical economics, starting with 258–9; "no problem good", problem of 254–5; pluridisciplinarity, call for 255; post-autistic economics, curriculum of 255; public health systems, and fairness 253–4; "social analysis 72" experiment, Harvard 256–8; student protest, France June 2000 250–1; teachers, role of 255; textbooks 255–6, 259–60; thematic courses 255–6; undergraduate economics pedagogy 255–6
Tetreault, M.K.T. 239
Third World: economic reform campaigns 157–8; laissez faire capitalism 147; national liberation movements 152
Thompson, E.P. 198
Thucydides 206
Titmuss, R.M. 200, 201
Tobin, J. 161
Tomass, M. 182
Tooke, J. 209
Tool, M.R. 2
Traweek, S. 69
Tribe, K. 2

UADPhilEcon, University of Athens: classic texts, systematic reading of 286; demystification, as aim of pluralism 278–9; economists, required gifts of good 284–5; first year courses 286, 289–91; Greek Civil War, to pluralist doctoral program 281–3; mainstream economics, teaching at highest level 279–80, 284; objectives of 285–6; philosophical-*cum*-historical approach 284; philosophy of 284–5; postgraduate economics, pluralist agenda for 278–9; second year courses 286–7; structure of 285–91; student body 288; success of 287–8
underconsumption, crises due to 146
undergraduate economics education: accountability, issue of 226; calls for change, in economics education 223, 224–5; civic engagement movement 226, 227; conversation, promoting 222–6; economics education, expanding 221; higher education trends, role of 226–9; learning outcomes, as key component 222; liberal education movement 226–7; multiple paradigm approach 222–3; non-lecture pedagogical practice, assessment of 230; nonmainstream approaches, lack of exposure to 222; pedagogical practices, choice of 230; service-learning 228–9; single paradigm approach 222; student outcomes, measurement of 229–30; teaching commons 225–6, 230–1; undergraduate research 227–8, 229; voices, empowering 231
Underwood, D.A. 4, 222
Ungurean, S. 199
Union of Radical Political Economics (URPE) 23, 24–5
utility of confrontations, Mill's vision of: epistemological thesis, of Mill 79; individualism, promotion of 79; pluralism, Mill's concept of 78–9; pluralism, two senses of 78–9, 80–1; theoretical pluralism, positive and negative arguments for 79–80; truth, and knowledge 80

Van Bouwel, J. 4, 83, 89, 97n1; feminist economics, and social relationality 110–11; isolationism 109–11; mathematical methods 111; motivation, for pluralism 109; old Institutionalism 110; ontological conception 110; social ontology 111; uncertainty, and post Keynesians 110
van Dalen, H.P. 224
Van Staveren, I. 207, 215n2
Varoufakis, Y. 11, 101, 292n4
Veblen, T. 50, 53, 54, 55–6, 58, 164, 165–6
venture capital investment 134
Vesterlund, L. 247n7
Voltaire 97n3, 97n16

von Mises, L. 181
Vromen, J. 4

Waller, W. 6, 28, 48, 49, 56
Walstad, W. 223
Ward, L. 56
Watts, M. 221, 244
Weber, L.E. 226
well-being of all 61–2
Wells, R. 242
West, J.P. 190
Weston, S.C. 236
Whalen, C. 54
Whalen, I. 54
Widmaier, W. 236
Wilber, C.K. 224
Williams, C. 189, 209
Williamson, O.E. 48, 49
Williamson, T. 136

Wink, C. 61
Wismer, S. 160, 170
Witt, S. 210
Wolff, R.D. 2, 5
Wolfson, M. 159n1
Wootton, B. 53
working class, and laissez faire capitalism
    147–8
World Bank 158
World Systems theory 159n1

Yates, J. 133, 141n4
Ythier, J. 215n2

Zelizer, V.R. 198
Ziegert, A. 228
Ziliak, S. 261n11
Zolatas, X. 161

For Product Safety Concerns and Information please contact our EU
representative  GPSR@taylorandfrancis.com
Taylor & Francis Verlag GmbH, Kaufingerstraße 24, 80331 München, Germany